# Advance Praise

"*GaYme Changer* is a unique overview of the rise of LGBT+ inclusion in global workplaces and beyond. With rich stories and background analysis, it demonstrates how LGBT+ equality is not only a moral imperative but also a dynamic driver of growth, cultural change, and business success. Jens Schadendorf's book is an insightful and compelling read – essential for every leader and those driving inclusion at all levels."
**Antonio Zappulla, CEO, Thomson Reuters Foundation, London**

"Global developments and new role models, corporate social responsibility and the economic benefits of LGBT+ diversity and inclusion – all in one. *GaYme Changer* is unique – a must-read!"
**Professor Christoph Lütge, Peter Löscher Chair of Business Ethics, Technical University of Munich**

"*GaYme Changer* is the book we need in these turbulent times. Jens Schadendorf eloquently tells the story of how the LGBT+ community and their allies are transforming the global economy – a potential example to all marginalized communities. Among other things, he shows how senior business figures are key in this journey, and how there is an inclusion dividend. For both reasons, more top executives must get on board. Fortunately, Schadendorf's book clearly marks out the way with fantastic leadership examples. I highly recommend it."
**Todd Sears, Founder and CEO, Out Leadership, New York**

"*GaYme Changer* provides new insights into an exceptional journey: the rise of the LGBT+ communit~~y in global~~ workplaces, supported by a growing number of allies, net~~works and cross-corporate part~~nerships. With compelling narratives o~~~~ors from both individuals and organiz~~~~he bigger picture, Jens Schadendorf sh~~~~equality delivers a return. It is good for ~~business~~ ~~to~~ do."
**Christian Klein, CEO and Member of the Executive Board, SAP**

"In our lifetime, we have witnessed significant changes in the visibility and acceptance of the LGBT+ community. Jens Schadendorf has tracked this transformation in the business world, and demonstrates – with a keen eye and compelling examples – why businesses want LGBT+ employees to belong. His stories inspire as much as the data. There is real power in understanding how individuals, companies, and other organizations have pushed for greater inclusion and begun unlocking the 'holy grail' of optimal organizational culture."
**Erin Uritus, CEO, Out & Equal Workplace Advocates, Oakland/Washington, DC**

"Jens Schadendorf uses a mixture of inarguable facts and strong storytelling to demonstrate the positive impact the LGBT+ community is having on our economies as well as our societies. In so doing, he writes persuasively on the power and importance of inclusion and diversity for any organization to be competitive and remain a home for top talent. I hope it will be read by the yet-to-be enlightened as well as those of us who already prize the LGBT+ community as an integral part of our workforce."
**Tobias C. Pross, CEO, Allianz Global Investors**

"*GaYme Changer* deals with a minority that has too long been rejected by the majority, but that has increasingly made exceptional contributions in the fields of business, science, and art. In a stirring book, Jens Schadendorf reports on extensive research that he carried out on five continents, delivering a fascinating picture of these contributions and their immense value for the development of business, society, and human culture. This book is a must-read for all who want to understand the evolution of society and come to an unbiased judgment."
**Professor Hans-Werner Sinn, President Emeritus, ifo Institute of Economic Research, and Chair Emeritus, Economics and Public Finance, Ludwig Maximilian University Munich**

"More and more business leaders have come to understand that LGBT+ inclusion in the workplace and far beyond helps create not only a better world but also better companies. With deep analysis and rich accounts of innovative businesses, new organizations, best practice, LGBT+ activists and their allies, Jens Schadendorf provides readers with a unique global perspective. *GaYme Changer* is also a wake-up call to companies to stay relevant and contribute positively to society."
**Tarique Shakir-Khalil, Partner, PwC, Paris**

"The LGBT+ community has made great strides in the global business arena in recent years. Jens Schadendorf takes you by the hand on a tour of the entrepreneurial players pushing for change, among them a fast-growing number of allies. By sharing fascinating backgrounds and amazing stories he shows specifically how progress was made. Yet, this progress is not universal. The world needs more GaYme Changers. This book is an inspirational call-to-action to make this happen."
**Sander van 't Noordende, Global Executive, former Group CEO, Accenture, and Board member, Out & Equal Workplace Advocates**

"*GaYme Changer* is the analytical picture of a stunning development and a sweeping and compelling set of stories. What emerges is the power of individual and collective actions in leveraging business to accelerate progress toward human rights, LGBT+ equality, and inclusion."
**Beth Brooke and Dan Bross, Co-Chairs, Partnership for Global LGBTI Equality**

"Jens Schadendorf has written an amazing book showing how people and organizations globally are working for LGBT+ workplace equality, making both business and the societies we live in better. The overarching analysis is intertwined with rich human stories of the individuals involved. *GaYme Changer* is an essential and truly enjoyable read."
**Alexander Dmitrenko and Naosuke Fujita, Co-Founders and Co-Chairs of LLAN (Lawyers for LGBT & Allies Network), Tokyo**

"What a journey in less than a decade! From 'hide your pride' to 'LGBT+ diversity is key.' That's the essence of Jens Schadendorf's book, which I found both insightful and inspiring. It demonstrates perfectly how much mindset shift is possible in economy and society. *GaYme Changer* is a must-read for anyone seeking to drive and establish positive change."
**Natalia Oropeza, Chief Diversity Officer, Siemens**

"Anyone who is serious, or even curious, about being an ally to the LGBT+ community, or is part of the community itself, should read *GaYme Changer*. It has the inspiring stories, deep background insights, and tools essential to help drive the change needed for a more LGBT+ -inclusive world."
**Suki Sandhu OBE, Founder and CEO, Audeliss and INvolve, London**

"In *GaYme Changer*, Jens Schadendorf has expertly put all of the pieces of the puzzle together and gives us an easy-to-read insight into the complex landscape of LGBT+ workplace inclusion."
**David Pollard, Co-Founder and Executive Director, Workplace Pride Foundation, Amsterdam**

"*GaYme Changer* shows very clearly how LGBT+ inclusion and equality pay off – for businesses, economies, societies – and everybody. A strong book and right up to date."
**Dr. Stefan Schuppert, Managing Partner for Germany, Hogan Lovells**

"Jens Schadendorf's narrative in *GaYme Changer* is fascinating. Looking at a wide range of entrepreneurial individuals and organizations around the globe, he shows that today companies can only succeed by creating a culture of inclusion. In India, the revocation of Section 377 by the Honorable Supreme Court in September 2018 marked the beginning of a new era for the LGBT+ community, their allies, and Corporate India. I am positive that *GaYme Changer* will inspire leaders and companies to take straightforward action to further advance LGBT+ equality in the workplace and beyond."
**Sindhu Gangadharan, Senior Vice President and Managing Director, SAP Labs India**

"Jens Schadendorf makes it clear that global companies and organizations must step up on LGBT+ inclusion. Leaders need to be more vocal, as their voices carry into the rooms where future policy is made. Being a *GaYme Changer* not only benefits LGBT+ people, it also supports greater equality in gender, race, cultural background, religion, physical and mental ability, etc. This book is a must-read for everyone who wants to move the needle."
**Leon Pieters, Partner, Deloitte, and Board member,**
**Workplace Pride Foundation, Amsterdam**

"*GaYme Changer* is a fantastic combination of global analysis, colorful stories, and best practice from LGBT+ leaders, allies, and companies about the importance and benefits of advancing inclusion at work for all. Moreover, it spotlights the realities LGBT+ employees face in the workplaces where they spend most of their lives. This book is a must-read for all corporate activists fostering a culture of equality – in whatever function, in whatever industry, on whatever hierarchical level."
**Christine Rauh, Managing Director, Accenture, and Executive**
**Sponsor of the firm's Global Pride (Employee) Network**

"Profound analysis of a fascinating development and colorful stories on creating business and social value and on individual empowerment: *GaYme Changer* is a must-read for true business leaders, allies, and LGBT+ people at all levels, and a call-to-action on working for diversity, inclusion, and corporate citizenship in an era where all this is much needed."
**Lawrence Spicer, Vice President, Royal Bank of Canada (RBC), Toronto**

"In his new book, Jens Schadendorf combines fascinating analysis with colorful depictions of the individuals and global organizations fighting for LGBT+ equality on business and ethical grounds. It also adds up to a compelling discussion of some our era's key questions: the power of disruptors in making organizations evolve, the responsibility of companies beyond profit-making, and the reinvention of stable societies, with inclusivity as a basis for economic and social growth."
**Fabrice Houdart, Co-author of the UN LGBTI Standards of**
**Conduct for Business, and Managing Director at Out Leadership,**
**New York**

"Formerly marginalized LGBT+ communities globally are now connecting and mobilizing in fast-increasing numbers, finding allies, partners, and resources. In *GaYme Changer*, Jens Schadendorf has traced this breathtaking development, showing how new individual, corporate and other organizational role models are amplifying their amazing stories, accelerating cultural change in workplaces and society. As the successful Taiwanese campaign for same-sex marriage has inspired other Asian LGBT+ communities and their supporters, this fascinating book will inspire the world."
**Jay Lin, Founder and CEO, Portico Media and
GagaOOLala, Taipei**

"With concrete examples and authentic testimonials, Jens Schadendorf shows that the long stigmatized LGBT+ community has not only become part of daily economic life, but is now a unique driver in the business world, embedded in fast-growing global networks and innovative partnerships. This book is a real eye-opener and a source of inspiration for all."
**Ludo Swinnen and Pavel Šubrt, Co-founders,
East meets West, Vienna, and EGLCC (European LGBTIQ
Chamber of Commerce), Brussels**

"A great overview – with gripping stories about LGBT+ people and their allies in the global business arena and how they are making the world better, both economically and for every individual."
**Stuart Cameron, Founder and CEO, Uhlala Group, Berlin**

"*GaYme Changer* beautifully ties in LGBT+ human rights with the business and economic case for equality, all supported by fabulous examples of how this is being realized in different parts of the world. It provides a great insight into the importance of businesses in enabling inclusive society and shows how they can reap benefits from it. It's a book of action and hope for a better world and it's a must-read."
**Ramkrishna Sinha, Co-founder, Pride Circle, India**

"Profound research, great storytelling, fascinating details, and, at the same time, the big picture: *GaYme Changer* is an exceptional account of how the rainbow community and their allies in the arena of global workplaces have developed – and of their creativity, challenges, and successes."
**Albert Kehrer and Dr. Jean-Luc Vey, Co-founders and Chairs, Prout at Work Foundation, Munich**

"Compelling analysis and amazing stories on the economic, social, and individual benefits of LGBT+ inclusion in the business world: *GaYme Changer* is a fascinating call-to-action and must-read."
**Alberto Padilla, Board Co-Chair, London Business School's EurOUT and Founding Board Member, Out Investors**

"*GaYme Changer* is a must-read for employers and any individual wanting not just to understand a spectacular development but also to shape it in their own economic interest: the rise of LGBT+ equality at work and in society, led by companies, creative organizations, global institutions, LGBT+ activists and their allies. The world is not perfect but, as Jens Schadendorf shows, despite the remaining obstacles, it can get better."
**Marta Fernández Herráiz and Óscar Muñoz Hernández, Co-Executive Directors, REDI (Red Empresarial por la Diversidad y la Inclusión LGBTI), Spain**

"It makes business sense to engage for LGBT+ inclusion, and as Jens Schadendorf shows, great progress has been made globally while new challenges emerge. *GaYme Changer* provides colorful stories and deep insights to the global movers and shakers – individuals, companies, and institutions – working hard to make LGBT+ equality a reality in workplaces and societies."
**Luke Andrews, Co-founder, South African LGBT+ Management Forum, Johannesburg**

Published by
**LID Publishing Limited**
The Record Hall, Studio 304,
16-16a Baldwins Gardens,
London EC1N 7RJ, UK

info@lidpublishing.com
www.lidpublishing.com

A member of:

businesspublishersroundtable.com

All rights reserved. Without limiting the rights under copyright reserved, no part of this publication may be reproduced, stored or introduced into a retrieval system, or transmitted, in any form or by any means (electronic, mechanical, photocopying, recording or otherwise) without the prior written permission of both the copyright owners and the publisher of this book.

The English language edition was arranged by Maria Pinto-Peuckmann, Literary Agency, World Copyright Promotion, Kaufering, Germany.

© Jens Schadendorf, 2021
© LID Publishing Limited, 2021

Printed by Gutenberg Press, Malta

ISBN: 978-1-912555-95-6
ISBN: 978-1-911671-20-6 (ebook)

Cover design: Matthew Renaudin
Page design: Caroline Li

# GAYME CHANGER

# CHANGER

## HOW THE LGBT+ COMMUNITY

## AND THEIR ALLIES ARE CHANGING

## THE GLOBAL ECONOMY

# JENS SCHADENDORF

MADRID | MEXICO CITY | LONDON
NEW YORK | BUENOS AIRES
BOGOTA | SHANGHAI | NEW DELHI

For Karsten

# Contents

## Introduction

## Part I

Barilla's pasta war, a global turnaround, and a new social positioning

## Part II

A surprising initiative in Davos, hide-and-seek at the top,
and an economic message to the world for the years ahead

## Part III

Globally and locally: A growing network of organizations

## Part IV

Changing cultures, a revolution among the young,
and its impact on the business world

# Introduction

## Out of the shadows and into the light – The economic power of human recognition

We live in turbulent times. Immersed in what is happening around us, we often do not notice major shifts we are a part of, even when we contribute to them ourselves, maybe substantially.

This book is about recognition and the long struggle of a group of people to be acknowledged and included as equal members of diverse societies wherever they are around the world. Not all, but many of those societies have long promised members equal rights, chances, and opportunities to make something of their lives, thrive, and rise – even the opportunity to give something back to the communities they are part of. But as always, a promise is one thing, reality another.

Over time, this group's struggle has reached places where we spend a lot of time and that are not only essential to survival, but also to purpose, creativity, and productivity: workplaces, local and global markets, and economies.

The group, I am speaking of, is, of course, the LGBT+ community, an umbrella term that includes lesbians, gays, bisexuals, transgender, intersexual, and queer people, plus others with sexual and gender identities different from the norm defined by the majority.

The major shift I am referring to is the steadily increasing contributions of this community to improving not just their own lives, but also the businesses and societies they belong to. They have made those businesses and societies better in numerous ways, via the many roles that they and their supporters fill: as employees, team leaders, top executives, entrepreneurs, consultants, investors, lawyers, customers, media figures, students, lecturers, researchers, staff in nonprofits and nongovernmental organizations, activists, citizens, family members, friends – ultimately, as agents of change.

This is not to say the world has become a perfect place for the LGBT+ community and its growing number of straight allies. It has not. For cultural, religious, legal, power, and/or other reasons, often with deep historical roots, many parts of the globe – including some in liberal Western societies – still do not acknowledge them and their struggle for recognition as human beings and economic actors. It did not take the COVID-19 pandemic to remind us that, especially in times of major crisis, the most vulnerable, which still includes many members of longtime minorities and underrepresented groups, tend to be affected and suffer most. The struggle is not yet over.

However, I have good reason, I think, to argue in this book that the LGBT+ community is now a powerful factor in the global economy, one that is not going to be returned to the shadows and cannot be ignored.

## A turning point

It all began with the Stonewall riots during the summer of 1969, when gay and trans people fought back after being severely persecuted by New York City police. But the learning curve, always steep, has accelerated dramatically in roughly the last seven or eight years, during which time it has also become increasingly global.

In retrospect, 2013–14 represented a key moment of change when advancing LGBT+ equality in the workplace took on a new momentum. Many factors have played a part, as I will relate in this book, but four stand out:

1. For decades, the United Nations (UN) had not engaged substantially with the issues of LGBT+ equality and the world of business. But in 2013, the UN Free & Equal Campaign was launched by the UN High Commissioner of Human Rights, beginning a process of informing and educating in order to fight bullying, harassment, hate speech, violence, and other forms of discrimination against LGBT+ people. This unprecedented campaign continues to this day. Only four years later, the UN LGBTI Standards of Conduct for Business followed, managed under the umbrella of the Free & Equal Campaign. The number of companies that signed grew quickly, reaching over 300 at time of writing.

   With these two breakthrough UN initiatives, the ideas of LGBT+ rights perceived as human rights and key to global business not only arrived prominently on the global stage, but both ideas were also thought of together – another milestone.

2. In the fall of 2013, the first global LGBT+ out executive role model list was launched by British social business INvolve, published at the time by the *Financial Times* (now by *Yahoo Finance*), recognizing the strong internal and external engagements of out business leaders in matters of LGBT+ diversity and inclusion (D&I). It stimulated further rankings, including editions in Australia, France, and Germany, for example. Stuart Cameron, who started the German rankings, now co-managed with local Prout at Work

Foundation, sums up their value as he sees them: "Visibility creates confrontation with clichés, may enable positive development of normality, and can ultimately lead to tolerance, acceptance, and real inclusion."

The lists have contributed substantially to an increased awareness and visibility of out executives and out future leaders, as well as supportive straight allies. Media coverage has been strong from the start and ranked companies and role models have proudly marketed their success internally and externally, especially on social media. Present in all industries, across all hierarchical levels, ages, ethnicities, and genders, workplace activists and others who were inspired by them now represent a growing cohort of well-networked and impactful GaYme Changers.

3. Also in the fall of 2013, Guido Barilla made offensive homophobic remarks on Italian radio, initiating an unprecedented public outcry globally, marking a shift of values and expectations and pushing the global Italian pasta primus Barilla to start a spectacular and to-this-day credible LGBT+ D&I turnaround.

The Barilla story, which I tell in detail in Part I of this book, stands as a warning for companies: in a fast-paced, globalized, digital-media, and networked world, there is growing pressure on companies to take sides for equal LGBT+ rights and opportunities through convincing and verifiable D&I efforts. If they do not do so, they run the risk of suffering economic damage. At the same time, the story of Barilla's cultural transformation is an object lesson in just how quickly a company can manage true cultural change – if it correctly reads the runes, acts courageously, and is helped by the right people and organizations, including civil rights activists and LGBT+ nonprofits.

4. In January 2014, a historic breakfast took place at the annual meeting of the World Economic Forum (WEF) in Davos, Switzerland. Set up in partnership with the large US LGBT+ nonprofit Human Rights Campaign, it was initiated by two American billionaire investors, one of whom had a gay son. It was "only" a nonofficial, offsite event. But it was also a landmark occasion at which, for the first time, LGBT+ equality was discussed at the high mass of the global business elite, and it was the talk of the town at Davos that year.

This fast-growing awareness at the top level was strongly supported only a few months later by a prominent member of the business elite: ex-BP CEO Lord John Browne, publishing his book *The Glass Closet: Why coming out is good business.* Only around seven years earlier, this former British superhero, who had led BP to unprecedented success, had experienced a spectacular fall. It was connected to his long-hidden homosexuality and the end of a relationship to a former rent boy, and was brutally covered by the media. In a peculiar way, *The Glass Closet* marked an amazing comeback on the global stage. No other top business figure had, up to then, both come out – though involuntarily – and drawn attention to the financial benefit of LGBT+ D&I, much less in such an elaborate way. His book shone a spotlight on this in the media for the first time, drew a wide corporate audience, encouraged support from straight leaders and ultimately had a domino effect beyond business. This impact was amplified by Apple CEO Tim Cook who, only some weeks later in October 2014, came out as gay in a remarkable article on *Bloomberg*, which received global attention and was widely discussed. At around the same time, some other top executives also came out, for example, Jim Fitterling, today Dow's CEO.

In retrospect, the year 2014 was a starting point in urging global business leaders and the WEF itself to put LGBT+ inclusion on the official agenda in Davos, where Browne's, Cook's, and Fitterling's peers meet annually. The impact of the historic breakfast and Browne's, Cook's, and Fitterling's actions contributed to a substantial change of conversation there and led to fast-increasing numbers of offsite and official WEF events around LGBT+ equality, all connected to either economic and/or human rights arguments for inclusion. Eventually, only five years later, the launch of the new Partnership for Global LGBTI Equality (PGLE) was celebrated in Davos.

Today, the PGLE is formally connected to the WEF, counting major multinational companies as founder members. Human rights NGOs, LGBT+ nonprofits, and the UN High Commissioner of Human Rights are supporters. The year it was founded, the Partnership also took on the task of further advancing the diffusion and operationalization of the UN LGBTI Standards of Conduct for Business. It now bridges big global businesses, the WEF, the UN, and human rights advocacies – a stunning constellation, unimaginable some years ago.

## A journey

Writing a book like this is more than just typing – it involves research online and in libraries, interviews, travel, and discussion with friends and other trusted sounding boards. And then there are the moments when you retreat to friends or your partner, exhausted by trying to find the right words.

Even with a fairly fixed table of contents to fill, it can be a journey into the unknown. Having been in book publishing for many years – as an editor, program strategist, publishing director, advisor, and author – I knew this but still, even with a German version to build on, developing this English-language book I found I was facing unknown territory again, with new interviews, research, and writing, making it a completely new work. I took the leap. Now, *voilà*, it is done.

The journey was exciting. I have conducted researched on five continents. From Munich, where I live, I have traveled to New York, Johannesburg, Moscow, London, Paris, Rome, Hong Kong, Brussels, Vienna, Berlin, Seattle, Manchester, Frankfurt, and Amsterdam. I have connected to many other places digitally; for example, India, Japan, Canada, Spain, Mexico, Poland, the Czech Republic, Switzerland, Liechtenstein, Australia, and Brazil. I have participated in conferences, award ceremonies, panel discussions, and workshops, sometimes as the only external participant.

I have conducted numerous interviews, face to face, by phone, Skype, or Zoom. Sometimes the conversations were straight to the point, sometimes they took unexpected turns. Sometimes tears were shed, for example, when seasoned top managers suddenly recalled memories of long-gone suffering or when interviewees from cultures hostile to LGBT+ people talked about being harassed, stigmatized, and even beaten. Sometimes there were also tears of joy.

## Powerful arguments

Almost always there was an open spirit of support and serious engagement – condensed into an interest in helping to further underscore what in recent years have become the main arguments for advancing LGBT+ equality: from a human rights perspective it is the right thing to do, and at the same time it is good for business, economies, and society as a whole.

Not to advance it would mean, at least in the long run, losing talents, customers, business partners, the support of diverse communities and cities, productivity, sales, revenue, profits, GDP, taxes, public goods, and much more.

In my research to understand the change, several key factors emerged. There are many more in this book's analysis and stories around dynamic individual, corporate, and other organizational GaYme Changers, but here are some of the most important:

- Unlike their predecessor generations, the young have fast-changing values and expectations around corporate social responsibility, equality, inclusion, justice, human rights, open working cultures, and sexual and gender identity. They influence all parts of society, including the world of work.

- There is growing awareness that merely making LGBT+ D&I work internally is not enough, since the young perceive companies as part of society, with responsibilities, and expect them to support LGBT+ nonprofits taking care of the more vulnerable.

- Essentially there are two incentives for businesses to do well at LGBT+ D&I. First, companies that are genuinely LGBT+-friendly – and not "pinkwashers" – do better externally, with customers, and many other stakeholders, who, in the main, will no longer tolerate businesses failing on this. Second, more open and diverse corporate cultures are better internally – for employee wellbeing, at productivity, innovation, and more. For both those reasons, they also do better at attracting and retaining the strongest talents.

- Many global corporates across many industries have become strong drivers of LGBT+-related change in their workplaces and beyond. This can include becoming members or supporters of the fast-growing number of national and global organizations working for LGBT+ equality, such as nonprofits, social businesses, networks, coalitions, student clubs, equal marriage campaigns and chambers of commerce, sometimes even in places with legislation and culture hostile to LGBT+ people. In doing all this, and doing so with increasing speed, competing within industries to be best in class, companies are responding to the changing values and expectations.

## More research

For some time now, research and business results have shown that companies and other organizations that practice sustained, systematic, and flexible LGBT+ diversity and inclusion management thought of together with social responsibilities gain a major advantage in a highly competitive world. In an era when there is so much pressure to create and innovate, smartly managed diverse perspectives are crucial to success. The more equal opportunities LGBT+ people have, the more they become healthy, learning, and productive change agents.

Evidence of the cost of LGBT+ exclusion on a macroeconomic level has grown recently. It comes, for example, from Kenya, with research demonstrating that anti-LGBT+ discrimination in the country may be reducing GDP by up to 1.7%. This is mainly due to poor health outcomes, lost tourist dollars, and underutilized human capital,[1] as a study by London-based nonprofit Open for Business (OFB), a coalition of global companies working for LGBT+-inclusive businesses, cities, and societies, has shown. Based on these findings, OFB's local country director Yvonne Muthoni can now contribute to convincing Kenyan business and political leaders that laws and initiatives against anti-LGBT+ discrimination would also be good for them.

A 2014 study on India showed similar harm to GDP. Finally, in 2018, Section 377 of the Indian criminal code, which criminalized, among other things, same-sex intercourse between adults, was dropped. Living and working as a member of the LGBT+ community remains tough, with discrimination and violence high. However, the change allows businesses and other organizations, especially in places like India's IT hub Bangalore, much more freedom to drive the inclusion and empowerment that will ultimately deliver both social and economic benefits.

Social business Out Leadership, for example, offers a global perspective for companies. It is a vanguard working for LGBT+ equality in companies on economic grounds. Headquartered in New York, it was founded by former Wall Street banker Todd Sears more than ten years ago. It is growing fast and today counts over 80 member firms across several industries. It engages on four continents and reports a compelling "$5.2 trillion LGBT+ market opportunity."[2]

While there is evidence of LGBT+ representation having declined somewhat during the COVID-19 pandemic, the trend toward greater inclusion is not going into reverse any time soon.

A new Deloitte Global Millennial Survey partly conducted during the pandemic found that young people "continue to push for a world in which businesses and governments mirror [their] commitment to society, putting people ahead of profits."[3]

The message is clear: inclusion, equality, and empowering LGBT+ people pays off on all levels.

## A watershed moment

In the light of these developments and findings, the main advice to companies and lawmakers must be the following: even in the face of prejudice, unconscious bias, open hostility, resistance, or crisis, it is *always* and *everywhere* economically, socially and ethically beneficial for businesses, communities, cities, and societies to invest in compelling LGBT+ diversity and inclusion management. This includes credible socially responsible action.

Making this investment confers on each individual LGBT+ person the respect that they deserve – which is as much as anyone else deserves. It also nurtures the development of a dynamic, modern, and highly competitive – yet humane – business world. There is economic power in human recognition.

Erin Uritus is CEO at Out & Equal Workplace Advocates, a leading US-based nonprofit that has been promoting LGBT+ equality in the workplace for about 25 years, mainly focusing on the US. With regard to her country, which is, in many ways, a global LGBT+ trendsetter, she rightly summarizes that in recent years the LGBT+ community and their allies have very successfully made the case that businesses and their employees benefit from more LGBT+ inclusivity: "We've seen that in the trajectory of companies who have changed their human resources and benefits policies, and the growing number of companies who step up for our community when we need their public advocacy."

But Uritus is also looking beyond this success: "The next frontier is for these companies to be able to effectively translate the decisions that they have made at the leadership level to every corner of their firm." It is "one thing to have a culture of belonging at corporate headquarters in New York or London. It's harder to have that translate to the factory floor, to storefronts in rural areas, and across political borders."

Uritus' view is understandable, particularly in light of the harsh and growing cultural and political divide the US has been experiencing for some years now. And there are similar tendencies in other democracies.

David Pollard, co-founder and Executive Director of Amsterdam-based Workplace Pride Foundation, which is very internationally focused, adds more on the global perspective: "In the greater context of the social changes taking place with the Black Lives Matter movement, the #MeToo debate, and the pandemic," he sees the world as being at a watershed moment, with businesses and governments likely to take a completely new look at LGBT+ inclusion in the workplace. "I think," he says, "that everyone will realize that we are in a period of social change as big as or greater than 1968, and that all stakeholders are going to have to adapt to the new reality of being more inclusive around the world."

Pollard could be right, and LGBT+ inclusion could be a substantial part of this social change – with strong support from not just the corporate arena, but also the political sphere. There are signs of a new momentum. Recently, in November 2020, the European Commission announced the first-ever strategy for advancing LGBT+ equality in the 27 EU member states, with their roughly 450 million total inhabitants. Just two weeks later, only a month after his election, then President-elect Joe Biden, in a short speech to the International LGBTQ Leaders Conference, committed to building the "most pro-equality administration in history" and pledged to "usher in a new era of LGBTQ rights."

Both announcements sound promising – not just for Europeans and Americans, but for the world. Still, promises only mean something when they are kept. Economic actors such as employees, entrepreneurs, customers, and investors know this well – as do citizens.

# Part I

**Barilla's pasta war,
a global turnaround, and
a new social positioning**

# 1. Offensive words and an outcry

On a late summer evening in early September 2013, Guido Barilla, head of the venerable pasta company that bears his family name, is interviewed on Italy's *Radio 24* on the program *La Zanzara*. The interviewer is known for directness, but nobody is forced to say anything they don't want to.

Guido Barilla, born in 1958, married to his second wife and father of five children, first speaks in detail about the company's long history in the field of pasta. It's a clear success story. Barilla is widely known. The Parma-based brand stands for culinary quality, the pleasures of Italian home cooking, healthy Mediterranean cuisine, and dining with loved ones. Many people also know Wasa, the premium crispbread from Sweden also belonging to the Barilla Group, along with other well-respected brands.

Except for a short period in the 1970s, the soon-to-be 150-year-old Italian company has always been in family hands. Today, 85% belongs to Guido Barilla and his siblings. The family does not make a fuss about their wealth, seek the limelight, or cultivate exaggerated vanities in public.

But Guido Barilla discusses more in this interview than just noodles and sauces. Asked why the pasta supremo does not want to advertise using depictions of homosexuals, he describes his understanding of family. His remarks, which I summarize as follows, are noteworthy to say the least:

On Barilla's values:
> We have a slightly different culture. For us the "holy/sacred
> family" remains one of the core values of the company. Our
> family is the classic, traditional family.

On the pasta eating habits of homosexuals:
> If homosexuals like our pasta and our advertising, they will eat our
> pasta. If they do not like them, they will eat someone else's pasta.

On advertising with a gay family:
> I would not do a commercial with a homosexual family. Not
> because of lack of respect toward homosexuals – who have the

right to do whatever they want without disturbing others – but because we want to talk to traditional families where the woman has a fundamental role.

## "Us" against "them"

The words of the patriarch are unambiguous. They draw a clear line: on one side is the "us" – the guardians of the "real," of, as it were, "holy/sacred" family values – and on the other is the "them," those who are attached to an open or an alternative family concept or are just single.

Guido Barilla says nothing against same-sex marriages in the interview but expresses strong opposition to adoption of children by same-sex couples. And, as noted, he says that if gays and lesbians do not like Barilla, they should eat other brands.

In family-orientated Italy, where the word of the Holy Mother (Catholic) Church is still important and women and men know their place, he probably thought that's what mattered – if he thought anything at all.

But in the media, especially social media, the story quickly becomes hugely negative for the pasta company. Just as fast, there are boycott calls from politicians, LGBT+ activists, and others – and not just in Italy, but throughout Europe and the world. The critics' charge is as clear as the head of the family and company's message had been: Barilla is discriminating against gays and lesbians; it is homophobic.

"Gastronomic homophobia is something we haven't seen before," Franco Grillini, head of the LGBT+ organization *Gaynet Italia*, pointedly remarks. "That niche has now been filled by Guido Barilla." Founded in 1998, Gaynet Italia is an association consisting mainly of journalists and members of cultural institutions. One important activity is providing training courses on sexual orientation and gender identity to journalists and other media and cultural actors, which includes publishing guides and other materials. Gaynet also operate the online news site *Gaynews.it*. The pasta boss did not realize, Grillini goes on, that the Italian family has profoundly changed in recent years. And he suggests that "60% of Italians should no longer buy their pasta because they do not belong to a traditional family."[1]

The elderly, now-deceased Nobel literary laureate Dario Fo, who decades ago appeared in ads for Barilla himself, launches a petition with the headline, "Tell Barilla: Where there is love, there is family." The petition has the form of an open letter, beginning with the words "Dear Guido Barilla" and ending with these:

*Guido, your company has come to define Italy – an Italy that is also made of unmarried couples, extended families, and families with LGBT parents.*

*That's why I ask you to take this opportunity and to return to the spirit of those commercials I starred in during the 1950s. That's why I ask you to end this controversy and be an ambassador of equality for all.*

*I ask you, Guido, to reflect the true Italy of today and become an ambassador of equality and a voice of the present. And I ask you to commit to an upcoming advertising campaign from Barilla, where the family can finally be represented in all its infinite and wonderful shapes of our times.*[2]

The petition is signed by more than 100,000 people.

## Battleground

But there is more. The hashtag #BoicottaBarilla not only becomes one of the most widely used Twitter hashtags in Italy, but – as #BoycottBarilla – also takes off globally. It put the billion-dollar company, founded in 1877, in extreme difficulty. According to its own data, at that point Barilla had 30 production facilities worldwide and produces 1.7 million tons of food, which were sold in around one hundred countries.[3] In the US, Barilla made about $430 million in pasta sales in 2013, corresponding to a market share of 30%,[4] making this its second most important market. And while Barilla earned most of its revenue in its home country around 20 years ago, the proportion is now less than half, so its global sales matter hugely.

The fierce reactions around the world threaten not only Barilla but its subsidiaries: Wasa and other high-turnover brands such as Harrys (French toast), Gran Cereale (Italian wholemeal biscuits), and more. They could easily be drawn into the boycott whirlwind.

Barilla USA quickly apologizes on its Facebook page. But is it credible?

The Harvard University Dining Service (HUDS) announces that it will stop serving Barilla pasta. Representatives of GLAAD, the influential US LGBT+ nonprofit organization with a special focus on the media, comments critically. Golden Globe award winner Mia Farrow tweets: "Now that we know that pasta CEO G. Barilla is homophobic, it's a good day to say that DeCecco is far better anyway."[5]

Other competitors like Bertoni, San Remo, and Buitoni posts social media messages supporting all types of families. The *Huffington Post* runs a feature itemizing "12 pasta brands that haven't pissed off gay people."[6]

Germany, an important pasta market, with its more than 80 million inhabitants, also becomes a battleground. Competitor Bertolli takes a boldly original stance, publishing on its Facebook page a motif of "same sex" pasta pairs with the slogan "Love and pasta for all," which is very well received. As early as 2009, the manufacturer of pasta and pasta sauce had already run a commercial depicting a gay couple and now – gleefully – it refers to it again.

## Culture war or a new path?

So, what to do? Join battle in a culture war? Although Barilla receives support from socially conservative and church-related circles, especially in Italy, the danger for the company is obvious. Will it get worse?

This is what Claudio Colzani fears. Barely a year in office as CEO of the Barilla group, his extensive previous experience is relevant in this crisis, especially with regard to the US business and to diversity management. Before he became the boss in Parma, Colzani, who studied Philosophy in Milan, worked for about 25 years for Anglo-Dutch consumer goods company Unilever – most recently as CEO of Unilever France, and in the US, where he was not only Chief Customer Officer but also part of the diversity committee.

On a drive from Milan to Parma for a dinner with Guido Barilla, Colzani tells *Bloomberg*, he follows the live interview on the radio and is horrified. Thirty minutes later he is sitting with Barilla in the restaurant, but the food is secondary. The main thing is to make the company head understand his interview's consequences.

To clarify the company hierarchy: Guido Barilla is Chairman, his two brothers Luca and Paolo are Vice Chairmen, and all three are something like leading board members. Colzani reports to them – with the Barillas, as owners, having the final say.

When Guido Barilla and Colzani meet, the shit storm online and ensuing wave of boycott threats has yet to take off. Colzani is worried about possible market share losses, "but I was much more worried about people perceiving Barilla as an out-of-date brand,"[7] he said later to *Bloomberg*.

## Dangers to reputation

When, finally, the full force of reactions hit home at Barilla, multiplying boycott threats notwithstanding, it hardly affects turnover at first. This is quite typical. As Mary-Hunter McDonnell, then Assistant Professor of Strategy at the McDonough Business School of Washington, DC's Georgetown University, tells the *Washington Post*, the danger for companies from boycotts lies not to short-term profits, which they rarely affect directly. Rather, the reputational harm can have drastic effects long term.[8] So Colzani at this point becomes highly attentive to possible changes in Barilla's brand reputation, which has been stable for years.

Only a few months later, his concerns are shown to be justified. In the 2014 ranking from the Reputation Institute, Barilla falls 21 places from 32 to 55.[9] The reputation capital the company has built up over many years is threatening to melt away. The damage is felt especially in the US, the UK, India, Australia, and Brazil. "That was a nightmare scenario," Kasper Ulf Nielsen, executive partner and co-founder of Reputation Institute, tells *Forbes*.[10]

At that time, to be a candidate for its international reputation list, a company had to be well known in the 15 countries surveyed, with revenues exceeding $6 billion in the United States or $1 billion globally. The survey aims to quantify how companies are viewed by consumers, looking at trust, admiration, feeling, and overall reputation. The institute found that 85% of consumers would buy from a company with a good reputation. Only 9% would buy from a company with a bad reputation.[11]

But it is not just reputation that is about to become a serious problem for Barilla. Internally, some employees, including managers, register shock – as do family members and friends, as CEO Claudio Colzani relates. Guido Barilla, generally very reserved in his appearances and communications, comes to understand that he has made a big mistake and offended a lot of people.

## A journey begins

Colzani calls former colleagues for advice. He enlists the support of Korn Ferry, a major consultancy focused on human resources (HR) management and related organizational matters, and US public relations agency Edelman. It is clear that a superficial image enhancement will not be enough.

What happens next can, depending on one's point of view, be interpreted as self-interest-driven rapid re-education or sheer opportunism. As I have no inclination to moralize, I take the first view – not least because Barilla's action is incisive, effective, and comprehensively convincing.

The Barilla Group begins a journey of learning and change that is careful yet quick. It is also particularly revealing in its detail. Here is an old family company from a deeply Catholic country in which globally operating family businesses are central to innovation and growth, a company selling not software, financial services, luxury items, or consultancy, but everyday culinary products, including one that is especially well-loved.

Barilla's story is worth telling just because the transformation was ultimately so huge. But it also serves as a valuable introduction to LGBT+ business issues, showing how an old stalwart can become credibly more open, modern, diverse, inclusive, and socially responsible.

The fundamental transformation begins at the end of September, when Guido Barilla apologizes in a video on the company website. This is only the first step.

He offers to exchange ideas with LGBT+ community representatives, to listen and learn about the blind spots that underlays his remarks. Not everyone wants to talk to him. Many fear being misused for PR purposes. In the end, however, he manages to meet LGBT+ activists in Italy and the US several times.

## 2. Starting to learn: The realities of family and home life

There was a particular focus on arranging such talks for Barilla in the US, given the importance of this market. Here, Guido Barilla sought to get to know the environment, other forms of family, and the lives of LGBT+ people in general.

Among other things, he held talks with representatives of the Tyler Clementi Foundation, an organization well known to the parents of LGBT+ children in the US.

### A student's death and how his parents honor him

Tyler Clementi was an 18-year-old student at Rutgers University, New Jersey, who, in September 2010, jumped off the George Washington Bridge, which connects New Jersey and Manhattan. Not simply a response to a perceived lack of meaning in life, his suicide was caused by malicious homophobic cyberbullying, including webcam pictures secretly taken by his roommate. It provoked nationwide shock and grief, with President Barack Obama and Secretary of State Hillary Clinton, among others, expressing their horror. Attention to bullying and cyberbullying against young LGBT+ people increased when at least three other US teenagers took their own lives for similar reasons that same month.

About half a year after Tyler's death, the Point Foundation decided to award a Tyler Clementi Point Scholarship to honor him. The foundation had been supporting talented LGBT+ students for many years through various grants and is the largest organization of its kind in the US.[12]

In 2011, Tyler's parents, Jane and Joseph Clementi, also decided to do something to honor their son and give meaning to his otherwise senseless death. They established the Tyler Clementi Foundation to promote acceptance of LGBT+ teenagers and others excluded from society, educate about all forms of bullying and cyberbullying, and support research and development on the causes and prevention of suicide. The foundation has been very active since its inception.

Research shows that suicide rates among LGBT+ adolescents, compared to heterosexual adolescents, are significantly higher.[13] A study published at the end of 2018 evaluated survey results from

2.5 million young people between the ages of 12 and 20 from ten countries. The risk of suicide was more than three times higher among homosexual adolescents than among their heterosexual peers, more than four times higher among bisexuals, and around six times higher among transgender adolescents. One of the authors, Ester di Giacomo from the Italian University of Milano-Bicocca, sees the main explanation for this as being the social stigmatization of LGBT+ people and the concomitant, inseparable difficulty of accepting oneself as one is.[14] This reflects the mainstream research view.

This is what Guido Barilla learned in his discussions with the foundation – that humiliating, bullying, suicide threats, and suicides are part of life for families with LGBT+ children.

## Italian conditions

In Italy, only shortly after his offensive remarks, the Barilla boss held a meeting with representatives of LBGT+ organizations. They included, for example, the aforementioned Gaynet Italia, *Equality Italia*, *ArciLesbica*, which opposes discrimination against lesbian women, *Famiglie Arcobaleno*, which works for LGBT+ parents and families, and *Arcigay*. Founded in 1985, Arcigay is the main Italian LGBT+ nonprofit and largest in terms of number of volunteers and activists. In the meeting, Guido Barilla apologized and promised to start a profound learning journey in his home country too.

Just a few weeks after his controversial statements, he received an object lesson in just how pernicious homophobia and discrimination is – and not only for young LGBT+ people. In the first session of the Italian parliament immediately after the interview, Gianlucca Buonanno of the right-wing party Lega taunted two openly homosexual parliamentary colleagues with a fennel bulb, then tried to physically attack one of them. In Italian, fennel can imply extreme contempt for homosexuals.

The following month, a 21-year-old gay medical student who had been bullied called ten suicide hotlines before jumping from the 11th floor of an old pasta factory in Rome. Later, a message from him was found: "Italy is a free country, but there is homophobia." It was the third suicide of its kind in Rome that year.[15]

Italy is anything but a paradise for LGBT+ people compared with Europe as a whole, as can be seen from the work of ILGA Europe, the nongovernmental organization based in Brussels and part of ILGA World (see box), each working for LGBT+ equality.

## ILGA Europe/ILGA World[16]

ILGA Europe is a kind of umbrella body for more than 600 organizations from 54 countries in Europe (and to a very small extent Central Asian countries such as Armenia and Azerbaijan). It is currently supported by the European Union. It advocates for human rights and LGBT+ equality, uses strategic litigation in European courts to advance LGBT+ rights, and aims to strengthen them in Europe (and Central Asia) by supporting its member organizations and other LGBT+ groups on advocacy, fundraising, strategic communications, and organizational development.

Since 1996, it has been an independent legal entity, but is also part of ILGA World. ILGA World was founded in 1978 as IGA (International Gay Association), changing its name eight years later to ILGA (for International Lesbian and Gay Association) and today sees itself as a fighter for LGBT+ people's rights globally.

ILGA World was, among other things, an early advocate for the removal of homosexuality from the WHO list of diseases. On May 17 1990, today celebrated as the International Day Against Homo-, Bi- and Transphobia (IDAHOBIT), the umbrella organization was able to celebrate achievement of this goal.

ILGA World now brings together some 1,500 organizations from around 150 countries. Its headquarters are in Geneva, where the World Health Organization (WHO) and the United Nations High Commissioner for Human Rights are also based.

An example of ILGA World's recent activities is the release, at the end of 2020, of the State-Sponsored Homophobia Report, 14th edition, a global legislation overview. And in June 2020 the nonprofit launched its new World Map on Sexual Orientation Laws in 20 languages, including Chinese, Arabic, Russian, Swahili, Japanese, Tagalog/Filipino, Malay, and Polish.

## Modest progress

One important thing ILGA Europe is doing is producing annual rankings and detailed reports.

Their Rainbow Europe Ranking examines laws and policies in 49 countries using 69 criteria divided into six categories: equality and non discrimination, family, hate crime and hate speech, legal gender recognition and bodily integrity, civil society space, and asylum.[17] Scores range from 100% (full respect for LGBT+ human rights = complete equality) to 0% (no respect for LGBT+ human rights = very strong discrimination).[18]

Looking at just the 27 EU countries, Malta, Belgium, Luxembourg, France, and Denmark currently lead. Spain is in sixth place, and Germany 12th. Italy has been far down the rankings for many years, currently 23rd, with only Bulgaria, Romania, Latvia, and Poland doing worse.

In the context of all the 49 countries examined, Italy ranks even worse: 35 – lower than Kosovo, Hungary, Serbia, Albania, and Georgia. Switzerland, in which almost 9% of the population speaks Italian, ranks poorly too: 23rd. (All figures as of December 2020.)

One example of Italy's slowness: at the time of Barilla's interview, the legal designation of a registered civil partnership did not yet exist there, only being introduced three years later – compared to, for example, Germany, which has had it since around 2001.

So no wonder that, in his interview with *Bloomberg*, Colzani said Guido Barilla's remarks reminded him powerfully that Italy's LGBT+ debate has started "very, very late compared to many other European countries." The reason was clear to him: the strong influence of religion.[19]

## Catholicism, morals, and business: Dolce & Gabbana

About 70% of Italians are Catholic,[20] even if they don't all go to church. Just how strongly the resulting mentality is rooted in Italian society and thus in its companies, is usefully demonstrated by Domenico Dolce and Stefano Gabbana of the Dolce & Gabbana fashion house, who are worth billions. Although today they are just business partners and friends, they were, for a long time, a couple, something they made public as early as 1999.

In an interview in the Italian magazine *Panorama*, however, they too declared that, "The only family is the traditional one." Only about a year and a half after Guido Barilla's radio remarks, the entrepreneurs went even further. They expostulated with *Panorama* against same-sex adoptions and parents, and denigrated children. They spoke of "rented wombs," and "children of chemistry,"[21] and made disparaging remarks about in vitro fertilization, the reproductive technology Elton John and his husband David Furnish, for instance, used to have their two children.

Again, there were boycott threats and outrage: from Elton John himself, from Victoria Beckham, Courtney Love, Madonna, Ricky Martin – himself a gay father – and from tennis star and lesbian icon Martina Navratilova. In the months that followed, there were also heated arguments between Elton John and the designers.

But though they had made themselves the object of massive criticism in the LGBT+ community, the turmoil was less fervid. Partly, this is about the difference between a mass-market culinary product and expensive fashion. But also, crucially, the line "us" versus "them" was not as easy to draw.

Finally, the designers rowed back. In a *Vogue* interview, Dolce, in particular, apologized and reversed his position, now praising modern science and saying the most important thing for him was people's happiness. Children, he said, are simply children. Gabbana, meanwhile, even said that he himself had thought about becoming a father.[22]

After half a year, the dispute with Elton John was settled. Perhaps the sudden change of mind was financially motivated, a hypothesis supported by the brand producing a collection of t-shirts depicting various parental pairings. But in the same *Vogue* interview, the designers also focused on their Catholicism. Dolce, who comes from Sicily, is particularly devout. He is convinced that certain decisions that other homosexual men and women may make are not open to him because of his faith.

In contrast to Dolce, Gabbana is not a regular churchgoer, but even born as he was in metropolitan Milan, he grew up embedded in Italian Catholic culture. "Our two mothers wore medallions of the Virgin in their bras for protection," he said.[23]

## A difficult environment even for companies willing to change

So this is the socially conservative environment Barilla inhabits, where even two gay, economically independent fashion designers adhere to the ideal of the "traditional" family, with concomitant discrimination against LGBT+ people.

All companies in Italy face the same challenge. "It's difficult to talk about something in our country where people might think about sexuality," says Giovanna Spinazzola. Spinazzola has worked for some 20 years for BNL, the Italian arm of BNP Paribas. The big French banking group operates in more than 70 countries, with about 200,000 employees and various brands.

Spinazzola works as a marketing manager at the still quite new Italian headquarters in Rome, where I met her at an LGBT+ business conference. She co-founded the Italian branch of BNP Paribas' LGBT+ employee network just under four years after the outcry against Barilla.

"We receive strong support from our CEO, Andrea Munari," says the southern Italian marketing expert, stressing the importance of top management support, "And we are also learning a lot from other national offshoots of our global network within the group, especially those in the US and UK, which are much further along. But we must not forget we are in Italy. There are cultural differences. Things are moving slowly in our country, even in companies. They are, of course, a mirror of society." But, she says, "We at BNL have achieved a lot in a short time, for example with training sessions to raise awareness of language in connection with LGBT+."

Another Italian manager working in the capital, who asked not to be named, agrees, adding, "Here in Rome, we also have the Vatican." This inspires, he says, great resistance to more LGBT+ acceptance in almost all areas – especially compared to more cosmopolitan Milan, the country's business stronghold.

Spinazzola says she is not deterred. It is imperative, she feels, for companies to become active and remain so. The outcry against Barilla is a warning, she says, to businesses – especially, but not only, Italian ones – about what can happen if their LGBT+ policies fail to keep up in a globalized world.

## Help from Parks and Ivan Scalfarotto

In order to support the learning process, not just in the US but also in his home country, Guido Barilla finally decided to turn to *Parks – Liberi e Uguali* (Parks for short – the rest of the name means "free and equal"), a nonprofit LGBT+ organization based in Milan. For more than a decade now, Parks has been helping paying member companies and organizations improve LGBT+ inclusion in their workplaces.

A brief note on the name Parks: it pays tribute to Rosa Louise Parks, the African American civil rights activist arrested in Montgomery, Alabama on December 1, 1955, for refusing to give up her bus seat to a white passenger. This led to the Montgomery bus boycott, one of the main triggers for the black civil rights movement, which ended the so-called Jim Crow state and local laws enforcing racial segregation in the Southern US states.

When Barilla approached Parks, they worked especially with global businesses not headquartered in Italy but with a strong presence there. If the now-troubled pasta maker became a member, this could be a signal to other Italian-headquartered organizations. Guido Barilla's first contact at Parks was Ivan Scalfarotto, an iconic activist for LGBT+ equality in Italy and globally. In 2010 he founded Parks, and 2015 and 2016 made the British *Economist* Global Diversity List, featuring the 50 most important personalities active, influential, and effective in the fight for greater diversity and inclusion.

Scalfarotto has not only worked for several banks, including Banco Ambrosiano Veneto and Citigroup, for which he was Head of HR in London, he has also been politically active for many years as a member of a party that in 2007 became the social democratically-oriented Partito Democratico (PD). The PD is best known for its former leader, the ex-Prime Minister Matteo Renzi. Scalfarotto served for some time as deputy party leader, was elected to the Italian parliament, of which he remains a member to this day, and served for a few years as Under Secretary of State in Renzi's cabinets.[24] In 2013, when Scalfarotto became a member of the Italian parliament, he started to nurture a successor at Parks. But when Guido Barilla asked to speak to Parks, Scalfarotto was still fully active there.

Guido Barilla could hardly have found a better contact in Italy than Scalfarotto, himself gay with a long history of LGBT+ activism, in addition to his wide experience of the world of global business at close quarters and his familiarity with Italy's political mechanisms.

In fact, there was also no real alternative. Parks was unrivalled in Italy in terms of the work it had done – and still is today.

A Parks collaboration with Barilla to support a journey to better LGBT+ inclusion was established and continues to this day.

# 3. GLAAD's script for acceptance and David Mixner's surprise

The most important impetus for Barilla's learning journey, however, originated from the US. Guido Barilla knows the country well. As a student he spent a year at a US high school. Later he studied philosophy in Milan, but also spent time at Boston College. After his studies and before he entered the family business, he also worked for several years at various US food companies.

As part of the reaction his interview provoked there, he received in invitation from GLAAD, the aforementioned nonprofit LGBT+ organization focused on the media, to meet with LGBT+ community members and "get to know how traditional we really are," Rich Ferraro, one of the organization's spokespersons, told *USA Today*.[25]

His mother, Linda, added Ferraro, had launched a Change.org petition focused on her neighborhood supermarket. Parts of the petition I quote here:

*As an Italian-American mom, some of my favorite memories are of sitting around the dinner table with my husband and our three sons on Sunday after Church. Lots of tomato sauce, lots of laughs, and lots of Barilla. In fact, there are several boxes of Barilla sitting in my cabinet right now. That is about to change.*

*My grandparents moved to Brooklyn, NY from Italy and taught me that family is more important than anything. I remembered that tradition when my son Rich was a teenager and cried at our dinner table as he told me he was gay.*

*I have a newsflash for Guido Barilla: I am proud of my gay son, and we are a traditional family.*

*Even though my sons are adults now, no one messes with any of my boys. I shop at Stop & Shop, and now that I dumped Barilla,*

*I think they should too. Please join me and urge Stop & Shop to take Barilla off their shelves.*[26]

Guido Barilla, already understanding more and more how outdated his old, exclusionary narrative was, accepted the invitation to speak with GLAAD. And the nonprofit organization was, in fact, perfect for him. GLAAD aims to be, in its own words, a "dynamic media force" promoting cultural change through changing narratives. It seeks, again in its own words, to "rewrite the script for LGBTQ acceptance" and to create "a world where everyone can live the life they love."[27]

Founded in New York in 1985 by gays and lesbians from the media industry, GLAAD's name was originally an acronym for Gay & Lesbian Alliance Against Defamation. Since 2013, the name has stood only for itself – without referring to gays and lesbians, making it clear that the organization also works for bisexual, transgender, and queer people.

The trigger for GLAAD's foundation was what the initiators saw as defamatory and sensationalist reporting on homosexuality and AIDS. The group started small, meeting at first in their homes. The first big success came in less than two years: The *New York Times* decided, after senior editors met with GLAAD, to use 'gay' instead of other more degrading terms. GLAAD subsequently urged news agencies and other television and print news sources to follow suit.

Soon it expanded to San Francisco and Los Angeles to influence how LGBT+ people are portrayed in films and TV shows. Since 1991, the GLAAD Media Awards have been presented year after year, recognizing English and Spanish-language media that meet GLAAD goals. In 2020, awards were given in about 30 categories, some in Spanish, including film, documentary, newspaper article, magazine article, comedy series, drama series, blog, digital journalism article, TV movie, TV journalism newsmagazine, comic book, and video game.[28] Among past award winners are numerous artistically and economically very successful films that can now be considered classics, including Oscar-winners such as *Philadelphia*, *The Hours*, *Billy Elliott* and *Brokeback Mountain*.

So it was clear: GLAAD could help Guido Barilla. The organization has been familiar with media-transmitted LGBT+ phobia, of which he and his company were now accused, for decades, and have proven strategies for fighting it.

## A meeting in Manhattan

David Mixner was also very familiar with such strategies. The American was to play a central role in Barilla's journey – to his own surprise; they did not get off to an easy start.

Mixner, born in 1946, is an activist, author, playwright, and consultant, and a speaker on civil rights, HIV/AIDS, and LGBT+ issues. His decades of advocacy on civil and LGBT+ rights have garnered him worldwide recognition for years. The recipient of numerous awards, he worked for Martin Luther King, Jr., among others, and was active in the front line against the Vietnam War. He has advised six US presidents, including Bill Clinton and Barack Obama. He has taught at Harvard, Oxford, Stanford, and Princeton, and appeared on theater stages with his own programs. For example, he created three performance pieces – *The Mixner Trilogy* – that dealt with the fights of his life. Yale University holds the David Benjamin Mixner Collection, his personal archive of books, papers, films, and other materials relating to his involvement in civil rights issues. *Newsweek* once called him the most powerful gay man in the US. So Guido Barilla could hardly have found a better advisor on LGBT+ lives.

However, the activist refused to even speak to him for a long time. In an interview for *Bloomberg*, Mixner told Thomas Buckley his version of the encounter with the Italian.[29] He said he had joined the boycott and refused meetings four times because he was – as he also said on YouTube – "tired of people apologizing for statements and not following it up with action."[30]

In the end, he only agreed to a meeting in a Manhattan restaurant for the sake of a friend in the PR industry. He wanted to keep it short, but unexpectedly the planned hour stretched into four. Mixner talked about his experiences as a gay man of a certain generation: lost jobs, being the target of hate crimes, and years of alienation from his family. Barilla told of his family's long fight against injustice, including his father's struggle as a member of the resistance against the Italian fascists.

Contrary to the US activist's expectations, the two men understood each other. Mixner found Barilla "to be a man of great integrity, real honesty."[31] He believed his apology and that he was serious about making a real change for himself and his company. And so, in the end, Mixner agreed to support Barilla's journey. Many in the LGBT+ community disapproved, he said, "But I told them that the purpose of a movement is to change minds."[32]

# 4. Almost a miracle: A radical transformation

Only about two months after the devastating interview, the company announced a drastic shift. On its website, Barilla now stated that diversity, integration, and equality would always be part of its culture, values, and ethics. This would apply to the performance of all the company's employees, regardless of age, physical condition, gender, origin, religion, and sexual orientation. At the same time, it would be Barilla's task to support the idea of diversity.

Some of this can be found in an internal strategy paper from years before. Nevertheless, there are new formulations on D&I that include LGBT+ people and that – unmistakably – (aim to) leave behind an old image and culture. No one would have believed this alone, but it did not end there. Barilla began to put its money where its mouth was.

## Internal measures

It created the new position of Chief Diversity & Inclusion Officer, reporting directly to CEO Claudio Colzani and heading the D&I Advisory Board, which was also new and now had 12 members. Two external advisors, one of them David Mixner, were also appointed to this board, which met quarterly. It is said that since the Manhattan meeting, Mixner has become Guido Barilla's most important confidant in all D&I matters.

Colzani wanted to create the D&I Advisory Board, consisting of external consultants and internal employees. "However, it was not that easy to find external experts who were willing to join the Board," says Kristen Anderson. Anderson is a chemical engineer who, based in Singapore, headed Barilla R&D in Asia, Africa, and Australia when she was asked to become Chief D&I Officer and return to Parma in 2016. She has held the position since.

"At Barilla, the D&I Board member roles are not designed as separate jobs," Anderson explains, "Instead, each of us has a leadership role in another function *and* a D&I Board member role ... we want to embed the D&I mindset and culture as a way of doing business." Anderson herself is Chief D&I Officer but also has a position in the communications and external relations department.

The D&l Board members represent the regions in which Barilla is active worldwide. Together, they started work on an action plan for the journey to a new open, inclusive culture. One of their first measures was to develop an employee survey in collaboration with Korn Ferry. Launched in eight languages, it aimed to better understand Barilla's D&l strengths and potential. The survey is now conducted every 18 to 24 months.

Another important early measure was to give employees (about 8,400) in Europe, Asia, and North and South America training in D&l and sensitization to unconscious prejudices (for more on these, see Part IV, Chapter 1). These were for all employees: executives, managers, office and sales employees, and factory workers.

In addition, Barilla promoted creation of employee networks, or employee resource groups, (ERGs), among them the LGBT+ network *Voce* ("Voice"). Another, called Balance, promotes gender and work/ life balance, and there is a network of Latinos and African Americans, called *Alleanza*. Today Barilla has 15 ERGs around the world. Each has an executive sponsor and approaches are flexible. In Russia, currently, there is a focus on diversity of leadership styles and reducing hierarchy. In Greece, an ERG called *Armonía* ("Harmony") works for more inclusion of refugees, people with disabilities, and the LGBT+ community.

A brief note: the term "employee network," or "affinity group" is increasingly being supplanted by "Employee Resource Group" (ERG), now preferred in most parts of the corporate world, including at Barilla. Some companies also use the word "Business Resource Group" (BRG). Both terms, ERG and BRG (or others in a similar vein), aim to make clear that the networks (increasingly should) serve a resource function – thus, a business function – for example, to better promote the desired cultural change toward a better appreciation of diversity and more successful inclusion using the specialist knowledge gathered by these networks. Such knowledge can be useful. A simple example: a company's LGBT+ ERG might help develop a product, marketing, and sales plan to target LGBT+ customers. Or it might help in recruitment processes.

Barilla also announced that it would expand its health services to include the families and relatives of transgender employees and officially became a member of Parks. In fact, many of the new measures benefitted from Parks' competencies. Through their membership, the pasta makers were able to access the nonprofit's networks, learn best practice from other companies, and take on Parks' D&I training recommendations. Parks also provided support in setting up an LGBT+ ERG and for special challenges such as accompanying transition, the process an individual goes through of changing gender presentation and/or sex characteristics to accord with one's internal sense of gender identity. There are also annual conferences at which representatives of member companies meet in person and offer lectures, workshops, and discussions. These usually happen at a member company premises. Since joining, Barilla has been there every year.

## External measures

Barilla now also works with several LGBT+ rights nonprofits and foundations, especially in the US, including the Tyler Clementi Foundation. (The list of its sponsors includes Google, Twitter, AT&T, Estée Lauder, Morgan Stanley, and more.)

The Italians also support New York City's Ali Forney Center, the largest community center for homeless LGBT+ youth in the US, working with people between the ages of 16 and 24. In 2019, it helped more 1,400 individuals.[33]

Also in the US, Barilla supports GLAAD, for example, on Spirit Day, held on the third Thursday of every October. This was initiated in 2010 by Canadian teenager Brittany McMillan in response to a spate of suicides related to bullying of LGBT+ youth that year, including Tyler Clementi's. Supporters wear purple to honor LGBT+ suicide victims and show solidarity with LGBT+ youth.

## "Very unusual": Barilla's CEI ranking

Barilla's transformation did not go unnoticed. In fall 2014, the *Washington Post* dedicated a special article to it,[34] shortly after the company's first-time ranking on the Corporate Equality Index (CEI).

The CEI is the most important benchmarking tool in the US on corporate policies and practices for LGBT+ employees and external stakeholders, taking into account both companies' internal policies and external commitment. It is compiled annually by the influential US LGBT+ nonprofit Human Rights Campaign (HRC) based in

Washington, DC. For the fiscal year ending March 2019, HRC, Inc. and HRC Foundation list total revenues of more than $70 million.[35]

Prior to 2014, Barilla had not even asked the HRC to evaluate it. Now, about 12 months after Guido Barilla's unfortunate interview, his company achieved the top score of 100, allowing it to use the coveted label "Best Places to Work for LGBTQ Equality."

For many this was a huge surprise – even more so since, of the nearly 800 companies evaluated that year, less than 50% achieved this highest rating. "It is very unusual for a business to take on the full range of CEI criteria in one year," said Deena Fidas,[36] then director of the HRC's Workplace Equality Program and the index. (Today, she works for Out & Equal Workplace Advocates; for more, see Part IV, Chapter 5.)

I interviewed Fidas during a research trip for this book to Seattle. Some people would certainly make legitimate assumptions about Barilla's motives, she said. But it is irrefutable that they now have strong LGBT+ policies and practices. This and the speed of Barilla's LGBT+ turnaround should be a model for other companies, she added.

The HRC regularly reviews its evaluation criteria and has become more demanding over the years. The results of the 2020 CEI, for example, showcased how companies are not only promoting LGBT+-friendly workplace policies in the US but also helping advance LGBT+ inclusion in workplaces abroad. Based on a system of comprehensive self-reporting with verified data submitted to the HRC, companies are analyzed and evaluated on five broad categories including nondiscrimination policies, employment benefits, organizational competency and accountability around LGBT+ D&I, public commitment to LGBT+ equality, and responsible citizenship.

Despite the tougher criteria, for the 2020 index more than one thousand companies asked to be evaluated, the number having risen for years. The same goes for the proportion that achieve the perfect score: almost seven hundred companies in 2020.[37]

## "It's okay to learn"

David Mixner had a similar assessment to Fidas'. Guido Barilla was honestly horrified by the effects of his expressed personal convictions, Mixner told the *Washington Post*. But now, he described Barilla's D&I initiatives, on the whole, a "miracle." He added, "I have never seen anything like that."[38]

Seth Adam, a GLAAD spokesman who had also met with Guido Barilla, echoed this. No one, he said, had the right to say discriminatory things, but saw it as important to recognize when someone develops. "I do think it's okay to learn, and I think we've seen that in elected officials to everyday families."[39] So why not in companies and their managers?

The *Post*, in fall 2014, scrutinizing Barilla, identified its rapid D&I turnaround as a powerful symbol of a generally emerging change. It quoted communications expert Bob Witeck on this. Witeck was co-author of *Business Inside Out: Capturing millions of brand loyal gay consumers*, the first marketing book on the target group of lesbians, gays, bisexuals, and transsexuals published in 2006. He helped me interview those responsible for the world's first LGBT+ leadership program at Stanford University, which I will report on briefly in Part II, Chapter 4.

Witeck pointed out in the *Post* that in the past companies had been worried about offending groups *opposed* to homosexuality. Two decades earlier, for example, he had helped American Airlines deal with public criticism of their decision to market to homosexuals. At the time, he advised the company simply to declare that it had made a good business decision.[40] But that was then. Witeck is convinced, as he told the *Post*, that it is now positive for some companies to openly support LGBT+ rights – especially in the eyes of many young people, who would consider statements like Guido Barilla's "stupid and backwards."[41]

## Different values, different costs and benefits, different decisions

In other words, new generations have new values with respect to LGBT+ people. Companies out of step with this can get into trouble. Where they previously might have profited from discrimination against LGBT+ people, they are now stigmatized for it.

Discriminatory companies risk being condemned by the general public and by stars like Dario Fo or Mia Farrow, whose critical statements on social media are increasingly impactful. They also risk losing out in the talent market, becoming unattractive to future young talents in an ever-more-competitive global economy and in consumer markets.

As Rich Ferraro from GLAAD pointed out in 2013, talking about Barilla in *USA Today*, "The public backlash shows that homophobia is bad for business today because we're living in a world where LGBT people are respected and accepted." He went on, "That wasn't the case five years ago."[42]

Of course, this higher level of acceptance is still a long way from being established in many socially conservative parts of the US, let alone much of the rest of the world. About 70 countries still criminalize homosexuality in various ways, some of them vicious. But the story of Barilla's transformation showcases a development that suddenly became visible in 2013–14, especially in liberal Western countries and companies. In a fast-paced, globalized, digital-media and networked world, there is growing pressure on companies to take sides for equal LGBT+ rights and opportunities through convincing and verifiable D&I efforts. If they do not do so, they run the risk of suffering economic damage. Barilla's story and a great deal else I will discuss in this book indicate that, globally, it is LGBT+ diversity and inclusion that has the wind at its back.

## A new promise and its credibility

Another lesson to be learned from Barilla is this: to cope with such changing values, expectations and, thus, also talent, consumer and public opinion markets, companies must orient themselves as quickly as possible around three increasingly important criteria for success in modern business. They must promise to:

1. Respect and value individuals as they are, inside and outside the company, even if they are LGBT+
2. Grant each individual protection and equal rights and opportunities in work and potential development, even if they are LGBT+
3. Create a working environment that is open and inclusive for a wide range of people, including those who are LGBT+, and contribute to a public climate in society that is also characterized by openness and inclusivity.

And they must keep these promises. For Barilla, recognition by the globally respected HRC gave it the desired credibility boost for its still nascent cultural change, internally and externally, and in many parts of the world. It sent a strong signal to current employees, to potential hires, and to the pasta-buying public at large.

But clearly achieving the top score only once would not have been enough. Barilla's progress has therefore been checked by the HRC every year since. The firm has continued to receive top marks. While in autumn 2014 Barilla still stood for a sensational LGBT+ D&I turnaround, today – about seven years later – it stands for a credible perpetuation of cultural change.

# 5. Turning away from Milton Friedman: The business of business is – what?

Barilla's LGBT+ turnaround being sparked by media coverage and public opinion points to another development driving corporate LGBT+ D&I. It is linked to the changed economic considerations just described. I mean the rediscovery of corporate responsibility and – in this context – the rise of the guiding principle of corporate social responsibility (CSR) and related questions on business ethics.

From this standpoint, it is no coincidence that Barilla is positioning itself as a social actor supporting nonprofit organizations and charitable foundations. Starting its journey, the company stated:

*As a socially responsible company that serves and respects diverse consumers, we now have to expand our commitment. Our goal is to do better by becoming a global corporate citizen and leader in diversity and inclusion, internally and externally.*[43]

It is worth briefly reviewing the idea of CSR – with specific reference to D&I in general and LGBT+ D&I management, and Barilla's transformation in particular.

## CSR, Klaus Schwab's mission, and a Nobel Prize winner's "unwitting puppets"

The definitions of what CSR today means are numerous, if not endless. Briefly summarized, here are four crucial defining aspects:

1. CSR is a principle of self-regulation for profit-oriented businesses that aim to contribute to societal goals like, for example, protecting the environment, furthering education, or working for human rights.

2. In recent years, companies' CSR initiatives have lost more and more of their initial voluntary spirit to increasingly become integrated in corporate strategies that focus on a (long-term) contribution to a firm's reputation and its business (models and success).
3. Also in recent years, companies have come to be seen as not distinct from society, but as deeply influenced by local community cultural traditions, values and formal and informal institutions, while also deeply influencing them. As part of this development, CSR has come to be thought of together with business ethics, thereby addressing the intersection between business and society to square economic with social and ethical responsibilities for the people, environments, and communities/societies affected by them. The business ethics part of CSR looks at the moral logic and the ethical principles, rules and regulations to be applied to companies to meet these responsibilities.
4. Companies committed to CSR address all stakeholders' interests in the societies in which they operate. Through their use of CSR as a guiding business principle, companies express a specific basic morality in their behavior toward society. They do so through ethical action, both complying with legal and regulatory environments and doing more than is required by law. Their work can, for instance, include advocacy/activism, philanthropy or charity work, either through direct engagement or financial or other forms of support.

The idea that firms have to be socially responsible is quite old but has a volatile history. It was severely on the back foot for quite some time, especially from the '80s to the mid-2000s.

In the modern era, it was in the '50s and '60s that the idea of CSR gained momentum, mainly triggered by the expansion of large corporations. Howard R. Bowen's landmark book *Social Responsibilities of the Businessman*, published in 1953, is the first comprehensive work on social responsibility and business ethics, and is still considered a seminal work on modern CSR. Other crucial early contributions come from William C. Frederick, starting in 1960 with his article *The Growing Concern Over Business Responsibility*.[44]

In 1971, Klaus Schwab founded the World Economic Forum (WEF.) The German – then in his early 30s – wrote a book in which he outlined his understanding of the role of companies and managers in society. It can be regarded as a kind of intellectual basis for the WEF that is also reflected in Schwab's first Davos Manifesto, launched in 1973. (It was adapted only in 2019, still reflecting a similar spirit.) Only about a page long, the 1973 Manifesto aimed to be a "code of ethics for business leaders." It said that "the purpose of professional management is to serve clients, shareholders, workers, and employees, as well as societies, and to harmonize the different interests of the stakeholders."[45] It also demanded that the management

> *… must assume the role of a trustee of the material universe for future generations. It has to use the immaterial and material resources at its disposal in an optimal way. It has to continuously expand the frontiers of knowledge in management and technology. It has to guarantee that its enterprise pays appropriate taxes to the community in order to allow the community to fulfill its objectives. The management also has to make its own knowledge and experience available to the community.*[46]

With this idea of a company's (and its managers') social role, Schwab clearly set himself apart from others early on. In particular, he was rejecting the idea of shareholder value maximization as a firm's governing principle, strongly promoted, for example, by the very influential Nobel Prize in Economic Sciences winner, Milton Friedman.

In the more of 50 years of its existence, the WEF has made a rapid ascent. In its current mission statement, it claims to be the leading "international organization for public-private cooperation," engaging "the foremost political, business, cultural, and other leaders of society to shape global, regional, and industry agendas."[47] It also claims its "activities are shaped by a unique institutional culture founded on the stakeholder theory, which asserts that an organization is accountable to all parts of society."[48]

In the public eye, however, the WEF is today mainly considered a global business power center or even a kind of secondary UN with a strong focus on business and the global economy. And this is not just because of its spectacular annual January meetings in Davos, Switzerland. (I will talk more about the WEF in Part II, Chapters 1 and 8, showing how it, too, after decades of silence and resistance, changed course on LGBT+ equality.)

Even if one disagrees that the WEF is a – or *the* – global economic power center, Schwab has clearly become one of business's most influential string-pullers. But, interestingly, this has not meant his stakeholder capitalism found favor – at least until recently. Rather, it has been Friedman's shareholder value maximization that prevailed in economies and many companies over decades – including some of the big players that are heavily involved with the WEF.

## A long-lasting focus on shareholder value maximization

Friedman's mantra, "the business of business is business" gave rise to an imperative for companies and their top managers that I summarize as follows:

> Focus on profit maximization and direct all business activities toward shareholder interests: their invested capital's maximization. If this conflicts with the interests of other stakeholders such as employees, customers, suppliers, politicians, the general public, etc., ensure shareholder interests take precedence. Acting thus, you also benefit society, as if guided by an invisible hand.

In the '70s, around the time Schwab started propagating his stakeholder/society-oriented approach, Friedman asked provocatively what it would even mean to say businesses have a responsibility. "Businessmen who talk this way are unwitting puppets of the intellectual forces that have been undermining the basis of a free society these past decades."[49] Only people could take responsibility. Managers were not in charge to balance the interests of shareholders and other stakeholders. In his seminal book *Capitalism and Freedom*, Friedman called the idea of social responsibility a "fundamentally subversive doctrine."

This spirit of a general sociopolitical and economic change was already clearly shining through here, driven forward resolutely only a short time later by the strongly formative governments of Margaret Thatcher in the United Kingdom and Ronald Reagan in the United States. In particular, Thatcher's famous dictum, "There is no such thing as society," is Friedmanism at its purest.

The shareholder value idea prevailed well into the 2000s, especially in Anglo-Saxon countries and companies, but with globalization, it had strong influence almost everywhere, including continental Europe, fast-emerging Asia, and economically volatile Latin America.

## Changing course

Now this idea has been materially called into serious question. Markets can fail, and they can do so with devastating consequences for economies and individuals, if failure correcting rules and regulations and their reliable enforcement are missing. In addition, subsequent policy measures aiming to limit the harm can cause additional problems in the long run. The global financial crisis in 2008 and its dramatic economic and social consequences revealed the excesses. Almost everywhere, the gigantic losses produced by excessively risk-exposed financial sector and capital market actors were borne by taxpayers in the form of government bailouts and controversial central bank programs. Friedman's promise that shareholder value maximization would automatically benefit society suddenly looked horribly naïve – at best.

In response, and as part of increasing concerns about widening inequality and the environment, a demand for CSR has begun to be felt. This means, to reiterate my previous definition, that companies – legitimately geared to making a profit – should assume responsibility toward all social stakeholders by taking actions that go beyond what is prescribed by law and contribute to societal goals.

As part of this development, the young especially are sending a clear message, reflected in several studies. The Lovell Corporation's Change Generation Report 2017, produced in cooperation with Guelph University, for instance, found that Canadian Millennials (or Generation Y) and their successors, Generation Z, ask much more than their predecessors about the significance of (potential) employers' actions, beyond mere career goals.[50]

The US-based Pew Research Center, which for many years has been engaged in research on age cohorts, defines Millennials as those born between 1981 and 1996, and Gen Zs as those born after 1997, while Generation X comprises the cohort born between 1965 and 1980 and the Baby Boomers are those born between 1946 and 1964.[51] The distinctions offer useful orientation – although the boundaries between the generations are likely to vary somewhat both internationally and across studies by different institutes.

One Lovell study finding is striking: income no longer makes the top three most important determinants of career choice. Job satisfaction and CSR do. These generations want to work for companies that help make a "better world," not *outside*, but *in* society, responsible, for example, for safeguarding the natural foundations of life and the equality and inclusion of diverse workforces.

If companies do not meet these expectations, the young are apt to turn away from them as customers, employees, or potential employees. As the Baby Boomers retire, the employment issue in particular represents a threat.

These are exactly the risks Barilla was confronted with and sought to understand after Guido Barilla's unfortunate radio interview. Their involvement with the Tyler Clementi Foundation, GLAAD, the Ali Forney Center, and similar nonprofits can be seen as a reaction to these changed expectations among the young. And it must be seen as a result of Barilla's learning that if a company wants to be perceived as "smart and modern" instead of "stupid and backwards," it has to focus on all stakeholders and follow CSR as a guiding business principle.

## 6. A CEO's demand: "Contribute to society or risk losing our support"[52]

CSR is used today interchangeably with many other terms such as corporate citizenship, corporate sustainability, stakeholder management, multistakeholder, or stakeholder approach. Whatever the terminology, hardly a medium-to-large company, listed or otherwise, remains that does not publicize its CSR activities. For some time now, it has been riskier not to present business as socially responsible.

This is also reflected in more and more corporate leaders taking a stance on CSR – going far beyond previous polished boilerplate. Probably one of the most impactful is from Laurence (Larry) Fink, Chairman and CEO of global investment management giant BlackRock. Founded by Fink over 30 years ago, it today has about 16,000 employees in more than 35 countries (as of December 2020).[53]

In January 2018, Fink's annual letter to the CEOs of the world's largest listed companies openly criticized the failure of "many governments ... to prepare for the future, on issues ranging from retirement and infrastructure to automation and worker retraining."[54] This would, he said, mean citizens turning less and less to government for support, instead increasingly demanding:

> ... that companies, both public and private, serve a social purpose. To prosper over time, every company must not only deliver financial performance, but also show how it makes a positive contribution to society. Companies must benefit all of their stakeholders, including shareholders, employees, customers, and the communities in which they operate.[55]

Fink added that firms should now ask themselves what role they play in the community, how they manage our impact on the environment, and if they work to create a diverse workforce.[56] The social function of companies in society, the idea of sustainability and of diversity are, thus, grouped – which is in evident alignment with the younger generations' values.

BlackRock is the world's largest asset manager with $7.81 trillion in assets under management (as of September 2020),[57] a volume roughly equivalent to the spending of the US government in 2019.[58] So what Fink says always carries weight, all the more so because his company influences the filling of top management positions in many large companies through its investments.

Fink's letter is – like previous and subsequent annual letters – still accessible on BlackRock's website. It made waves, inspiring articles and discussions in leading media outlets and the business world. A year after it was sent, Andrew Ross Sorkin commented in the *New York Times*, accurately, I think, on its impact, saying that it was "an inflection point in the long-simmering argument over the state of global capitalism." In response, CEOs would have begun "explicitly talking about their companies' 'purpose' – not just in high-minded mission statements but in government filings and investor reports."[59]

## Pushing the rise of CSR, commitment, and purpose

Essentially, one can interpret the fast rise of company social commitments in recent years as a powerful rediscovery of the idea Klaus Schwab has propagated since founding the WEF in the 1970s: that a company must be responsible to all stakeholders, not just primarily or solely to its shareholders, and must contribute to societal goals.

In recent years, the rediscovery of CSR has been supported by a fast-growing body of research, investigating relevant strategies and tools and their impact on economic performance. In developing its strategy for an LGBT+ turnaround, Barilla was able to draw on this general increase in CSR knowledge.

Fink – his letter written about four years after Barilla started to transform – was by no means early in his call for CSR, although he was very early among asset managers. But his statement made the topic much more visible and a much higher priority at the top levels of big global corporates.

The letter was given even greater force by the fact that BlackRock had for many years acted more as a passive, or apolitical, investor, not putting much pressure on individual companies and their leaders to take society into account. Of course, as Sorkin wrote in the *New York Times*, companies often talk about their social responsibility, but most of it is marketing or to appease politicians' regulatory zeal. He was right.[60] But this time things were different because Fink was a businessman talking to businesses, including companies in which BlackRock controlled huge investments, and promising consequences. The *New York Times* summarized, "BlackRock's message: contribute to society or risk losing our support."[61]

## Criticism

Some praised Fink, especially because of his progressive sociopolitical message, which included aspects like ethics, diversity, inclusion, equality, social responsibility, and social purpose. *Barron's* even called him the "new conscience of Wall Street."[62]

But Fink was also criticized. For example, at that time, BlackRock was an important investor in the weapons industry, i.e. gun makers and retailers. Specifically, it was the largest investor in gun makers and retailers such as Sturm Ruger and American Outdoor Brand, which owns Smith & Wesson, and the second-largest shareholder in Vista Outdoor. Were such investments appropriate for a company seeking to advise global corporates on CSR?

A couple weeks after the letter, BlackRock dealt with this. Though officially citing as motivation the recent school shooting in Parkland, Florida,[63] it said it would reexamine its gun market holdings.[64] Some weeks later, it announced it would offer clients the option of investing in funds that exclude weapons manufacturers and retailers. It also announced it would more actively engage with gun makers, potentially voting against some of their management's goals.

In his subsequent annual letter to CEOs in January 2019, Fink made his message even stronger, expressing his frustration about the state of the world, fast-growing uncertainties, eroding trust in institutions, and the lack of reliable future-oriented political leadership, and outlined the consequences for companies. "Fueled in part by social media, public pressures on corporations build faster and reach further than ever before." Stakeholders would push companies "to wade into sensitive social and political issues – especially as they see governments failing to do so effectively."[65]

What would be needed was both profit and purpose. Profits would be essential "if a company is to effectively serve all of its stakeholders over time – not only shareholders, but also employees, customers, and communities." Purpose, on the other hand, would unify management, employees, and communities. It would drive ethical behavior and create an essential check on actions that go against the best interests of stakeholders.[66]

The second letter not only called again for diversity (on boards of directors) and focus on environmental risks, it also spoke specifically about Millennials, saying that attracting and retaining the best talents would increasingly require a clear expression of social purpose. "We have seen some of the world's most skilled employees stage walkouts and participate in contentious town halls, expressing their perspective on the importance of corporate purpose." This development would grow as Millennials and their successors came to occupy senior positions. To support his argument, Fink quoted Deloitte's study on Millennial workers in which more than 60% said "improving society" is more important to them than "generating profit."[67]

But Millennials are not only the fastest-growing age cohort among workers and consumers; they will also soon inherit gigantic sums from the Baby Boomers, much of which they will seek to invest. This is particularly important for investment firms like BlackRock.

In response to his second letter, there was again some public approbation, including from leading academics, for example, the Harvard Business School.[68] But there was also a stream of criticism from conservative media. *Fox Business* disparaged both the letter and remarks Fink made to his own employees shortly after,[69] in which he said his firm would change its hiring and perhaps also its compensation structure to advance diversity. In five years, Black-Rock should not be "a bunch of white men."[70]

Critics quoted by *Fox Business* went as far as to call Fink's commitment to diversity a form of "corporate socialism."[71] One *Fox* interviewee, Charles Elson from the University of Delaware, said, it was "fundamentally not the role of a public company, and it's unfair to investors who may not agree with his politics. A CEO shouldn't use house money to further a goal that may not create economic returns."[72]

Of course, what one sees here is the old Friedmanite idea of shareholder value maximization as the one and only guiding business principle. For some, it might have sounded like an echo of the past, but clearly the attitude was not dead. It had become substantially weaker than it was before the global financial crisis, but it was still alive.

It seems, however, time is not on Friedman's side. Recently, amid the COVID-19 pandemic, the new Deloitte Global Millennial Survey supported social responsibility and even reinforced it. The study explored the views of more than 27,500 Millennials and Gen Zs, both before and after the onset of the pandemic. It summarizes, "They continue to push for a world in which businesses and governments mirror that same commitment to society, putting people ahead of profits, and prioritizing environmental sustainability."[73] And "while views of business continue to decline, Millennials and Gen Z will actively support companies that make positive impacts to society."[74]

The survey also found that job loyalty to employers among the two young age cohorts would increase as companies addressed employee needs, mentioning factors like D&I, reskilling, and sustainability. And it found that the preference among the young for businesses with a social focus was reflected in their purchasing habits, especially, but not only in view of the impact of the pandemic. For example, about 60% of the interviewees said they planned to buy more products and services from large businesses that have taken care of their workforces and positively impacted society during the pandemic. And even more, about three-quarters, planned the same with regard to smaller, local businesses.[75]

## United Nations' contributions

It's not just the young who support Fink's demand. Another powerful global force is doing so – and has done for some years: the United Nations.

It is right that initiatives adopted by UN institutions don't stipulate to what extent the world must align with them – even if formal signing processes imply strong commitment. However, if such initiatives are matched by similar or complementary approaches from states and organizations, this represents a strong global development that big global players like BlackRock and many others must react to and work with. Such is the case with regard to the UN's approach to CSR.

The UN's attempts to urge businesses to engage socially go back only about two decades but intensified after the financial crisis. A first milestone was the UN Global Compact, announced by then UN Secretary-General Kofi Annan at Davos in January 1999. The initiative called on firms of every size, everywhere in the world, to align strategies and operations with ten universal principles guaranteeing human rights, labor rights, environmental protection, and anti-corruption.[76] Principle 1, for instance, demands that businesses support and respect the protection of internationally proclaimed human rights.[77] And the UN also offers operational suggestions on how companies can adhere to this principle very concretely. The Global Compact, or simply, the Compact, started small, in a pilot phase with 44 companies.

Another important step was the launch of the UN Guiding Principles on Business and Human Rights, unanimously endorsed by the UN Human Rights Council in 2011.[78] They encompass 31 principles and are basically a three-pillar framework. One pillar addresses the state's duty to protect human rights. The second focuses on the responsibility of corporations to respect human rights. The third deals with the need for greater access to remedy for victims of business-related abuse.[79] The Guiding Principles represent the first-ever corporate human rights initiative endorsed by the United Nations.

As part of the aforementioned Global Compact, a third important milestone with major relevance was the 2030 Agenda for Sustainable Development. Adopted at a UN summit in 2015 with heads of state from 193 countries, the Agenda came officially into force at the beginning of 2016. A core section is the 17 Sustainable Development Goals (SDGs), which are linked to 169 concrete subtargets and 232 indicators.

Countries signing the Agenda commit to make measurable efforts to achieve these goals and targets by 2030 in order to end poverty, eliminate inequalities, and combat climate change. The overarching goal is to ensure that "no one is left behind."[80]

Companies and nonbusinesses (such as academic institutions, business associations, cities and municipalities, civil society organizations, and many more) can apply to become part of the Compact. Its website offers many options for businesses to contribute, such as that companies sign an open letter, provided on the website, calling on academic institutions to make human rights part of management education.[81]

Another option is to develop and implement human rights policy as part of overall company strategy. The Compact website says, "enlightened companies" will "recognize that it is not only the moral thing to do, but also the smart thing to do for their business."[82] It offers instructions and examples.[83]

Having started with only a few companies, the Compact has grown quickly into the world's largest corporate sustainability initiative,[84] with sustainability understood as an umbrella term close to CSR. Today more than 10,000 companies headquartered in 160 countries representing more than 70 million employees and more than 60 local networks have become part of it.[85]

BlackRock formally signed up to the SDGs in April 2020[86] with a letter of commitment from Larry Fink to UN Secretary-General António Guterres.

## Relevant also for LGBT+ equality in the corporate world

The adoption and broad support of the Global Compact in general and of the SDGs in particular can serve as a (further) legitimization for companies to focus on social commitment, responsibility, and purpose as guidelines for their business.[87]

The SDGs do not explicitly refer to LGBT+ rights or to ending anti-LGBT+ discrimination or violence. The same applies to UN Guiding Principles on Business and Human Rights. But based on the view that human rights apply regardless of sexual orientation and gender identity – as is explicitly acknowledged in the wake of some UN activities that I will outline in Part II, Chapter 8 – LGBT+ rights clearly must be seen as being implied by the SDGs.[88]

Goal 10, calling for reduced inequality, is one example. Two sub-targets are: "By 2030, empower and promote the social, economic, and political inclusion of all, irrespective of age, sex, disability, race, ethnicity, origin, religion, or economic or other status" and "Ensure equal opportunity and reduce inequalities of outcome, including by eliminating discriminatory laws, policies, and practices and promoting appropriate legislation, policies, and action in this regard."[89]

Barilla initiated its LGBT+ turnaround even before the UN adopted the SDGs and was, thus – in view of their strategy of also supporting LGBT+ nonprofit organizations – fully state-of-the-art when the SDGs came into play.

But beyond all that, in 2017 the UN made its commitment to LGBT+ rights explicit with the "Standards of Conduct for Business. Tackling Discrimination against Lesbian, Gay, Trans, & Intersex People," also known as the UN LGBTI Standards of Conduct for Business or the Standards for short. Companies signing the Standards make a voluntary commitment to comply. Essentially, this commitment is directed at internal policies and practices on the one hand, and toward external implementation in markets, societies, and communities on the other. The Standards were and still are another major milestone in the UN's efforts to bring companies' business interests and human rights together. In this case, it was the first time the UN encouraged companies specifically to visibly commit on engaging with LGBT+ equality in not just the workplace but also the markets, communities, and societies in which they operate. Internal dimensions of LGBT+ engagement and externals connected to CSR are thought of together. (For more on the Standards, see Part II, Chapter 8.)

Barilla reacted fast to this new UN initiative. At the end of January 2018, at a WEF event attended by then UN High Commissioner for Human Rights Zeid Ra'ad Al Hussein, a news item was disseminated: Barilla had signed the UN LGBTI Standards of Conduct for Business, which had only been announced the previous year.

Since their launch, more than 300 companies worldwide have committed to the Standards. Barilla was the first company in Italy to do so. In the limelight of a world mega event, the firm presented itself as a prime mover.

It also made a statement related to the ethical commitment involved, putting together business interests and social responsibility.

In a press release accompanying the signing of the Standards, Barilla stressed it would not only be "the world's top pasta producer" but also committed to "the battle against homophobia and LGBTI discrimination in the workplace." This would be a mission Barilla would pursue "with the same passion and the same sense of social and ethical responsibility that has made it a food industry benchmark for millions of people, and with which it has become a global promoter of healthy eating and nutrition worldwide."[90]

# 7. Playing "let's pretend" with pinkwashing

Quite a few companies still use CSR superficially, merely to polish their image. The spin can take the form of elaborate websites, social media campaigns, and nicely designed reports. But with increasing research into CSR, and the growing demand from citizens, workforces, future talents, and customers comes pressure for CSR commitments to be transparently substantiated.

We may very soon even see a different – and legally binding – form of accounting and reporting for companies that combines traditional financial figures and CSR-related figures, the latter carrying hard benefit and cost tags. These figures may reflect a company's "true" positive or negative effects on society – in all areas, including equal rights and inclusion of LGBT+ people and other underrepresented communities.

## Misusing the rainbow

A subcategory of CSR image polishing, "pinkwashing," describes strategies aimed at promoting products, brands, or companies through the appealing appearance of being LGBT+-friendly without really being so.

The discussion about pinkwashing – especially the misuse of the rainbow symbol – intensified after the summer 2019 celebrations in many countries marking the 50th anniversary of the Stonewall uprising (see box on page 51).

## The Stonewall riots, rainbow-colored Pride events and business

The Stonewall riots were a series of spontaneous demonstrations and violent conflicts between, on the one hand, homosexuals and transsexuals (or members of the LGBT+ community as we would now say), and police officers on the other. The first clashes broke out in the early hours of June 28, 1969 as a result of a police raid on the Stonewall Inn scene bar on Christopher Street in New York City's Greenwich Village. In the days that followed, the conflicts escalated. More and more homosexuals and transsexuals clashed with more and more police officers. Only after five days did the situation calm.

Raids on fashionable bars, especially gay bars, were commonplace in New York and other US cities in the 1960s. The police ascertained the identity of the visitors and arrests were often made for "indecent behavior," sometimes with charges and convictions following. The outbreak at Stonewall was the first time a large group of LGBT+ people resisted the police and risked arrest.

Today, the uprising is regarded worldwide as a central turning point in the community's struggle for legal and social equality, and for respect and recognition. It is commemorated every year in many places around the world with parades or marches, mostly in cities, usually but not only during the summer months. It is not uncommon for political, arts, and scientific programs to take place for a few days or longer in the period immediately before the parades, for example with LGBT+-related exhibitions, discussions, workshops, film festivals, and more.

In many parts of the world, LGBT+ events with parades and programs have long been called Gay Pride or just Pride, while in some countries they may have different names; in Germany, for example, most are (also) called CSD (for Christopher Street Day).

Over time the focus of these events shifted from "gay" to LGBT, LGBTI, LGBTQ, or similar. This reflects the way what was once referred to as the "gay community" has expanded over the years to cover the concerns of other sexual and gender minorities, with increasing solidarity across the subcommunities.

Also, for some time, the month of June has been known by many as Pride Month, and it has become common among LGBT+ community members and their allies to wish each other a "Happy Pride Month," mainly in the English-speaking (democratic) sphere, and in the English-speaking world of global business. In other parts of the world, though, mainly in the Southern Hemisphere, depending on the seasons, other months have come to be celebrated as Pride Month.

Very early, the rainbow became a crucial symbol. In 1977, activist Harvey Milk had been elected to the Board of Supervisors in San Francisco, making him one of the first openly gay people elected to political office in the US. As part of his plans for the Gay Freedom Day Parade in San Francisco, he was looking for a symbol to make participants feel part of a community. He commissioned gay artist Gilbert Baker, who created the rainbow flag, used for the first time in June 1978. Originally it had eight stripes, including one in pink. Over the years, it went through various changes, but for decades now it has had six stripes: red (for "life"), orange (for "healing"), yellow (for "sunlight"), green (for "nature"), indigo (for "serenity"), and violet (or "spirit"). It is usually flown horizontally, with the red stripe on top and violet at the bottom, to mirror a natural rainbow.

Pride parades, with their rainbows, have gained ground in many regions around the globe. Most were originally big city events, but from the 1990s onward, they also became fixtures in many medium-sized and smaller cities. As part of this, the meaning of the rainbow has changed or at least expanded. Beyond standing for LGBT+ pride and equality, it has come to symbolize respect for diversity and inclusion more generally.

As part of the Black Lives Matter movement in summer 2020, there were demands that the flag should again have eight colors, adding brown and black. Designs like this appeared at some (virtual Pride) events that year and on social media. Others demanded that light blue and light pink – used on the flag symbolizing the trans community – should also become part of the rainbow flag. Designs reflecting this also appeared at some (virtual Pride) events that year and on social media.

There is a business angle to Pride events and the rainbow: over the years, cities have fast come to understand that they can attract tourists with the party atmosphere of these colorful, creative, youthful, and cosmopolitan parades. They have become a major revenue generator for hotels, restaurants, bars, and much more. They are important for the cities' purses directly and also for their image of modernity, tolerance, openness, dynamism, and innovation. More and more cities are presenting themselves as LGBT+-inclusive, often competing with each other by running elaborate marketing and media campaigns for their Pride events to attract as many visitors as possible. The rainbow is used for all of these. (For more on LGBT+-friendly cities, see Part III, Chapter 5.)

The growing economic dimensions have also become important for the Pride organizers themselves. Mostly nonprofit LGBT+ organizations, they have come to understand that the more companies there are running parade floats, the better it is for their finances.

There is also growing controversy over whether the commercialization and hedonism of the Pride events contradicts their original remit: reminding people of the political and civil rights struggle for legal, social, and cultural LGBT+ equality, which has not come to an end.

In particular, it is often alleged that many large international companies (and other organizations, including some political parties) misuse Pride and/or the rainbow, pretending to support the LGBT+ community, profiting from products or logos temporarily adapted with the rainbow colors, but doing nothing of real substance.

## A quick checklist as an action plan

Obviously, selling rainbow-colored products, illuminating the headquarters of a company in rainbow colors once a year, or participating in Pride events in t-shirts with rainbow-ized company logos doesn't prove a firm's commitment to LGBT+ issues.

On the other hand, achieving the top score in the HRC's CEI, as Barilla has repeatedly done, is a good indicator that a company has reached a credible level of LGBT+ friendliness because the

HRC looks at both internal policies and practices and external social commitment.

Globally the CEI is the most important index because, step by step, it is getting tougher and relates to the most important market in the world, the US. But to become a top scorer a company must be US-based or have a US subsidiary. However, numerous companies headquartered outside the States with a subsidiary there also win CEI top scores but do little for LGBT+ equality in their home countries.

Of course, in some countries, national organizations working for LGBT+ equality in the workplace (and in society) have developed their own indexes, ratings, and labels, for example in the UK, Australia, Germany, France, Italy, Spain, the Netherlands, and Hong Kong or, more recently, in emerging markets such as Mexico, Chile, and South Africa.

Here is a general checklist of eight indicators that a company is credibly LGBT+-friendly. They can also be interpreted as an action plan for sustaining LGBT+ D&I.

---

### Eight indicators: a quick checklist to avoid pinkwashing – and a brief action plan to become credibly LGBT+-friendly

1. The top management/board of directors backs and supports LGBT+ D&I strategies internally and externally, including in public announcements, by signing commitments, attending/holding conferences and other events, in speeches, on the company's website, and in social media.

2. The company has a holistic D&I strategy addressing all relevant D&I dimensions and is managed by a D&I department (or by HR or other bodies). Where applicable, it includes blue-collar workers. The D&I dimension of LGBT+ is part of this strategy, with specific contact people for all topics around sexual orientation and gender identity, including LGBT+ policies and practices, membership in or cooperation with external organizations working for LGBT+ inclusion, programs around straight allies, and intersectionality (i.e. bridging different

---

diversity dimensions such as gender, ethnicity age, LGBT+), etc. The strategy includes regions, markets and communities that are difficult or even dangerous for LGBT+ people. Its success is measured.

3. There is an LGBT+ employee network, perhaps referred to as an employee resource group or affinity group or similar. This is supported by the top management and the D&I, HR, CSR and communications departments (or similar in smaller firms). It has one or preferably several senior sponsors – LGBT+ themselves or straight allies, and diverse in gender and ethnicity – a management across the regions the company operates in, and its own budget and/or other accessible resources. Ideally, there are also programs and initiatives that include straight allies and foster intersectionality, bringing together LGBT+ people with other affinity groups such as women's networks, groups centered around ethnicity, and more.

4. As part of a company's human resources strategy, there are measures especially focused on LGBT+ people, such as: LGBT+-related questions in employee surveys; self-directed LGBT+ career events or participation in external LGBT+ career events; encouragement of LGBT+ people and their allies to become role models for an open and tolerant corporate culture that values LGBT+ inclusivity; development of career paths that take entrepreneurial LGBT+ activities into account; equal benefits for same-sex partners; programs and benefits for LGBT+ people that need special support, such as trans people; awareness, unconscious bias, language sensitivity, mentoring, and other forms of training for all employees, including managers and blue-collar workers.

5. There are policies and practices that promote supply chain D&I, including the D&I dimension of LGBT+ to ensure that external suppliers meet high internal LGBT+ D&I standards too.

6. There is a more or less constant internal and external stream of company communications and events around LGBT+ issues, not just some once or twice a year. This also includes the celebration of LGBT+ and ally role models at all levels and across all regions a company is operating in.

7. In order to foster internal learnings, the company participates in external benchmarking initiatives, screenings, rankings, and indices, is engaged with organizations working for LGBT+ inclusion at work, and supports research on LGBT+ topics.
8. To reinforce acting socially responsible, there is financial support for the work of external LGBT+ nonprofit organizations or other forms of engagement for LGBT+ issues in the society and communities a company operates in, especially, but not only, in regions where it is difficult for LGBT+ people.

Of course, many things on this list are internal and difficult for an outsider such as a customer or other external stakeholders to spot, so it may be difficult for them to make an assessment. Also, companies come in different sizes, with different products or services, market values, financial resources, ownerships, headquarters, structures, and, especially, depending on where they are in the world, legal obligations. Not every company can be LGBT+-friendly in the same way and with the same depth. Nevertheless, one can summarize: only if a company copes with many or most parts of the above eight clusters in some way can it also be credible when marketing rainbow-ized products or presenting itself prominently at Pride or other LGBT+ events.

As we have seen, advised by civil rights activist David Mixner (and others), Barilla resisted the temptation to treat its engagement only as a marketing strategy. Its transformation into an LGBT+ champion is thus not just a matter of risk management and reputation laundering in the face of a public outcry. Rather, while commercial concerns were clearly one initial driver of change, the company can also be seen as having substantially adapted to changing societal expectations – especially among the young – and become responsible to its stakeholders in matters LGBT+ beyond what is expected by law, including contributing to societal goals.

## 8. The Thomson Reuters Foundation and a new LGBT+ media platform

Some of Barilla's LGBT+-related work stands out because the pasta maker is supporting new initiatives. Here is an example I stumbled upon by chance. Researching this book in New York, I was invited by Antonio Zappulla of the Thomson Reuters Foundation (TRF) to an event at the foundation's office in Times Square. I had got to know the Italian a few weeks before at an LGBT+ side event in European Parliament rooms in Brussels.

Zappulla, who is openly gay, was the foundation's Chief Operating Officer at that time, but a few months later, he was appointed CEO. In 2018, he ranked first in the OUTstanding LGBT+ Role Model list's category "Third/Public Sector." (For more on these lists, see Part II, Chapter 4.)

For quite some time already the Italian had been considered an influential LGBT+ leader, well connected in Britain, but also globally. For example, the trained journalist who before joining the foundation had worked for more than ten years as producer and then executive producer for *Bloomberg TV*, is on the steering committee of the Reuters Institute for the Study of Journalism at Oxford University. He is also an ambassador for One Young World, an influential global network of young leaders and a member of the Board of Trustees at Open for Business (OFB), a London-based coalition of major corporates, which works for LGBT+ inclusion globally (for more on OFB, see Part III, Chapter 5.)

His employer, the TRF is the nonprofit arm of Thomson Reuters, the world's largest news and information services provider. Established in 1983, the foundation is headquartered in London, where Zappulla has lived for many years, and registered as a charity in both the UK and US. Today its work is targeted at media freedom, more inclusive economies, and raising human rights awareness.

This includes LGBT+ issues. For example, the TRF works with a pro bono legal network, connecting civil society organizations and social enterprises with lawyers willing to provide legal advice for free. In its annual report, the TRF tells how it brought Equality Illinois, an LGBT+-rights NGO, and global law firm Kirkland & Ellis together. The firm produced legal research backing up advocacy to ban "conversion therapy" for LGBT+ minors in Illinois – with a happy ending. In 2015, the Youth Mental Health Protection Act was passed and included the ban.[91]

The Manhattan event Zappulla had invited me to was special, the launch of *Openly*, a digital news platform. It aims to be "the most important source of information for anyone interested in LGBT+ issues," as Zappulla put it.[92] It would be the world's first platform "dedicated to fair, accurate, and impartial coverage of LGBT+ stories with global distribution through the *Reuters* wire," covering a wide range of topics, such as changes in legislation, violence and discrimination, health, human rights activism, and corporate and economic issues.

## Tackling the "echo chamber approach"

This was an ambitious project for the Foundation. And, also at the NYC event, it was announced that its sponsor would be ... Barilla. *Openly* was Zappulla's own idea, one he had had in mind for years. "When it comes to LGBT+ content, the current news landscape is very fragmented, insular, and lacking in credibility," he explained. Most LGBT+ community media coverage tended "to be conducted through an LGBT+ lens, resulting in an 'echo chamber' approach." This could make it "akin to advocacy and [lacking in] journalistic authority." Also, at this point, it was mostly provided by "a limited number of small web-only outlets, predominantly offering content with a US or UK focus."

With respect to the English-speaking (media) world, all this is certainly true. And it is much the same in France, Germany, Italy, and smaller states, sometimes with few, if any, dedicated LGBT+ news outlets.

*Openly* is headed by Hugo Greenhalgh, for many years editor of the *Financial Times*. In addition, there is a reporter and web producer, Rachel Savage, whose work has appeared in the *Economist* and the *Guardian*, among others.[93] Both are "part of a global news team at the TRF with more than 45 journalists," Zappulla says. This team produces the original news, supported by a network of around 300 freelancers on all continents."

The global reach is extensive. The platform offers its original news via the Reuters news service, delivering to an audience of one billion readers worldwide every day. This news is available on openlynews. com and also in a special section of the TRF website, news.trust.org/ lgbt, as well as via other channels such as *Apple News*, *Google News* and *Facebook Instant News*. *Openly* also uses its Twitter account as a further channel.

## No interference – and a good start

It was at the New York launch that Zappulla announced Barilla would be the new platform's main supporter. The information was also discretely but clearly given in the launch's press release and on the *Openly* site.

Since *Openly's* start, as he does to all partners of foundation projects, Zappulla has reported to Barilla on developments. Every six months, he sends Barilla's D&I leader Kristen Anderson the data on the platform: number of articles, number of pick-ups by other global news outlets, and number of unique page views. "Barilla is not interfering in anything," Zappulla says. "This is a professional collaboration with great mutual respect."

That respect was based on prior collaboration. Already the foundation and the Barilla Center for Food and Nutrition had jointly awarded a media prize: the "Food Sustainability Media Award,"[94] recognizing journalists for outstanding contributions on the topics of food and sustainable eating. (The award is currently under evaluation.)

In addition to producing original news, *Openly* aggregates articles, news, and event information from external sources and makes them accessible on the platform. Every morning, the editorial team searches the internet, social media, and other sources to find the latest, most informative and trustworthy stories and analyses from all over the world.

"Our aim is to only use reputable sources like *The Economist*, *Financial Times* and the *New York Times*," Zappulla says in a telephone interview a couple months after we met in New York. But *Openly* also wants to make sure that the stories are geographically distributed. "The *South China Morning Post* (one of the leading English-speaking media sources in Hong Kong), the *Globe and Mail* (Canada's second-largest daily newspaper), and the English-language *Jakarta Post* all play a prominent role." If one visits *Openly's* sites today, one can also find articles from the *Independent*, the *New Statesman*, and the *Jewish Telegraphic Agency*. There is also news from sources like *Sports Media LGBT+* or the *Bay Area Reporter*, the oldest permanently published LGBT+ weekly newspaper in the US.

During the first ten months after the launch, the new service reached readers, viewers, and users in more than 50 countries, including many nations with difficult conditions for LGBT+ people. It has also achieved some scoops. One was being the first to report on new laws in the Sultanate of Brunei that mandated not just the death penalty but stoning to death for same-gender sex. This led to a worldwide outcry and – initiated by George Clooney – boycott threats against luxury hotels owned worldwide by the Sultan's ruling family or the Brunei Investment Agency.[95] Many global corporates joined this boycott, some without announcing it publicly for reasons of compliance. "The office of the UN High Commissioner for Human Rights contacted us after the publication," Zappulla says. The attention the article garnered triggered a statement by the UN High Commissioner for Human Rights, Michelle Bachelet, who condemned the law as a setback for human rights only days after publication of the article.[96] A short time later, the law was suspended with a moratorium.

A second scoop was *Openly*'s news in October 2019 that Uganda was going to pass a bill imposing the death penalty for gay sex.[97] Again there was an outcry and a lot of pressure from major aid donors. In the end, the government – fearing economic consequences – withdrew the bill.[98] "These are encouraging stories, facts, and figures," Zappulla says. Above all, for him they show "that there is a real demand for independent, fact-based LGBT+ news and information."

When the platform was launched in September 2018, Barilla signed up to support it for three years, but Barilla's head of D&l Kristen Anderson now says, "What *Openly* creates with such high quality is critical. The coverage is fantastic and very relevant to the global LGBT+ community." Recently, therefore, Barilla has committed to support *Openly* for another three years until 2024.

## A connection to the UN

With its *Openly* engagement, Barilla is building on its support for the LGBT+ nonprofit organization GLAAD. As mentioned earlier, GLAAD's work focuses particularly on changing old, often clichéd and prejudiced images of LGBT+ people in the US media.

The support for *Openly* is also fitting because at the NYC *Openly* launch, the Thomson Reuters Foundation had two presenting partners from the UN: the Human Rights Office and the LGBTI Core Group.

The LGBTI Core Group is an informal group of UN member states and a few other member institutions, co-chaired by Argentina and the Netherlands. The box on the next page shows the full list of member countries (as of December 2020). Others include the Office of the UN High Commissioner for Human Rights, Human Rights Watch, and the LGBT+ human rights NGO OutRight, short for OutRight Action International.

OutRight, based in New York City, was founded in 1990. It often works with the UN. For example, OutRight Executive Director Jessica Stern, representing the organization, gave the first UN Security Council briefing on LGBT+ human rights violations. OutRight is also substantially involved in managing the Core Group and serves as its secretary.

Established in 2008, the Group aims at helping to improve LGBT+ rights and protection worldwide within the UN framework. It has branches at the UN sites in Geneva and New York, the latter especially active with regular meetings, informal networking and agenda setting within the UN, and more.

So Barilla's commitment to *Openly* is linked not only to the Thomson Reuters Foundation, but also to the UN's human rights efforts, to which it had already shown commitment eight months before *Openly*'s launch. As mentioned, it was the first Italian company to sign the United Nations LGBTI Standards of Conduct for Business.

> ## Member countries of the UN LGBTI Core Group
>
> | | | |
> |---|---|---|
> | Albania | Argentina | Australia |
> | Brazil | Cabo Verde | Canada |
> | Chile | Colombia | Costa Rica |
> | Croatia | Ecuador | El Salvador |
> | France | Germany | Iceland |
> | Israel | Italy | Japan |
> | Luxembourg | Malta | Mexico |
> | Montenegro | Nepal | Netherlands |
> | New Zealand | North Macedonia | Norway |
> | Spain | Sweden | United Kingdom |
> | Uruguay | USA | (European Union) |

# 9. To Germany with start-up aid from Milan – and also to France

It is clear that, while the top CEI rating Barilla has achieved for many years looks good in other countries, it cannot really replace national credibility tests. In a globalized economy, national characteristics and local imprimaturs still matter.

Three years after its first CEI success, Barilla also became active in Europe's largest economy, Germany, a major pasta market.

## The Prout at Work Foundation

One central contact for companies in Germany on LGBT+ D&I strategies and measures is the Prout at Work Foundation. Among many other things, the foundation offers companies use of the label "Prout Employer," if they meet certain requirements. These are much less demanding than those required by the HRC and CEI, but the basic message is the same.

Albert Kehrer has been the foundation's chairman since it was established. He runs it with a small team from Munich, where he lives with his husband, and where the foundation is based. For the foundation's work, Munich is not a bad location. Many large German corporates, such as Allianz, BMW, or Siemens, are head-quartered in Bavaria's capital, and there are also numerous leading consulting companies, global law firms, and other global giants such as Microsoft, IBM, Salesforce, and Amazon with larger offices. Deputy Chairman Jean Luc Vey works in Frankfurt, another important German business center with similar contact points, which also helps.

Prout at Work began in 2006 as an informal association of people from LGBT+ employee networks in companies, plus *Völklinger Kreis* – the association for gay managers, entrepreneurs, and self-employed people in Germany – and *Wirtschaftsweiber*, the business network of lesbian managers and professional specialists. Participants sought to learn from each other's D&I work and support companies on LGBT+ activities.

Kehrer and Vey, two of the prime movers, soon saw that loose affiliations were not enough. In 2013, they established a foundation with the two of them as private founders and a few large companies on board. The time seemed favorable. Although Germany was lagging far behind Anglo-American LGBT+ developments, it was visibly changing too. That summer, Europe's largest LGBT+ job fair, Sticks & Stones in Berlin, Germany, was held for the fourth time (for more on the fair, see Part IV, Chapter 7). Moreover, Barilla had shown what could happen if companies failed to read the runes. The boycott threats had happened in Germany too.

So Kehrer and Vey had some momentum. They were also very well connected and knew their stuff. Kehrer had previously started D&I primus IBM's LGBT+ employee network's German branch, then been a diversity manager at auditing giant KPMG. Vey, an innovation manager at Deutsche Bank in Frankfurt, was an active member of dbPride, the bank's LGBT+ network. For years, the bank had been considered particularly proactive and experienced on LGBT+ D&I, nationally and internationally in finance industry strongholds such as New York and London.

In many conversations and meetings, the two men finally managed to win over eight global companies, covering a broad range of industries and, as of the end of 2019, employing over 1.5 million people globally. These were:

1. Technology, management consulting and professional services giant Accenture: about half a million employees
2. BASF, the world largest chemical producer, headquartered in Ludwigshafen, Germany: over 110,000 employees
3. Commerzbank, the country's second largest listed bank: about 48,000 employees
4. Deutsche Post DHL, the German multinational package delivery and supply chain management company: over 540,000 employees
5. Deutsche Telekom, one of the world's leading integrated tele-communications companies with global brands such as T-Mobile: over 200,000 employees
6. IBM, the tech and services icon: about 350,000 employees
7. SAP, Europe's largest and the world's third largest listed software company, based in Walldorf, Germany: about 100,000 employees
8. White & Case, one of the leading corporate law firms, present on all continents: a high four-digit number of employees.

Soon after Prout at Work was set up, Google joined as another donor. The foundation's advisory board includes several further company representatives.

At the end of 2013, Kehrer and Vey were ready to launch. With the foundation established, the focus broadened. The fight against discrimination, homophobia, biphobia, and transphobia at work was now on the agenda. Prout at Work is, as its website says, committed to ensuring "that all working environments are open to all people, regardless of their sexual orientation, gender identity, gender expression or sexual characteristics."[99]

## A call from friends in Milan and a conference in Rome

As explained earlier, Parks's goals for Italy are very similar to those of Prout at Work for Germany.[100] The connection was made: "Barilla had asked Igor Suran from Parks in Milan for advice on who to approach in Germany and he called us," reports Vey.

Suran was the successor aforementioned Parks founder Ivan Scalforetto had been nurturing, a friend from their days at Citigroup. Suran has become the primary Parks contact for Barilla. A native Croatian, he has lived in Milan for over 20 years and, prior to his involvement with Parks, held various management positions at Citigroup. As an Executive Director of Parks, he is today responsible for strategy and operational decisions.

During research for this book I experienced Igor Suran in action. In May 2018, BNP Paribas was holding its second global LGBT+ business conference. Having taken place in London two years earlier, this time it would be held at the still quite new headquarters of BNL, BNP Paribas's Italian arm, in Rome. Italy was a strong symbolic choice both because of Barilla's scandal and turnaround and because, as previously noted, the country lags behind in Europe, especially the EU, on LGBT+ rights. Numerous representatives of the group's LGBT+ employee network's national branches were flown in, from sites including São Paulo, Hong Kong, New York, London, Paris, Munich, Lisbon, and Montreal. The huge investment sent a strong signal to the entire banking group that LGBT+ D&I mattered. Furthermore, at the Roman headquarters, the event was held very prominently near the entrance. Every bank employee and visitor entering or leaving could see what was happening: conference participants speaking with each other with rainbow lanyards, loud rock music playing during breaks, and rainbow posters everywhere.

It was an internal event. But I was allowed to attend as a neutral participant for research. The program was rich. Among other things, I experienced not only an emotional speech by Andrea Munari, BNL/ BNP Paribas's CEO and Chairman of the Board, in which he talked very personally, with tears in his eyes, about his family's experiences of exclusion. There was also a focused presentation from Suran on the progress of LGBT+ equality in workplaces in Italy, again summarizing the benefits for companies and the economy.

## Recent progress

Though it remains difficult with Italy's conservative social environment, efforts to improve LGBT+ inclusion in the workplace are progressing. Parks, at any rate, has attracted many globally operating member companies in around ten years of existence.

The companies contribute to Parks financially through their membership fee and other forms of support. In return, they use the organization as a meeting, networking, information, and learning platform and seek strategic and operational advice on successful LGBT+ D&I management.

Since 2013, Suran and his team have also managed an LGBT+ diversity index for companies, the first of its kind in Italy. It is based on a questionnaire that differentiates between large firms and small and medium-sized companies. The index measures a company's success in implementing D&I policies for LGBT+ people and in creating an LGBT+-inclusive culture. It also enables companies to compare levels of LGBT+ equality – in general and in detail – and to encourage each other to improve in the face of growing pressure for change.

As part of index work, Parks also awards prizes in different categories. In 2018, Accenture was celebrated as most LGBT+-inclusive large company. Vector, an automotive supplier active in over 25 locations worldwide with around 2,500 employees and headquarters in Milan, won in the category "Best Small- or Medium-Sized Company."

Among the more than 90 Parks member organizations, there are well-known banks, insurance companies, consulting firms, IT and software groups, law firms, pharmaceutical companies, consumer goods firms, and others (see box, as of December 2020).

---

## Parks – Liberi e Uguali, Italy: selected member companies

**Banks, finance, insurance, investment:**
Allianz Partners, Aon, Aviva, AXA, Banca d'Italia (Central Bank), Barclays, BNL (BNP Paribas Group), Citi, Deutsche Bank, HSBC, Sace Simest, State Street, Unicredit

**Consumer goods, fashion, furniture, travel:**
Barilla, Coca-Cola, Costa, Danone, Gucci, Ikea, Nestlé, Proctor & Gamble

**Communication, media, technology, software:**
Consoft, Discovery Italia, Google, IBM, Microsoft, Oracle, Sky, TIM/Telecom Italia

**Consulting (management, auditing, technology, HR):**
Accenture, Alix Partners, Bain, Boston Consulting Group, Deloitte, EY, Lang & Partners, McKinsey, PwC

**Law firms:**
Clifford Chance, Freshfields Bruckhaus Deringer, Hogan Lovells, Linklaters, Simmons & Simmons, Scorcelli & Partners

---

**Industry, energy:**
3M, Baker Hughes, Dow, Enel, GE, Philips
**Pharma:**
Johnson & Johnson, Lilly, Pfizer, Sanofi

"As Parks, we have received a particular boost from the law on civil partnership (*Union Civile*)," Suran says. Companies have felt a sharp increase in the need for advice as a result, because equal treatment is now required for benefit claims and numerous other regulations. "Since the law came into effect in spring 2016, we have noted an increase of more than 50% in members."

And Barilla? The company has not yet received a Parks award. But Suran has been a frequent guest in recent years for meetings with members of the Barilla D&I Board, speeches, strategic and operational advice, and much more. The firm's employees and managers also participate in Parks' trainings, workshops, and conferences. Some time ago, Kristen Anderson, Barilla's Chief Diversity Officer, became a member of Parks' Board, which is currently made up of seven representatives of member companies, plus Suran.

"A very trustworthy cooperation on many levels," Suran says of Barilla, agreeing with David Mixner that it is going through a "really credible change." Suran knows Mixner well, seeing and speaking to him regularly. Around the time the *Unione Civile* became law, Parks (and Barilla) sponsored a performance by the American at the Elfo Puccini Theater in Milan. Mixner's show – *Oh Hell No!* – was about the LGBT+ movement's fight for equality and his associated life. The auditorium was full. Italian *Vanity Fair* ran a long interview with the activist in which he praised the Italian government of the day and spoke of a "long struggle."[101]

## Getting to know each other: civil society and business

When Suran called Prout at Work Vice Chairman Vey in fall 2017, he got straight to the point. He wanted the German foundation to help bring Mixner and Barilla together with members of the LGBT+ community in Germany – as soon as possible.

Since joining Barilla as an external D&I Board member, Mixner had been traveling to a new country for Barilla about every six months. Germany was now the next stop. "We knew about the change at Barilla," Vey says. "However, like others, we asked ourselves: are they serious?" adds Kehrer. In the end, both decided, "We'll help first and see how things develop."

Barilla wanted the meeting to be a closed event without publicity. It was to take place in Cologne, Germany, where the Barilla's Central European headquarters is based, Germany being this region's main market. Mixner and a Barilla delegation, including D&I boss Kristen Anderson, invited ten people to a restaurant.

Half the party was made up of people from large companies. In addition, there was Vey and representatives from *Aidshilfe* (the major German AIDS NGO), *LSVD* (a major national LGBT+ association), and *VelsPol* (the LGBT+ police service network). Sarah Ungar traveled from Essen, headquarters of her employer Thyssenkrupp, the German global industrial engineering and steel giant. Born in 1981, the human resources specialist joined the company as a young male trainee in 2006. A few years later, she completed her transition. "I could suddenly just be me," she says. For a long time, she was a Thyssenkrupp manager but now works as an HR director for a Rolls-Royce Group company.

"Don't be a victim," David Mixner told her in Cologne, but there was no risk of that. She had co-founded the LGBT+ ERG at Thyssenkrupp, fighting for more visibility and inclusion in the company. She was also a frequent panelist and interview partner on LGBT+ issues in the media. Above all, she knows what she's fighting for: transgender people like her often have a difficult time at work, especially when they decide only in adulthood to live in the gender with which they really identify. Almost everywhere in the world the unemployment rate is above average for transgender people. They also face discrimination in everyday life much more frequently than lesbians or gays. "Now it's your turn," Mixner told everyone in the Cologne restaurant – meaning, "You are now the generation that must drive the change forward."

Holger Reuschling, then a middle manager at Germany's second largest bank, Commerzbank in Frankfurt, and a spokesperson for its LGBT+ ERG, sat next to Mixner. Above all, Reuschling, Ungar, and the other attendees experienced him as both charismatic and an attentive listener. "David Mixner not only wanted to understand what companies are doing in Germany in the area of LGBT+ inclusion," Reuschling said, "he was even more interested in the everyday life of LGBT+ people, with respect to discrimination, protection, and the experience of freedom. Listening to these local stories and then thinking about appropriate activities for Barilla – this was Mixner's approach."

Activity at Barilla's German headquarters began with a gentle overture to the German LGBT+ community: Nina Tsilomanidis, key account manager for Barilla in Germany and member of the firm's D&I Board for Central Europe, gave a short interview to a local gay website in summer 2018. She said, for example, that Barilla supported "equal marriage" and gave same-sex couples the same benefits as heterosexual ones, such as for weddings, parenthood, deaths in the family, etc. She also reported on the D&I Board's composition and work and talked about Voce, the LGBT+ ERG, then with over 150 members in Italy, the US, Germany, and France, Barilla's major markets. (It now has over 300 members, with Italy as the largest chapter. Of the around 8,400 employees globally, about 5,000 work in Italy.)

## The German boss gets on board and the work begins

Shortly thereafter, some of Barilla's colleagues attended the Prout at Work annual conference, among them Tsilomanidis, with further meetings and discussions between Barilla Germany and Prout at Work following. Finally, Kehrer and Vey traveled to Cologne in January 2019 to sign an agreement setting out Barilla's strategic LGBT+ goals and stipulating regular reviews. It also gave Barilla permission to use the "Prout Employer" label in Germany in exchange for the company committing on concrete next steps.

It was Claus Butterwegge, head of Barilla for Germany, Austria, Switzerland, and Poland, who signed. Barilla posted a photo on LinkedIn showing Kehrer, Vey, and Butterwegge holding the Prout Employer certificate with a message saying they were proud to be the first food industry business to partner with Prout at Work. Work started immediately. Kehrer and Vey met with additional representatives from Barilla's German D&I department, including Tsilomanidis, to discuss steps for 2019.

Kehrer and Vey are drawing up similar annual plans with all Prout Employers, the total number of which has grown rapidly. By end of 2014, when the Prout Employer initiative was launched, eight companies were on the list; by end of 2016, 21; by 2018, 35; and by December 2020, 47 (see below).

---

## Prout at Work Foundation, Germany: Prout Employers

**Banking, insurance, finance:**
AXA, Commerzbank, Deutsche Bank, ING, Deutsche Börse

**Consumer goods, food:**
Barilla, Beiersdorf, Coca-Cola

**Communication, media, technology, software:**
Bertelsmann, Discovery, Deutsche Telekom, Google, IBM, Kantar, Orcale, SAP, Tech Data

**Retail, transport, logistics:**
Deutsche Bahn, Deutsche Post DHL, Metro, Otto, Rewe, Sodexo

**Pharma:**
Bayer, Boehringer Ingelheim, Pfizer

**Industry, energy:**
Airbus, Audi, BASF, Continental, Covestro, Robert Bosch, RWE, Siemens, Thyssenkrupp, Vinci Energies

**Consulting (management, auditing, technology):**
Accenture, Campana & Schott, EY, KPMG, Oliver Wyman, PwC

**Corporate law firms:**
Clifford Chance, Dentons, Hogan Lovells, Linklaters, White & Case

---

The plans Kehrer and Vey draw up with their Prout Employers can vary greatly. They depend on the size of the company in Germany and on the industry. Global law firms, for example, are very different from large consulting, IT, or pharmaceutical companies. It also matters whether a company is just starting its journey, is more advanced, or is already a true LGBT+ professional. It also makes a big difference in which parts of the world a company is headquartered and operating and with how many people. Further factors are whether a company has many blue-collar workers and how much the education levels differ within the organization.

One measure agreed between Barilla and Prout at Work was for it to take part in a Prout at Work LinkedIn campaign advocating for LGBT+ inclusion in the workplace.

The foundation celebrated its fifth birthday in February 2019, just a few weeks after agreeing to the partnership. On this occasion, one of Prout at Work's founding businesses, corporate law firm White & Case, hosted an event with Barilla Germany's D&I leader Tsilomanidis appearing as a panelist.

That summer, for the first time, members of Voce were at Pride Cologne, Germany's largest Pride event, with more than one million participants. They were there with other LGBT+ ERGs under the Prout at Work umbrella.

That same summer, Tsilomanidis traveled to Vienna to speak about Barilla's diversity turnaround at an LGBT+ business conference as part of the Europride program. Europride is the central European Pride event held every year since 1992, hosted in a major European city.

It was also decided that Barilla's boss in Germany, Claus Butterwegge, would attend Prout at Work's next "Dinner Beyond Business." The foundation has been organizing this exclusive dinner for some years. The host is a Prout at Work member company, so the location changes each time, though not the format: an LGBT+ top manager with global influence gives a presentation or is interviewed, followed by Q&A sessions and informal discussions. The guests are handpicked, mostly board members and other high-ranking business representatives. In the end, due to a short-notice business commitment, Butterwegge could not go, so Tsilomanidis attended instead.

## Increased activity in France

In France, another important market, the Italians increased activities too. Barilla France sponsored another roundtable with Mixner and representatives from other companies, employers, and NGOs. Again, they discussed local national attitudes around LGBT+ inclusion to work out Barilla's approach.

As in Germany, the firm became a member of the local organization working for LGBT+ inclusion in the workplace: *L'Autre Cercle*. L'Autre Cercle's goals are about the same as those of Prout at Work and Parks, but its organizational setup is a bit different, with less-active company members and fewer services offered. Although founded early, in the late '90s, it is still working with volunteers. Overall, France, continental Europe's second-largest economy, is significantly less advanced on LGBT+ workplace inclusion than Germany and, especially, the UK and the US. (For more on France and L'Autre Cercle, see Part II, Chapter 5).

In 2019, Miloud Benaouda, Barilla's Western European Regional President, spoke at a L'Autre Cercle's event. His high level of LGBT+ D&I engagement also put Benaouda on that year's first edition of France's LGBT+ and ally role model rankings, set up by L'Autre Cercle, copying British global lists (for more on these rankings, see Part II, Chapter 4). Benaouda was ranked as a straight executive ally visibly supporting LGBT+ inclusion.

The French chapter of the the firm's LGBT+ ERG *Voce* is quite active, and Barilla France also works with the local *Fondation Le Refuge* – "Shelter Foundation." Set up almost 20 years ago, it aims to combat isolation and suicide among LGBT+ youth aged 14 to 25, and support LGBT+ people in cases of homophobia, transphobia, and family breakdown. Some of its services are similar to those of New York City's Ali Forney Center, the largest community center for homeless LGBT+ youth in the US (see earlier this section, referring to Barilla's affiliation). Barilla France sponsored foundation events such as cooking classes for LGBT+ youth at the firm's Paris headquarters with one of Barilla's local *chefs de cuisine*.

Barilla's LGBT+ journey in France and Germany is still in an early phase, while in the US and Italy, Barilla's two most important markets, it is much further ahead. How will it continue?

# 10. "Take a traveler who chooses the wrong path"

At the company's employee meeting in December 2018 in Parma, Italy, Barilla showed a three-minute film that today is the first item one sees when visiting the company's D&I site. Accompanied by soft music, it shows a range of ethnicities and ages, women touching each other tenderly, parents caring lovingly for children, David Mixner on stage, Igor Suran in conversation, Mixner and Guido Barilla hugging and laughing, lots of greenery, relaxed people in charming Italian streets.

A female voiceover tells a story in English, her words subtitled in Italian:

*Take a traveler who chooses the wrong path. If the path makes him discover things about himself – and about the world – that he never would have known and that make him a better person – can we still say that path was the wrong one?*[102]

## "Change catalyst"

The narrator continues that the company chose the wrong path, then embarked on a five-year learning journey. The events that led to the path have come to be seen as a "change catalyst," the voice explains.

The images tell the story of the company becoming one that embraces diversity and inclusion – in particular, diverse sexual orientations and gender identities. Barilla has taught us, the voiceover continues, that love does not differentiate by gender, religion, or ethnicity. The rainbow flag with the word "Voce" on it appears, with members of the LGBT+ employee network of that name.

Shortly before the end, American Jessica Sharpe comes into frame. She is not only the film's narrator, but Voce's spokesperson and one of its two founders. When she joined Barilla in 2012, she was not out, she tells the audience. Quoting the company founder back in the 19th century, saying no Barilla employee should ever be ashamed, she was proud of what had been achieved and that she was now coming to work every day as her true, authentic self.

A lot of positive feeling. Too much? Not necessarily. The story, people, and organizations involved, the facts and details of Barilla's development as I have told in this book so far speak for themselves. And there is more. Barilla now has a website to support, educate, and develop its suppliers within the framework of a D&I program designed specifically for them. The company is thus looking at the entire supply chain to encourage its suppliers to engage in D&I that meets its new standards. Whoever visits the site as a supplier is greeted by eight tiles. One shows a Barilla flag, a US flag, and a rainbow flag.

CEO Claudio Colzani also says on the company website that he has embarked on a major transformation based on the three key concepts of international expansion of the business, centrality of the customer, and promotion of diversity and inclusiveness. With respect to the last of these, he adds that Barilla's D&I journey "starts with the recognition that supporting diversity and inclusion is the right thing to do and it is also good for business."[103]

## Two women on a box

Two further milestones reflect Barilla's ongoing transformation.

In 2016, YouTube star Hannah Hart became a "pasta girl." As part of its Passion for Pasta campaign, Barilla launched a video series dubbed *While the Water Boils*, for which Hart interviewed celebrities. Each interview lasted the time it took to cook pasta: about five minutes. As Hart is openly lesbian, Barilla's work with her was reported around the world.

Two months before Barilla showed this work at its headquarters, at the Pasta World Cup in Milan, Guido Barilla did what he had vowed never to do five years before: advertise with a homosexual couple. He unveiled a limited edition of his group's most popular product, Spaghetti n. 5, featuring two stylized women holding hands. On the other side of the box are the two women's heads with, between them, a single strand of pasta, joining their lips. A kiss thus seems imminent.

The design is by Olimpia Zagnoli, a designer who had long boycotted the Italian company over the notorious interview. In search of unconventional ideas, the group approached her and chose this design.

In media both social and traditional, the package and the story behind it were widely circulated, not least by the designer herself. From opposing Barilla, she has become a supporter – one willing to extensively communicate her new opinion. Barilla has changed and so has she.

Barilla has not received much praise from its critics for its efforts in recent years, says CEO Claudio Colzani. "They say, 'You're OK. You're still in repair mode.'" But that would be "a fair comment. We'll always try to improve ourselves before telling others we're fine."[104] Chief Diversity Officer Kristen Anderson agrees that good progress has been made, but that there is "still a lot of work" ahead.

As the voice in the corporate film says, "The journey has only just begun."

## It goes on

One year later, by the end of November 2019, Voce had arranged that Thomson Reuters Foundation CEO Antonio Zappulla would travel to Barilla's headquarters in Parma. "It was the first time that he shared his own story in his country of birth, gave background information on *Openly*'s idea, results, and impact, and presented his thoughts on how media and information can contribute to making societies more inclusive," Anderson says. Zappulla appeared on stage with Parks Executive Director Igor Suran and Barilla's Chief Supply Chain Officer Antonio Copercini who is also Voce's executive sponsor. They discussed the continuing challenges of LGBT+ inclusion in Italy, Barilla's approach, and lessons from other companies. "Our largest event hall, *Sala Manfredi*, holding 100 people, was packed," Anderson says, with herself and Colzani attending.

Recently, the company's most credible D&I supporter, David Mixner, has publicly retired from many of his activities but has decided nevertheless to remain on the firm's D&I Board. "Of course, we are very happy about that," says Anderson, who speaks to Mixner regularly. "We would like him to stay on the Board as long as he wishes to do so, because he is an instrumental part of our D&I journey."

Amid the COVID-19 pandemic, in spring 2020, Parks boss Suran held a virtual event around the use of potentially exclusionary language. At around the same time, Voce initiated a Zoom networking roundtable, open to all Barilla employees. It was moderated by Suran, and Mixner took center stage, sharing news of the pandemic in New York, where he is based. "This was a moving event, about human vulnerability and resilience," says Anderson. "It was also about what is important in life and how we can be more inclusive every day. And it was about moving forward – in a spirit of optimism and open-mindedness."

# Postscript with a diva: *È pronto*

When in the past the great Sophia Loren, iconic Italian diva and a world superstar, was asked about the secret of her beauty, her answer was always, *"Pasta e amore"* – "Pasta and love": a plate of spaghetti every day for a firm décolletage, flawless skin, and full lips. It led to her publishing a cookbook entitled *In cucina con amore* – "In the kitchen with love" – which was re-released in 2013 on the occasion of her 80th birthday.

So she was the perfect protagonist for a spot by the very young Italian fashion label GCDS featuring the liaison of old pasta traditions and a fresh, colorful spirit.

In some way, GCDS – the initials stand for God Can't Destroy Streetwear – is a symbol of Italian manufacturing that is energetic, a bit eccentric, multicultural, and youthful. This is reflected in its style: casual, at times ironic, oversized, and usually unisex, with bright colors and pop graphics.

When Barilla started its LGBT+ journey, the company didn't even exist, but created by two Italian brothers in Milan only in 2015, it is growing fast, presenting its quite expensive pieces at the Milan and New York fashions weeks.

Barilla contacted Giuliano Calza, GCDS's creative director and one of its two founding brothers, asking it to design a special tribute-to-Barilla collection for fall/winter 2019/20 and to reinvent its classic packaging for a limited edition.

This is how the famous blue Spaghetti n. 5 box turned a striking fuchsia pink with both brands present on the bold packaging. At the same time, in October 2019, the related special collection was launched with unisex clothes and all-over prints, including hooded sweatshirts, wool hats, and t-shirts. On all of them, Barilla's logo is very visible.

In parallel, a campaign started to go viral, centered around a high-gloss advertising video entitled *"Dinner's Ready."* The video features top black model Aweng, trans Youtuber Nikita Dragun, and drag queen Violet Chachki, a winner of the iconic TV show *RuPaul's Drag Race* – a cast from a diversity handbook.

Alongside all of these: Sophia Loren.

After various scenes around the city, the entire group – or alternative family? – gathers around a long, richly laid table, with Loren at its head, calling everyone to dinner. Putting a pot of spaghetti on the table she shouts, "*È pronto!*" At the right bottom corner, Barilla's special pink pasta box can be seen, fitting right into the colorful *mise en scène*.

There is an Italian colloquialism that reads, "*Di che pasta sei fatto?*" meaning "What are you made of?" It seems Barilla has found some open-minded answers.

# Part II

**A surprising initiative in Davos, hide-and-seek at the top, and an economic message to the world for the years ahead**

# 1. The global leaders' high mass – with breakfast at Microsoft

In January 2014, Guido Barilla was still struggling with the devastating response to his interview, and it was not yet even remotely clear if his company's LGBT+ turnaround would succeed. Around that time, a slightly different LGBT+ furor was reported from snowy Davos, Switzerland. It was a caesura with great impact and became part of the global trend I am describing in this book.

As always that winter, great numbers of the world's elite gathered for their high mass in the Eastern Alps: the annual meeting of the World Economic Forum (WEF). There were top executives and senior managers from multinational corporations, influential leaders from management and technology consulting firms, heads of state, prime ministers and cabinet members, leading representatives of supranational organizations such as EU, UN, and major central banks, heads of influential foundations, and selected young leaders.

In all, around 3,000 participants usually attend the global mega event. The international media coverage is huge and the Forum itself sends streams of information in writing and pictures around the globe.

But what information? For a long time, there was resistance to even mentioning LGBT+ D&I at the WEF. That January, things suddenly began to change – albeit not, initially, with official WEF support. In fact, the change occurred *despite* their lack of support.

## Alpine inspiration and the art of agenda setting

Davos is a pleasant ski resort, almost 1,600 meters above sea level. I know the area quite well as a result of my time studying in Switzerland. Many others know it for a completely different reason: a century ago, it inspired the genial Nobel Prize winner Thomas Mann's monumental novel, *Magic Mountain*. For about 50 years now, however, it has been about the WEF summit.

"Committed to improving the state of the world"[1] is the WEF's promise. Certainly, the agenda reflects key global issues and has huge influence. In most cases, this is about challenges that international companies need to approach strategically. Some want to influence

topics on the official agenda for the Forum's annual meeting. Competition for such influence is fierce.

The same applies to side or "off-piste" events outside the official program, like breakfasts, lunches, dinners, and other informal meetings, many of them offering keynote addresses by renowned speakers, presentations of new research, or panel discussions. A lot of companies and other organizations attach great importance – and duly allocate funds generously – to such peripheral Davos formats because they can host and hence influence them more directly.

## Taking a risk

A significant version of this happened in January 2014 when several influential WEF member companies took the initiative outside the official program and issued invitations to what would become a historic Davos breakfast. The title was unambiguous: "The Global Struggle for LGBT+ Equality."

HRC was one of the partners helping to set up the panel, but the prime movers were billionaires Daniel Loeb and Paul Singer, both from New York City and frequent Davos attendees. Loeb is founder of the hedge fund Third Point, and a philanthropist through his Third Point Foundation. Singer is founder of the hedge fund Elliott Management Corporation and a philanthropist through his Paul & Emily Singer Family Foundation.

Singer and Loeb had originally approached the WEF wanting to stage an official dialogue on LGBT+ rights in Davos, but they bit the granite hard and were thus forced to seek an alternative away from the formal agenda. That they met with rejection was not surprising. When *CNN* anchor Richard Quest asked aforementioned WEF founder Klaus Schwab a few years ago why LGBT+ issues were not yet on the docket at Davos, his reply was that there were many important issues, but you couldn't cover them all. Of course, this is true *prima facie*. Nevertheless, Schwab could be asked whether he resisted discussions and initiatives on LGBT+ challenges primarily because the Davos guest list includes numerous representatives from, for example, Africa, the Caribbean, and the Muslim world, where homophobia and serious legal reprisals against sexual minorities remain rife. Was he wary of alienating them? – especially the

leaders in the rich oil-exporting countries such as the Arab states, Russia, and China?

Even if Schwab would deny such political opportunism, it is still legitimate to ask whether the WEF here was really fulfilling its remit. After all, it is not just a neutral, nonprofit organization. Rather, it gives two commitments: one, to make the world a better place, and two, to spot economically important trends in good time to serve its members, especially companies.

In retrospect, it is clear that on both these counts, the "official" WEF has long fallen short on LGBT+ D&I issues and has, thus, fallen short as a global leader.

## Full house

In the end, the Global Struggle for LGBT Equality breakfast took place in a packed house. "We did not expect so many people to show up but were happy that they did," said Dan Bross, another of the breakfast's organizers, when I met him in New York for our own extended breakfast. The guests at the WEF event had included dozens of top decision-makers from business, politics, and society – a very satisfactory start for the hosting partners.

At that time, Bross had been a Microsoft senior director for sixteen years. In this role, he was responsible, among other things, for managing Microsoft's relationship with a range of key external stakeholders including the WEF. He also oversaw the company's CSR and human rights work.

The pioneering breakfast took place directly across the street from the main conference center, in a building Microsoft had been using for years for its own events with customers, civil society organization partners, public officials, academics, media leaders and others. For the duration of the WEF annual conference, the premises have therefore for many years been called the Microsoft Meeting Center. "When the hosts and I were speaking about the possibility of such an event," said Bross, "the location of the meeting center was a happy coincidence since, as Microsoft, we were able to provide fairly centralized facilities in Davos."

The panel for the breakfast was moderated by Fareed Zakaria, presenter of the weekly TV show *Fareed Zakaria GPS* on *CNN*, and columnist for, among others, the *Washington Post*. Born and raised in India, the award-winning journalist is regarded as impartial, highly competent and, the same time, opinionated. With a view to attracting global attention at Davos and in the media, he was a clever choice.

Not only was the event extremely well attended, it boasted a particularly high-level endorsement: Navi Pillay, the United Nations High Commissioner for Human Rights, agreed to give the opening speech.[2] She got directly to the point, relating by way of introduction how when she took office, she was repeatedly urged *not* to deal with "this topic" – and how she flatly rejected this advice.

The mother of two and member of the ethnic Indian minority had suffered under the Apartheid regime in her home country, South Africa, and had been an active LGBT+ ally from an early age. During her term in office – from autumn 2008 to autumn 2014, the longest of any UN High Commissioner of Human Rights to date – a remarkable amount, much of it decisive, was accomplished with regard to LGBT+ rights at the United Nations. I will talk a bit more about that in Part II, Chapter 8.

## Unexpected advocates

Most of the panel participants were LGBT+ human rights activists but alongside them, the main drivers to make this event happen, Singer and Loeb, were also speaking.

Singer, especially, talked about his personal motivation to finally put LGBT+ issues on the agenda in Davos, even if only unofficially for now. His son Andrew, then in his early 20s, had informed him in the late 1990s that he was homosexual. Singer's primary reaction as a father had been to admit that he knew nothing about life as a gay man or, indeed, a member of any sexual or gender minority. While studying medicine at Harvard, Andrew had become an activist for LGBT+ rights and inclusion, HIV/AIDS education, and more. His son's enthusiasm in his struggle had also gripped the rest of the family, including the father, giving rise to the latter's activism.

Singer's work in this regard is remarkable to some in two ways. First, as a hedge fund manager and active investor, the billionaire is considered a controversial figure in the finance industry. *Fortune* once described him as one of the "smartest and toughest money managers."[3] Others have criticized him for his aggressive methods, for example his practice of purchasing distressed securities – i.e. tradable financial assets with a high risk of becoming worthless – from states and companies and then pursuing full payment in court.

Second, Singer is as an active member of the Republican Party, often donating a lot to electoral campaigns, including presidential ones. Singer tried to prevent Donald Trump from becoming president, favoring a Republican competitor. However, after Trump's election, Singer supported the inauguration ceremony (and continued the support thereafter).

On the other hand, Singer wants to convince fellow Republicans to support same-sex marriage, reasoning that it would well fit within his "framework of freedom" and contribute to "family stability." At a time when the institution of marriage has virtually collapsed in the US, he sees it is a "lovely sign" that so many same-sex partners want to marry.[4]

It has been estimated that Singer had already donated tens of millions of dollars to the LGBT+ rights movement. For example, he supported the Human Rights Campaign's global activities. He also supported several campaigns to legalize same-sex marriage, including in New York City, Maryland, and New York State, where the legislation passed in 2011. The year after that, he provided a million dollars to start American Unity, a Political Action Committee with the mission of encouraging "Republican candidates to support same-sex marriage, in part by helping them to feel financially shielded from any blowback from well-funded groups that oppose it,"[5] as the *New York Times* wrote. Singer also funded the American Unity Fund, a nonprofit that aims at advancing "the cause of freedom for LGBTQ Americans by making the conservative case that freedom truly means freedom for everyone."[6]

## Everything starts with a good breakfast

The media response to the 90-minute event was huge. A personality as dazzling as Singer naturally attracts attention: extremely rich as an investor through his own efforts, controversial in his methods, an active Republican, and at the same time an enthusiastic pro-LGBT+ activist, inspired to be so by his gay son.

Also of interest was the other super-rich investor behind the event, Daniel Loeb. Loeb has no known family ties to the topic and, also in contrast to Singer, has supported Democrats in senate campaigns, as well as Barack Obama's presidential campaign. In common with Singer, however, he had also previously promoted LGBT+ issues, such as the ultimately successful fight for same-sex marriage in New York State and, like Singer, he had funded the American Unity Fund. In 2015, the year after the historic Davos breakfast, Loeb and Singer would also donate substantially to launch "Freedom For All Americans," a permanent bipartisan campaign aiming to bring together "Republicans and Democrats, businesses large and small, people of faith, and allies from all walks of life"[7] to secure full protection against discrimination for LGBT+ people in states and local communities in the US.

Anyone looking back at the Davos event today would notice that the panel speakers called for more equality and inclusion for LGBT+ people, with specific reference to human rights. However, Singer and Loeb's passionate involvement also conveyed its relevance to the economy – strengthened by the personal presence at the event of numerous US senators and top business executives such as Coca-Cola CEO Muhtar Kent, Virgin founder Sir Richard Branson, EY top executive Beth Brooke, Accenture top executive Sander van 't Noordende and Microsoft President Brad Smith.

## A turning point and the first small breakthroughs

The breakfast was one of the most talked-about events in Davos that year. It marked a turning point, with LGBT+ issues suddenly brought to the fore on one of the most important stages of the global economy – with powerful, influential and, for many, unexpected advocates.

In January 2015, when the global elite met again in Switzerland, the effects of these influences became apparent, with a delicate but clearly visible breakthrough. *Fortune* ran a striking headline: *Gay rights takes center stage in Davos.*[8]

In an article for the WEF website published shortly before the annual meeting of the Forum, aforementioned Sander van 't Noordende, at that time and for many years a Group CEO at Accenture – a job, he had stepped away from by the end of 2019 – stressed that the LGBT+ topic was now "on the radar" of the world's top business leaders.[9]

It has to be said that visibility on the formal agenda was still very modest. The only relevant event was on page 103 of the official, extremely long program – one of the last events on the afternoon of the last day of the congress. Its title, "The Diversity Dividend," spoke to how organizations can embrace diversity to drive innovation and sharpen their competitive position. It gave three bullet points on this, only the second of which referred to LGBT+ inclusion.

So, a single bullet point with the four letters LGBT, placed under a very general heading: it couldn't have been more hidden. In addition, quite a few Davos visitors would already have left by the time of the event or simply been too exhausted by the previous four or five days.

Sander van 't Noordende, who was considered one of the most active senior out top executives globally at that time – known, among many other things, for having appeared at the WEF for many years as an openly gay Group CEO – was aware of all this. Yet he was right that this event on the WEF's official agenda was a breakthrough – as he knew from his familiarity with the small signs indicating formal change in the political world of the Forum and measured against the its clear reticence in previous years.

The Dutchman was also right for a second reason. There was another event not on the official agenda that, nevertheless, made waves. On the heels of the historic side-event breakfast the year before, Accenture now organized a historic afternoon panel session at Davos to shine a spotlight on LGBT+ issues and the challenges companies encounter with them across their global operations: Improving the State of the LGBT Workforce.

On the panel were three frequent Davos guests: aforementioned Beth Brooke from auditing and consulting giant EY, at that time one of the most senior out lesbian top executives; António Simões, out CEO at HSBC Bank, UK; and Sander van 't Noordende. The panel was moderated by *CNN* business journalist Richard Quest. It was the first time at the annual meeting of the WEF that this topic was taken up with a strict business perspective and at a high level, although again just in an informal session. Nevertheless, this premiere was again much talked about at the Forum.

That these further steps toward significant higher visibility were possible at Davos had a lot to do with events in the months before, which I will describe in the next chapter.

## 2. The courage of a business journalist and the second life of a CEO

Every now and then I watch *CNN*, especially its business reporting, especially during the WEF's annual meeting, and especially when Richard Quest is the presenter. He often appears at Davos in a thick winter jacket with various guests. Or he does the odd disguise surprise, turning up, for example, in the uniform of ice hockey team HC Davos, the arena of which is located directly next to the congress center, the WEF's main venue.

No question about it, the guy's a showman. I find the Liverpool-born New Yorker with the raucous voice wonderfully entertaining and at the same time superbly informative. Not only is Quest one of *CNN International*'s most popular presenters, he also hosts the weekday business show *Quest Means Business* and other formats.

But that's not all. As well as being a highly regarded international business journalist, the late-50s anchor is also one of the very few who is openly gay. When he received an offer in 2006 to switch to the English-language Arabic news channel *Al Jazeera*, Quest declined because he would have felt out of place there as a Jew and homosexual.[10] Thus, it was no coincidence that Accenture had chosen Quest as moderator for their first panel on LGBT+ workplace issues at the WEF.

For a business journalist, Quest's openness about his homosexuality is still courageous today. It was even more so some 15 years ago. In mid-2014, however, he took his clarity on the issue even further. In his own globally broadcast business show, he dealt extensively with homosexuality among business leaders – uniquely, to my knowledge, in programming of this kind anywhere in the world at that level.

The historic Davos breakfast only some months previously would likely have given him a tailwind. But the topic had become spectacularly interesting, especially in the Anglo-American world, for another reason: around that time, ex-BP CEO John Browne published his book *The Glass Closet: Why coming out is good business*. It represented an impressive comeback for a former business superhero after a spectacular fall some seven years earlier.

## A true story about two lives

Brown's departure from BP made for quite a story. The son of a British Army officer and a Jewish-Hungarian woman who had survived Auschwitz but many of whose family had been murdered in the camps, Browne served as BP's top boss for 12 years until 2007. He had joined the company in the mid-'60s as a university trainee and enjoyed a steep career trajectory. When he became the company's CEO, he catapulted it into a new era.

Because of a strict cost regime, some major accidents, including a refinery explosion, a salary of his own in the millions, and alleged "Sun King airs and graces," he was not uncontroversial during his tenure. But under him, BP's market value increased fivefold in just over a decade. From an operation of limited size and market power, it became a global oil and gas giant with, today, some 70,000 employees in almost 80 countries.[11]

Beyond the successful businessman, ennobled by the Queen as Lord Browne of Madingley, was another John Browne. Despite the confidence conferred by class, elite education, and business success, this one was in hiding. Browne had realized he was gay while still at boarding school, but for about 40 years he had kept his sexual orientation secret in public life.

And then the veil on this second life was pulled aside spectacularly. Browne had been in a relationship for a few years with the Canadian Jeff Chevalier, a former rent boy whom he had met in 2003 through an escort agency. The couple lived a status-oriented private life in a milieu of well-known personalities, including prime ministers, other high-ranking politicians, and world-famous artists. They had a private jet, butler, chauffeur, and several residences, and gave frequent dinner parties. Somehow, despite the ostentatious opulence, Browne kept the relationship secret.

When it ended, Browne continued to support Chevalier financially for a while, but at some point, he wanted to stop. Chevalier responded with blackmail, using Browne's in-the-closet status against him. When Browne was no longer willing to pay, Chevalier took the story to the sensationalist conservative tabloid newspaper *The Mail on Sunday*.[12]

Browne fought back by accusing his ex-lover of alcohol addiction and drug abuse, allegations that were medically refuted. A restraining order, with which Browne had hoped to prevent the story reaching the public, was lifted in response to Browne's own lies about how he had met Chevalier. The *Mail on Sunday* finally ran its scoop in May 2007: *The true story about Lord Browne – by ex-rent boy lover.*[13]

The ensuing scandal was huge. Browne, already on the point of retiring, resigned early, thereby giving up millions in claims against BP from a severance package and more. Just a few months earlier, Browne had traveled to the annual meeting of the World Economic Forum with, at that time, nothing to separate him from the many hundreds of other CEOs and chairmen in attendance. Now, suddenly, he had plunged to undreamt-of depths, himself speaking of shame and shock at the revelations.

## Media coverage with a homophobic tone

It didn't end with a single news item. The *Mail on Sunday*'s sister paper, the *Daily Mail*, with a daily circulation of millions, was "aggressively leading the coverage of my sensational exposure," as Browne wrote later.[14] In one month it published more than 12 articles on the drama, by his count.[15] Other media outlets also pounced on the story and reported it incessantly. The UK media, much of which is notorious for its viciousness, characteristically showed no mercy in tearing down a man whose contributions to the British economy they had long celebrated.

In retrospect, Browne recognized that when there are changes at top management level in a large company, public and media interest is legitimate. However, he also believed that details of his personal life were exaggerated just to increase news media profits.

Perhaps he was right. But in his job as BP boss, Browne had got to know the media well and had used them to pursue his own goals, including his fame as a dynamic, visionary, successful BP boss. What weighed more heavily was that his downfall, as he said, was partly celebrated in homophobic tones.[16] Anyone who has read any of the articles must surely agree.

Beyond new professional activities and goals, Browne's return to public life was relatively swift. He wrote books, one of which was his autobiography, *Beyond Business*, published three years after the scandal and garnering a lot of attention. It seemed he wanted to regain interpretative sovereignty over his life and, in particular, his professional successes, which had received some criticism both before and after his departure from BP. In *Beyond Business*, Browne also provided some very personal insights into his inner life and the circumstances that led to his departure, but predominantly laid out his rise at BP and the transformation of the group under his leadership.

In 2014, however, seven years after his spectacular downfall, Browne wrote *The Glass Closet: Why coming out is good business*. This time, LGBT+ inclusion in companies was the sole focus, promoted on economic grounds.

The times had changed as well with respect to the media's reaction. The British Guardian immediately published an interview with him, headlined, *Lord Browne: 'I thought being gay was basically wrong.'*[17] Other major media also covered the book, which Browne promoted intensively in the UK and the US.

## Lord Browne's focus: the economic rationale – to be managed top down

On the one hand, Browne's book is a reappraisal of his personal history after a few years' gap. Particularly touching is the first chapter, entitled "Hide-and-Seek," in which he describes his scandalous fall – up to the blackmailing by his ex-partner – and the high personal costs of his double life. He reflects that the dramatic events surrounding his departure marked a turning point in both his professional and personal lives and showed the consequences of not being authentic.

However, Browne's history as the closeted head of one of the largest British companies and major global player is really just a starting point. He brings his experience together with that of other LGBT+ leaders and experts and looks at it in the light of both recent practice in companies and research findings on the economic advantages of not hiding one's true self.

In an interview with the *New York Times*, Browne admitted his "greatest regret in life is that I wasn't honest while I was chief executive." He had led "a great company for many years, and not to let people see who I was, was a big error." People "need to see role models. I could have left BP in a very different way." He now also thought that his concerns about how deliberately coming out might negatively impact BP's business were misplaced and that BP would have been better off if he had come out earlier.[18]

Browne's book was sending a clear message arguing for the LGBT+ inclusion business case: companies benefit economically if they cultivate a culture that is open and appreciative toward diverse people in general and toward LGBT+ people in particular. In such a culture, LGBT+ people no longer need to waste their energies on hiding their sexual orientation and gender identity. Instead, they can work without fear and make a career as LGBT+ people who are authentically themselves. Companies should therefore activate these resource potentials. Enabled by focused top-down management, they should promote a working climate open to diversity for everyone, including LGBT+ people. In the end, everyone benefits from such a culture: LGBT+ employees do better because they feel better and are able to focus on their work, not on hiding; that means the company does better and that's better for all other employees.

To get LGBT+ inclusion right, i.e. to create and sustain the desired working climate and culture, Browne suggests seven actions. The first is:

- To actively set direction from the top, making LGBT+ D&I a senior management and thus a strategic task.

Then:

- Let LGBT+ employees know they must take active ownership of this journey too
- Create and support LGBT+ employee resource groups
- Encourage straight allies to be part of the cultural transformation
- Set concrete goals and measure against them
- Identify role models and tell their stories again and again
- Set clear expectations for those working in "conservative" countries, i.e. in countries where life – as a local or assigned LGBT+ employee – is dangerous or even criminalized.[19]

The Barilla transformation, described in Part I of this book, was aimed precisely at achieving the desired open inclusive culture, and some of Browne's recommendations Barilla eventually took. But when Browne's work was published in spring 2014, the pasta company was still groping its way out of its self-imposed public shaming. The HRC top rating that later publicly certified their first successes on their way to becoming LGBT+ champions had not yet been awarded.

Whether Browne's book had any direct effect on the conversation around Barilla, the timing was unquestionably apt. In any case, both events, along with the Davos breakfast, act as barometers of a clear change taking place internationally.

## Prestige support and global impact

This view is also backed by the unprecedented support Browne's book received from global leaders. It was published with endorsements from a long list of high-profile supporters. These included (heterosexual) CEOs of large multinational companies, such as the financial giants Goldman Sachs and Standard Chartered, the consumer goods group Unilever, and the advertising and PR giant WPP. These influential global players represented many billions in market capitalization and sales and hundreds of thousands of employees.

There were also statements from Beth Brooke, Sir Richard Branson, and David Petraeus. Petraeus is the retired four-star general who was previously, among other things, commander-in-chief of the US forces in Afghanistan and director of the CIA. Branson, legendary British founder and Chairman of the Virgin Group, had, just a few months earlier, already attended the Davos breakfast. And as mentioned, just some months later, EY's top out executive Brooke would be on the first panel discussing LGBT+ in the workplace at the WEF's annual meeting.

Browne's subject was, of course, controversial even in liberal Western societies at that time, impacting the Anglo-Saxon world and, to a lesser extent, other liberal Western countries. But that pales into insignificance when you take into account that most of those praising the book were leaders in companies also operating in areas where LGBT+ people are persecuted and/or criminalized – places like Nigeria, Kenya, Saudi Arabia, Qatar, Jamaica, Malaysia, Brunei, and Pakistan. The message would potentially reach managers and employees in branches there, as well as local leaders and legislators, the business community, and media, and, crucially, the vulnerable LGBT+ community and their families and friends.

The supporters' numerousness and prestige thus set an extraordinary example. That CEOs and other top decision-makers would dare to break cover on this issue would have been hard to imagine just a year earlier. Furthermore, it is not easy at the best of times to persuade board members and top decision-makers to write even short statements praising books. Board offices and communications departments often block such requests without even passing them on to their bosses. Even when they do get through, the bosses usually object, especially when the requests are for books or authors that might appear controversial. I myself worked for a long time as an editorial and publishing director at large business and nonfiction publishers and often experienced this.

So the support from top leaders was also a coup for Browne himself. With a loud bang, he had made it clear that at least some major global corporations and their bosses were now courageous enough to express broadly visible public support for LGBT+ diversity and inclusion in everyday working life for economic reasons. Conversely, the list of book supporters considerably strengthened the impact of Browne's book and its message on the media, on business, and on the general public.

What a change for the scandal-hit man from seven years ago – and, with the focus on economic benefits, a different but complementary focus from the historic breakfast at the WEF where human rights arguments prevailed.

## Gay business hits the airwaves

*CNN* business journalist Richard Quest reinforced the effect, taking on the subject of Browne's book in a very personal way. On his program, he discussed not only homosexuality among company bosses and managers, but also his own coming out. Before it, he said, he had spent a lot of time feeling anxious, worried about what his family, friends, colleagues, and viewers would think. "Would the fact that I'm gay affect my creditability as a business journalist? Would you watch the program differently?"[20]

Unlike Browne, who remained closeted throughout his long working life at BP, Quest was able to report on his own experiences before and after. In this way, he underlined Browne's economic arguments on lost productivity with his own experience. In front of a large TV business audience, he related how energy-consuming worrying about all this had been:[21] "Thinking like this saps energy, it drains confidence, it takes a toll on productivity, it's exhausting!"[22] Of course, he knew that everyone goes their own way and has to decide for themselves when the time is ripe to come out. But he also knew that in his case, "the worst fears never materialized. All in all, professionally, I know the work I do here every day is better because I'm honest about who I am."[23]

The concerns that Quest outlined are familiar to anyone who has ever agonized about coming out on the job – and to every family member, friend, colleague, or ally with whom such an individual has discussed the matter. But now the public, especially the business public, was hearing from the horse's mouth that high-ranking business journalists like Quest could suffer from such anxieties, and from Browne that managers at every level could too.

At the top level at which these men operated, the fear may be particularly intense because senior people may feel they have a lot to lose. The following figures would seem to support this argument: up to mid-2014, the time of Quest's broadcast and Browne's book's publication, very few CEOs or top managers had identified themselves publicly as LGBT+. On the FTSE 100, which tracks shares in the 100 largest businesses on the London Stock Exchange, only one company at that time, the fashion group Burberry, had an openly gay CEO, Christopher Bailey. On the S&P 700, which tracks 1,200 of the world's largest listed companies minus the 500 US companies included in it, no CEO had come out as LGBT+. Thus the *New York Times* in May 2014 had good reason to publish an article titled *Where are the gay chief executives?*[24]

Critics, perhaps with some validity, accused Browne's book of displaying the same magisterial self-regard he had previously displayed as BP boss. Others believed that Browne, as a privileged child of the British upper classes, had had a softer landing than others might have. In fact, he has found his way back into business. He is currently Executive Chairman of L1 Energy, an oil and gas investment company indirectly controlled by Russian-Israeli billionaire Mikhail Fridman, and also holds various supervisory board positions. But what about Browne's ex-lover, Chevalier, whom he may not have treated very well? Shouldn't LGBT+ rights be allied to equal rights, opportunities, and respect for everyone, regardless of pay grade, status, and social standing?

Nevertheless, Browne was the first broadly visible top business leader to collapse the two sides of his double life and highlight the economic benefits of LGBT+ diversity and inclusion for businesses. For the first time, this concern was being widely discussed in the media. And by having heterosexual leaders support him in his marketing efforts, Browne not only reached a large business audience across hierarchies, but also had an impact beyond business.

## 3. An executive's journey from the man to the woman she has always been

The same year Barilla initiated its LGBT+ turnaround and John Browne began writing his book, Swiss businesswoman Angela Matthes started a new chapter in her life, showing that a CEO – albeit of a very small local unit – can successfully come out as a transwoman. Matthes had prepared for this with great care.

During research for this book, I met Matthes, CEO of Baloise Life Liechtenstein, at a panel discussion at IBM premises in Munich, Germany. The stories shared on the podium, including those of IBM and SAP executives, were complex and interesting, but Matthes' was particularly special. Afterwards, we arranged to discuss it in more detail later.

Her story is worth telling not least because it took place in the insurance industry, starting in Switzerland and ending in Liechtenstein, the wealthy German-speaking microstate in the Alps with less than 40,000 inhabitants. The industry and both locations are highly conservative.

Matthes had been working for the same company – the only one in her professional life – for about 30 years before she finally decided to transition: the over 150-year-old Baloise Group. It operates in several European countries with over 7,000 employees, revenues of around nine billion Swiss Francs (as of the end of 2019) and a major but not exclusive focus on insurance. The Group is headquartered in Basel, in the German-speaking part of Switzerland.

Matthes joined Baloise aged just 15, made a career, then continued her education with an Executive MBA among other things, and achieved promotions to several leading management positions – all this as a man, at least in the eyes of others.

In 2013, the parent company sent Matthes, now in her mid-40s, to Balzers, a community of 4,500 in Liechtenstein, where the local Baloise Life unit is headquartered. The subsidiary, which specializes in pensions and income-related life insurance, was small, with about 25 employees. Matthes was to be their CEO.

The task that awaited her was not easy. A restructuring had reduced staff by around half. "And then, after nine months, a new CEO comes along again, and that was me," Matthes told the German edition of *Forbes*, "... one could still feel the uncertainty."[25] Her first few months were mainly about overcoming this, stabilizing employees, and motivating them for the future.

## A plan

What no one suspected was the other matter of concern to Matthes: she finally wanted to live in the gender identity she had felt was hers since childhood, as she later told the Swiss radio magazine *Spirit*, which deals with religious and ethical issues.[26]

She had a plan. Parallel to her assignment in Liechtenstein, she began training for an Executive Master's in Consulting and Coaching for Change at the elite management forge INSEAD in Fontainebleau, France. She wanted to use the training both to expand her qualifications and to protect herself if Baloise did not support her decision "that this transition had to happen."[27] In Liechtenstein she was still perceived as a male CEO, but on the program in France she was a step ahead. She said later, "In March 2014, I was already in Fontainebleau as Angela," telling her colleagues on the program, "I am trans, but have not yet completed the transition."[28] This outspokenness further accelerated her inner process, in which she was accompanied by a therapist.

## Support from Basel

Two months later, she set up three meetings at the group's headquarters in Basel: with the head of the human resources department, with the chairman of the board, and with her direct superior, the Baloise Group CEO. The central subject of all three meetings was Matthes' decision to live and work as a woman from the fall onwards. Her interlocutors were surprised but thanked her for her trust and immediately offered support.[29]

Help in such a situation is not always given so easily. In his book, for example, in a chapter titled "Transgender Taboo," Lord Browne tells of Maggie Stumpp, a chief investment officer in the US, then known as Mark, who told her boss she wanted to undergo transition surgery. Her boss' reaction: "Maggie, we love you and whatever you want to do is fine." And then, says Stumpp, he ran out "like the *Road Runner* cartoon" into a bar.[30]

The story indicates the great embarrassment with which even supportive people can react to transitions. It was possible Matthes would also have to deal with embarrassment, even fear among colleagues, employees, and later also customers and business partners. And she was aware of this.

## A parallel: the Transparent series

But it was not only *her* time to start a "new" life. Perception of transgender people had begun to change around this time, especially in liberal Western societies. One sign of this was the premiere of Amazon's *Transparent* series in February 2014 – just one month before Matthes left for France. It immediately made a splash because of its great quality and wit. Many people around the world ultimately watched it in various languages.

The title is a pun, collapsing "*trans*gender" and "*parent*." The series revolves around the Pfefferman family after Mort, the father, decides to live her gender identity as Maura. The series was an extraordinary artistic and commercial success, with further seasons following and many awards. One was from GLAAD, the aforementioned LGBT+ nonprofit focusing on the media.

## Lisa Sherman's perspective

Lisa Sherman saw the success of *Transparent* as deserved. In a panel discussion at the WEF in Davos – three years after the historic breakfast there – she talked about the importance of quality LGBT+-related films and series in general and *Transparent* in particular.

For a few years now, Sherman has been the head of the Advertising Council, or Ad Council for short, a national nonprofit headquartered in New York, founded in 1942. On behalf of various institutions, including NGOs and US government agencies, the Ad Council produces nonpartisan material on social issues, collaborating with ad agencies, storytellers, and media platforms working pro bono. It has launched many campaigns related to the COVID-19 pandemic, for example. The Ad Council website says it is led by the "belief that creative marketing can solve complex social issues."[31] Sherman is thus not only a successful businesswoman, she is also an expert on how images, moving pictures, and stories can be powerful agents of change.

With regard to the LGBT+ community, especially, Sherman knows what she is talking about. In 2005 she joined the US media giant Viacom, where she launched *LogoTV*, the first cable network for LGBT+ audiences. She came out late in her career, after almost 18 years. Like Browne and many other leaders, she had long led a double life. With family and friends, she was out, but not at work. She even had a photo of her best friend Bob in her office to seem like a male partner. With respect to her real partner, she mastered the "black art of pronoun puppetry,"[32] as she called it, meaning that she used "him," "he," and "we" to avoid "her" and "she."

She long thought coming out could mean "career suicide." It was only on her last working day with her previous employer in the late 1990s that, aged 39, she had the courage to come out to her CEO. A Harvard Business School case study published as early as 2008 describes how Sherman left Verizon, where she had served as a successful executive for many years, "because of the negative views of gays and lesbians expressed at a diversity training workshop, and her final meeting with Verizon CEO Ray Smith to describe the challenges she had faced."[33] The case study also describes the actions that Smith finally took to change the LGBT+-unfriendly culture Sherman had revealed to him. Finally, it describes Sherman's successful subsequent career at Viacom, including the launch of *LogoTV*.

## Real stories from real people

Sherman said on the podium at Davos that new generations are living different stories from those of their predecessors. The stories presented in the media about LGBT+ topics should continuously be updated to promote equality and inclusion and help overcome old stereotypes. Of course, the reality of LGBT+ people has always been multifaceted, but never so visibly in daily life. There is no doubt that this will continue to grow.

Sherman demanded that the color and richness of LGBT+ life be reflected across media, from movies to ads. In developing characters for these, you need, she said, "real stories from real people." To her, *Transparent* was a particularly successful example, as anyone who has seen an episode will immediately understand This is no freak show about a "tranny," but the depiction of a full life – funny, touching, sometimes sad, always convincing. When clichés do appear, they are immediately shown up and subverted.

This kind of high-quality storytelling in the media is much needed given the heterosexual mainstream's scant knowledge of transgender people, who make up about 0.5 to 1% of every society (for research on the gender revolution among the young, see Part IV, Chapter 2) and prejudice against them is particularly high.

From that viewpoint, *Transparent*'s capacity to increase acceptance of transgender people – and sexual and gender minorities in general – cannot be underestimated. Series with relatable, multi-layered characters become part of viewers' lives much more than cinema films, for example, with great potential for lasting effects in overcoming stereotypes. As I mentioned above, Browne's book had a chapter titled, "Transgender Taboo." The quality and success of *Transparent* helps render that taboo less powerful. It also offers transgender people credible role models for their own lives.

Meanwhile, its artistic and economic success incentivizes further programming in the same vein. Accusations from several women of on-set sexual assault against lead actor Jeffrey Tambor may have killed the series prematurely, but not the prospect of making more money from it and similar shows – nor its contribution to learning and understanding more about trans people and their families' experience of their transitions.

## Transition at home – "suddenly" a mother of two sons and an activist at work

When Lisa Sherman made her statements in Davos, Wenche Frederiksen was confronted with a lack of information too – especially about her own situation. Frederiksen, who is based in Oslo, Norway, has worked for consulting giant Accenture for about three decades now, almost two of them in the human resources and diversity and inclusion arena. Today, she leads Accenture's D&I activities in the Nordic states, which includes – in her firm's world – Sweden, Denmark, Norway, Finland and Latvia. In her role, she has, among other things, pushed for active LGBT+ networks in all those countries and made Accenture the first company in Norway to provide LGBT+ awareness training. She was also a key driver in organizing Norway's first Oslo Pride Business Forum.

A short time ago, Fredriksen experienced a major change in her private a life that also impacted her work as a D&I manager. When they were young, Fredriksen and her husband adopted two little children from Colombia. "For many years, I have thought I have a son and daughter," the Norwegian says, "But in 2016, our eldest, at that time aged 21, came to me and said: 'Mom, something is wrong.'"

It turned out that the person she had thought to be her daughter identified as her son. "This at first came as a shock to me." Although, due to her role, Fredriksen was a knowledgeable and empathic D&I expert, she came to understand that she did not know enough about trans people and transitions in general. "And of course, I was worried about what this would mean for my child. Would he be bullied? Would he find a life partner?" At the same time, she says, "there was also this feeling of deep love for our son. And as a family we all committed that we would do all that would be necessary to support him in his journey."

Fredriksen's son now has his own apartment and a girlfriend and is happy, working as a personal trainer. Fredriksen, for her part, has become an even more dedicated LGBT+ inclusion advocate internally and externally. She has also been invited to many companies, "to share her story as a proud mom," she says, "to inspire them to start focusing on LGBT+ workplace inclusion, get them engaged with networks and more."

"Due to the changing values of generations with respect to sexual and gender identity," she adds, "and also due to social media and new smart media coverage of trans and nonbinary people, knowledge and awareness have increased fast in recent years." Nevertheless, many challenges for trans people and their families remain, including lack of knowledge, prejudice and biases.

On the other hand, an increasing number of global companies have made trans inclusion a major D&I topic, providing trainings, guides and ally programs. "As we do," says Fredriksen – who regularly joins the global meeting of Accenture parents of trans children, which takes place every month virtually.

## Many discussions

Angela Matthes understood the significance of informing her colleagues about the step she was taking and decided it required more than just a simple internal memo or explanatory note – especially since, having been with the company for about 30 years, she was well known across the group. She wanted to communicate in good time, carefully and as personally as possible, fostering knowledge, trust, and strong relationships.

After the three meetings with the company's bosses, she conducted around 150 individual and group discussions over a period of three months and thus ensured her colleagues were on board. In mid-August 2014, a symbolic division was made: a farewell party on a small scale, which her therapist had advised her to give. "I gave away all my neckties and came back two weeks later as Angela,"[34] she says. At the end of August, the company finally sent out the official internal communication and the press release.

On September 1, she took up her old/new CEO job, a position she successfully fills to this day, as Angela Matthes. She has never regretted her decision, and reports feeling happier, healthier, and more active.[35]

## And beyond the only role model?

There are currently just two items on the Baloise Group's website on LGBT+ D&I. One is a very short note on "Jump!" the company's still-new LGBT+ employee network, without any reference to related activities, such as social media or Pride parade presence. The other is a link to the aforementioned radio interview with Matthes.

So her company, only a bit smaller than Barilla in employee numbers, has supported her journey, but clearly still has some catching up to do to be visibly and credibly LGBT+-friendly, let alone be seen as leading in that respect in Switzerland (see box).

## Certifying LGBT+ friendliness in Switzerland

Compared to its large neighbors, Germany, France, and Italy, companies based in Switzerland are lagging far behind on LGBT+ D&I. But there is progress here, too. In fall 2018, for instance, the "Swiss Label LGBTI" was launched, developed mainly by two partners.

One was *Network*, the Swiss association for gay managers, self-employed people, artists, and students. It is subdivided into eight regional chapters, two of which cover the French-speaking part of the country, Geneva and Lausanne, the most recent representing the Italian-speaking part, Ticino. Switzerland has a bit less than nine million inhabitants speaking a variety of languages. Its major languages are German (spoken by some 65%), French (by around 23%), and Italian (by around 8%).

The second partner was *Wybernet*, the Swiss network of lesbian employees, specialists, and managers from the private sector, administration, and independent entrepreneurs. In setting up the label, the two leading partners were supported by some other LGBT+ nonprofits, such as the Transgender Network Switzerland, Pink Cross (advocating for gay and bisexual men), and others.

Once a year, the Swiss Label LGBTI distinguishes Swiss organizations in business and administration (including cities, universities, and state agencies) that are particularly open and tolerant toward the LGBT+ community. They are presented in two categories: organizations of below and above 250 employees.

In 2020, the award recipients in the latter categories were Accenture, Allianz Suisse (the Swiss arm of global German insurance giant Allianz), EY, Johnson & Johnson, Swiss (a subsidiary of German Lufthansa Group), and the City of Zurich. Only one company founded and headquartered in Switzerland received the label: Schindler, one of the world's leading providers of elevators, escalators, and moving walkways.

Especially with regard to the young, it remains to be seen whether Baloise Group will be able to quickly become appealing enough as an employer to attract the best talents, namely the young, high-potential talents crucial for long-term success.

For some years already, students at Swiss universities have been pushing for change, especially at the internationally respected University of St. Gallen, known for its excellent bachelor, master, and doctoral programs in business; at ETH Zurich, appreciated in particular for its quality in the fields of technology and natural sciences; and at the University of Zurich.

UniGay, the LGBT+ students' association at the University of St. Gallen, for example, is small but quite active. It sets up dinners with professors and lecturers, holds meetings with fellow LGBT+ clubs at foreign universities such as Madrid, and establishes contacts to LGBT+ ERGs such as those at Swiss business icons UBS bank and Novartis, and premiere consultancies such as BCG or McKinsey. Every year, members of UniGay join Zurich Pride as guests on the UBS truck. And for almost ten years, there has been a UniGay alumni network too.

Also crucial is Get Connected, a Swiss platform for advancing the exchange of experiences between LGBT+ students and professionals. The platform is hosted at St. Gallen and managed by students and former students, operationally supported by UniGay and the LGBT+ associations of ETH Zurich and Zurich University. Get Connected welcomes LGBT+ students from all fields of study and also LGBT+ professionals from all sectors and industries. It provides a mentoring program for young LGBT+ people and manages events via a panel discussing selected LGBT+ issues. The last event before the COVID-19 pandemic was centered around an anti-discrimination law and co-hosted by Get Connected; UniGay; the association of LGBT+ students in Zurich (z&h); the association of lesbian, bisexual, and queer women at universities in Zurich (L-Punkt); Accenture; and Homburger, one of the leading corporate law firms in Switzerland.

As for Angela Matthes, from time to time she shares her story in small interviews, on panels, and in speeches. Long term, this is not enough for Baloise to develop and showcase true LGBT+ friendliness. Nevertheless, since Matthes made her journey visible in 2014, she has become a role model – for colleagues at Baloise and beyond.

## 4. A gift from God, a Portuguese in London, and the rise of role model lists

The same applies to Apple CEO Tim Cook but in a different, more spectacular, and more globally impactful way. In the fall of 2014, the boss of one of the most valuable and admired companies in the world showed himself as who he was: a gay man and top business leader.

The temporal proximity to previous events that year was hardly a coincidence. Cook would have noticed the historic Davos breakfast and Browne's book – and understood the message. In any case, he sent a strong signal himself at this inflection point of high-level global corporate LGBT+ visibility.

His article in *Bloomberg* was entitled, *Tim Cook speaks up.* And that's what he did, very clearly and, above all, very personally. For years, a lot of colleagues at Apple had known Cook was gay, and it didn't seem to make a difference how they treated him, he wrote. He felt privileged to work in a company that valued creativity and innovation and knew that it could only succeed if people's differences were embraced. Although he had never denied his sexual orientation, he had not publicly confirmed it until now. "I'm proud to be gay, and I consider being gay among the greatest gifts God has given me," he wrote.[36]

He did not consider himself an activist, Cook went on, but knew how much he had benefited from the sacrifices of others. Privacy had always been very important to him. But if it helped someone to hear that Apple's CEO was gay so that they were more likely to admit who they were, or if it gave comfort to someone who felt alone, or if it inspired people to insist on their equality, then making a public statement about his homosexuality was worth compromising his own privacy.[37]

Cook also put forward some very open thoughts about how being gay might have affected his personality and his skills as a top manager. It had given him, he said, a deeper understanding of what it meant to be in a minority and an insight into the challenges that people in other minority groups faced daily. "It's made me more empathetic, which has led to a richer life," but it had also been tough and uncomfortable at times, which had "given me the skin of a rhinoceros, which comes in handy when you're the CEO of Apple."[38]

## Arrogant abuse of power or responsible citizen-boss?

Cook's article made a big splash – in the US, Europe, Asia, all over the world. And it caused some controversy, too. In its wake, Jochen Wegner, editor-in-chief of *Zeit online*, the news site of German liberal-progressive quality weekly *Die Zeit*, called me. He drew my attention to an article in the liberal-conservative Swiss *Neue Zürcher Zeitung (NZZ)* in which the author basically accused Tim Cook of abuse of power and arrogance. She respected Cook's performance as the CEO of Apple, but he was not a politician or civil rights activist, and should, therefore, according to the article's subtext, keep quiet about his homosexuality. Wegner asked me if I wanted to comment on this.

I did feel this needed an answer and said, "Yes." To me, the *NZZ* journalist's view was basically influenced by the very narrow Milton Friedmanite view of how corporations and their managers should do business described in Part I. Ultimately, in my answer on *Zeit online*,[39] I took a perspective partly influenced by social responsibility as a guiding business principle, as outlined earlier in this book.

Summarized and here modulated a little, the answer went like this: my colleague is wrong. A boss, whether of a medium-sized company or Apple CEO, is not just a boss who works his way up in the company. Rather, as a functionary of his organization, he is always and everywhere at the same time to be understood as a citizen of society, which he influences with his presence, actions, and statements. In the finely differentiated categories that have been known since the French Revolution at the latest, he is therefore, to put it briefly, not only an "economic citizen" (*bourgeois*) but also a "social and political citizen" (*citoyen*) or – for short – "citizen in society."

This already applies to any straight member of a company's board of directors who attends a gala evening with a wife or husband, as well as to Tim Cook when he talks about his homosexuality. In everything they do and say – or don't do and say – they are setting an example. In all these things, they are both leading "economic citizens" *and* leading "citizens in society," exercising their rights and power, with concomitant responsibilities toward the company *and* society. In this respect – precisely because of their prominent position as functionaries and citizens – they are always political in what they say and do, whether they like it or not and whether they are aware of it or not.

Cook therefore, with his words in *Bloomberg*, is not abusing his power. The opposite is true, precisely because with his statements on his homosexuality, he shows that he sees his company and himself as part of society. To frame it a bit more specifically: because Cook's words draw attention to the basic foundational values of modern, competitive, yet human societies – that promise equal rights and opportunities – he was using his power socially responsibly.

Seen in this light, Cook should be praised, not criticized, for his statements, for having acted as an ideal "citizen" boss for the company's almost 150,000 full-time employees worldwide – including its LGBT+ employees. And at the same time, he should be praised for having presented himself as role model for millions of customers, thousands of Apple suppliers, business partners, shareholders, and stakeholders – including LGBT+ people and their straight allies.

## A demand for a leader to take "personal responsibility"

António Simões followed in the Apple boss's footsteps just a few days later. Previously employed by Goldman Sachs and McKinsey, the Portuguese joined financial giant HSBC as Head of Strategy in 2007 at the age of 30. Soon after that, he was appointed a Young Global Leader of the World Economic Forum and has attended its annual meeting in Davos since then. Another three years later he was promoted at HSBC to become the bank's CEO in the UK and Deputy Chief Executive of HSBC Bank plc, the Group's principal UK and continental European subsidiary.

At an event hosted by Deutsche Bank in London, he criticized other top LGBT+ managers who have not yet come out. "We're in London, we're in 2014. It's not acceptable that we take for granted all the work done by others."[40] The similarity of Cook's and Simões' statements are evident. But the then 39-year-old HSBC man went a bit further than Cook and added that LGBT+ business leaders had a "huge personal responsibility" to come out[41] and showcase themselves as role models.

Simões embodies a different generation from Cook, who is around 15 years older. And the former knew what he was talking about. In contrast to Cook, Simões had made a name for himself as an openly gay top decision-maker even before his remarks and had also been involved in many ways in supporting LGBT+ equality. (This is not to say that Cook's courage in speaking up later in his career should be judged lesser. It is not, precisely because he belongs to an older generation that has undergone a lot more discrimination and stig-matization, both open and hidden.)

## Authenticity, empathy, and leadership skills as competitive advantages? Or: "My husband will divorce me"

In fact, it was not the first time that Simões had spoken publicly about his sexual orientation. He had done so in a video message to HSBC employees the year before and on many other occa-sions. There is no doubt that he is a professional when it comes to media communication.

For example, some weeks after the London event, he gave an interview to *Expresso*, a magazine in his Portuguese homeland, which again made waves. "If we want to live in a true meritocracy, the only thing that should matter is what you can do," he said. "I think being gay is an advantage," he stressed, explaining that it had helped him to become a more authentic, empathic, emotionally intelligent person and this had helped him rise to the top.[42]

Simões here again takes up some of Cook's thoughts, the former having reflected on how his homosexuality had affected his person-ality and his skills as a top manager. Cook mentioned as advantages empathy, a better understanding of the challenges of other minorities – and thus of people's differences in general – and that, in dealing with rejection, he had developed the aforementioned "skin of a rhinoceros."

In fact, Cook and Simões drew attention to leadership talents and abilities that have gained ground quickly in recent years. More and more, authenticity, empathy, and emotional intelligence are consid-ered important qualities and skills for successful managers today. Nearly all renowned business schools and leadership programs now offer methods for reflecting on one own's emotional, social, commu-nicative capabilities and relationships.

This also applies to the LGBT+ Executive Leadership Program launched by the Stanford Graduate School of Business in 2016. The first of its kind at a leading business school, it has been offered every summer since, with the number of participants increasing year by year. As one of the main benefits, its website promises "Lead with strength. Lead with impact. The LGBTQ Executive Leadership Pro-gram teaches you how to do both – authentically, effectively, and confidently." And it promises: "Learn how your LGBTQ identity influences and strengthens your personal leadership style. Assess and refine your interpersonal skills to become a more authentic leader."[43] This echoes Simões in his understanding of being openly LGBT+ as a potential career and leadership benefit.

In the summer of 2019, the roughly 200-year-old business school ESCP (*École Supérieure de Commerce de Paris*) began to offer an intensive program along these lines, too. The first of its kind in continental Europe, it was run in English out of ESCP's location in Berlin, though the school was founded in France where it is still headquartered and has its main activities. Run in cooperation with the German Prout at Work Foundation, the program's main promises are "LGBT+ leadership – increase your impact as a leader for more business success" and to "develop an authentic approach to leading your employees."[44]

Simões, whose involvement in LGBT+ issues has made him publicly known as a man who is married to a man since 2007, in his aforementioned interview with *Expresso*, revealed that nevertheless he would be asked once in a while about how his wife is. "Sometimes I say, 'My husband also works in the financial area' or 'My husband will divorce me if I don't get home in time to walk the dogs.'"[45] Quite an authentic answer – disrupting a cliché with a smile.

Simões, who lives with his husband and their two children, has recently been hired by the Spanish Santander Bank to become a member of the Group management committee, reporting to the Group CEO. His main job is to serve as regional head of Europe, covering Spain, the UK, Portugal, and Poland.[46]

He had been a CEO at HSBC and this move meant he lost the title, at least formally. That may change again soon. In the interview some five years ago, he said, "I hope – in fact, I am sure – that we will have a lot more gay CEOs for generations to come."[47]

## Role models and their rankings

During his professional career, Simões has become a true role model. This was formally acknowledged when he made the top rank on the first OUTstanding list showcasing the most visibly and impactfully engaged LGBT+ out executives. Twelve months later, in 2014, he made second place, after then Burberry CEO Christopher Bailey.[48] And in 2015, he placed third after Alan Joyce, CEO of Australian airline Quantas, and Inga Beale who came top, the first woman and the first openly bisexual person to do so. Beale had also been the first woman appointed CEO of the more than 300-year-old Lloyd's of London insurance market.

When this ranking, initiated in the UK, premiered in fall 2013, it comprised 50 people and offered for the first time an overview of LGBT+ role models in the business world. Because of its strong resonance in media, companies, the D&I community, and the LGBT+ community, the list was soon expanded to 100. Further lists followed, including those of straight allies at the executive level, young LGBT+ role models ("Future Leaders"), and an LGBT+ top 30 list for the public and third sector.

The criteria for ranking on the OUTstanding lists has become tougher over time. Currently, they include a candidate's activities to make the workplace an LGBT+-inclusive place; activities outside the workplace to contribute to positive change for LGBT+ people; prizes and awards received; and seniority and influence in the business or work environment (although the seniority criterion does not apply to young LGBT+ role models). At the end of the nomination process, a jury decides on the final ranking. John Browne has been on the jury since the lists were established, along with other high-caliber individuals.

Another jury member is Suki Sandhu, one of the leading players in promoting LGBT+ equality, primarily in the British business arena and to some extent in other parts of the world, especially the US. The openly gay Sandhu is the founder and CEO of London-based executive search firm Audeliss focussing on diverse senior talent, i.e. women, ethnic minority and LGBT+ leaders. He is also founder and CEO of social business INvolve, working for D&I in the corporate world through events, consultation, and programs.

Beyond Audeliss and INvolve, he is also engaged in human-rights-related activities. For example, he has launched The Suki Sandhu LGBTQI Asia Fund to support activism in Asia. He is also a Board member at OutRight, short for OutRight Action International, the New York-based NGO I referred to earlier, which advocates for LGBT+ human rights in the US and globally. For his various engagements, Sandhu has been ennobled by the Queen with the Order of the British Empire (OBE).

His business INvolve mainly consists of three initiatives focused on ethnic minority, gender, and LGBT+ D&I respectively: EMpower,

HERoes, and OUTstanding. INvolve is also present in Dublin and New York, but its main activities are in the UK. Beyond D&I-related events, consultation, and programs around these three initiatives, Sandhu has initiated annual role model lists for all of them and has been on their juries since they launched.

His venture OUTstanding, which has given the LGBT+ role model lists their name, is set up as a membership organization for international companies and, according to its own information, works with a good quarter of companies on the FTSE 100, the leading British stock market index.

## Media partners – what works?

For the first five years, the *Financial Times* was the media partner and publisher of the OUTstanding lists. Since 2019, the new partner has been *Yahoo Finance*. It remains to be seen whether this change will have an impact on the perceived objectivity of this list, which long benefited from its association with the premium *Financial Times* brand. The new partner may deliver a positive marketing effect in the US and more media power too, because *Yahoo Finance* has for some years belonged to Verizon Media, part of multinational telecommunications giant Verizon Communications.

The number of candidates who wish to be part of the list has increased quickly from year to year, as has the interest of companies in being associated with those ranked on the lists. The same applies to related external and internal marketing activities. LGBT+ managers, straight allies, and future leaders who have been honored with inclusion in the rankings as role models are usually celebrated extensively, both publicly and internally. Above all, the enormous response in social media can be followed very closely on international portals such as LinkedIn, Twitter, Facebook, and Instagram.

## Truly global?

The OUTstanding lists aim to have a global appeal. On the one hand, they do already, because the Western English-speaking cosmos that is their base, especially the US and UK, has set most of the business trends for decades now, including those around more recent concerns like LGBT+ D&I. On the other hand, they are not yet truly global.

The first lists, especially, were clearly and overwhelmingly dominated by role models from that same Western Anglo-Saxon cosmos, again mainly the US and UK, but also Australia and Canada. Either the role models' companies were headquartered in these countries or the role models were nationals of them.

This "bias" is also visible in OUTstanding's Hall of Fame (see box), launched some years ago. Currently (as of August 2020), there are 12 members. All of them belong to the Anglo-Saxon universe, and only two have a non-Anglo-Saxon national origin: Portuguese António Simões, who has spent most of his professional life in the British capital and/or in US- or UK-based companies; and Dutch straight ally Paul Polman, who from 2009 served for about ten years as the CEO of Unilever, the British-Dutch multinational consumer goods company, headquartered in both London and Rotterdam.

### OUTstanding's Hall of Fame – three selected members

OUTstanding's Hall of Fame honors leaders who are visible, sustaining, and inspiring champions for the advancement of LGBT+ inclusion and equality in the workplace. Such leaders are either part of the LGBT+ community or straight allies. Here is a brief look at three of them.

Martine Rothblatt, born Martin to a Jewish family in Chicago in 1954, initially became a lawyer and worked on communications satellite law and life sciences projects. In her private life – still as Martin – she became a husband and father. While she continued to pursue her career, in 1994 she finally came out as transgender and changed her name to Martine Aliana. Today, as she relates, she is still happily married to the woman who became her wife roughly four decades ago.

Her coming out was not the only drastic change in her life. Only two years later, Rothblatt founded United Therapeutics Corporation and, as CEO, led it to become a billion-dollar biotech company listed on the NASDAQ. At the time, she also became a very vocal and visible transgender rights activist, which included sharing her own story, for example in a now-famous TED talk in 2015.[49] She also attended one of the annual LGBT+ Pride receptions given by

President Barack Obama at the White House, expressing ongoing support for the fight for LGBT+ equality during the eight years of his presidency.

Rothblatt has written books, too. Her most often quoted is *Apartheid of Sex: A manifesto on the freedom of gender*. In it, she strongly opposes societies forcing people to be – or identify as – either male or female. She calls such regimes "sexual apartheid," comparing them to the South African Apartheid system that, according to her, forced people into two racial categories, white and black/nonwhite. Rothblatt claims that it is known from anthropological science that race is fiction, even though racism is real. At the same time, it is known from cultural studies that the idea of separate male or female genders is also a socially constructed fiction. To Rothblatt, the reality is a gender fluidity that embodies the entire continuum from male to female. She herself, she says in aforementioned TED talk, sometimes feels more woman, sometimes more man, and can change her gender several times a day.[50] (For more on the gender revolution among the young, who are increasingly living out Rothblatt's description of gender fluidity, and on companies' responses to this changing gender reality, see Part IV, Chapters 2–6.)

Anthony Watson is a second inhabitant of OUTstanding's Hall of Fame. From the UK and today in his mid-40s, he has worked in senior executive roles at the intersection of technology and business. For example, he has worked in banks such as Wells Fargo and Barclays, and as Chief Information Officer at Nike. In October 2014, he placed 19th in *Fortune* magazine's "40 under 40" ranking, which lists the world's most powerful C-level executives under 40, and he was the only openly LGBT+ person included. In January 2016, the British newspaper *The Telegraph* named him the most powerful LGBT+ business leader in the UK. A bit later, he was also appointed chair of the Labour Party's Business and Enterprise Council.[51]

Currently, he is engaged in a variety of ventures. He is founder and CEO of TBOL, which has offices in London, Luxemburg, and New York. TBOL is a startup, bringing together "veteran banking experts, leading creative innovators, and visionary technologists [...] working quietly" on "building the future of finance," as Watson's LinkedIn business profile says. Not quietly at all, for many years Watson has also been a human and LGBT+ rights activist. Ranked several times on OUTstanding's Out Executive role model list, he has also received a variety of awards for his services to the LGBT+ community. For example, since 2013 he has been engaged at GLAAD as a member of the Board of Directors, Chair of the Finance Committee, and treasurer. As mentioned in more depth in Part I, Chapter 3, GLAAD is the world's largest and influential LGBT+ nonprofit with a focus on the media.

Finally, Claudia Brind-Woody is the third inhabitant of OUTstanding's Hall of Fame I want to introduce here as an example. An American, she joined IBM in 1996 and has worked for them in Finland and the United Kingdom as well as the US. Currently, she is a Vice President and a Managing Director for global intellectual property licensing at the company and is a senior advocate across many LGBT+ networks. For many years she has been considered one of the most powerful lesbian women in business. And for many years, too, IBM has been a global leader in furthering LGBT+ inclusion in their workplaces and in promoting the idea of a related business case globally.

US icon IBM began its LGBT+ D&I journey as far back as 1984. On May 1 of that year, it showed "sexual preference" as a diversity characteristic for the first time in one of its company magazines[52] – a starting point for including this diversity dimension in its D&I activities, first in the US, then step by step globally. An LGBT+ timeline on the company's LGBT+ D&I website begins that year and stretches to the present. It shows in detail the firm's development to becoming a fast-moving LGBT+ champion.

It is no coincidence that in the past decades the company has received a stream of awards for pioneering modern LGBT+ D&I. Its activities to this end have included running mentoring programs; developing LGBT+-friendly products, services and programs; strategically addressing LGBT+ customer segments; serving companies wishing to reach LGBT+ customers; and more. In the last few years, its LGBT+ leadership has been challenged by some other companies, such as Accenture or SAP, for example, but IBM continues to be a highly innovative LGBT+-friendly actor.

Brind-Woody has been one of the leading out figures framing and pushing her firm's agenda internally and externally. Like IBM, she has received a variety of awards for her LGBT+ activities and achievements, including being highly ranked on several role model lists. She contributed to Lord Browne's aforementioned landmark book, *The Glass Closet*. And she also sits on a variety of boards for nonprofits working for LGBT+ equality in the workplace, for example, US-based Out & Equal Workplace Advocates and Dutch Workplace Pride Foundation, both engaged in LGBT+ inclusion at work for many years already. (For more on Out & Equal see Part IV, Chapter 5; on the Dutch foundation see Part III, Chapter 4.)

Only in recent years have the OUTstanding role model lists become a bit more global, but still not much. If there are Japanese, Germans, French, Italians, or other nationalities on the lists, they still mostly work for global players from fields like financial services, consulting, law, and others predominantly shaped by the Western Anglo-Saxon cosmos, or they work in London or New York.

Also only recently, the idea of creating, publishing, and marketing LGBT+ (and straight ally) role model lists has been exported to other countries, starting with Australia in 2016, for example (for more on Australia see Part III, Chapter 4.)

Germany, after a very short pilot in 2017, followed, celebrating the third edition of its lists in October 2020. The German lists were inspired by the OUTstanding rankings, but Suki Sandhu didn't play an active role in setting them up. This was different in France, the second-largest country in continental Europe after economic powerhouse Germany. In both countries, the focus of the list was not global, but national. Let's first have a quick look at Germany, then France.

## Initiating German rankings

Stuart Cameron, a Bavarian with a Scottish name, is highly entrepreneurial. He is the CEO of Uhlala Group in Berlin, a leading social business working for LGBT+ inclusion in the workplace. In contrast to the German Prout at Work Foundation, which – as shown at length in Part I of this book – has a similar purpose, Uhlala is not a nonprofit. Under the umbrella of Uhlala, the openly gay Cameron operates several projects, brands, and services for financial return.

His best-known initiative is Europe's largest annual LGBT+ job and career fair, Sticks & Stones in Berlin, usually attended by about 3,000 people and more than 100 companies and other employers. Another is the global LGBT+ leadership contest RAHM, a three-day event that takes place two to three times a year in different locations such as Berlin, London, or Toronto, each time hosted by a global company. (I will get back to Cameron and these two initiatives in Part IV, Chapter 7.)

One of Cameron's further initiatives started in spring 2017, when he launched Germany's Top 10 LGBT+ role model list, not limited to economic players. He wanted something similar to the OUTstanding lists for his country and decided that initially he would do something on a small scale to raise awareness and build from there. In 2018, he joined forces with the Prout at Work Foundation, which had approached him for a cooperative effort, to launch the first professionally compiled role model list of Germany's Top 100 Out Executives. The criteria for inclusion were similar to those used by OUTstanding. And following the British in another respect, the jury, along with the founding partners, included representatives from leading German companies.

## A tedious beginning

"2018 was not a bad start for our list of 100," says Kehrer, Chairman of Prout at Work Foundation, "but it was also very tedious." The Germans had known that getting 100 role models courageous enough to show their true faces in public would not be easy. German LGBT+ executives and other leaders are more fearful and hesitant than their colleagues in the US, Great Britain, Australia, and Canada.

In contrast to the English-speaking world, for example, hardly any companies proposed a candidate. "We sent out mailings, phoned a lot. But many of the people we had our eye on just didn't dare," says Kehrer. "It was frustrating at times," confirms Cameron. "Undoubtedly, in Germany there are still many concerns that it could damage your career." What was missing, above all, were top people from the board room. "They exist, but they don't dare. It's time for that to change."

Cameron is right. And for an example of how it should be, you don't need to compare only with US and Britain. "Let's just have a look at Workplace Pride, founded and led by our colleague David Pollard in Amsterdam," says Kehrer. The Workplace Pride Foundation is a nonprofit with similar goals for the Netherlands as Prout at Work has for Germany. The Netherlands has only 17 million inhabitants compared to 83 million in Germany and Workplace Pride has not initiated a role model list yet. "But you can meet a wealth of out LGBT+ top executives at the major Workplace Pride annual dinners," Kehrer says. "What Dutch bosses can do should also be possible in Germany." (For more on the Netherlands and Workplace Pride, see Part III, Chapter 4.)

"With regard to straight allies of LGBT+ inclusion, things are similar," Jean-Luc Vey, Prout at Work Vice-Chairman adds. "In this group, too, far too few from the top echelons are visible and audible in this country" – at least compared to the US, Britain, or the Netherlands.

On the other hand, when the first German lists were published in the fall of 2018, the impact in the media was strong and increased visibility for LGBT+ equality and the importance of role models. "That's what we wanted," says Cameron, "because visibility creates confrontation with clichés, may enable positive development of normality, and can ultimately lead to tolerance, acceptance, and real inclusion."

In contrast to the OUTstanding lists, there is as yet no role model ranking of straight allies for LGBT+ workplace inclusion. "But we have plans to start them soon," says Jean-Luc Vey. The year 2019 saw the second edition of Germany's Top 100 Out Executives. There was "at last some movement through active applications from companies," the Prout at Work Vice Chairman summarizes, "and more movement on the top floors, too, although not enough." The same applied to a new list in 2019, the Top Out Future Leaders ranking, inspired by an equivalent OUTstanding ranking focusing on young LGBT+ activists in companies and organizations.

For the 2020 rankings the Future Leader list was changed to become the Top LGBT+ Voices ranking. "We are learning," admits Vey. "The focus just on the young was too narrow for Germany. What about those who are older than 35 years and, for example as team leaders or highly skilled experts in their job, are pushing for better LGBT+ inclusion?"

## Reasons for optimism

"So far, there is still a lot of potential for improvement reflected in the next years' list editions," says Uhlala man Stuart Cameron. But he also has good reason to be optimistic. Not only were both the response and quality of the candidates significantly higher than the year before, the 2019 ranking also made headlines for showing not just six women in the top ten but three actually leading the list. Given that there is a certain dominance of gay white men in the LGBT+ business community in terms of activity and visibility almost everywhere globally, the 2019 German ranking sent a strong signal for greater diversity within these circles.

Eva Kreienkamp took first place in 2019, after taking second the year before. She holds a degree in mathematics and has had a colorful career. Recently, she was appointed board chair of Berlin's huge public transport organization. Previously she was, among other things, a co-managing director of public transport in the city of Mainz, worked for a start-up, founded a gender and diversity marketing and market research company (together with her wife and another partner), wrote a book about gender marketing, launched the country's first international gender marketing congress, and co-founded FidAR, a nonprofit advocating for more women on supervisory boards and leadership roles in Germany.[53]

Of particular interest was also, for example, the woman in third place, Anastasia Biefang, a Lieutenant Colonel in the German army. Her father was an air force officer, she joined the military in 1994, studied pedagogy at the University of the German Army, graduated, served in several military functions and, after more than 20 years, came out as a transwoman and bisexual. She transitioned and has since been on several tours of Afghanistan. Until recently, she was commander of an IT battalion and the first-ever battalion commander with a trans background. Through her various engagements,

Biefang has become one of the most visible leadership voices engaging for LGBT+ equality in general and inclusion for trans people in particular, far beyond the German army.

Incidentally, her inclusion on the German ranking also highlights the fact that, in contrast to the British OUTstanding Top 100 LGBT+ Out Executive list, which confines itself to business, the German ranking draws from all other employers as well. (A short note: for a couple years now, OUTstanding has managed a separate LGBT+ Out Executive ranking covering the public and third sector, as I mentioned briefly earlier.)

When in October 2020 the list's third edition was published, Biefang climbed to second place – this time again with six women in the top ten, but with a gay man, Nico Hofmann, in the lead, after placing 12th the year before.

To some, Hofmann's rise came as a surprise, because, for decades, he had not been engaged in advancing LGBT+ equality. Hofmann, who is in his early 60s, is not only an award-winning movie director, producer and screenwriter, one of the most influential in his country, he is also the head of Ufa, a major film and television production company and subsidiary of billion-dollar German media giant Bertelsmann. After a long and successful career, he decided just a short time ago to engage visibly for LGBT+ inclusion. Among other things, since its launch in 2017, he has supported Bertelsmann's employee network be.queer. He has also been a very visible supporter of the Queer Media Society (QMS), a new German network of queer media people working to stop discrimination against LGBT+ people in the media industry and to change representation of LGBT+ people in the media itself. He has also become a frequent speaker and guest on panels dealing with these issues. (For more on QMS's American role model GLAAD see Part I, Chapter 3.)

Finally, Cameron has another reason to be optimistic. The growth of his own social business Uhlala Group over more than ten years is a strong sign that Germany is taking off when it comes to LGBT+ workplace inclusion. As host of the aforementioned Sticks & Stones career fair in Berlin and the global LGBT+ leadership contest, RAHM, both overwhelmingly attended by the young, Cameron knows firsthand that many of those younger cohorts are pushing for change by living it. In a few years, some of them will be candidates for the executive ranking.

# 5. French progress – slow at first, but now new rankings and other initiatives are building momentum

The first role model list edition in France, published in spring 2019, was initiated and managed by L'Autre Cercle, the leading local organization working for LGBT+ workplace inclusion, which I referred to earlier. As with the British and German rankings, the French equivalent aims at increasing visibility.

L'Autre Cercle pursues the same goals as other European nonprofits like Prout at Work in Germany and Parks in Italy. However, as already mentioned, it is much less sophisticated in the services and support it offers employers, is still a volunteer organization, and counts significantly less employer support.

When it comes to LGBT+ inclusion in the workplace, France still lags behind compared to the other two leading European economies. The UK is very advanced, and even Germany has, as we have seen, caught up significantly in recent years.

In a way, France's slower progress is surprising since the country was an early mover. L'Autre Cercle was founded as far back as 1997. In 2012 it partnered with consultancy Accenture to set up a major event focusing on LGBT+ D&I policies, which led to the *Charte d'Engagement LGBT+* ("Charter of LGBT+ Commitment.")[54]

The Charter's idea, goal, and approach were similar to the Declaration of Amsterdam, launched in 2011 by L'Autre Cercle's Dutch cousin, the very impactful, globally oriented Workplace Pride Foundation (see Part III, Chapter 4). When – managed by L'Autre Cercle – the French Charter was finally inaugurated in January 2013, nine private and public-sector organizations signed, with more soon to follow. Today, about 140 public and private organizations have committed to the Charter (as of February 2020), representing about 1.3 million employees.[55]

## Cultural obstacles

L'Autre Cercle was founded and issued its Charter of LGBT+ Commitment before the Prout at Work Foundation in neighboring Germany was even launched. Nevertheless, initiating and sustaining LGBT+

journeys in French workplaces has remained tough. Signing the Charter is one thing; transforming cultural attitudes is quite another.

Sometimes even the signing can be difficult. When, in fall 2015, Paris-headquartered global banking group BNP Paribas publicly announced that it would commit to the Charter, there was severe protest from thousands of employees, complete with a petition. The furor was quickly taken up by groups close to the political extreme right and by conservative Catholics. BNP Paribas, however, signed. Today, among companies with French roots, BNP Paribas is, on a global level, one of the most advanced in LGBT+ inclusion.

The continuing difficulties in the country may have to do with a cultural trait that, in a work context, separates the private sphere more strongly from the professional than in the Anglo-Saxon world, for example. "To go on a stage in a professional setting and say: I am gay and I want to be at work with my whole, my true, my authentic self, is in some ways alien to French culture," Armand Jouhet says. "I don't want to stereotype, but I think, we, as French, also don't think in categories of 'community.' It's culturally not easily accepted to build a social group within an organization based on characteristics that are perceived as strictly personal. It's you, as an individual – and it's the employer. That's it."

Jouhet, still in his mid-30s, is a senior consultant at Strategy&, which belongs to the PwC network. Among other things, he holds bachelor's and master's degrees in management from HEC Paris (*École des Hautes Etudes Commerciales*). HEC belongs to the *Grandes Écoles*, the small group of prestigious higher education institutions in France. Since 1999, it has had its own LGBT+ students and alumni club, In&Out, the first to be set up in a French business school. Among other things, the club organizes conferences on campus, called DiversiTalks, inviting professionals to talk about LGBT+ workplace issues. Jouhet is still a club member and today serves as a mentor, "advising students," he says, "on specific issues they might face, for example related to homophobia on campus."

## Companies' new gradual progress

He is also part of *Réseau des Réseaux* (RdR for short, "network of networks"), an informal network of LGBT+ ERG representatives from Paris companies. Jouhet manages their regular afterwork meet-ups.

"Recently, there has been a fast-growing number of people interested in being included in the RdR mailing list and attending our get-togethers," he says.

The companies represented cover a wide range of industries, such as banking, insurance, automotive, manufacturing, consumer goods, logistics, transportation, consulting, communications, media, IT, and more. This wide range and the increased number of individuals interested in attending RdR's get-togethers reflect a general tendency: for some time now, more and more French companies have been intensifying work for LGBT+ inclusion in their workplaces and beyond.

This also applies to global corporates headquartered in France. Sometimes they begin by being active in their offices abroad, in countries more open to conversations around LGBT+ issues, or they combine these activities with their engagement in France. For example, Sodexo, the French catering and facility management giant, with more than 450,000 employees worldwide, works with Prout at Work in Germany as well as with L'Autre Cercle in France, and is also active in other countries such as the US. AXA, the world's largest insurance company headquartered in Paris, also works with both these organizations and with Parks in Italy, with their cousin organization in Spain and others (for more on Spain, see Part III, Chapter 4).

The luxury goods group LVMH, with its more than 140,000 employees worldwide, signed the UN LGBTI Standards of Conduct for Business in March 2019. That summer, it also held a party in an opulent New York setting with its openly gay star designer Marc Jacobs. And a bit later, it was one of very few European firms to become a member of New York-based social business OL, which has around 80 member firms and focuses on the top executive levels (for more on OL, see Part III, Chapter 1).

Or take the major banks BNP Paribas and Societé Générale (SG). Like LVMH, AXA, and Sodexo, both have signed the UN LGBTI Standards of Conduct for Business, and their American subsidiaries both also regularly achieve the perfect score of 100 in the HRC's CEI.

BNP Paribas works with Parks and L'Autre Cercle too and hosts an internal LGBT+ conference, to which I referred in Part I. In summer 2018, it was also spectacularly visible as one of the main supporters of the Gay Games in Paris, sponsoring it with a six-figure sum and flying in BNP Paribas LGBT+ delegations from several countries. The Gay Games has taken place every four years since 1982, with over 10,000 athletes participating most recently. It is globally considered the most important LGBT+ sporting event. In 2022, it will be held in Hong Kong.

Employees from BNP Paribas and SG also appear on the OUT-standing role model lists, though it must be said, these individuals are almost never actually French, but almost exclusively Anglo-American. One of the few exceptions is Vincent François, who works for SG in London as a senior manager in auditing. He is considered one of the most important LGBT+ assets and role models in the organization.

SG is also becoming more active in other areas. Ezequiel Corral provides an example. I met him in New York, where he has been working for the bank for several years, currently a manager in auditing corporate and investment banking. Corral, born in Argentina and openly gay, is considered an important driver of the bank's LGBT+ activities. President of the company's LGBT+ employee network for the North American continent, in just two years he has overseen a tenfold membership increase, including straight allies. He has also introduced LGBT+ mentoring programs and helped to establish local LGBT+ employee networks in the bank's Chicago and Mon-treal branches. It is down to him that, year after year, the bank has achieved the perfect 100 score on the HRC's CEI.

## More research, a conference and a new generation

There is more that indicates a gradual change in France. For example, recently, L'Autre Cercle partnered with Ifop (*Institut Français d'Opin-ion Publique*), a major international polling and market research firm headquartered in Paris, to launch the second edition of the survey *Inclusion of LGBT+ people in the workplace in France*.[56] Two further partners were consultancy PwC and *France TV*, the large state-owned public national television broadcaster.

About seven years after the launch of its Charter, L'Autre Cercle ran the survey, taken in fall 2019 and published in February 2020, to learn more about LGBT+ people's situations in public and pri-vate organizations. One finding was that while more companies are advancing LGBT+-inclusive policies and practices, one LGBT+ per-son in four has been the victim of at least one LGBT+-phobic attack at work. Another was that within those organizations that have signed the Charter, 84% of the workforce would feel "comfortable" if a colleague came out. On the other hand, almost half (49%) of LGBT+ people prefer to remain discreet about their sexual orientation.[57] The mere fact that French companies and media now support such up-to-date research as a basis for next steps on LGBT+ workplace inclusion reflects improving awareness and progress.

For some years, the country has also played host to a conference called LGBT Talents. It is managed by Escape, the students and alumni club for LGBT+ people and allies at the ESCP, which I referred to earlier. Founded in 1819, it is thought to be the oldest business school in the world and is owned by the Paris Chamber of Commerce.

The student-led one-day event LGBT Talents brings together students, professionals, and activists to discuss different facets of LGBT+ inclusion at work and in the world. In 2019, for the conference's third edition, consultancy BCG was the Platinum sponsor, with further sponsors such as Accenture, Bloomberg, ESCP, GE and IBM, plus the global law firms Eversheds Sutherland and Herbert Smith Freehills. (For more on the world's largest student-led LGBT+ conferences, ROMBA in the US and EurOUT in the UK, see Part IV, Chapter 9; for more on LGBT+@Work, another major conference in Spain, see Part III, Chapter 4.)

Thomas Cusson, a senior analyst in Accenture's consulting practice, who holds a master's degree in engineering from the prestigious *École Nationale Supérieure d'Arts et Métiers* in Paris – Arts et Métiers for short – is one of LGBT Talents' co-founders and main organizers. Beyond that, he has not only been an active supporter of the aforementioned Réseau des Réseaux, but is also frequently visible in the media.

In summer 2019, for example, he contributed to an article in the liberal daily *Les Echos*, a leading financial newspaper that belongs to the aforementioned LVMH Group. There, he pointed to the fact that in French engineering schools, "no action is taken in favor of the LGBT community."[58] Cusson, who graduated from Arts et Métiers only in 2016 and today is still in his 20s, stressed that the LGBT+ topic does not exist in his alma mater, even though it is the leading engineering school in terms of student numbers.

He tried to change this while he was a student but was unsuccessful because of self-censorship by other LGBT+ students anxious about becoming visible.[59] In other schools, there is also resistance from the management, Cusson reports. "When we talk to them about equality, engineering schools focus on gender mix and often neglect other forms of inequality," he explains, "And then, there is a strong culture of separation between professional and personal life, as can be found in large industrial companies. As a result, many consider the LGBT+ issue to be an intimate one."[60] In this, he highlights the same peculiarly French attitude as his Réseau des Réseaux colleague Jouhet.

Cusson's strong engagements very early in his career were recognized with a special award when the first French LGBT+ role model list was launched in 2019. This brings us back to the development and launch of the French rankings, following British-global, Australian, and German lists.

## French rankings – support, media, and the president

For its role model ranking premiere, L'Autre Cercle partnered with OUTstanding to learn from Suki Sandhu – who was also part of the jury – and his team. Not surprisingly, the criteria for acceptance as a candidate and for ranking on the lists were roughly similar to OUTstanding's. Cooperating partners were French banking giant BNP Paribas and the two global law firms, Herbert Smith Freehills and Eversheds Sutherland. The initiative also benefited from the patronage of French President Emmanuel Macron, a particular coup for the organizers.

Committed to a high level of transparency, L'Autre Cercle published a comprehensive and transparent 23-pages overview for the media of the whole list project, including some detailed figures and analysis.[61] In the end, 60 of the 115 accepted list candidates found their way onto three lists: 20 on the executive straight allies list, 20 on the LGBT+ executive list and 20 on the LGBT+ leaders list, covering the ranks below executive levels.[62]

In line with the way French companies and other workplaces are far behind the Western English-speaking world on LGBT+ inclusion and equality, the visibility of LGBT+ executives, other leaders, and straight allies remains comparatively low. The organizers therefore did not start with rankings showcasing 100 or even 50 role models. In fact, many French companies – and especially their LGBT+ executives – held back from seeking nomination, while Anglo-Saxon companies in France were more active. Almost 80% of candidates were either executive allies or LGBT+ leaders. And only about a fifth were candidates for the LGBT+ executive list, which is the most important for increasing visibility at the top.

Another critical factor in the French role model data was the strong bias toward only one of the country's 18 regions: the Île-de-France, which is basically the wealthy Paris region, making up about 30% of national GDP. Seventy-five percent of the accepted role model candidates came from there. Since France, in contrast, for example, to Germany, is a very centralized state, this is not surprising. But it is also a challenge for the future because LGBT+ inclusion and visibility has to focus on companies and other employers across the nation in order to set really effective examples.

Another challenge for future list editions – and for LGBT+ inclusion as a whole – is that about 75% of the candidates for the two LGBT+ lists (the exception being the allies list) were men.

However, the L'Autre Cercle team and its partners still had reason to celebrate. The project pushed awareness of LGBT+ inclusion and created visibility for role models in companies and other organizations in France substantially. Much increasing the impact on the public and the business community, L'Autre Cercle had cooperated with two premium media-partners: business and finance site *La Tribune* and public-service radio broadcaster *Radio France*, the country's leading radio group with seven national and forty-four local stations and over fifteen million daily listeners.[63] Both provided substantial coverage.

For the list's second edition, L'Autre Cercle used the role models from the first to campaign on social media. In October 2020, when France was hit particularly hard by another wave of the COVID-19 pandemic, L'Autre Cercle managed to organize a digital ceremony to honor 95 new role models. It took the form of a TV program recorded at the *Radio France* studios in the presence of Elisabeth Moreno, Minister Delegate to the French Prime Minister, in charge of equality between women and men, diversity and equal opportunities. Further partners were leading global players such as insurance giant Aviva, Atos, BNP Paribas, Orange, Renault, and Pfizer. *La Tribune* was once again the second media supporter.

This time, there was also a fourth list, *Jeunes Diplômé·e·s LGBT+*, ranking young LGBT+ role models already pushing for inclusion in their first jobs or as graduate students. Compared to the British and

German lists, this is a true innovation. There is a similarity with the OUTstanding LGBT+ Future Leaders ranking launched in 2015, but the new French list focuses on even younger LGBT+ activists, allowing it also to acknowledge LGBT+-related activities at university.

This seems smart because it takes into account the rapid societal values change driven by the young I talked about in the Barilla story. One day these young leaders may have risen to the top – or at least to the middle. Being acknowledged and honored for their engagements now, may help them achieve later positions of prominence and influence.

## 6. A middle manager and father coming out late and leading with trust

Although visibility at the top executive level is helpful if not vital in pushing for more LGBT+ D&I workplace inclusion, not everyone can or has to reach the top to be a role model. In daily working life, middle managers, including team and project leaders, are a lot more present, not just in meetings but also informal settings such as the water cooler or at lunch.

Holger Reuschling was just such a middle manager. His story shows how valuable a company's ERG can be in supporting an employee's coming out. "Even after my private coming out, I led a double life in my job for another ten years. Gay with my boyfriend in my circle of friends, straight in the bank," says Reuschling. "At some point, that didn't work anymore." About ten years after his private coming out, he decided to leave the closet at work too.

The large bank Reuschling worked for had been taken over in 2009 by Commerzbank, Germany's second largest private bank by total value of its balance sheet. At that time, it already had an LGBT+ employee network, but Reuschling did not know this and did not yet want to come out.

Reuschling came from "a conservative middle-class background" and grew up in a rural area. At 16 he had his first gay experience, a secret two-year love affair with a boy from his village, ending the relationship shortly before graduating high school. "I just didn't want to admit this to myself," he says. From that point on, he focused only on his job. He was ambitious and successful, quickly ascending to management and then a succession of further promotions.

## Private dramas

Privately, too, everything seemed to be going well. "I got married, our daughter was born – a gift," he says. "I thought a successful banker needed a family." But in 2004, aged 34 he fell in love with a man. Now he was honest with himself. It was a painful process full of self-doubt but, only a short time later, he privately took the consequences. "I owed this to my family," he says, "but also to me. The situation tore me apart." Talking to his wife was not easy. Both agreed not to inform their daughter, then five, for the time being. He left and moved in with his boyfriend.

A few years later, when he had a firm relationship with another man, whom he later married, Reuschling also told his daughter. There were tears, but the discussion was successful, and their relationship became more intimate. From then on, she came to visit frequently and soon had her own room. "It could have turned out differently, but I was lucky," says Reuschling. "I always wanted to be a good father. And the way it looks today, I have succeeded."

## A master of disguise and the costs of a double life

Nobody in the bank was yet aware of these private dramas. Reuschling was becoming, as he says, "a master of disguise." When colleagues in the city met him with his boyfriend the latter was passed off as "the best buddy." Even when talking about weekend experiences, this "best buddy" line was occasionally used. "A neighbor" was another option.

His divorce was no secret at the bank, so sometimes he invented a female partner when talking to colleagues and customers. At least he could continue to talk about his daughter at work. "I love her, but sometimes I wonder if I haven't used her as a distraction in conversations in the bank from time to time – unconsciously, of course." That didn't feel good in retrospect. At some point he also begun to wonder if his colleagues were talking about him behind his back.

In 2013, he decided to build a house with his partner – now his husband. At work he talked about the construction of the house but didn't mention who he was building it with. The couple wanted to finance the build together, but Reuschling went to an online provider instead of his own bank. "Less personal questions, more anonymity."

"Sure, I was afraid I'd give myself away," says Reuschling today. "I was also afraid that the half-truths I told would contain contradictions. For example, how I spent Christmas." Again, we see the stress and wasted energy: the cost of thinking twice. At first, Reuschling had felt these costs rather less because he was simply happy about his new life. But the longer the situation lasted, the more he suffered from this schism between the private and professional world. "But I also tried to repress this suffering." It was only in retrospect and after years that he realized how much it had affected him.

## The importance of trust

The "creative stories" are particularly critical for a manager, because they go to the essence of what makes for successful leadership: trust. "I was a sales executive, the face of the bank. So I had to communicate honestly – with team members, with colleagues, with customers. And that's what I wanted," summarizes Reuschling. "I myself am a trust guy. I prefer to trust, and I prefer that I can trust other people, though not naively."

A good ten years ago, German management philosopher Reinhard Sprenger put this in a nutshell with a bestseller in German-speaking countries, the title of which, translated, reads: *Trust Leads: What really matters in a company.* Sprenger's interest is the "instrumental value" of trust in a company, its creation and in its day-to-day effects. Economically and in simple terms, more trust between leaders and those being led means less costs in the interaction between them.

"Trust saves time and effort," says Reuschling. He has no doubt that "the teams that I led after my professional coming out were, in my perception, closer to me and ultimately more successful."

Strong trust is particularly valuable when the tasks are complex and urgent – as many are in the age of globalization and digitization, with their constantly growing competitive and innovative pressure.

In large restructurings, especially, which, because of today's fast-changing markets, have become routine in many companies, managers must motivate employees to follow new structures and processes. Trust here is of the essence.

So loss of trust is a key worry about coming out for someone in Reuschling's position. At worst, it could write off trust capital developed over many years. Breakdown of trust is a breakdown in leadership and, as such, threatens not just the manager's success but that of the company. Ultimately, if a manager is no longer a successful leader, the company will likely no longer require their services. The sense of risk may even be sharpened by the manager's other working relationships, with colleagues of equal and higher rank. Considered in this light, the fear Reuschling felt becomes all too painfully intelligible.

Furthermore, to talented, ambitious managers who spend a lot of time at work, professional success is crucial for self-image. Will an existential crisis, even a depression, follow? Reuschling confirms the difficulty: "Some of my colleagues on the same hierarchical level approached me after my professional coming out and asked why I had lied to them for so long. It took some very long discussions afterwards to find common ground again."

## Risks versus benefits

Given the risks, modern psychological research is very clear that everyone should decide for themselves when to come out professionally. In cases of doubt, it also recommends seeking external professional and, if necessary, psychological advice. In particular, if a working atmosphere is not experienced as sufficiently open, possibly even being potentially dangerous, the risks may have to be given greater weight than the hoped-for positive effects.

Also, older managers may be held back by past atmospheres of prejudice. Prior to 2007 when he was outed, ex-BP CEO John Browne's cost-benefit analysis on coming out had lacked the economic arguments he later himself put forward (and which have been further substantiated since). For much of his career, the situation in his country, and in all liberal Western countries and companies, were less open to LGBT+ people and issues than they are now. Born in 1948, Browne had seen criminalization, violence, and open hatred of gays and other, more subtle forms of stigmatization and exclusion. All had shaped him, as he himself says, to the point of self-hatred – condensed in the sentence previously quoted: "I thought being gay was basically wrong."

And there may simply be personal circumstances, a point Reuschling backs up: "Of course, my private situation – above all my concern for the good relationship with my daughter and her well-being – influenced my decisions not to come out of the closet professionally for so long."

## Inspiration from a professional soccer player

Such complex emotional challenges faced by some middle-aged or older experienced managers are almost certainly better tackled with support – something more and more companies are beginning to offer, whether for compassionate reasons or because they understand it is ultimately in their economic interests to do so. Such help is not always firmly institutionalized, for example, coordinated by the HR department, but "in my case, Arco, our LGBT+ employee network, played a decisive role," Reuschling reports.

The trigger, however, was something quite different: Thomas Hitzlsperger's coming out in German liberal-progressive quality weekly *Die Zeit*. Born in Bavaria in 1982, Hitzlsperger had an illustrious career in both English and German soccer, including being part of the German team that made Vice-European Champion in 2008. In early January 2014, some time after retiring, he came out, saying he had only realized he was gay a few years before. No male professional soccer player of equivalent standing had previously come out.

A brief note: previously, British forward Justin Fashanu had been the first professional player to come out – way back in 1990. His achievements were on a lower level but coming out then was also substantially more challenging and made harder by Fashanu being black and coming out during his career. Eight years later, he committed suicide because of false allegations against him. In 2020, Fashanu was inducted into the British National Football Museum Hall of Fame. His niece Amal Fashanu set up the Justin Fashanu Foundation "tackling discrimination out of football"[64] to honor him.

Hitzlsperger's revelation made major media waves for weeks (for more on Hitzlsperger and his career in sports business, see box).

## Thomas Hitzlsperger – a steep career rise in the business of sports after coming out

After some weeks, the media furor around Thomas Hitzlsperger's coming out in January 2014 eventually died out. But though Germany's culture is basically skeptical and slow to open up, something began to change. A taboo had fallen: being gay in the tough, male world of professional soccer – in a country where soccer has been the by far most important sport for decades.

In addition, and perhaps even more importantly, Hitzlsperger's career after his courageous coming out has sent a strong signal to the very competitive, sports-oriented global business world. Coming out did not hinder him in pursuing a career in media and sports business at the highest levels. At the 2014 World Cup in Brazil just a few months after his coming out, Hitzlsperger was already a TV sports commentator on Germany's most important TV morning show. During the following World Cup 2018 in Russia, he again filled the commentator role to high praise.

Meanwhile, in 2016, he had become part of the management of Stuttgart, though initially in a small, representative function. This was the club for which he had played when they became national champions ten years earlier – a success partly down to his spectacular goal in the last game of the season. Only a short time later, he was promoted to head of the club's youth center. In February 2019, he was then made sports director of the professional player department and only a few months later, he became a member of the board, in charge not only of sports issues but also strategy and communications. His (comparatively smaller) ambitions as a TV expert had to end with the club management appointment, due to possible conflicts of interest. Finally, in summer 2020, under Hitzlsperger's leadership, Stuttgart once again ascended to Germany's highest soccer league, the *Bundesliga*.

This was an extraordinarily rapid ascent in a business that has long been considered macho and conservative. There are probably very few, if any, similarly fast-paced career paths for an out former professional sportsman directly into top management.

It is all the more impressive given that Hitzlsperger is only in his late 30s – and not only quickly proved excellent in his new job, but also sought to make a difference beyond it. For a long time now, and unnoticed by many, he has been socially committed. For example, he is an ambassador for the Magnus Hirschfeld Foundation, founded by the German Federal State to counteract discrimination against LGBT+ people in Germany. It is named after the German medical doctor, international pioneer of sexual science/ sexology and co-founder of the first homosexual movement, Magnus Hirschfeld. Because he was gay, socialist, and Jewish, and because of the subject of his research, he had to flee the Nazis, only to die in Nice a few years later.

Hitzlsperger is also sponsor of Ubunta Africa, a project that supports HIV-positive children in South Africa. He has also supported campaigns by the initiative, *Gesicht zeigen. Für ein weltoffenes Deutschland* ("Show your face. For a Germany open to the world"), which fights against racism, xenophobia, right-wing extremist violence, and anti-Semitism. For some years already, he has also been an Ambassador for Diversity for DFB, the German soccer association which is the largest national sports association globally. In October 2020, for his engagements against homophobia, sexism and racism in stadiums, clubs and society, Hitzlsperger was awarded the "Federal Cross of Merit" *(Bundesverdienstkreuz)* by the German Federal President.

## Support from the company network

Hitzlsperger's coming out was the push Reuschling ultimately needed. As he puts it: "Finally, a visible role model." He registered at Arco's internal forum, knowing this was a safe space. With more than 400 members, Arco is one of the largest LGBT+ employee networks in Germany, very active both inside and outside Commerzbank. It is also open to straight allies.

Though this does not always allay the fears of long-term closeted employees like Reuschling, Commerzbank has been strongly committed to LGBT+ friendliness for some time and been honored for it with the prestigious German Max Spohr Prize. This is an award from Völklinger Kreis, the roughly 30-year-old German association for gay managers, entrepreneurs, and self-employed persons. Every two years, it honors one company and one public institution in Germany for exemplary D&I management, but especially for measures and programs to promote LGBT+ diversity and inclusion,[65] including supporting the activities and visibility of LGBT+ ERGs. The prize is named after German publisher Max Spohr, one of the first worldwide to publish books on homosexuality, starting in 1893. Until his early death in 1905, he lived with his wife and three children in the city of Leipzig in Eastern Germany, from where he ran the publishing house he founded and where a street was named after him in 2001. From what we know, he himself was not gay and he was therefore an early "straight ally."

When Commerzbank received the prize in 2010, Reuschling says he "didn't realize this, but today I suspect that I unconsciously kept it away from me." Though it was clearly perceptible internally and externally, for many years he also failed to perceive the visible support from various Commerzbank board members for LGBT+ diversity and inclusion or the Arco network's events, workshops, reports, and involvement in Pride. "I was kind of blind and resisting noticing all of this," says Reuschling.

But with Hitzlsperger's inspiration, he not only logged on to the Arco portal, he also wrote an article there. He began his post quoting an article in the leading German quality daily, liberal progressive *Süddeutsche Zeitung (SZ)*, in which a diversity researcher and business psychologist discussed the costs of a double life, and an openly gay entrepreneur told his own story, relating his struggles around late coming out with remarkable openness:

*... I am not a top manager, only a sales middle manager, but I can understand [the SZ article] in many ways.*

*I am (privately) openly gay, have a great partner with whom I have built a house and share my life. My daughter is part of our life and very often with us.*

*However, despite my private coming out, something has long prevented me from moving around the bank so openly ... Maybe it was the fear of being perceived and treated differently and losing face. I was always the ambitious, successful banker and showcase leader ...*

*Socially we are not yet at the point where it is 'normal,' and I can understand anyone who does not come out in a certain position for fear of loss of reputation, disadvantages, or attacks.*

*Even if I don't advertise the fact that I'm gay, I don't want to make a secret of it (in the bank) and so I now stand for a new normality in dealing with homosexuals and aim to be a role model.*

*That's why, by the way, I registered with you a few days ago, even though I noticed during my first search that the number of managers in your organization is actually very small ...*

Within a very short time, there were numerous reactions from colleagues and other managers:

*Hello Holger,*

*Thank you for your contribution. Great! I'm particularly attracted to this site because I have a manager here who still carries a lot of fears, but at least thanks to 'his own overzealous post of his own wedding on Facebook' has now been 'forced to be out by his own initiative' at least once in the branch. The response of his own employees: they were STINKING mad that he had excluded them from his personal special event and that they could neither join in the excitement nor vote on who was allowed to go to the registry office and who had to stay in the branch.*

*As for him marrying a man ... no problem.*

*That shows me we're definitely way back at the base. As it looks like on the upper floors ...*

"I was surprised by what happened. I hadn't expected that," says Reuschling, who also posted in the Arco forum himself repeatedly. Only four days after his first post, he wrote another, in which his doubts and fears became particularly clear:

*Oh man ... this week has shown me once again very clearly how difficult it is for me to move around the bank openly.*

*In April I will take a new job as a manager ... this week in the evening we were invited by our new boss in Frankfurt to the first meeting.*

*It felt like a rather conservative and elitist circle ... at least I couldn't bring myself to talk about my partner at the meeting.*

*Even when a colleague asked me whether I had a woman at my side again, I said yes and talked about 'her' the rest of the evening ...*

*Somehow it pisses me off and I'm angry at myself ... the chance would have been there.*

*I firmly intend to 'let my pants down' at our off-site in March ...
in the well-understood sense ... otherwise this hiding will start all
over again ... and I don't feel like it.*

*On the other hand, doubts are beginning to arise again,
about whether I shouldn't keep my gayness out of the bank more ...
What do you think?*

Colleagues reacted quickly. One exemplary response:
*Hi Holger,*

*Of course, only you can make this decision for yourself, but I
read in your lines that you don't want to hide, don't want to hide
again. I think at first there will be surprised faces, but ultimately
one of them will be yours. Because your expectations will be
completely overturned. You will certainly have colleagues who turn
away, but also those who are with you, who support you and take
you as you are.*

*I wish you courage, strength, and the maintenance of your pride
in your life, your daughter, and your partner. They are the most
important things, and those who turn away are unimportant.*

*Take a deep breath and just let go.*

## Letting go – in a management meeting

Over a period of several months, hundreds of supportive comments
appeared from colleagues, with frequent interjections from Reuschling himself. He also conversed directly with colleagues in the
LGBT+ employee network, especially Christian Weis, one of the
former Arco spokespersons. Weis had also been with the bank for
many years, but, in contrast, had come out very early, as a 17-year-
old trainee.

Weis, a good ten years younger than Reuschling, had had good
experiences with his out status in every respect, never experiencing
any career disadvantages. "But my personal experiences and those
of many Arco colleagues are one thing," says Weis, adding, "everyone lives their own lives. Just as a professional coming out is to be
respected, so is staying in the closet."

Discussions also took place with his partner, with whom Reuschling had moved into the new house in the meantime, and with
friends. In the end, Reuschling decided to come out at work as well.

He used a promotion to head of the business-customer service in the Frankfurt area to come out. This was a good eight months since Reuschling's first post in the Arco Forum. Now his new supervisor asked him and his five colleagues to introduce themselves in five-minute presentations, with reference to things they were particularly proud of.

Reuschling was the last to speak. He was well prepared, took his courage in his hands and, at the end of his presentation, said he had been living in a steady relationship with a man for ten years. He was especially proud of the fact that after his difficult coming out to his family, he still had a warm and intimate relationship with his daughter, now 14 years old. "Afterwards, there was a period of silence," Reuschling says.

Again, he used the Arco forum and posted about the experience. And once again, discussions took place there and he received encouragement. He also discussed his coming out at the off-site meeting with his new boss who was, says Reuschling, "relaxed and encouraged me to continue on my way. For me, it was a relief."

## A celebration – and then back to work

The relief translated into action immediately. A few weeks after coming out at work, Reuschling finally entered into a registered civil partnership with his partner, with "a celebration in a small, very dignified setting." (Same-sex marriage in Germany has only been possible since October 2017.)

A few days before this, his colleagues kidnapped him for a stag party, organized with help from some of his long-time executive peers. On the day of the ceremony, colleagues old and new stood in front of the registry office and toasted the couple. There were gifts, including one from his new management colleagues and new boss.

Soon everything went back to normal. Reuschling has since been repeatedly promoted. Later he became one of the spokespersons for the bank's LGBT+ ERG, setting up several initiatives, hosting the global LGBT+ leadership contest RAHM at the bank's site in Berlin (more on RAHM, see Part IV, Chapter 7) and other events.

In the fall of 2019, after almost 30 years, he decided to leave the bank in order to set up his own business as a consultant for the small- and medium-sized companies he knew well from his various functions in the bank. "Coming out at work was definitely one of the most difficult decisions of my life – and one of the best," says Reuschling. "It was an excellent one for the bank, too. Now, it is excellent for my consulting clients." Inspired by his story in the German edition of this book, some articles were published about him. Far from this having a negative impact on his business, he has been fully booked since, even in the challenging times of the COVID-19 pandemic. And recently, he was elected to the board of Völklinger Kreis, the aforementioned German gay managers association.

Also in the fall of 2019, around the time he set up his own business, he made Germany's Top 100 Out Executives ranking, honoring his LGBT+ activism at Commerzbank. He is still in close contact with his former colleagues and consults on the bank's LGBT+ activities.

# 7. Some days in Lisbon and a new global alliance

Consultancy is also McKinsey's field, though generally at a much higher level. In summer 2018, it took a significant step for the advancement of LGBT+ D&I. At considerable expense, it hosted a major Lisbon event called the Alliance, ambitiously claiming to be something like a "Davos for LGBT+ executives." Its website commits "to advancing LGBTQ+ equality and achieving greater acceptance in the workplace and in society."[66]

## A long history – and a new openness

For many, McKinsey has long been known for its great reluctance to share information, its elite image, and alleged preference for tough cost-cutting programs, ignoring a firm's responsibility beyond a narrow business focus. There are also rumored secret networks of former McKinsey consultants in top corporate positions. True or not, in matters LGBT+, the consultancy has recently become significantly more willing to share information and innovate visibly.

This may be due to the younger generations' changed values, reflected upon already in this book (see Part 1). McKinsey too is struggling to get as many high-quality candidates as possible in their recruitment and talent pipeline. In the age of increased desire for authenticity, openness, and being one's true self, too much secrecy may no longer be a good strategy – especially with respect to LGBT+ issues.

As well as the Alliance website, McKinsey now has another summarizing its LGBT+ activities, with more detailed information than many companies share. The site not only informs users that GLAM, the company's global LGBT+ network, is celebrating its 25th anniversary in 2020, a video also tells the story of its foundation. It features Brian Rolfes, today a partner in charge of global recruitment and part of the GLAM leadership.

I spoke with the Canadian in summer 2018, just before the Alliance premiere and a few weeks before he made the OUTstanding LGBT+ executive role model list top 20. Talking about GLAM's start, he related how, in 1995, 14 colleagues, including himself, met in a McKinsey partner's Washington, DC apartment aiming to push the company to the LGBT+ forefront. Rolfes is in the video, which shows the "historic" email sent by the partner inviting the others to his home. He had joined McKinsey the same year – and suddenly found himself becoming a GLAM co-founder.[67]

The video shows further McKinsey LGBT+ milestones: 1997's inaugural GLAM conference in New York, the first global virtual GLAM conference in 2001, the first straight ally groups in Dubai and Washington, DC in 2011, the 2017 signing of the UN LGBTI Standards of Conduct for Business, the Alliance launch, regular achievement since 2006 of the HRC top score on their CEI, and more.[68]

Today GLAM boasts almost 1,000 members worldwide, plus about 5,000 heterosexual allies, not in GLAM, but Friends of GLAM. 6,000 of the approximately 30,000 McKinsey people means nearly a quarter of partners and employees are narrowly or broadly LGBT+ involved.[69]

## The Alliance's start

About two years before the Alliance premiere in Lisbon, McKinsey had started to run executive master classes, helping freshly hired or promoted LGBT+ (senior) executives thrive in their new roles.

Part of these classes' work was – and is – doing pro bono work for the LGBT+ community.

It was some alumni from these classes who thought of coming together on a broader scale.[70] Their idea was taken up spectacularly. For the Alliance premiere, over 100 LGBT+ leaders from 19 countries flocked to the Portuguese capital for a Wednesday evening and a full Thursday. They came mainly from the private sector but some were from public and social bodies.

The event's theme was clear: LGBT+ D&I on a personal, organizational, and societal level[71] – including the business case for it. To ensure participants were well prepared, McKinsey even sent out a reading list of eight books. There were classic works such as *Blindspot: Hidden biases of good people* by Mahzarin R. Banaji and bestsellers like *Shackleton's Way: Leadership lessons from the great antarctic explorer* by Margaret Merrell and Stephanie Capparell.

With more direct relevance, there was also Kirk Snyder's *The G Quotient: Why gay executives are excelling as leaders ... and what every manager needs to know*, first published in 2006. That year, *Harvard Business Review* put it on its recommended business books list. From his extensive surveys and research with 1,000 employees from four different US industries, Snyder revealed surprising results: a strong correlation between leadership by gay managers and the job satisfaction, commitment, and workplace morale of their primarily heterosexual employees. For gay leaders, these three categories' values were significantly, even extremely, higher than for heterosexual ones. Snyder derived seven tenets of successful "Q-Quotient Leadership" from this. He called them principles, but they are better understood as skills or capabilities: inclusion, creativity, connectivity, adaptability, intuition, communication, and collaboration.

Thus, about 15 years ago, there were already empirical and theoretically sound studies that – albeit differently from more recent research on LGBT+ diversity – focused on inclusion's benefits. The focus solely on homosexuality looks insufficiently diverse now, and the findings might be read today as stereotyping, albeit very positive stereotyping. Nevertheless, unlike old, negative LGBT+ caricatures, they are based on rigorous empirical data. And, as the subtitle says, they contain potential lessons for all managers.

## Premium networking and business

Among the top executives on stage in Lisbon, sharing personal coming-out stories, talking about LGBT+ challenges in their companies and developing visions, were representatives of Pepsi, Red Bull, IBM, and Sodexo.

Katrin Suder put in an appearance to share her experience as an openly lesbian mother of three, as a high-ranking McKinsey alumnus, and as a former State Secretary in the German Federal Ministry of Defense. During her time in this last job, diversity became a strategic leadership task in the German military. In 2018, Suder, a physics PhD, was ranked top on Germany's first Out Executive role model list. Today, she heads the German Federal Government's Digital Council, which includes several digital experts and cabinet ministers, plus Chancellor Angela Merkel.

The Alliance holds another influential German LGBT+ ace: Ralph Breuer, a partner in McKinsey's Cologne office. A customer experience and loyalty expert, in his day job he implements marketing and sales practice in Europe. He also manages GLAM in Europe, and has built up the Friends of GLAM. In the fall of 2020, he ranked third on Germany's second role model edition.

Freshly appointed global McKinsey boss Kevin Sneader was in Lisbon to give the closing remarks, sending a strong symbolic signal. A Canadian-born Scot who lives with his wife and family in Hong Kong and is McKinsey's first Jewish leader, he knew just how important the group was.

Almost all the event guests were current or potential consulting clients. If they weren't in diversity, they were in even more lucrative fields such as strategy, digitization, or major corporate transformation. The Alliance was thus a fitting name. Although the event was LGBT+-focused, it also facilitated networking, deepening relationships and personal ties, and building alliances – thus strengthening future business.

## Stability and engagement: Lawrence Spicer from the Royal Bank of Canada

Lawrence Spicer, Royal Bank of Canada (RBC) Vice President, who explained the program and reading list to me in detail, was enthusiastic in retrospect: "Very interesting people, very interesting subjects, excellent networking opportunities."

Spicer, in his mid-50s, has been with his husband for decades, but professionally came out late, after 18 years at the bank. He was the first visibly gay executive there and is the Executive Chair of RBC's Pride Canada employee resource group, fostering annual growth of 10% for the last five years. He also helped launch a bank mentoring program, connecting LGBT+ employees with LGBT+ executives and allies. This led to an enterprise-wide LGBT+ event in 2017, hosted by RBC's CEO and senior executives.

Spicer also procured bank funds for Start Proud/*Fier Départ* (formerly "Out On Bay Street"), a Canadian young professionals' leadership organization that facilitates professional development of LGBT+ students moving from school to career, in order to build a national LGBT+ network. Further sponsors include Canadian companies and global brands such as HSBC, Unilever, IBM, Accenture, BCG, Deloitte, EY, PwC, and McKinsey.[72]

As his long-term commitments, both private and within the bank, suggest, Spicer likes stability, and he radiates this in public. I met him in London in summer 2018 at RAHM, the aforementioned LGBT+ leadership contest (for more, see also Part IV, Chapter 7). A member of the RAHM jury, he liked it so much that he went all out to get his employer, the RBC, to host the first RAHM in North American the following year in Toronto. There were also plans for a 2020 event in Vancouver, postponed due to COVID-19.

In London, in conversation and in his jury work, I experienced Spicer as an open, creative, level-headed and forward-looking leader. At RAHM he benefitted from having participated in the world's first LGBTQ Executive Leadership Program at the renowned Stanford Graduate School, in 2017 (see Part II, Chapter 4). He was one of the program's spokespeople and gave interviews about it, for example to the *Financial Times*.[73] Today, he is still an active alumnus.

The program's cost is currently $13,000, plus travel and accommodation. "A large investment of my bank," says Spicer, "and a rich source of knowledge for me as a manager, and for self-reflection as a gay manager." Especially after participating in the Stanford program, one thing was clear to him: "I want to be a visible role model for other managers and for young LGBT+ people, as do many of the people I met in Lisbon at the Alliance event." Recently, he adds, he has been asked by a few senior executives from Canadian companies in different sectors to be an "'external coach' on D&I specifically focused on LGBTQ issues and leadership challenges."

In the OUTstanding LGBT+ executive role model list, with its criteria and competition getting tougher every year, his achievements have been recognized by inclusion in the top 100 four years in a row.

## Figures and numerical deficits

Let's get back to the Alliance. Diana Ellsworth, previously a teacher at a public middle school, now a McKinsey partner in their Atlanta office,[74] was part of the 20-strong team behind the Alliance. She developed and hosted the inaugural event in Portugal and co-leads GLAM. "We all know that individuals from the LGBTQ community can face barriers – sometimes visible, sometimes invisible – in life and in work,"[75] she says in a McKinsey article. "But it is surprising how many people, still today, are 'out' in their personal lives but not at work."[76] LGBT+ visibility was a key issue for the Alliance. Of the estimated 455 million LGBT+ people worldwide, McKinsey reported in Lisbon that only about 27% were out,[77] meaning around 332 million were not. (For another global study focused on coming outs of the young, see Part IV, Chapter 1.)

Discrimination's consequences are not just borne by individuals but by the economy and thus whole societies. In 2014, US economist M.V. Lee Badgett conclusively demonstrated this for the first time. In a highly acclaimed World Bank case study, she showed the costs of stigmatization and discrimination against LGBT+ people in India, including health disparities and workplace discrimination. Her findings suggest, for instance, that LGBT+ people stigmatized and discriminated against at work are much more prone to depression, suicide, and HIV than the rest of the population. Badgett showed that these factors alone could create up to a 1.4% GDP loss.[78]

## Next steps

In September 2019, McKinsey held another Alliance event, this time in Florida,[79] again hosted by Diana Ellsworth. "We want to see how LGBTQ+ leaders' sense of strength and experience are similar and how they're different from their non-LGBTQ+ peers,"[80] she said, echoing Kirk Snyder's *The G Quotient*, "This will help illuminate for organizations how they can foster LGBTQ+ employees into leaders and avoid unintended roadblocks."[81]

The Alliance is not then primarily a glamorous event for executives. Rather, as the report on the second event suggests, it highlights work to be done, e.g. data needed to inform the LGBT+ D&I business case. This became even more evident on the its new website, promoting, for example, data collection on LGBT+ youth to support them in education, at work, and in their private lives. Starting as an event, the Alliance has thus become a community with a stream of communication and project work between annual events.

The 2020 gathering was to take place in Tokyo during the Paralympics but had to be cancelled due to COVID-19. The Alliance – as McKinsey says on its website – now offers regular virtual gatherings, including smaller working groups to address crucial impact areas.[82] And there is mutual support across the group, with a view, among other things, to driving progress on issues facing the broader LGBT+ community.[83]

McKinsey publicly stresses that it targets LGBT+ senior leaders from prominent public, private, and social institutions to join the Alliance. They become members not as organizations' representatives but individuals working "through their respective networks and platforms."[84] However, McKinsey also states that the Alliance currently (as of July 2020) counts "140 companies and other organizations" as members, as well as about 200 members representing over 20 different countries.[85]

Of course, McKinsey, as a profit-driven company, has interests beyond good works and social progress. It also has a legitimate interest in doing good business with companies, state agencies and other institutions. The Alliance may not directly aim at that but will certainly contribute to it in the long run. In that sense it is a strategic initiative that bridges business goals and work for social good.

# 8. Growing support from the UN and a long-prepared partnership at the World Economic Forum

Improving the world is the primary mission of the UN and, though in a very different way, also of the WEF. The UN, as we saw in Part I, has, since the 2008 financial crisis, become significantly more active in marrying human rights with companies' interests and social responsibilities. The basis of this is the Universal Declaration of Human Rights with its 30 articles affirming equal rights for every human being. Signed in 1948 in Paris, the Universal Declaration of Human Rights, though not legally binding, has influenced international treaties, national constitutions, and more.

## Navi Pillay, the UN Free & Equal campaign, and an outspoken archbishop

With respect to LGBT+ equality, the UN started late, but then accelerated fast. A lot happened especially during 2008 to 2014 – Navi Pillay's term as UN High Commissioner for Human Rights – laying the groundwork for more in the years to come. We previously met Pillay giving the keynote address for the landmark 2014 Davos breakfast.

In her LGBT+ activism at the UN, Pillay partnered with then UN Secretary-General Ban Ki-moon, to whom she formally reported and who came to understand too that LGBT+ rights were human rights. After some preparatory work, during which resistance had to be overcome at the UN, Pillay, in her function as High Commissioner, published a 60-page brochure in 2012. Its title was vague – *Born Free and Equal* – but its subtitle was clearer: *Sexual orientation and gender identity in international human rights law*.[86] It described legal obligations to protect LGBT+ human rights and was designed as a tool to help states better understand those obligations and how to fulfill them. It was also aimed at civil society activists and others who want to hold governments accountable for human rights violations.[87]

In parallel, Pillay and her team prepared a worldwide awareness and education campaign unique in its form. In doing so, she was taking up one of the recommendations of her own UN study.

143

The name of the campaign, echoing that of the brochure, was Free & Equal.

The goals were clear: to work against homophobia, biphobia, and transphobia; to create more awareness and respect worldwide for LGBT+ equality; and to initiate legal reforms in line with the recommendations in the UN study. In 2013, a few days before May 17, the International Day Against Homophobia, Biphobia, and Transphobia (IDAHOBIT), the UN uploaded its first Free & Equal campaign video on YouTube: *The Riddle: new anti-homophobia message from UN human rights office.*[88]

As part of IDAHOBIT, Pillay spoke in The Hague, the city where she had been a judge at the International Criminal Court a few years earlier. She referred to the upcoming campaign and showed the video.[89] Both she and UN Secretary-General Ban had already talked about the need for more public education to combat homophobia at its roots, she said. This was primarily the responsibility of governments and was best addressed with the active participation of civil society, "But I believe that the United Nations can and should do more to promote this process."[90]

The Free & Equal campaign was launched in Cape Town in July 2013. Pillay's fellow countryman, the retired Anglican Archbishop, anti-Apartheid fighter, human rights activist, and Nobel Peace Prize winner Desmond Tutu addressed a press event for it. Known for his bold statements, Tutu didn't disappoint: "I would refuse to go to a homophobic heaven. No, I would say sorry, I mean I would much rather go to the other place ... I would not worship a God who is homophobic, and that is how deeply I feel about this." He added that to him this campaign was similar to the campaign against racism in South Africa. "I am as passionate about this campaign as I ever was about Apartheid. For me, it is at the same level."[91] Tutu has continued to actively support the campaign over the years.

Other well-known personalities have supported Free & Equal since: tennis legend Martina Navratilova, out for decades; Bollywood actress Celina Jaitly; and Puerto Rican pop star Ricky Martin, also openly gay for many years. There is also ex-basketball professional Jason Collins, who, in 2013, was the first active player in the NBA to come out and has stated that his jersey number, 98, worn for years, commemorated the brutal 1998 homophobic murder of college student Matthew Shepard in Wyoming.[92]

Despite being received with great reluctance, even rejection, in countries where LGBT+ people are persecuted, criminalized, or even killed, the campaign took off quickly (see box).

## The UN Free & Equal campaign and its impact

Since Free & Equal's 2013 inception, the UN has launched national campaigns in over 30 countries in every global region. In 2018, for example, it was the turn of Albania, Brazil, Cape Verde, Cambodia, Dominican Republic, Guatemala, Macedonia, Mongolia, Peru, Serbia, Timor Leste, and Ukraine.[93]

Every spring, the UN campaign team presents new facts and figures for the previous 12 months.[94] Its analysis shows the campaign increasing its impact year on year. In 2017, it reached over 2.4 billion social media feeds worldwide with videos, graphics, and fact sheets – parts, as always, of global mini and nationally adapted campaigns. In 2018, the total social media feeds reached increased again. Some Free & Equal videos are among the UN's most viewed ever.[95]

There have been global mini-campaigns on transsexual youth, on myths surrounding bisexuals, and on the 70th anniversary of the Universal Declaration of Human Rights. On May 17, 2018, the IDAHOBIT, the campaign also raised awareness of LGBTI allies. A campaign video went viral on the Chinese social media platform Weibo, being seen by over 21 million people in the week of its launch.[96]

Since its inception, the campaign has produced a series of constantly updated compact digital fact sheets on LGBTI people's situations. They are available in Arabic, Chinese, English, French, Portuguese, Russian, and Spanish. Topics include violence, criminalization, discrimination, and bullying of LGBTI people, and frequently asked questions on sexual orientation and gender identity, and on transgender, intersex, and bisexual identities.

## The UN LGBTI Standards of Conduct for Business

The Free & Equal campaign is designed for the long term. It was continued by Pillay's successor Zeid Ra'ad Al Hussein and, beyond his term of office, at the time of this writing, is still going.

Zeid, a prince of the Jordanian royal family, was also in office at the time of another UN LGBT+ milestone: the launch of the aforementioned "Standards of Conduct for Business. Tackling Discrimination against Lesbian, Gay, Bi, Trans, and Intersex People," or UN LGBTI Standards of Conduct for Business[97] or Standards for short. In fact, it was Zeid's idea to formulate them. In his letter introducing the Standards, he stressed that the original idea for developing them came from a panel discussion he was involved in at the WEF's annual meeting in Davos in 2016.

The Standards aim to bridge the gap between LGBT+ rights as human rights and the business world, and further boosted the accelerating pace of LGBT+ inclusion in business globally. Based on input from hundreds of companies in a wide range of industries and other stakeholders, they were developed over several months, coming into force in September 2017.

The Standards' starting point was the conviction that violence and discrimination against LGBTI people could not be overcome by governments (and the UN) alone and that companies should and could play a role globally. The aim is to support companies in promoting diversity, respect, and equality internally and externally – which will also be to their own economic benefit – by providing an initial orientation for achieving this goal.

"The decisions that companies make – on personnel, resources, investments, supply chains, or even marketing themselves – have a real and strong impact on human rights,"[98] Prince Zeid said, publicly launching the Standards at Microsoft's New York headquarters. To raise awareness globally, similar launches, with lots of social media attention, took place in Mumbai, London, Hong Kong, Geneva, and Melbourne.[99]

## The United Nations LGBTI Standards of Conduct for Business

The Standards, launched in 2017, require that companies:

Always:

1. **Respect human rights.** More specifically, this means that companies "should develop policies, exercise due diligence, and remediate adverse impacts to ensure they respect human rights of LGBTI people." They "should also establish mechanisms to monitor and communicate about their compliance with human rights standards."[100]

In the company/at the workplace:

2. **Eliminate discrimination.** More specifically this means that companies "should ensure that there is no discrimination in their recruitment, employment, working conditions, benefits, respect for privacy, or treatment of harassment."[101]

3. **Provide support.** More specifically, this means that companies "should provide a positive, affirmative environment so that LGBTI employees can work with dignity and without stigma."[102]

In the marketplace:

4. **Prevent other human rights violations.** More specifically, this means that companies "should not discriminate against LGBTI suppliers, distributors, or customers, and should use their leverage to prevent discrimination and related abuses by their business partners."[103]

In society/in the communities:

5. **Act in the public sphere.** More specifically, this means that companies "are encouraged to contribute to stopping human rights abuses in the countries in which they operate. In doing so, they should consult with local communities to identify steps they might take – including public advocacy, collective action, social dialogue, support for LGBTI organizations, and challenging abusive government actions."[104]

## Only a general commitment – but a major milestone

The Standards can be regarded as a quantum leap in interaction between the world community and the global business sphere. Currently more than 300 companies have signed up (as of December 2020), representing the world's largest CSR initiative on LGBT+ issues.

The Standards are unmistakably formulated in such general terms that they can theoretically be signed by all companies, whether large or small, global or local. The only decisive thing is that, by signing, a company makes visible externally and internally a voluntary commitment to LGBT+ equality, nondiscrimination, and human rights.

This is exactly what the Standards are sometimes criticized for: their wording's generality makes it difficult to check the voluntary commitment is being observed. A 52-page UN brochure lays out background, objective, and some explanations, but this does not go very deep.[105]

However, there were ways to ensure greater commitment. Stonewall, the UK-based LGBT+ equality charity, already had an established program for companies, helping businesses transform operations to improve LGBT+ lives, both in the UK and throughout companies' global footprint, including supply chains etc. Stonewall had also helped develop the Standards. With their launch, it produced a compact toolkit to support companies implementing them, e.g. in aligning companies' existing LGBT+ policies with the Standards. The German Prout at Work Foundation also launched a detailed pragmatic guide to how companies could be fully compliant with the Standards. The Dutch nonprofit Workplace Pride did the same and broadcast a webinar about it. Other organizations working for LGBT+ equality at work released similar guides.

## 2016 – stunning dynamics in Davos and Joe Biden pushing top business leaders

The Standards were also made part of a new WEF project. Who would have thought it, after the Forum's long years of near total resistance to LGBT+ issues? But, as if a leash had been cut, from 2014, the pace of change had suddenly accelerated.

To recap: in 2014 there was the "unofficial" Microsoft breakfast. Then, in 2015 for the first time, the issue crept, as a subcategory, onto the official program. The same year, in an unofficial side-event, LGBT+ workplace inclusion was, for the first time, discussed publicly at the Forum, and by three top out global business leaders.

Then things accelerated fast. In 2016, there were not one but two events on the official program. One was asking, "How can companies support the LGBT agenda in order to promote a more diverse workforce and a more inclusive corporate culture?" [106] It was the first official World Economic Forum diversity discussion purely focused on LGBT+ issues and was moderated by *Thomson Reuters*' journalist Carmel Crimmins. Panelists included again EY's Beth Brooke and HSBC's António Simões, both of whom we have met in this book, plus Luxembourg's Prime Minister Xavier Bettel (still in office today) and Canada's Scott Brison, then President of the Treasury Committee. With both on stage, the event was also the first where openly gay politicians discussed the topic at Davos.

The second official event that year took place in the Media Village: the first-ever Davos media briefing on LGBT+ issues. Moreover, it was moderated by the forum's Head of Media Content, constituting another first: a WEF representative appearing in an official capacity to talk about LGBT+ issues.

There were also further unofficial events in 2016. The most important, again hosted by Microsoft and organized by the HRC, was with then US Vice President Joe Biden, who had been vocally committed to same-sex marriage and LGBT+ rights for years. Never before had a high-ranking politician been so explicit and detailed on LGBT+ issues at Davos as this. And never before had such a large number of top decision-makers gathered to listen. These included board members, founders, and other executives from global business heavyweights, e.g. Accenture, Airbnb, Alcoa, Coca-Cola, Deloitte, Dow, EY, Mastercard, Microsoft, and UPS.

This was just prior to Donald Trump's election as US President and was part of Biden's last vice presidential appearance at Davos. With great passion, which can still be experienced on the net,[107] he stressed that regarding LGBT+ rights, the world looks to top business leaders. "You have more impact in the world than the US government, the Supreme Court, or the White House," he said, calling on his listeners to work massively for change. Countries where LGBT+ rights were lacking should not be written off with cultural justifications, he said. Such justifications do not exist.

If top business leaders spoke up for LGBT+ rights directly, it would happen: "You can change the terms of debate," he said, "You actually put governments on notice."[108]

International coverage of Biden's appearance was widespread, especially in the Anglo-Saxon world,[109] but he also left a strong impression elsewhere. Today his comments are considered an outstanding milestone impacting world business leaders.

## Three models for LGBT+ inclusion in a globalized world

Another 2016 Davos premiere was Zanny Minton Beddoes, also speaking on LGBT+ business issues. The mother of four had then for just a few months been editor-in-chief of the *Economist*, a position she still holds at time of this writing. A couple months after its appearance at the WEF, the *Economist* would start a new conference format, "Pride and Prejudice," addressing LGBT+ D&I in businesses. Conferences have taken place since in locations such as London, New York, and Hong Kong.

In Davos, Beddoes moderated a discussion launching a report by Sylvia Ann Hewlett and Kenji Yoshino, *Out in the World: Securing LGBT rights in the global marketplace*,[110] published by the Center for Talent Innovation (CTI). Both Hewlett and Yoshino spoke. Hewlett is an economist, CTI founder, and talent management expert, and author of award-winning books. Yoshino, a professor of constitutional law at New York University (NYU), has also authored several bestsellers. Among these is *Covering: The hidden assault on our civil rights*, a highly praised memoir, published in 2007, in which – drawing on his life as a gay Asian-American man and his career as a legal scholar – he argues that the pressure to conform poses a threat to civil rights.

The key question posed and answered by Hewlett and Yoshino was what companies supporting LGBT+ rights should do in territories that reject those rights. Their report, among other things, introduced three possible models for companies operating in LGBT+-unfriendly territories. (see box). Only a few days after the end of the Forum, Hewlett and Yoshino reinforced the favorable response to their appearance with an article in the *Harvard Business Review* on the event and the results of their study: *LGBT-inclusive companies are better at 3 big things*.[111]

This was not the only impact of this session in Davos. It was also here that then-UN High Commissioner of Human Rights Prince Zeid got the idea of developing the global LGBTI Standards of Conduct for Business.

## How global companies can become more LGBT+-inclusive everywhere: three models of engagement

In their report, *Out in the World: Securing LGBT Rights in the Global Marketplace*,[112] Sylvia Ann Hewlett and Kenji Yoshino describe three models of corporate LGBT+ engagement tailored to different local legal and cultural environments. They also show that in anti-LGBT+ countries, corporates tend to choose from and move between these models.[113]

In the "When in Rome" model, companies are, as I classify them, "local rule followers." They adhere to local legal norms and create exceptions to their otherwise pro-LGBT+ policies. For example, though they have D&I programs, they do not include LGBT+ issues. That includes disallowing the establishment of local LGBT+ ERG chapters. The model lets companies avoid potential backlashes from local governments and other institutions. It is often used where LGBT+ people face significant legal or safety risks – but has the disadvantage that it neglects inclusion of local LGBT+ employees.[114]

In the second model, the "Embassy" approach, global companies focus on creating an inclusive workplace internally for their LGBT+ employees. For example, they adopt a nondiscrimination policy, offer equal benefits for same-sex partners, provide training on LGBT+ topics, establish a local LGBT+ ERG chapter, promote mentoring, and sponsor social activities for LGBT+ employees (and their allies). Companies often use this approach in locations where the cultural and legal climate is unwelcoming to LGBT+ people in principle but does not pose severe legal or safety risks. It enables global companies to support LGBT+ employees, but when those employees leave the safe haven of the embassy, they continue to face discrimination. The company does not seek to change local laws or attitudes.

In the third model, the "Advocate", businesses aim to influence the local climate or culture, even the laws. In strong contrast to the "When in Rome" rule-follower model, this approach means companies aiming to contribute to changing external rules. For example, they can lobby local business bodies and governments, support local LGBT+ nonprofits and activists, participate in local Pride events, and more. One concrete example is the lobbying conducted by businesses for marriage equality in Australia, Ireland, Taiwan, Japan, and the Czech Republic, based on economic arguments.

## A blog explosion on the WEF's website

Something else was changing at the WEF: a series of blogs on the Forum's website on LGBT+ issues began shortly before the 2016 meeting. There had been articles on this topic before, but very few. By comparison, the range of authors, subjects, and regions that appeared in just a few months around the 2016 Forum represented an explosion. The momentum has not, at the time of this writing, abated. The blogs often covered regions that were anything but LGBT+-friendly.

Here is just a small selection of subjects for the period: an overview of the status of LGBT+ rights globally,[115] the "real cost of LGBT discrimination,"[116] "the real story" of the LGBT+ community in the Middle East.[117] Titles included, *The fight for LGBT rights has just begun,*[118] *What role should business play in promoting LGBT rights in Africa?,*[119] and *Why Commonwealth countries need to wake up to LGBT rights.*[120] The countries referred to include many from Africa, the Arab world, and Asia, where LGBT+ people are socially stigmatized and/or legally criminalized.

One of the earliest Davos blogs in this vein was by then Microsoft Senior Director Dan Bross. We have met him before, as a facilitator of the first Davos breakfast. Bross's post, *My 30 years of being out and proud in leadership,*[121] told of his personal journey as a gay businessman – beginning with dark valleys in the 1980s as a manager with an oil and gas company in Houston, Texas. He wrote of that time, "I was gay by night and straight by day" – just like ex-BP CEO

Lord Browne, whose double life was to be so stunningly exposed some 20 years later. In contrast to Browne, however, Bross decided to leave his homophobic professional environment – which he had gotten to know as such – in the 1980s. In the following ten years, he devoted himself instead to work in the LGBT+ and HIV/AIDS communities in California, Washington, DC, and New York City. And then he found his way to Microsoft, where he was, for almost two decades, a successful out executive, one with direct influence on his company's human rights and LGBT+ activities and also serving as co-executive sponsor of the firm's LGBT+ ERG GLEAM (Gay and Lesbian Employees At Microsoft). There would be more to come for Bross, as I will relate in a moment.

Today the blog series has run to countless new contributions. As the WEF has developed into a powerful communication and social media machine in recent years, the power of these blogs can hardly be underestimated, even far beyond Davos.

## The Partnership for Global LGBTI Equality

Davos 2016's momentum continued the following year, officially and on the side. Again in contrast to the earlier restraint, there were now suddenly debates on support for transgender people in business and society, intersex children, and nonbinary young people. (For more on the younger generations' gender revolution, see Part IV, Chapters 2–6.)

In fall 2017, top managers from seven major global companies sent a letter to WEF founder Klaus Schwab, wanting to fully and permanently integrate LGBT+ inclusion into the WEF system. The time was right. Only shortly before, the UN had launched its LGBTI Standards of Conduct for Business.

Schwab quickly agreed. And in January 2019, a formal WEF press release announced the launch of the Partnership for Global LGBTI Equality (PGLE) as a new formal project within the WEF – a spectacular change in just five years since the rebellious off-site breakfast initiated by two US billionaires.

The Partnership's 16 founding member companies are: Accenture (see box on next page), BCG, Cisco, Coca-Cola, Deloitte, Deutsche Bank, EY, Edelman, Johnson & Johnson, Mastercard, Microsoft, P&G, PepsiCo, PwC, Salesforce, and Scotiabank.

## Accenture's white-collar activism in Davos and beyond

For many years, consultancy giant Accenture has been very visibly pushing for LGBT+ inclusion, and has received several awards for its endeavors. One of the drivers of this development was Sander van 't Noordende, whom we have briefly met before. Until recently and for a long time, he was not only a Group CEO at Accenture but also the main sponsor of the company's global Pride network.

As such, he pushed for strategically structured LGBT+ D&I internally and externally, stimulating and supporting a variety of global and local initiatives, programs and studies. Since 2015, Accenture has hosted its own LGBT+ Davos events, with panel discussions, presenting research and more, mostly with van 't Noordende on stage. He has also regularly written blogs on the WEF's website and, on behalf of his company, he was one of the signatories of the letter to WEF Executive Chairman Klaus Schwab that sparked the Partnership for Global LGBTI Equality (PGLE).

Van 't Noordende's contributions while at Accenture were recognized by inclusion in the OUTstanding LGBT+ Out Executive ranking several times. After over three decades, he left the company at end of 2019. His involvements remain numerous, however. Among other things, he is an investor and holds several board positions, including one at LGBT+ nonprofit Out & Equal. (For more on Out & Equal, see Part IV, Chapter 5.)

His departure meant a new start for Accenture's executive visibility with regard to global LGBT+ equality. Now there are new lynchpins. One is Marco Ziegler, a native German who has been with Accenture as a consultant for over 20 years and is a senior managing director focused on key relationships with Fortune 100 companies across several industries. Alongside his core job, Ziegler is now Accenture's global Pride employee network co-sponsor and also the firm's representative on the PGLE Steering Committee.

He seems well prepared for the role. For many years, he has been one of the main drivers of Accenture' Pride network in North America and still serves as its executive sponsor. He has also led and participated as a faculty member in Accenture's

North American "LGBT+ Leaders Learning," a leadership training program with which he is still engaged. Ziegler has also worked with the HRC, has spoken at client events on his firm's approach to LGBT+ inclusion and has, among other things, supported the development of client LGBT+ ally programs. In 2020, already in this new role as global co-sponsor of his firm's Pride network, and amid the COVID-19 pandemic, Ziegler arranged a cooperation with GLAAD to take their annual awards ceremony digital and help them reach a larger audience (for more on GLAAD, see Part I, Chapter 3). In his private life, Ziegler is a visible activist, too: He is married, lives with his husband and their two children in the Greater New York area, and serves on the Diversity Board of his children's school, representing the LGBT+ community.

Accenture's second new high-end LGBT+ front person is Christine Rauh, who has been with her employer for more than 14 years. In her day-to-day job, she is a managing director and consultant working on cloud-based solutions for clients in a variety of industries. Alongside this core position, Rauh, who lives in Zurich, Switzerland with her wife, now serves as the firm's global Pride network's co-sponsor too. Recently she, together with Ziegler, co-authored the report *Visible Growth; Invisible Fears: Getting to Equal, 2020: Pride* about challenges to overcome in making workplaces more LGBT+-inclusive.[122]

Prior to her new role, Rauh led Accenture's Swiss Pride network chapter, growing it from just two members to over 250, including many straight allies, within three years. On behalf of her firm, she received the Swiss LGBTI Label award (for more on this see Part II, Chapter 3). Like Ziegler, she has been engaged for many years in the company's global LGBT+ Leaders Learning sessions. Rauh, a native German, is also her firm's representative on the board of German Prout at work Foundation, of which Accenture is a founding member and to which I have referred frequently in this book already.

Beyond these broadly visible changes at the LGBT+ top ranks, there is internal continuity in the middle leadership tier at Accenture, for example, represented by Javier Leonor-Vicente.

Researching this book, I met the very active native Spaniard several times, mostly at conferences where his firm was a sponsor. With the firm for over ten years, Leonor, who lives with his Dutch husband in Amsterdam, was in 2018 appointed to Accenture's global D&I team leading the LGBT+ programs on all continents – no small task in a firm of over half million people.

For example, there is a global internal mentoring program that continuously expands to new countries, including some that are difficult or even hostile to LGBT+ people such as China, Singapore, Russia, or Poland. And there are the aforementioned LGBT+ Leaders Learning sessions, with senior Accenture LGBT+ leaders teaching. Many of these trainings, which take place across the globe, are set up with support from and in cooperation with local LGBT+ nonprofits. Recently, there were sessions in Warsaw, Buenos Aires, Chicago, Tokyo, New York, and – just before the lockdown due to COVID-19 – São Paulo.

A further key program aims to increase the number and activity of straight allies, currently reaching the high level of 125,000 people. Yet another enables employees to self-identify by their sexual orientation and gender identity voluntarily in countries where this is legally possible. The aim is to provide more accurate data so as to better design and monitor LGBT+ D&I programs focused on recruitment, retention, and career development. There are also sponsorships for events and other engagements that advance LGBT+ supply chain diversity and regular studies investigating the current state of LGBT+ inclusion at work and beyond, including best practice examples and continuing challenges.

As I have been arguing, discrimination on the basis of sexual orientation and gender identity is not only a violation of fundamental human rights but also has a negative impact on individuals', companies' and countries' long-term economic prospects. The PGLE recognized this in the press release accompanying its launch, referring to a 2017 UNAIDS study estimating "the global cost of LGBTI discrimination at $100 billion per year. Businesses have an important role to play in respecting and protecting human rights through fostering workplace inclusion for LGBTI people."[123]

Some months after its launch, the Partnership established a Steering Committee in which all founding member are represented and that is co-chaired by two "neutral" key figures.[124] One of them is Dan Bross. I have described parts of his background already, but here's a bit more relevant to the new job. At Microsoft, for many years, Bross was in charge of developing and managing the firm's global CSR program.[125] Among other things, he founded and led the Microsoft Technology and Human Rights Center, in which capacity he managed the company's adoption of the aforementioned UN Guiding Principles on Business and Human Rights.[126] (For more see Part I, Chapter 6.) He was also in charge of his firm's engagement with socially responsible investors, CSR organizations, UN agencies, the WEF, and more.[127]

## A powerful woman and the "It gets better" campaign

Certainly, Bross was well prepared to take up his role as PGLE's Co-Chair. The same applies for the Partnership's second Co-Chair, Beth Brooke, but in different ways. For some years, she has been considered one the world's most impactful out senior executives, although in coming out, she was a late starter. Until the age of 52, like many others of her generation, she feared negative impacts on her career.

Brooke began working for auditing and consulting giant EY in 1991. In her many years there, she had public policy responsibility for its operations in over 150 countries, was global sponsor for the firm's D&I efforts and spearheaded the formation of its corporate responsibility group. During the presidency of Bill Clinton, she left EY for two years to work in the Department of the Treasury, responsible for all tax policy matters related to insurance and managed care. Today, among many other engagements, she still co-chairs the International Council on Women's Business Leadership, founded by Hillary Clinton.

In 2013 and 2014, she ranked second and third, respectively, on the first two OUTstanding LGBT+ Out Executives role model lists and is now part of its Hall of Fame (see Part II, Chapter 4).[128] And in January 2015, she was on the first panel at the World Economic

Forum to discuss LGBT+ issues, after she had – just a few days earlier – published a highly acclaimed article in *Fortune*: *Why I am proud to be gay – at home and at work*.[129]

Not long ago, so much attention for Brooke as a top out lesbian leader would have been unthinkable to her. At one point – for more than a decade – she was married to a man. Only when, in her early 30s, she transferred to Washington, DC after ten successful years in Indianapolis did she gradually understand she was gay.

It took another 20 years before finally, in 2011, at over 50, she came out at EY and only a very short time later also publicly. It surprised her almost as much as everyone else. The trigger was the social media campaign "It gets better," now widely known to many globally. US journalist, author, and LGBT+ activist Dan Savage and his husband, Terry Miller, started the project in 2010, reacting to several US suicides of young people bullied because they were or were perceived to be LGBT+. The campaign quickly found numerous prominent supporters, among them Barack Obama; Joe Biden; Hillary Clinton; pop star Gloria Estefan; US presenter, comedian and lesbian icon Ellen DeGeneres; and Neil Patrick Harris, star of the worldwide hit TV series *How I Met Your Mother*, who is openly gay in real life.

In short video sequences, they and many tens of thousands of others supported LGBT+ youth in feeling confident and happy in who they were. The initiative was so successful that numerous national offshoots followed, including in Switzerland, Austria, Italy, Finland, South Africa, and several South American countries.

Like many other companies, EY was involved from the start of the campaign, and Brooke, then still in the closet, agreed to participate.[130] In several interviews, including one with me, she has described how this played out. She was approached as a supposed heterosexual to make her own short video. Preparing her remarks, she decided that she couldn't be inauthentic in a message to children – and finally came out on camera.

When Brooke retired in 2019, after an almost four-decade career, she had become one of the most visible, networked, and active out lesbian senior executives worldwide. She was also instrumental in setting up the Partnership for Global LGBTI Equality linked to the WEF, which, as mentioned, she now co-chairs (while also sitting on several boards). For more than a decade, the US business magazine

*Forbes* repeatedly listed her as one of the most powerful women in the world – something that changed only with her retirement – and not with her late coming out.[131]

## Truly global at the highest levels

On its website, the Partnership states its mission: "... to accelerate equality and social and economic inclusion for lesbian, gay, bisexual, transgender, and intersex people."[132] It works in collaboration with the WEF's Center for New Economy and Society, both focusing on three goals. The first is to operationalize the UN LGBTI Standards of Conduct for Business by providing tools and resources for companies. The second is to "organize and raise awareness of best practices and benchmarks to assist companies in meeting their commitments and responsibilities to global LGBTI equality." The third is to leverage the WEF's platform "to support committed business leaders in accelerating LGBTI workplace inclusion and promoting human rights for all,"[133] which again stresses that the business case and human rights approach should be thought of together.

These three goals might not seem to make a difference to what other organizations advancing LGBT+ inclusion in the workplace are doing. But the PGLE is doing it in alliance with the WEF at a very high, truly global level and is also working hand in hand with the Office of the UN High Commissioner for Human Rights to further advance and provide support to companies to operationalize the UN Standards of Conduct for Business. On its website, the PGLE also provides the list with all global Standard's signatories.

Beyond its 16 founding members there are not only further "ordinary" company members but also two major human rights organizations we have met before: Human Rights Watch and OutRight Action International, both also members of the UN LGBTI Core Group. Recently, the PGLE also added some further civil society organizations to their partner list, which I have referred to in this book frequently: HRC, GLAAD, ILGA, and Stonewall.

With this set of partners, which is expected to grow, the still quite new Partnership should be a vital force in advancing LGBT+ equality among top business leaders and global companies and maybe also influencing the LGBT+ equality agenda within the WEF and the UN – openly and/or behind the scenes.

# Part III

**Globally and locally:
A growing network
of organizations**

During the past few years, a rapidly increasing number of organizations have emerged working for LGBT+ equality and inclusion in the workplace and the corporate world. They include coalitions, chambers of commerce, partnerships, networks, social businesses, consultancies, nonprofits, and others.

We got a flavor of all this before in this book, especially from Barilla's LGBT+ turnaround story in Part I, in which we met operations with a national focus such as Parks in Italy, Prout at Work and Uhlala in Germany, L'Autre Cercle in France, or the Human Rights Campaign and Out & Equal in the US. Others, such as the Partnership for Global LGBTI Equality, in connection with the UN and the World Economic Forum, aim to cover the world.

Part III will look first at Out Leadership – a further leading organization working globally that I have referred to briefly before – and then at others engaging both nationally and internationally to help businesses advancing LGBT+ inclusion in the workplace and beyond. As will become clear, what we have seen so far was merely the tip of an impressively large and growing iceberg.

# 1. Out leaders on the street and a business story of growth

Todd Sears knows the United Nations and their LGBTI Standards of Conduct for Business well too. And he knows the top executives who congregate each year in Davos. He has to, since Out Leadership (OL) – the organization he founded in New York in 2011 and now chairs – is primarily focused on those leaders.

Sears began with a financial sector organization called Out on the Street (meaning Wall Street), then another called Out in Law. Three cross-industry LGBT+ talent initiatives followed.[1] Today, OL is an LGBT+ business network of global leaders but also, says Sears, "as a firm, we aim to make LGBT+ inclusion a strategic and day-to-day priority at the top levels of global companies.

"In fact, Out Leadership was established as a B corp, which means we are a 'social impact for profit business,'" he adds. "We reinvest all our profits in the company and over the past five years, we have donated 20% of our pretax profits to LGBT+ nonprofit organizations all over the world."

OL provides its paying member firms with services to strategically unleash the business potential of LGBT+ inclusion: summits and other events, strategic insights, research, a variety of programs, and more. It gives global corporations and their leaders the tools to create "Return on Equality®", a registered trademark Sears created some ten years ago.

## Out on Wall Street

OL's foundation grew out of Sears' experience as a gay man in finance in Manhattan in the late 1990s. Openly gay since his freshman year in college, he started work as an analyst on Wall Street immediately after graduating from Duke University. Just over a week after he began, his boss called a colleague "a f— faggot" right in front of him, Sears says. "I was shocked and decided to go back in the closet. But after eight months, I could stand it no more and left the firm – committed to never hiding my sexual identity again."

In subsequent years, he worked as an investment banker and financial advisor, later moving into diversity leadership at Merrill Lynch and Credit Suisse. OL's website says he "created the first team of financial advisors on Wall Street to focus on the LGBT+ community, bringing $1.5 billion in new assets to Merrill Lynch."[2]

Sears, today in his mid-40s and in a relationship for many years, started OL with only six member companies, all Wall Street investment firms. It now numbers over 80 global corporates across a large variety of industries – an entrepreneurial success story achieved in only a decade.

## Nonprofit support – for example, Williams Institute and Lambda Legal

Beyond his rise as an LGBT+ social entrepreneur, Sears works with several nonprofits. One is the highly regarded Williams Institute, or "Williams Institute for Sexual Orientation and Gender Identity Law & Public Policy" (UCLA School of Law). He became a board member about 15 years ago, before founding OL. The Williams Institute conducts research on sexual orientation and gender identity to deliver independent data to inform laws, policies, and judicial decisions that affect LGBT+ people.[3] Some have relevance for business and national or local economies.

For example, in May 2020, the Institute published a report titled, *The Economic Impact of Marriage Equality Five Years after Obergefell v. Hodges.*[4] Obergefell v. Hodges was the US Supreme Court's landmark 2015 ruling that the Constitution guarantees all same-sex couples the right to marry. At the time, 13 states forbade this. The ruling declared this not a states' rights issue, granting same-sex marriage rights everywhere in the country. Since then, the number of married same-sex couples has more than doubled, from an estimated 220,000 to 513,000. The report shows "that wedding spending by these couples and their out-of-state guests has boosted state and local economies by an estimated $3.8 billion and generated an estimated $244.1 million in state and local sales tax revenue." It also shows that this spending supported an estimated 45,000 jobs a year.[5]

The Williams Institute provides international research, too. In December 2019, for example, it published *The Economic costs of LGBT Stigma and Discrimination in South Africa.*[6] A further study, March 2018's *Links Between Economic Development and New Measures of LGBT Inclusion* used said measures to test previous findings linking LGBT+ inclusion to countries' economic performance.[7]

Another of Sears' nonprofit engagements is his board membership at Lambda Legal, for which he has raised funds for over 20 years. Lambda Legal Defense and Education Fund,[8] founded in 1973, is an American civil rights organization focusing on LGBT+ people and people living with HIV/AIDS. The nonprofit aims at influencing the political arena, societal education, and impact and strategic litigation. Impact litigation means bringing lawsuits to effect societal change. In 2015, for instance, Lambda Legal was a co-counsel in one of the cases making up Obergefell v. Hodges.

## Broad portfolio

Sears' engagement with the Williams Institute, in particular, fits with OL's approach: grounded in data and research, focused on top leadership, and business driven. OL's website often displays research – for instance, recently, a global study on the benefit of straight allies in companies' journeys to LGBT+ inclusion – and member firms are continuously provided with new LGBT+ related data.

The website also shows membership benefits, listing three areas of service and showing their availability on the continents on which OL is active: the Americas, Europe, Asia, and Australia.

In the first category, "Executive Events", there is a senior leader summit, a VIP dinner, and a CEO dinner. All take place on all four continents.

In the second category of benefits for members, Talent Accelerators, there are three talent initiatives. The first is called Quorum and aims at increasing LGBT+ representation on corporate boards. The second, OutWOMEN, brings together senior LGBT+ businesswomen. The third initiative, OutNEXT, is a global talent development program for young and/or emerging LGBT+ leaders, for which member companies can select high-performing and/or high-potential LGBT+ employees. Among other things, those selected participate in face-to-face and virtual events throughout the year. Program and event elements are interviews, lecture-style presentations, mentorships, access to up-to-date research, and more. In 2019, for example, they attended a global summit in New York and regional salons in different cities such as London, Hong Kong, San Francisco, and Sydney. In 2020, due to the pandemic, there was a strong focus in virtual sessions. That year, almost 400 emerging LGBT+ leaders from five continents joined the program.

In the third membership benefit category, "Strategic Insights", OL provides services on all four continents, such as "Public Policy Advisory", "Speaker Sourcing", "Advisory", "OutNEWS", "CEO Business Briefs", and more.

## Responding to operational and reputational risks

In 2015 at Davos, OL introduced its CEO Business Briefs to advise global business leaders on advancing and leveraging LGBT+ equality for business benefits in talent, customer, supplier, and other stakeholder markets, and to provide a research basis for doing so. OL started with six briefs and now provides them for more than 20 countries. According to the social business, they have been used by hundreds of CEOs globally.[9]

In May 2019, OL also launched the LGBT+ Business Climate Index,[10] measuring every US state's performance on LGBT+ inclusion. It goes beyond mere analysis of legal frameworks, aiming to measure the impact of government policies and cultural attitudes on LGBT+ people living (and working and buying) in each state. The goal is to quantify the costs of discrimination and the economic and business imperatives for LGBT+ inclusion, comparing across states.

Out Leadership set up the index with financial support from the Gill Foundation, one of the largest US funders working for LGBT+ people. It also worked with data partners, for example, the aforementioned Williams Institute and the United States Transgender Survey.

The index gives each state a score out of 100, based on 20 markers assessing LGBT+ people's lived experiences – in the workplace or other business-related environments. The premiere in 2019 showed Massachusetts and California in the lead, with around 90 points each, while South Carolina and Mississippi at the end ranked 49th and 50th with less than 33 points each. Based on the index results, OL also launched CEO Business Briefs for each of the 50 US states, expanding the idea of the CEO country briefs to smaller local entities.

The rationale for the index and briefs is to support global companies in understanding and responding appropriately to the operational and reputation risks of operating in places hostile to LGBT+ people. "Responding appropriately" in the US could, for instance, mean empowering executives to engage locally with development officials and other stakeholders on the negative economic impact of anti-LGBT+ discrimination.[11] The briefs should thus provide executives with structured arguments and data supporting the LGBT+ D&I economic and business cases, framed through local laws, cultural attitudes, and institutions.

"Respond appropriately" in an international context, meanwhile, could mean assessing options around the three aforementioned approaches a global corporate can take in nations unwelcoming to LGBT+ people: the When in Rome, the Embassy and the Advocate models (see Part II, Chapter 8).

It may be no coincidence then that Kenji Yoshino, one of the two study authors we met defining these models,[12] sits on OL's Global Advisory Board. Also on the Board are Beth Brooke and John Browne, both of whom I have referred to frequently.

Another Board member is Jim Fitterling from Dow, the US billion-dollar chemical commodity company. Born in 1962, he joined Dow's board in 2019, the same year he became the first openly gay CEO of a large industrial company, and the first board-appointed out CEO of a Fortune 100 company. In 2014, after a successful fight against cancer,

Fitterling, already a senior executive, had come out to Dow employees on America's National Coming Out Day, October 11.

He has since become an increasingly visible advocate for LGBT+ equality, both internally – not least as mentor of LGBT+ employees – and externally. For example, in 2016, when Dow was publicly campaigning against anti-gay rights legislation in US states such as Mississippi, Tennessee, and others, he was actively involved. Since the historic side-event breakfast at the WEF in early 2014, he has also frequently attended LGBT+ events at Davos. The OUTstanding Out Executive role model list reflects Fitterling's increased engagement in LGBT+ issues. In 2015, the first time he was part of the evaluation, he ranked 73. Only three years later, in 2018, he took first place, then placed third in 2019.

On occasion of the Coming Out Day 2020, Fitterling posted a short personal message on LinkedIn. Looking back on his coming out, he had overwhelmingly positive support, he said. "My fears were unfounded. I learned that fear will get me nowhere. So, whether it's coming out or embracing a more inclusive, sustainable world, let's put fear aside. Embrace progress. It will make us all better."

## Political or not?

A year after the first, in June 2020, Out Leadership shared its second index edition, now called LGBTQ+ Business Climate Index. Instead of using LGBT+, which, in many international business contexts outside the US is standard, as it is on OL's website, the new "Q," reflects increasingly common practice in the US.

In his introduction to the second edition, Sears wrote, "These briefs and metrics are apolitical, data-focused, and are meant to connect the dots between LGBTQ+ inclusion and equality and bottom-line impact."[13] Of course, the index is not apolitical at all. It wasn't the year before and it was even less so in summer 2020, when the world was hit by the coronavirus and the US was shaken by the Black Lives Matter movement and riots on the street against inequality and injustice. Passionate and furious debates about political failures of crisis management, related lack of support for the weakest and obvious economic, social, ethnic, and racial injustices intensified substantially.

While Sears could technically claim to be producing "apolitical briefs and metrics," he was also being explicitly political, writing, "This year, more than ever, it is important for us to focus on the impact of policy on equality. During this COVID-19 crisis, the LGBTQ+ population is disproportionately exposed."[14] He called "upon businesses to double down on inclusion during this crisis,"[15] meaning they should take on (social) responsibility where government is failing.

## High-end? Expensive? Global?

For some, the annual OL membership fee for companies might look high. This would be a false impression, says Sears. "We have a tiered global membership structure with our top membership tier being $50,000," he explains. "This is what many firms pay for a single table at a fundraising dinner one time a year and only in the US. When viewed by engagement, by region, and especially by return on investment, our membership is actually incredibly inexpensive. In 2020, we convene over 150 events on five continents with thousands of leaders and hundreds of CEOs, most of them virtual due to the pandemic."

In fact, OL's structure, reach, and offerings are quite unique globally. Until some five to ten years ago, there was still significant industry and US bias, stemming from Sears launching his social business with Wall Street banks and law firms, all with a global focus but strong US roots. But "since then, we have grown to over 80 member companies, representing more than 15 different industries, including consumer products, beverages, technology, fintech, media, industrials, asset management, advertising, private equity, hedge funds, global merchant services, and others," Sears says, "And since our start, our network of CEOs has grown to over 500."

Still, the number of member companies belonging in finance is high. This might also have to do with the fact that this industry – at least in the Anglo-Saxon world – has been at the forefront of advancing LGBT+ inclusion at work and beyond. This is not least reflected in quite active and well-managed volunteer networking platforms for LGBT+ people in the financial services industry in many global financial centers. Mostly, they bring together member of LGBT+ employee networks. In London, for example, there is Interbank, a forum for members of local LGBT+ ERGs, founded in 2002.[16] Hong Kong also has an Interbank forum and network of currently about 35 LGBT+ affinity groups from banks and financial firms. It was informally set up in 2006 and officially launched in July 2016.[17]

In New York City, where OL is based, there is Open Finance, founded in 2006. Currently, it counts about 5,000 individuals, belonging to about 50 participating firms' LGBT+ ERG's.[18] A significant number are also OL members. In 2019, Open Finance held their third forum, hosted by Bloomberg, with speakers such as John C. Williams, President of the Federal Reserve Bank of New York and OL's board representative Beth Brooke.

The strong engagement from the finance industry is also visible at OL's largest global sponsor, British-based HSBC banking group. Further members from the non-European Anglo-Saxon world are major Australian financial players such as National Australian Bank and Macquarie. There are also Japanese banks Mizuho and Nomura, both active on Wall Street (as of July 2020). Companies based in Europe include Schroders from the UK, another financial services company, French insurance giant AXA, and LVMH, the French luxury goods conglomerate I referred to earlier in this book (For a recent OL executive summit in Paris, see Part IV, Chapter 10.)

OL has grown fast, both in members and activities, increasing its industry and global scope substantially in the more than ten years since its foundation. There is still potential to enlarge membership of companies based in Asia, Europe, and Australia, but on all three continents, OL's activities have increased recently. If it continues its high rate of growth, OL should soon be what continental Europeans, Asians or Africans would consider truly global.

## 2. Crossing the lines – from France to the US, from distressing shame to fervid engagement, and from public service to private sector

Someone quite knowledgeable about this global journey is Fabrice Houdart. A Frenchman living in the US for more than two decades, Houdart was a Human Rights Officer at the UN until recently, a co-author of the UN LGBTI Standards of Conduct for Business and ranked second on OUTstanding's Top 30 LGBT+ Public Sector Leader list 2019. Now he is a managing director at OL, in charge of Global Equality Initiatives.

"I like crossing the lines," says Houdart, "not because it's fun, but especially when I feel that they need to be crossed." Now in his early 40s, for many years he has worked at the intersection of economics, business, and LGBT+ rights and equality. His story is worth telling in some detail. It's one in which he has indeed crossed lines several times, notably from public service at two global institutions, the World Bank and the Office of the UN High Commissioner of Human Rights (OCHR), to his hiring by Todd Sears.

## From Paris to DC and the World Bank – but with initial anxiety

He was born "quite privileged, into a white, wealthy, and bourgeois family," Houdart says. "My father was the CEO of a welding company, my mother was at home. In fact, my family was socially conservative. And that's still so today. In 2013, at age 92, my grandfather joined several family members to demonstrate against same-sex marriage even though they knew I was gay and had a partner."

In France, he "felt bad as a gay young man, although I had not come out yet, and I dreamt of reinventing myself by going to the US." That's what he did. After gaining his bachelor's in economics and management at Dauphine University in Paris, he earned an MBA from Washington, DC's American University in the early 2000s. At age 23, he joined the World Bank in Washington, DC, where he worked for around 14 years, dealing with developmental economics issues, covering Africa, including the Maghreb, the Middle East, and Central Asia.

When he joined the World Bank, he was in the process of coming out to his parents and friends. His concerned father warned that "being gay would irrevocably hurt my career prospects, which fed my existing insecurities," he says. "And while my brother was absent from this conversation, my mother hinted that it would be better if I stayed in the US."

For many years, he felt fragile at the World Bank. He was scared "that my colleagues and clients, who came from diverse cultural backgrounds and were often deeply religious, would discover the truth and take a dim view of me." Even after he became regular staff in 2004, giving him greater security both economically and visa-wise, anxieties remained. "I felt shame, fear, and inferiority around straight colleagues, particularly straight men, and terrified that something would reveal I am gay," he says, telling a story still all too typical, even in liberal Western countries. "I felt insecure in most business meetings, sometimes sweating because of anxiety and nervousness. There is no doubt that all this reduced my job performance, productivity, and career prospects significantly."

GLOBE, the World Bank's LGBT+ affinity group, had been founded in 1992, so very early, but "The network's beginning was not easy," says Houdart. "GLOBE colleagues told me that an executive had tried to block the announcement of the group's formation, saying, 'Next there'll be ads for wife-swapping clubs and nude mud-wrestling clubs.'"[19]

Houdart learned of GLOBE's existence quite soon after joining the World Bank in his first years, but steered clear, "because my struggle to survive and related demons were all too energy-consuming." Over time, he became interested and once he got involved, was soon all in, eventually being elected treasurer, then vice president, then president.

## "Conversion therapy": learning to fight for LGBT+ equality

"This happened amid a major controversy," Houdart says. The World Bank had added PFOX – short for Parents and Friends of Ex-Gays and Gays – to a list of suggested charities for employees to donate to. "This was, of course, insane," he says. He is right. PFOX, a US charity, says every human being is born heterosexual and promotes "conversion therapy," a pseudo-therapy that promises to "return" gay people to a "natural" sexual orientation. US ultra-conservative Christians push this especially, but there is also strong support in other countries, notably in Latin America.

Modern science, medicine, and psychology strongly oppose it, partly because the idea that everyone is born heterosexual is nonsense and partly because the therapy can cause severe long-term psychological damage, even increasing suicide risk. Recently, Germany, for example, led by its broadly respected conservative-progressive Minister of Health, Jens Spahn, banned "conversation therapy" for under-aged people, and there is an ongoing struggle to ban it for all ages.

Other recent bans have happened in Illinois, as I report elsewhere in this book, and, in July 2020, in Mexico City.[20] The UN Independent Expert on protection against violence and discrimination based on sexual orientation and gender identity has called for a global ban.[21] Recently, in December 2020, more than 370 religious leaders from around the world, including former Chief Rabbi of Ireland David Rosen and South African Archbishop Desmond Tutu, signed a declaration, calling for a global ban, too.

For Houdart, the scandal didn't end there: "The World Bank HR department even told us to be tolerant of the opposing view, which was even more insane because it was about damaging lives." To him, this was "another major moment of crossing a line. I started advocating for LGBT+ equality visibly." He realized "how unaware of LGBT+ workplace issues some of my colleagues were, and how necessary it was for us to step up."[22]

GLOBE ran an organization-wide survey, documented in the report *The Invisible Minority at the World Bank*, in spring 2011. It found that the vast majority of LGBT+ staff members "still hid their identity, feared discrimination from managers, experienced hostile treatment from coworkers, and felt insecurity in our various country offices," Houdart summarizes.

Again, there was a backlash. Bank staff members, including a World Bank senior vice president, wrote to management worrying the survey might restrict "their 'freedom to judge homosexual acts to be objectionable on moral, religious, and/or other grounds,'" Houdart says, knowing this view is still common in many places.

It only inspired him to further courage. He went beyond the more or less safe GLOBE circle and fully came out to the whole World Bank. He put his boyfriend's picture on his desk, shared his personal experience on the World Bank's Family Network, and sought ways to discuss the survey results and advocate for change.

"Coming out relieved me of the shame I had felt for so many years. Almost overnight I experienced a newfound self-confidence. That allowed me to have tough conversations with management on their passivity in fostering greater inclusion of LGBT people, both internally and in our mission as a development organization,"[23] he wrote in an article some years ago. "But more importantly, it gave me a true sense of pride, that I was worthy and belonged to this organization as much as anybody else."

## Development economics, sexual minorities, and a research program

Houdart's published numerous articles on the World Bank site between 2012 and 2014, including *Estimating the Global Cost of Homophobia and Transphobia, From India: Sexual minorities and the gender agenda*, and many more. And during the five years of his presidency, he led GLOBE "from a mere staff club to a real leader on LGBT+ rights," he says. "In spring 2015, I chaired a major meeting with delegates from several continents, representatives of NGOs concerned with the issue of sexual minorities and economic development. The then Bank President Jim Yong Kim was also there. This meeting finally led to the creation of a department devoted to these issues."

Working on topics around sexual minorities and economic development, Houdart successfully applied for a $250,000 grant from the World Bank's Nordic Trust Fund. Nobody at the World Bank who might ordinarily have led such a project wanted it because of the topic, so "I had to do this," Houdart says, "my first leadership experience – beyond my job as GLOBE's president."

The research delivered the first estimate of the cost of homophobia, inspiring Lee Badgett's 2014 World Bank socioeconomic study of LGBT+ people, the first of its kind.[24] So Houdart's work led directly to research on the economics of LGBT+ equality.

Badgett, formerly director of the School of Public Policy at Massachusetts University, is an economics professor and a co-founder and the first research director of the aforementioned Williams Institute. As a now leading economist on LGBT+ issues, she co-authored, among many other studies, the 2016 report, *Investing in a Research Revolution for LGBTI Inclusion*, supported by the World Bank and the UN Development Program.[25] It drew attention for the first time to significant knowledge gaps on LGBT+ rights, including the investment needed to get them on human rights and economic development agendas.

A lot research done subsequently is in line with the program laid out by Badgett and her co-author Phil Crehan, then LGBTI and Social Inclusion Consultant at the World Bank.[26] More recently, based on the growing body of research, much of it her own, Badgett wrote the book, *The Economic Case for LGBT Equality: Why fair and equal treatment benefits us all*. It was widely praised, notably by Janet Yellen, chair of the US Federal Reserve until 2018.

## Crossing the lines again: fathering twins, moving to NYC, and the intersection of human rights and business

During his years of growing impact at the World Bank, Houdart also took a personal step. "Now that I was fueled with all the energy of coming out and doing LGBT+ work, I recalled that I had always wanted to be a father," Houdart says. "To tell the truth, I wanted to begin with one child – a girl or a boy. Now I am so happy to have two." His twins, Eitan and Maxime – born in 2013 – are part of his public life, appearing in pictures on his social media feed and in blog posts, such as his *Confessions of a single gay dad*.[27]

In another big change, after 14 years, he decided to leave the World Bank in order to move, in 2016, to Manhattan, where he joined the Office of the UN High Commissioner of Human Rights (OHCHR). Immediately at the OHCHR, he was in charge of managing the aforementioned Free & Equal campaign for LGBT+ equality. But very soon another idea emerged that was driven by High Commissioner Prince Zeid and that I have referred in Part II already: the UN LGBTI Standards of Conduct for Business. Houdart contributed significantly to making the Standards a reality. He brought together relevant stakeholders around the globe to define them – businesses, nonprofits working for LGBT+ workplace equality, human rights NGOs, and others – and became one of the Standards' co-authors before they were launched in mid-2017. Finally, he also became their operational leader, managing them, traveling to acquire a huge number of new signatories, writing reports, speaking at company signings, and more. In the roughly two and a half years from the Standards' launch until he left the UN, he became their public face.

Inviting him to become a Managing Director at Out Leadership seems a smart move by Todd Sears. Houdart is not just well connected globally in all the ways we have seen. He is also a board member at several nonprofits, including LGBT+ human rights NGO OutRight frequently referred to before, and he is European, with the potential to bring new OL members from farther afield, as he did recently with French luxury giant LVMH.

Houdart could have left the "UN system" as he calls it, a bit frustrated. His cause's allies at the UN – the Obama Administration's support there, Ban Ki-moon, and Prince Zeid – are gone. Working for LGBT+ inclusion there has got tougher. As described in Part II, management, operationalizing and marketing of the Standards are now in the hands of – or at least strongly linked to – the Partnership for Global LGBTI Equality, led by private companies and connected to the WEF.

"I have come to consider that for the LGBT+ community, it is crucial to avoid complacency and start looking hard for new strategies and new allies," Houdart says. He is convinced that currently the engine for advancing LGBT+ equality is not governments and multilateralism, but the private sector. He may be right. A lot of the changes described in this book were driven by businesses – including his new employer OL.

On the other hand, the world is fast becoming more insecure. Agents in the political arena are going to change, and priorities may shift again quickly. We saw this after the financial crisis of 2008, and we are beginning to see it again with COVID-19, with the increasing conflicts within societies or between the US and China and in other regions of the world.

The private sector and markets alone do not make for change. Functioning state institutions and political leadership are always vital. The pandemic, with all its tragic failures of response in states like the US, Brazil, the UK, and others, has once again made this all too clear. As always, then, the future is open – including the future of multilateralism, embodied by the UN, the WEF and other institutions. One way or another, the experience capital Houdart has accumulated related to the public sector will be vitally useful to both his paid and nonprofit LGBT+ endeavors.

## 3. Vienna and Eastern Europe calling, and some new business chambers

Engagements driven by corporates mainly headquartered in the US, as members of global organizations like Out Leadership or the PGLE, are important. However, at an institutional level, they are just one transformative force in the international economy.

Further institutional forces such as workplace-related nonprofits, social businesses, and less formal networks have become increasingly active in recent years. I have referred to a few previously in the

US, UK, Germany, France, Italy, the Netherlands, and Switzerland. Almost all promote LGBT+ inclusion in the workplace with the only or main focus on their respective countries.

## East meets West's focus on Central and Eastern Europe

East meets West (EmW), in contrast, works across nations focused on a region. Initiated in Vienna in 2013, EmW is a registered non-profit network of LGBT+ professionals with a central focus on Central and Eastern Europe. It has grown fast, today encompassing around 1,300 LGBT+ people and straight allies, mainly from Central and Eastern Europe.

Focused on "advancing and supporting micro business initiatives in Austria and Central and Eastern Europe,"[28] its flagship product is the International East meets West Conference, held annually in June. Prague, the Czech Republic's capital, has twice played host (for developments in the Czech Republic, see box), but its permanent location is now Vienna. In 2020, it was virtual because of COVID-19.

### The Czech Republic: Prague Pride, a business forum, and a campaign

The Czech Republic has roughly ten million inhabitants and, among Eastern European states, ranks second behind Poland and before Romania for GDP (as of end of 2019). On LGBT+ human rights, it is far behind in Europe. In the 2020 ILGA Europe ranking,[29] which looks at 49 European states (see Part I, Chapter 2), it places 32nd. Nevertheless, companies' fostering of LGBT+ inclusion in the workplace and beyond have lately increased.

One the most important Czech platforms working for LGBT+ rights and inclusion in general is Prague Pride. The volunteer non-profit aims to promote a tolerant society, fight LGBT+-phobia, and raise awareness of the LGBT+ community nationally. Originally set up in 2010 to organize the city's Pride event, it has broadened its activities significantly. For example, it holds a run against homophobia and stigmatization of HIV+ sufferers, called Fun & Run. There is an LGBT+ peer-to-peer service, sbarvouven.cz, currently supported by Citibank and Vodafone.[30] Prague Pride also belongs to a coalition of five Czech nonprofits – one the local Amnesty International chapter – campaigning for marriage equality, not least with economic arguments.

Prague Pride was founded by Czeslaw Walek, one of the most prominent LGBT+ activists in the country and he is also involved in workplace-related topics. A lawyer now in his mid-40s, with Polish roots, he studied in Krakow, Antwerp, and Budapest. He specialized in human rights law and became active in various related initiatives, including one on Roma inclusion in the Czech Republic. From 2009 to 2011, he served as the Czech Republic's Deputy Minister of Human Rights and Minorities – while also founding Prague Pride. He has chaired the nonprofit since, and after he married his husband in the Netherlands some years ago, he also became Prague Pride's representative in *Jsme fér* ("We are fair"), the Czech equal marriage campaign.

Walek is also the Prague Pride representative at and driver of the Pride Business Forum. Launched in 2011, the Forum is the country's main platform pushing for LGBT+ workplace equality. It provides spaces to share best practice and network and recognizes LGBT+-friendly employers as "Pride Business Forum Heroes." It has become one of the most important get-togethers on LGBT+ workplace inclusion in Eastern European business.

Another important Czech protagonist is Adéla Horáková, who works with Walek closely on many LGBT+ engagements. Having obtained master and doctoral degrees in law, Horáková was for over ten years a lawyer at global law firms such as Clifford Chance and Dentons before she decided to become a D&I manager for Dentons' European offices. Currently she works as an independent consultant, mainly on LGBT+ inclusion.

Beyond that, she is engaged with the Pride Business Forum. There, aside from being on the jury for the main LGBT+ workplace equality awards, she is a moderator of the Forum's annual conference. She is also a member of the executive committee at PROUD, a Czech LGBT+ nonprofit with a wide range of activities including advocacy, research, legal counseling, and support for LGBT+ seniors.

Most of the time, though, she is both the legal counselor of the aforementioned Jsme fér campaign and its public face in the media. And while Walek heads the campaign and targets the business arena for support, Horáková leads the related lobbying work. Meanwhile over 70 international and local companies have expressed support.

Also, Walek and Horáková helped facilitate a meeting of 16 companies with the Czech Prime Minister on the issue of LGBT+ inclusion and the advantages (including the economic advantages) of equal marriage. To date, Jsme fér has collected about 100,000 signatures in support of it, but over two years after a bill was submitted to MPs there has been next to no movement on it in the Czech parliament.

Nevertheless, the fact that major parts of the local business world are visibly supporting the campaign indicates strong progress. This echoes the resonance of another initiative in the corporate arena, the Pride Business Forum Memorandum 2017+. Initiated by the Forum, it invites companies in the Czech Republic to commit to advancing LGBT+ D&I in the workplace and beyond. Signatories include multinationals such as IBM, Vodafone, Accenture, Amazon, ExxonMobil, Citibank, Microsoft, SAP and law firm Allen & Overy, and also local businesses.

EmW's overarching mission is to increase societal and business acceptance of LGBT+ people in Europe, again mainly in Central and Eastern Europe. "In our work, we have two pillars – a social or human rights one, and the business one," says Ludo Swinnen, a Flemish-Belgian, one of East meets West's co-founders, "Firstly, we want to promote that LGBT+ rights are human rights everywhere – not least in the Central and Eastern Europe region, where living and working as an LGBT+ person due to laws and cultural attitudes is a lot more difficult than in most parts of liberal Western Europe."

Pavel Šubrt, Swinnen's Czech co-founder, elucidates: "We bring together the LGBT+ community, corporate players, entrepreneurs, NGOs, nonprofits, researchers, diplomats, EU officials, straight allies, and other relevant actors. And very specifically, we also help NGOs in Central and Eastern Europe" (see box on next page).

> ## Central and Eastern European countries in which East meets West supports or is affiliated with NGOs
>
> | | | |
> |---|---|---|
> | Albania | Armenia | Austria |
> | Croatia | Belarus | Bosnia and Herzegovina |
> | Bulgaria | Czech Republic | Estonia |
> | Hungary | Kosovo | Latvia |
> | Lithuania | Montenegro | North Macedonia |
> | Poland | Romania | Russia |
> | Serbia | Slovakia | Slovenia |
> | Ukraine | | |

"As the second pillar," Swinnen says, "we look at businesses in a narrower way to support and strengthen LGBT+-owned firms, mostly small to medium. We also promote LGBT+ entrepreneurs as role models for other LGBT+ people." Šubrt adds that this "might have an even larger impact in local communities than role models working in large corporations. But, of course, we need both."

At their conference, Šubrt says they discuss subjects such as the business case for LGBT+ D&I or advancing LGBT+ diversity in corporate supply chains, as in their recent virtual conference with Nedra Dickson, Accenture's Head of Global Supplier Inclusion and Sustainability. They have also hosted Germàn Henao, face of the first-ever LGBT+ campaign, #LoveIsLove by Coca-Cola Hungary, and Austrian Alexa Michelle Schwarz, a former Volvo CRM manager turned transgender activist. They have also heard from voices further afield, relating, for example, conditions for LGBT+ people in Tajikistan, and showcased the Czech Republic's marriage equality campaign. They also provided a platform for first-hand accounts from Poland where the right-wing nationalist party PiS is now fostering widespread LGBT+ phobia (see box on next page).

## Polish business world progress – despite "LGBT-free zones"

Life and work for LGBT+ people in Poland has become more difficult in recent years. The ruling PiS party has not only strongly undermined the rule of law and the media's function of being a critical check on the government, it has also fought hard against so-called "LGBT ideology." The party is strong in the Polish regions and smaller communities, but weaker in large cities. It is most difficult for LGBT+ people in the Eastern part and in the countryside," a Polish interviewee who prefers to remain anonymous says. "The big cities are relatively safe for LGBT+ people, especially Warsaw, which hosts the country's largest Pride event. But you may get into trouble there too."

PiS has recently lost some support, but still managed to oversee an ugly development quite unique in Europe or even the world: the proclamation of so-called "LGBT-free zones." Regions and municipalities totaling about a third of Poland's territory have declared themselves unwelcoming to LGBT+ people and/or so-called "LGBT ideology." This has not only been supported by the PiS political agenda but has also been lobbied for by some orthodox parts of the Catholic Church in Poland.

Although it is clear legally that, so far, the declaration can only have a symbolic character, it is also clear that it can palpably stigmatize LGBT+ people and legitimizes bullying, harassment, hate speech, and even violence. In the 2020 ILGA Europe Rainbow ranking, which measures the legal and policy situation of LGBT+ people in 49 European countries, and to which I referred earlier in this book, Poland is only ranked 42nd.[31]

But there is growing resistance. Poland is a European Union member and in December 2019 the European Parliament, with a vast majority, condemned "LGBT-free zones." They violate the EU Charter of Fundamental Rights.[32] In summer 2020, the EU denied funds to six municipalities that had proclaimed themselves "LGBT-free zones."[33] Helena Dalli, the European Commissioner for Equality, tweeted, "EU values and fundamental rights must be respected … This is why six town twinning applications involving Polish authorities that adopted 'LGBTI free zones' or 'family rights' resolutions were rejected."[34] Later, European Commission President Ursula von der Leyen condemned the PiS party and LGBT-free zones strongly, stating, "Being yourself is not your ideology" and "I want to be crystal clear – LGBTQI-free zones are humanity-free zones. And they have no place in our union."[35]

There are also signs of pushback from the corporate world. For some time, representatives of companies' LGBT+ employee networks have been meeting, following models across Europe, in companies' offices. Companies include Cisco, State Street, Shell, Philip Morris, UBS, HSBC, IG, and Akamai. Most recently, for the first time, Polish LGBT+ NGO representatives also attended a meeting. Among those present were *My Rodzice* (We the Parents), the Polish association of parents of LGBT+ people; *Fundacja Kultura dla Tolerancji* (Culture for Tolerance Foundation); and *Fundacja Wiara i Tęcza* (Faith and Rainbow Foundation). The owner of queer.pl, a major Polish LGBT+ internet portal, also joined the meeting.

In March 2018, global media giant Discovery bought the private Polish TV station *TVN*, more liberal in its reporting than the public broadcasters, which are under PIS's thumb. "Poland is … particularly interesting at present," says the openly gay Christian Hug, a Discovery Vice President in charge of, among other things, inclusion, and a member of the company's LGBT+ ERG priDe. "Our network in Poland has been in existence since summer 2019, and we already have more than 220 members." Recently, those members created a kind of inclusion glossary for the media.

Since 2018, there have also been the "NatWest LGBT+ Diamonds Polish Business Awards", sponsored by UK-based National Westminster Bank. Awards are given in seven categories, including "LGBT+-Supporting employer of the year." The website says the awards are "to say thank-you to people and organizations making a real change for LGBT+ employees in Poland. It is high time big businesses recognize their role in supporting LGBT+ people inside and outside the workplace."[36]

## A Belgian and a Czech, four countries, and two generations

Swinnen and Šubrt are two gay men of different generations and from different parts of Europe, who met in Vienna while working at Raiffeisen Bank International (RBI), a large Austrian banking group. "Our working life at RBI certainly inspired us in setting up East meets West," says Swinnen, "Both of us had, for many years, a lot of direct contacts, such as traveling to these countries very often." "Vienna is also a large international city," adds Šubrt, "with a lot of exciting cultural influences from Central and Eastern Europe, including the Balkans. Wherever you go you might hear some Central or Eastern European language."

"In a way, at EmW, we are a small, fast, flexible, and professional family business, but aren't paid for it," Šubrt says, referring to the fact that he and Swinnen manage EmW in their free time. "We wanted to be independent," Swinnen says. "And in the beginning, there was also some skepticism in the bank. But this has changed since. Obviously, the fast-increasing successes especially of our flagship, the conference, were very convincing."

In fact, RBI finally became a sponsor. "In addition, a subsidiary, Raiffeisen Centrobank, focused on investment banking in Austria, Central and Eastern Europe, also joined the partner club, which included strong global brands such as Accenture, Johnson & Johnson, or Coca-Cola," the Belgian says. Centrobank, Austrian railway company ÖBB, and Hotel Group Novotel provided travel and accommodation support for the many participants from Central and Eastern European states, economically weaker than Western European countries, who otherwise couldn't have afforded to come.

After his business studies at Anglo-American University in Prague and his first career steps in the local financial industry, Šubrt, today in his mid-40s, joined the Raiffeisen Group in 2004 and now works in RBI's digital banking section as a transformation manager. He lives in Vienna and Prague with his husband.

Swinnen, in his mid-60s and about to retire, holds a law degree from the renowned Catholic University of Louvain, Belgium, and an Executive MBA in finance from New York University (NYU). After years in insurance in his home country, he worked in the financial industry in Slovakia, the Czech Republic, Romania, and Germany. Like Šubrt, Swinnen is married and has two homes. He and his husband travel to the second in Nice whenever they can.

## Further initiatives in Austria

While at RBI, Swinnen became a member of AGPRO, short for Austrian Gay Professionals, the local gay leaders network, an affiliated partner of EmW. In 2018, with Šubrt, he also founded BRich, a joint initiative of LGBT+ ERGs from Austrian businesses and other institutions, some state owned. BRich's main activity is regular get-togethers hosted by member organizations to discuss LGBT+ D&I.

Before that, Swinnen and Šubrt had also helped to set up Embrace, the Raiffeisen Group's still quite young employee network, which is now a member of BRich as well. Currently, BRich counts about 30 member organizations, with more than 100 people on its mailing list. Austria's working world, compared with many other Western European countries, especially Germany and the UK, still has some LGBT+ workplace equality catching up to do. Therefore, "this is quite a success within a relatively short period of time," Swinnen rightly says.

BRich joins Pride Biz Austria, a major local platform based in the capital Vienna that was initiated by the aforementioned AGPRO and QBW – short for Queer Business Women, a network of lesbian women in the working world. Pride Biz Austria bundles activities in the area of LGBT+D&I in business and the working world and acts as major contact body for companies and politics in the country. Every two years it awards a prize for scientific research dealing with LGBT+ people's workplace situation. Also every two years, it awards the "Meritus," a prize for companies and other organizations that are role models in LGBT+ D&I management. Among recent winners were IBM, Bank Austria and ÖBB (Austrian Railways). Meritus is sponsored by several partners, among them the Chamber of Commerce, Federal Ministries and the City of Vienna. There is also the LGBT+ Business Forum. Once a year, Pride Biz Austria partners with IBM to invite managers as well as HR and D&I officers to attend a half-day conference related to LGBT+ D&I management. This includes lectures, workshops, networking, and more.

## New business chambers – and a bit more Western European business perspective

As for Swinnen, all this activity in Austria is the past for him now. Recently, he decided to leave Raiffeisen and move back to his home city of Antwerp, after decades as a globetrotter in the world of finance.

"I am preparing my retirement in order to have more time for East meets West and other nonprofit work."

Swinnen will need the extra time: after 2018's East meets West conference, he and Šubrt released the Vienna Declaration, announcing, among other things, an imminent new venture, the EGLCC. On the face of it, the initials stand for European Gay and Lesbian Chamber of Commerce, modeled on American NGLCC, or National Gay and Lesbian Chamber of Commerce. NGLCC was founded in 2002 but changed in 2017 to include other sexual and gender identities, becoming the National LGBT Chamber of Commerce, but keeping the old initials. In some alignment with this approach, EGLCC's full name is European LGBTIQ Chamber of Commerce.

Unlike for East meets West, for EGLCC, Šubrt and Swinnen worked with other founders. One, from Stockholm, is Tobias Holfelt, founder and CEO of MB Market Makers, a small business advisory working globally. It specializes in inclusion, training, and (external) communication, including setting up conferences, ultimately focused on reaping profits in LGBT+ customer markets. Holfelt is also President of the Scandinavian Gay & Lesbian Chamber of Commerce, which he founded in 2016. Another partner is Norbert Michael Grillitsch and the Italian GLBT Business Chamber he founded. Grillitsch is German but has lived in Italy for many years and runs ModusMaris, a small business HR advisory working globally, too.

Finally, as a further partner, the freshly launched German chamber, GGLBC, also joined. For legal reasons, in Germany the term "Chamber of Commerce" was not allowed, hence the use of "Business Chamber" – the "BC" in GGLBC. The chamber is a registered nonprofit and headquartered in Cologne, one of the most liberal German cities and particularly LGBT+-friendly.

"We thought it was necessary to give our activities a bit more Western European flavor," Šubrt says. "After all," Swinnen adds, "this part of the continent is more advanced in LGBT+ equality, and one of our goals from the very beginning was to provide learning in strategies, tools, and best practices." East meets West serves as a kind of fourth business chamber for Central and Eastern Europe.

---

## The EGLCC – four founding members

- EmW – representing Central and Eastern European countries
- German Gay and Lesbian Business Chamber (GGLBC)
- Italian GLBT Business Chamber (IGLBC)
- Scandinavian Gay & Lesbian Chamber of Commerce (SGLCC)

---

## Female forces, an Ethiopian childhood, and a political spirit

With the German Chamber, Europe's largest economy by far joined the founder's club, but also brought more female visibility: the GGLBC is driven by an eight-member team, including Šubrt and Swinnen, with three lesbian businesswomen as their lead.

One is Annika Zawadzki, a BCG partner whom we will meet later as one of the co-authors of a major global study on young people coming out at work (see Part IV, Chapter 1). The other two are Fabienne Stordiau and Dawn River.

I met Stordiau at the East meet West conference's EGLCC launch in Vienna, summer 2019. "We as lesbians have to be more visible and vocal in the business world," she says. Lesbian women at work, especially in management, cope with quite different challenges from their gay colleagues, almost everywhere globally. Stordiau says, "As women, we are still confronted with old-fashioned patriarchal ideology. Our performance has to be really good in this men's world to make us visible – unfortunately this even applies with gay men, who are not always our true allies. So our struggle as lesbians is against being an underrepresented minority in not one but two ways: 1) being women, and 2) being members of the rainbow community. Many of us still fear exclusion – despite all the progress we have made in everyday life and at work."

Stordiau, born in 1966, certainly knows about being out of the ordinary. Born in Addis Ababa, the youngest child of a half-Ethiopian, half-Armenian mother and a Belgian father with Austrian roots, she grew up speaking six languages: German, English, French, Armenian, Amharic, and Italian.

"I learned early on what it can mean not to belong because you are different. And I learned early on how important it is to stand by yourself and how enriching diversity and inclusion can be." Nevertheless, she waited until she was 30 to come out, at first doing so in her private life only. As with some other examples in this book, this marked a turning point for her, not just in terms of the increased openness, but engagement with LGBT+ issues. Almost immediately she became a "convinced activist," as she puts it. She has since been involved in LGBT+ initiatives in Cologne and far beyond.

With the same degree of willingness to change things, she also transformed her professional life only a short time later. Age 33, she founded her own company, now called Allround Team. "Not because I absolutely wanted to become an entrepreneur, but because I absolutely had to work flexibly. I was a single mother."

Stordiau believes that, "Once you gain confidence in yourself, coming out is like a liberating blow, both personally and professionally." To her, "Every coming out, as private as it is, is always a political act – including a coming out in the workplace. I wish more and more lesbians would come out and have the courage to lead."

Her company has now existed for over 20 years. With over 40 employees, it has two offices in Cologne and a UK branch in Brighton. Stordiau's wife, Dawn River, with whom she has lived for many years, is the company's head of strategy. Both now help run the GGLBC – with Stordiau also acting as national representative in the European chamber.

Among the existing new European national LGBT+ chambers, currently the German chamber is the most advanced. It provides a self-registration process, draws attention to supplier diversity and offers member firms various services for advancing LGBT+ inclusion, in German and English.

## The North American model for Europe

"We got the idea of setting up our European chamber from our US friends, NGLCC,"[37] Swinnen reports. "But, of course, we had to adapt it a bit because Europe is quite different from the US. They have 50 states, all belonging to the US legally. In Europe, in contrast, we have the EU with some areas covered by European law. In parallel, we still have a lot of national law in the many sovereign countries, many of which are not part of the EU. And some of these also have hostile LGBT+ laws and/or cultural attitudes, especially in Central and Eastern Europe."

The US LGBT+ chambers of commerce system is quite elaborate and mature. The original idea was to create an organization supporting LGBT+ business owners and to showcase the diversity of LGBT+ talents. Today, NGLCC also works for LGBT+ equality in large corporates and in government agencies by advocating for the inclusion of LGBT+ businesses in their supplier programs.

Just two years after its inauguration, NGLCC launched a "diversity certification program," which proved successful and has been a nationally exclusive certifying body for LGBT+-owned businesses ever since.[38] Out Leadership, for example, lists NGLCC as a partner, and OL's website also it is an NGLCC-certified LGBT+-owned business, or LGBT Business Enterprise (LGBTBE).

Also, a couple years ago, the NGLCC celebrated a success. Companies seeking the top score on the HRC Workplace Equality Index (see Part I), must take notice: since 2017, the inclusion of LGBTBEs certified by the NGLCC in a company's supplier diversity program has been a criteria on the index.[39]

Overall, the basic criteria to be certified as an LGBTBE are simple: businesses must be at least 51% owned, operated, managed, and controlled by an LGBT+ person or persons, and this person or persons must be either US citizens or permanent residents. They must be independent from any non-LGBT+ business enterprise, must have their principal place of business or headquarters in the United States, and must have been formed as a legal entity there.[40]

The process of certifying an LGBTBE can be carried out by the NGLCC, and the national chamber waives the $400,00 registration if the candidate joins one of the affiliated local LGBT+ chambers of commerce, present in more than 30 US states. Membership of such a chamber automatically confers NGLCC membership. California alone has seven local chambers, but some states have none.

To finance its activities, the NGLCC offers paid membership to companies. Today there are almost 250 members, a broad cross-section of the US economy, including tech giants such as Apple, Facebook, Google, Microsoft, and Salesforce, icons such as Dow, IBM, and Goldman Sachs, many telecommunications and media firms, sports businesses such as Major League Baseball and the NBA and – criticized by many – Northrop Grumman, one of the world's largest manufacturers of weapons and military technology. Member companies with a non-US ownership background are rare, but include

Italian pasta-primus Barilla, Swiss pharma giant Novartis Japanese car maker Toyota, British energy colossus BP, and German chemical and life science multinational Merck.[41]

Partner members get access to certified suppliers, have the opportunity to share best practice in supplier diversity and will – as a side effect – be perceived as supporters of the LGBT+ (business) community. Beyond that, the NGLCC hosts, for example, an annual dinner and an annual business conference. "The atmosphere at these conferences we have visited is exciting and inspiring. Some-times there are more than 1,000 participants," says Šubrt, "But as EGLCC, we are still small, in an early phase, and have to learn a lot, and fast. The same applies to our national chambers in Sweden, Italy, and Germany."

## Chambers going global – networked

Other chambers have learned from the example too, for instance, in Latin America, India, Australia, and South Africa. The NGLCC Global division, formed in 2013, focuses on precisely these parts of the world – and on Europe – not least to enlarge the markets for US-based LGBT-BEs. The box on the next page shows NGLCC's national affiliates.

With the exception of India, Asian chambers are not included yet, although there is, for example, a quite active Filipino LGBT Chamber. Founded in 2016 with Dutch Government support, in 2018 it even launched the Corporate SOGIE Diversity and Inclusiveness Index (SOGIE stands for Sexual Orientation, Gender Identity, and Expression), as a tool for organizations to benchmark themselves against international and local standards of LGBT+ diversity and inclusion in the workplace. Missing are affiliated chambers, for example, from Japan, South Korea, China or from South East Asian countries such as Thailand and Singapore.

## NGLCC's affiliated national LGBT+ chambers of commerce

| | |
|---|---|
| Australia | Gay and Lesbian Organization of Business and Enterprise (GLOBE) |
| Brazil | Cámara de Comercio e Turismo LGBT do Brasil |
| Canada | Canadian Gay & Lesbian Chamber of Commerce (CGLCC) |
| Central & Eastern Europe | East meets West |
| Colombia | Cámara de Comerciantes LGBT de Colombia (CCLGBTco) |
| Costa Rica | Cámara de Comercio Diversa Costa Rica (CCDCR) |
| Dominican Republic | Cámara de Comercio LGBT de la Republica Dominicana (CCLGBTRD) |
| Ecuador | Cámara LGBT de Comercio Ecuador (CCLGBTE) |
| India | Rajmala Welfare Society (RWS) – India's Diverse Chamber |
| Italy | Italian GLBT Business Chamber (IGLBC) |
| Jamaica | Jamaica Association of Diverse Businesses (JADB) |
| Mexico | Federación Mexicana de Empresarios LGBT (FME-LGBT) |
| Scandinavia | Scandinavian Gay & Lesbian Chamber of Commerce (SGLCC) |
| South Africa | PLUS – The LGBTI Business Network (part of The Other Foundation) |
| Uruguay | Cámara de Comercio y Negocios LGBT de Uruguay (CCNLGBTU) |

## "This is only the beginning"

"This is only the beginning," Šubrt says. The EGLCC is now understood as the umbrella organization for all present and future national European LGBT+ chambers of commerce.[42] On EGLCC's website there is a self-registration tool, and the four EGLCC founder members have developed a guideline for setting up a local chamber of commerce as a member of the EGLCC.

"After having received a candidacy, we have a call with the candidate and send them our guideline," Swinnen explains. "This way, they can adjust their expectations to reality – and then we move on or not." So far there are currently more than ten candidate chambers. "But based on an internal analysis, we now have a short list of suitable candidates. These are from Belgium, France, Spain, Portugal, Slovakia, and Scotland," Šubrt says, "We have sent them an official invitation to participate in a six-month coaching we as EGLCC are providing. It consists of training, best practice from successful chambers, podcasts, and personal meetings. After these six months, they can officially become an EGLCC member chamber of commerce."

### The Economic potential of the region covered by the EGLCC

- Population: overall 356 million; LGBT+: 21.4 million
- Gross Domestic Product (GDP): overall €8.34 trillion; LGBT+: €500 billion
- Numbers of small businesses: overall 15.8 million; LGBT+: 948 thousand

Source: EGLCC, Guidelines, as of August 2020 (excluding Russia)

Being located in Belgium now, "is clearly an advantage," Swinnen adds. "Vienna is perfect when looking at Austria and the East, as Pavel will continue to do. But Belgium, with Brussels, is of course the home of the EU and from there Paris, London, and Cologne are just a train ride away. I am the West man now – for our EmW focus, but also for our European chamber work." Recently, Brussels has become the official legal headquarters of the EGLCC – now a foundation.

# 4. Mature economies' different stages: Japan, Australia, the Netherlands, and Spain

In addition to these transnational examples, several advanced, though culturally very different economies – Australia, the Netherlands, and Spain – offer models of how work can be done nationally for LGBT+ workplace inclusion. This is happening especially, but not only, in the corporate world. There is also rich Japan, taking an own, quite slow path, though with activities increasing recently.

## Japan

Among economically leading countries, in terms of advancing LGBT+ equality and inclusion at work and in society, for decades Japan has lagged significantly behind. Daily culture and legislation are not LGBT+-friendly, although here too the younger generation has begun to live their sexual orientation and gender identity differently and more openly than their predecessor age cohorts.

In parallel, for some time, there have been other signs of a gradual shift, visibly connected to the business world. "In fact, things have started to move," says Alexander Dmitrenko, who has lived and worked in the country since 2009, "The awareness is growing that there are economic arguments to change course."

Japan's fast-aging society is facing a quickly tightening labor market. According to a 2018 survey by Persol Research and Consulting and Chuo University, the country will be subject to a shortage of 6.44 million workers in 2030. This number is about five times higher than the Ministry of Health, Labor and Welfare had estimated a year before and equates to about 5% of Japan's 2017 population.[43]

"It is clear that this can and will impede Japan's increase of productivity and growth," Dmitrenko says. He is a native Ukrainian, got master's degrees from several colleges, such as NYU School of Law and University of Toronto and now holds a passport for Canada. Currently, he leads the "Global Investigations practice" at corporate law firm Freshfields Bruckhaus Deringer's Tokyo office, focusing on a wide range of regulatory compliance matters, such as anti-bribery, export controls, anti-money-laundering, cybersecurity, data protection, and human rights.

Having lived there for more than a decade now, Dmitrenko, who is openly gay, has fallen in love with Japan, its cities, nature, culture and people. More specifically, for some years already, he has had a Japanese partner. "From time to time, we take our dog and flee from exciting Tokyo to calm Hachijō-jima, an island in the Pacific, which administratively belongs to Tokyo, although it's about 350 kilometers away. I adore the ashitaba tea cultivated on Hachijō-jima – it's the best. We have a 'dacha,' a small house in the countryside," he says, using a word that betrays his Ukrainian roots." That's not all. "In fact, I am a cultural and tourism ambassador for this gorgeous remote place, something I am quite proud of. It helps me feel to be an accepted member of Japanese society as opposed to an outsider trying to tell the Japanese what to do," he adds.

Alongside his core professional work (and private love for Japan), Dmitrenko is one of the co-founders of LLAN, short for Lawyers for LGBT & Allies Network, set up in 2015. As one of its Co-Chairs, he has become a "white-collar activist" in matters of LGBT+ inclusion in Japanese workplaces.

In fact, LLAN has become a major driver of "equality for all." That's its mission statement, accessible on its website in Japanese and English. The nonprofit works "to promote the understanding of LGBT and other sexual minorities and to eliminate discrimination based on sexual orientation or gender identity," providing legal assistance and information, setting up or co-hosting events, supporting cross-company initiatives and more. It aims to "contribute to the realization of a fair society where all people may realize their full potential in safety and where due consideration shall be given to individual dignity and diversity."[44] Currently, LLAN has over 500 affiliated members which, says Dmitrenko, is "fast growth in just a short time, and we continue to grow."

## Cultural obstacles

For a long time, Japanese society has been considered quite homogeneous and, in some way, even hostile in taking up cultural or foreign influences. "Japanese culture at work and in society as a whole is significantly less open to change than, for example, Anglo-Saxon cultures and business," confirms Naosuke Fujita. He is also a LLAN co-founder and the organization's second Co-Chair, working closely with Dmitrenko.

Fujita knows what he is talking about. He holds a law degree from Waseda University, alongside Keiō University one of the most prestigious private Japanese colleges, and University of Michigan Law School. For more than ten years, he was a managing director and the General Counsel for Goldman Sachs Japan. "The coming out of a colleague in 2015 inspired me to help promote LGBT+ rights and awareness at Goldman Sachs and in Japan," he says. Among other things, within the frame of LLAN and while still with Goldman Sachs, he spearheaded a campaign to educate Japanese law firms on the economic benefits of credible LGBT+ D&I, inspiring many of them to modify their policies, e.g. ensuring that same-sex partners, although not allowed to marry, get the same benefits as married heterosexual partners.

In June 2017, the *Financial Times* recognized Fujita's contributions with the "Most Innovative General Counsel Award", honoring, among other things, his engagements related to LGBT+ inclusion in the Japanese law industry and to LLAN. Having retired from Goldman Sachs in 2020, he has since continued his work for LLAN as a straight ally activist in the business world.

The fact that just a couple of months after his retirement from Goldman Sachs, he was lured to become the General Counsel at highly prestigious Government Pension Insurance Fund (GPIF) did not change that. GPIF, established by the Japanese government, is the largest public fund investor in the country by assets and manages one of biggest pools of retirement savings globally.

## An index – and SoftBank as an example

Dmitrenko's and Fujita's initiatives are supported by the increasing diffusion of knowledge about the economic benefits of LGBT+ inclusion, and have been buoyed up by other developments. For example, the nonprofit work with Pride (wwP) joined forces with 24 companies and groups over a period of six months to develop an index measuring corporate efforts to support LGBT+ inclusion.[45] In June 2016, the first edition of what wwP has called the PRIDE Index was launched. With companies fighting to attract the best talents in the tight Japanese labor market, many are becoming increasingly engaged in working to meet the index's standards.

This is not limited to global corporates headquartered outside Japan. An example of local involvement is SoftBank, the Japanese multinational conglomerate headquartered in Tokyo, led by founder Masayoshi Son. One of the largest publicly traded firms in the country, it holds stakes in many technology, financial, energy and other companies and also runs Vision Fund, which, with about $100 billion in capital, is one of the world's largest technology-focused venture capital funds.

"The index has helped to raise awareness of changing Japanese corporate cultures," says Fujita. An example supports this view. Soft-Bank with its roughly 75,000 employees globally, is now publicly celebrating LGBT+ friendliness, communicating on its website, for instance, about receiving the PRIDE Index's "Gold" rating, which is the highest, three years in a row as of 2019. The firm also stresses that it supports the mission of Tokyo Rainbow Pride and that Soft-Bank employees and their families have participated in the parades in recent years. The interior of one of their branches, located along the parade course, a press release says, "was decorated with a rainbow theme" and employees handed out limited-edition shopping bags. They were also "engaged in awareness activities by wearing original t-shirts, and the company's LGBT initiatives were introduced in a panel exhibition inside the venue."[46]

SoftBank also issues marketing communications on its nondiscrimination policies, provides awareness trainings and much more, all necessary in reaching the top of corporate LGBT+ equality indexes such as the Japanese one too. Among other things, in October 2016, SoftBank further reports, it amended "its internal rules to recognize same-sex partners as spouses in line with the definition defined in its internal documentation, in addition to spouses recognized under Japanese law."

## Campaigning for equal marriage on economic grounds with strong partners

"One peculiarity of Japan's way of changing course is that the campaigning of businesses for equal marriage plays a crucial role," Dmitrenko reports. "Given the specificities of Japanese cultural resistance to outside influence, that's perhaps a very helpful move," Fujita adds, "because it touches a very basic human thing: family relationships, and, related to this, the promise of loyalty to 'our' group and stability, which for us, as Japanese, are highest values."

In September 2018, at LLAN's festive Annual Equality Gala, attended by over 250 people, the American Chamber of Commerce in Japan (ACCJ) launched one of its so-called "viewpoints," and it was a special one. The influential ACCJ was founded in 1948 and is a nonprofit membership organization within Tokyo, Osaka, and Nagoya, representing over 3,000 members from 600 companies and 40 countries.

With this viewpoint, ACCJ became a crucial player advocating for equal marriage on behalf of a growing section of the Japanese business world, whether domestic or headquartered outside the country. A press release summarized the core argument targeted at the Japanese government as follows: "Legalizing marriage equality would be economically good for business in Japan."

In fact, about 28 countries have currently legalized same-sex marriage, "including many of Japan's trading partners." Among the G7 countries, comprising the seven major developed countries – the US, the UK, Canada, Germany, France, Italy and Japan – all the others have equal marriage. In Japan, meanwhile, LGBT+ couples also have no legal marital protection, and national anti-discrimination policy does not exist.[47]

This has clear economic implications. "This disparity makes Japan a less attractive option for LGBT couples compared to many other countries vying for the same talent," argues an updated ACCL viewpoint on the issue two years later, "Correcting the inequality before the law would also conform with the global best practice and would allow Japanese companies doing business overseas, and international companies doing business in Japan, to apply the same standards and benefit guidelines to all their employees, regardless of their sexual orientation or current county of residence."[48]

Right from the start, the viewpoint's demand to the Japanese government was endorsed by the Australian & New Zealand Chamber of Commerce in Japan (ANZCCJ), British Chamber of Commerce in Japan (BCCJ), Canadian Chamber of Commerce in Japan (CCCJ), and Ireland Japan Chamber of Commerce (IJCC).[49] In their common position, the five chambers focused on tight talent markets and international competitiveness, emphasizing the business advantages of D&I for better use of human resource potential and increased productivity via minimization of minority stress and related psychological and health costs. In addition, they pointed out the positive impact on Japan's global reputation that would come from "demonstrating

its continued commitment to individual liberty and progressive ide-
als."[50] In a nutshell, the viewpoint's arguments stressed the business
and economic case for equal marriage in the country.

"LLAN has worked closely with the ACCJ and other entities to
ensure and expand support for this viewpoint," says Fujita. Dmitrenko, who was among its key initiators and authors, adds that they
also "learned a lot from the US, in particular from the Amicus Brief
submitted by 379 major corporations in support of marriage equality
before the US Supreme Court in 2015."

Since the launch of this joint initiative of the five chambers in
2018, over 100 companies have publicly committed to it, many headquartered in Japan, such as SoftBank, Panasonic, and Lixil (one of the
country's manufacturing giants). The number is steadily growing.
Currently, over 50% of the endorsing firms belong to the law, finance
and consulting industries. But there are also tech giants like Amazon,
Google and Microsoft and important European-headquartered players such as Swedish H&M, German Deutsche Bank, Swiss UBS, and
French LVMH.

Also, further chambers such as the DCCJ (Danish Chamber of
Commerce Japan), the SCCJ (Swedish Chamber of Commerce and
Industry in Japan), the BLCCJ (Belgian-Luxembourg Chamber of
Commerce in Japan), and the EBC (European Business Council
in Japan) have become supporters, along with major Japanese law
associations such as JILA (Japan In-House Lawyers Association) and
Women in Law Japan. In a country where the (large) group is (generally) perceived as a lot more important than the individual, this is an
important development.

Recently, there have been a television series and manga with
LGBT+ protagonists, reflecting to some extent an improving public
understanding of sexual and gender minorities. On the other hand,
the Ministry of Health, Labor and Welfare's recent survey of about
10,000 Japanese firms, all with over 50 employees, reveals that there
is still a lot to do. The survey focused on LGBT+ inclusion-related
policies. Of the around 2,400 companies responding, only 11% had
implemented measures targeting LGBT+ employees. The larger the
companies, the more likely they were to have such measures. But
over 70% of the responding companies believed – strongly or to
some extent – that their firm should create a workplace environment
accepting of sexual minorities.[51]

"You need patience," LLAN Co-Chair Dmitrenko says, "Our lawyers network has only been around for about five years now. Japan does not change fast, but it changes – if you act collectively."

"That's what we are doing," his Co-Chair peer Fujita adds, "working to change elements of the culture by respecting it."

## Australia

In Australia, which belongs to the top 15 of the world's strongest economies, Pride in Diversity is the most important local LGBT+ inclusion program, and it also has an index. The background to its formation is the establishment in 1985 of ACON, short for AIDS Council of New South Wales, Australia. Today, this is the country's largest not-for-profit health organization for people of diverse sexualities and genders. Part of its work focuses on making life and work more inclusive of LGBT+ people, in the service of which it runs various programs.

ACON's Pride in Diversity program was co-founded by two public partners – the Australian Federal Police and the Department of Defence – and six corporates: Goldman Sachs, IBM, Dutch-based ING bank, KPMG, Lendlease (an Australian property group), and Telstra, the multinational telecommunication giant headquartered in Melbourne.

As with some similar programs and organizations for other countries I have referred to, Pride in Diversity supports employers in advancing LGBT+ inclusion, focusing on issues around human resource management, organizational change, and workplace diversity.

In addition, it publishes the annual Australian Workplace Equality Index (AWEI). In its general goal and approach, AWEI, despite some differences, is similar to the indexes managed by the US-based HRC and the UK's Stonewall (for more detail on Stonewall, see Part IV, Chapter 6). Based on the index results, awards are handed out in various categories, with different levels of achievement recognized as gold, silver, or platinum.

Companies were also engaged when in 2017 the Australian Marriage Equality Campaign was launched, achieving its goal in December of that year. 851 firms publicly supported the campaign.[52] Later in this book, I will say a bit more about this initiative and one of its leading campaign managers, Tiernan Brady, who now works for corporate law firm Clifford Chance pushing to advance LGBT+ inclusion there.

Inspired by the idea of LGBT+ role model lists, as we have seen first compiled by British social business INvolve in 2013, an Australian ranking followed in 2016. It was consulting and auditing giant Deloitte that introduced the country's first list of 50 LGBT+ out executives. The second edition, for which Deloitte partnered with Google, was published two years later, in 2018. That year, the list included role models from large corporates, the public sector, government agencies, and also small-to-medium enterprises.

Finally, there is Out For Australia, a major nonprofit aiming to support aspiring LGBT+ professionals through events, role models, and more. One of its major initiatives is a mentoring program that helps graduate students and professionals, supporting them in their transition from university to the workplace, in career changes or in reaching other career goals.

Out For Australia has a long list of sponsoring and supporting companies. Currently, it includes a variety of global firms like Baker McKenzie, BCG, PwC, Accenture, and Deloitte, but also local operations such as TAL, one of the country's life insurers. It also issues awards at an event called 30 Under 30, run with BCG, aiming to draw attention to the next generation of LGBT+ role models.

Also addressing the country's youth a bit more lately is consulting firm Accenture. In a way this can be seen as a response to some recent Accenture research. Among other things, one of its findings was that 64% of Australian LGBT+ employees believe their gender identity/ gender expression or their sexual orientation has slowed their career progress at work. The report also says 19% remain closeted at work[53] – which on the one hand means that more than four-fifths are out – as the title of the report I have referred to earlier indicates: *Visible Growth; Invisible Fears: Getting to equal: 2020 Pride.*

In September 2020, Accenture announced that it was partnering with the Pinnacle Foundation. The foundation not only offers educational scholarships but also support from mentors – thought to be role models – who share the same academic and professional interests, gender identity, and sexual orientation. The consultancy committed for three years to be a Gold Partner and award "The Accenture Scholarship" to young LGBT+ Australians studying in commercial disciplines.

Overall, Australia is considered quite advanced in terms of companies fostering LGBT+ inclusion, visibly internally and externally. This also includes nonprofits on a city level, such as the Sydney Gay and Lesbian Business Association (SGLBA), one of the oldest organizations of its kind globally, set up as far back as 1981. Sidney is one of the country's largest cities, with more than five million inhabitants. Currently, SGLBA is sponsored by Australia Post, the country's postal service.[54] Among a variety of initiatives, programs, and events, it has the SGLBA Education Fund, providing financial grants to LGBT+ individuals "undertaking a course of study in a business or commerce-related discipline which meaningfully, substantially and demonstrably benefits their life or, through them, the lives of other people within the Australian community."[55]

## The Netherlands

Very advanced, too, is the Netherlands, not least due to the Amsterdam-based Workplace Pride Foundation, Workplace Pride for short, briefly referred to earlier in this book. It was in co-founded in 2006 by David Pollard, who is now its executive director. Pollard is a US American but has lived in Amsterdam for more than a quarter of a century, almost as long as he has been with his German husband: about 30 years.

Workplace Pride is known for being particularly active, innovative, transparent, and – beyond its focus on its home country – very globally oriented. The NGO's website is not in Dutch, only in English.

Although the Netherlands has just 17 million inhabitants compared to about 60 million in Italy, the Dutch nonprofit can boast a list of members almost as long as its Italian cousin organization Parks: currently about 70. In addition to numerous well-known multinational companies, including strong Dutch global brands such as Unilever, Heineken, Shell, ING, Philips, Booking.com, and Rabobank, Workplace Pride also has other high-level members such as several Dutch ministries, universities, and cities like Amsterdam and The Hague.

## Workplace Pride Foundation as a role model

Because of the depth and width of its membership structure and activities and its international scope, for many continental European cousin organizations such as German Prout at Work and Spanish REDI, Workplace Pride is a role model. As mentioned earlier, there is a regular exchange of experiences and ideas between these organizations. And sometimes there is also very practical support. When, for example, in fall 2018, Prout at Work decided to increase its level of international scope and organize its first English conference on LGBT+ inclusion, Pollard served as moderator during the day and also helped invite speakers.

Beyond a number of events, trainings, webinars, summits, and galas, Workplace Pride also conducts various surveys and works with universities to promote research. For example, it cooperates closely with Leiden University's Jojanneke van der Toorn, whose job title is Professor of LGBT Workplace Inclusion. "The chair was initiated by Workplace Pride," says Pollard. "It was created in 2016 as a joint effort between the university and our foundation, with Dutch Telecom company KPN as five-year-sponsor." The chair covers the whole range of LGBT+ work issues but focuses in particular on organizational psychology. "It is the only university chair in the world on this topic," Pollard says. On their website, Workplace Pride calls it the Workplace Pride Chair at Leiden University.[56]

Workplace Pride also produces a highly regarded global benchmark study on LGBT+ equality levels in member companies, intended as a tool for further fostering LGBT+ inclusion in the workplace. "The global benchmark study is an evidence-based survey in which participating organizations must provide actual proof to support their choices made on the multiple-choice survey," Pollard explains.

"It takes into account the global activities of participating organizations and not just in one country," says Marijn Pijnenburg, a business development executive for diversity, in particular LGBT+, at IBM. Here, the native Dutchman, who is based in Amsterdam and currently active in Europe, the Middle East and Africa (EMEA), is an expert. In his role, he covers organizations and events related to his job in 34 countries, including some with legislation hostile to LGBT+ people, such as Kenya, Morocco, Qatar and Russia.

Basically, Pijnenburg says, he advises IBM customers and top executives "on how to leverage human capital, diversity, inclusion, LGBT+ and collaboration to fostering innovation and driving business." He also manages IBM's partnerships with LGBT+/diversity organizations throughout EMEA, for example, with Diversity Pro in Slovakia or Pride Biz in Austria, and has already initiated several Diversity and LGBT+ Business Forums in this region.

Recently, in October 2020, "IBM was the first organization ever to score 100% in the global Workplace Pride benchmark's seven-year history," he adds. Pollard explains, "This is particularly relevant as we have continued to raise the bar each year to accommodate the changes in the workplace landscape for LGBT+ people." (For more on IBM's pioneering role in some areas of LGBT+ D&I, see Part II, Chapter IV.)

Pollard and Pijnenburg meet each other quite often. Since 2018, Workplace Pride has provided a forum called Global Leaders Council (GLC). Pijnenburg, who is in his late-40s and has worked with IBM for more than 25 years, has been a member of the GLC and a frequent guest for many years. GLC meetings are designed as a quarterly discussion amongst foundation members. "Their focus is mostly on international topics, but national and more general topics are also covered," Pijnenburg says.

Pollard and his team must also be considered exemplary when it comes to transparency around the costs and benefits of different levels of membership, itemizing both in detail on their website. Currently, there are three levels: €5,500 makes you a Member, €11,000 makes you a Partner, and €19,500 makes you a Leader.[57]

About ten years ago, in July 2011, Workplace Pride also launched the Declaration of Amsterdam for an LGBT Inclusive Workplace,[58] another innovation well ahead of what was happening elsewhere. Among the first signatories a couple months later, alongside a group of Dutch-based multinationals, were the city of The Hague (seat of the Dutch government), and global corporates such as Accenture, IBM, and Cisco.

As of the end of August 2020, the Declaration has been signed by 28 employers. Basically, it promotes:
- The creation of inclusive corporate cultures where LGBT+ employees feel valued, can be their authentic selves, and can realize their full potential
- The creation of working environments for LGBT+ people that go beyond minimum legal requirements
- Active and visible leadership from straight allies and LGBT+ role models to foster LGBT+ inclusion in the workplace.[59]

On its second page, the two-page declaration breaks down these general commitments with a call-to-action in the form of ten points, some recommendations, some commands, including a number that are quite innovative. The ninth, for instance, recommends that "Employers should dedicate a minimum of 1 Euro per employee in the organization to support LGBT programs and employee resource groups."[60]

## Strong support from executives

Furthermore, numerous top-level executives are involved and very visibly so, attending, for example, Workplace Pride's annual leadership awards gala, New Year's reception, or membership-only events during the legendary Amsterdam Pride celebrations. Attracting hundreds of thousands of visitors every year, these celebrations have become a mainstream mega event. Next to *Koningsdag*, or "King's Day," a national holiday marking the Dutch King's birthday, Amsterdam Pride is now the largest festival in the city. It is held annually on the first weekend in August in the city center, encompassing a large variety of events. The highlight is the Canal Parade, the carnival-like parade of imaginatively costumed or scantily clad participants in colorfully decorated boats through the canals of Amsterdam, covered widely by the media. Many companies are present with their own boats, inviting managers, employees, and clients, showing their logos, and displaying their openness and tolerance.

Global consultancy Deloitte has done this for a couple years, with the participation of Leon Pieters, who has been with Deloitte for more than 20 years. He is a partner there, has served in a variety of roles across Europe, the Middle East, and Africa, and worked for multinationals and global organizations in the US and all major European countries. Currently, he leads the firm's global consumer industry and mostly works with clients from the food and beverage industry, as well as serving some NGOs. For a number of years, Pieters has also been part of his firm's D&I council, and the sponsoring partner for the Dutch chapter of GLOBE, Deloitte's LGBT+ network.

Pieters, who has been with his partner for more than 20 years and is based in Rotterdam, appears on stage at Deloitte and externally quite often to talk about LGBT+ issues, for example, in internal webinars, in a live speech on stage within Deloitte worldwide, or at a conference attended by over 1,000 MBA students at Amsterdam University's business school in 2019.[61]

"When I share my story, I propagate very much to 'fully accept yourself' and to 'bring your authentic self to work,'" Pieters reports.

"When I became a partner at Deloitte some 15 years ago, I did not want to be perceived as 'the gay partner.'" So, although he was out at work from day one, he was not engaged in LGBT+ issues in the firm or in supporting the community for a long time.

However, as he relates in an article on Deloitte's website, "... the coming out of Apple CEO Tim Cook has inspired me. I feel like now I am in the position to take action. If I could only help one person by showing my face and telling my story, I consider it a success."[62] He realized, he says, that rather than hiding, he should use the "gifts, skills, and personality features" he had "been given as a gay man and leader. Just as Tim Cook has put it." (For more on Cook's coming out in 2014, see Part II, Chapter 4.)

At a certain point, Pieters consciously decided that he wanted to be a role model. "It took me 15 years, until age 29, to come out," he says, "In a pre-internet era and living on the countryside, I did not have any role models. Now, at Deloitte, I can be one – including bringing my partner to company events."

In fact, it's not just the big speeches on stage, but also the small things that make for change. Regarding his homosexuality, Pieters says, he has not had any real negative experiences within the firm, "aside from a few – not even bad intentioned – but nonetheless bad jokes. I always respond by pointing out that these kinds of remarks can be offensive. People often do not realize that."[63] And since 2018, Pieters has also been a nonexecutive member of the board at Workplace Pride, which Deloitte Netherlands has supported for many years.

## Helped by the Ministry of Foreign Affairs

Workplace Pride's strong commitment to internationalism is reflected in its Advisory Board, which currently consists of five members. One, for example, is Graham Sparks, a Brit who was with Shell for about 35 years, most recently as the firm's Chief D&I Officer. A second is American Claudia Brind-Woody, a top-level out IBM executive whom we have met before.

As far as internationalism is concerned, Workplace Pride's close connections to the Dutch government are sometimes helpful to it too, for example when it comes to organizing its international conferences on LGBT+ inclusion in the workplace. These innovative events, which started in Krakow, Poland, in 2015, bring together employers, employees, and civil society at locations around the globe, sometimes in countries that are or can be dangerous for LGBT+ people. Usually, they are held in the offices of a global company – Shell's in Krakow, for example.

The box gives an overview of activities from the conference's start:

---

## Workplace Pride – International events on LGBT+ inclusion in the workplace

- 2015: Krakow, Poland; and Prague, Czech Republic
- 2016: Bangkok, Thailand; and Paramaribo, Surinam
- 2017: Chennai, India; and Manilla, Philippines
- 2018: Hong Kong, China; Moscow, Russia; and Nairobi, Kenya
- 2019: Kiev, Ukraine; and Singapore
- 2020: Taipei, Taiwan

---

As the box shows, in 2018, Workplace Pride organized three events. One took place in Hong Kong with Accenture as the hosting partner and I attended. The event on LGBT+ inclusion in the workplace in Greater China, moderated by Workplace Pride Executive Director Pollard, was preceded by a reception at a wonderful colonial-style residence of the local Dutch Consul General,who also gave the event's closing remarks – strong signs of the Dutch government's commitment to the cause of LGBT+ inclusion abroad as well as at home.

In fact, the Netherlands' Ministry of Foreign Affairs is a frequent partner for Workplace Pride's international activities. This included, for example, an event in Moscow called Executive Roundtable: Putting Diversity and Inclusion on the Agenda in Russia. Out LGBT+ people in Russia are discriminated against, sometimes even exposed not only to hate speech but to brutal violence. In order to cope with this challenging local context (which I will address with respect to the Russian business world in more depth in Part IV, Chapter 10), the Moscow event took place at the Dutch Embassy, with the opening words spoken by the Dutch Deputy Ambassador to Russia.[64]

The official invitation showed, as host, the Government of the Netherlands with its logo, while Workplace Pride was listed as an organizer alongside local NGO Coming Out from St. Petersburg. Presenters were Shell, IBM, Accenture, and Sodexo, the French-headquartered food services and facility management giant.

Post-pandemic, Pollard has plans to set up a variety of conferences. One, for example, will take place in Denmark. As part of the Copenhagen 2021 World Pride festivities, there will be Human Rights conference, where Workplace Pride will organize the block related to the workplace issues. There are also plans for India, Romania, and Spain, here as part of the European Lesbian Conference, to take place in October 2021.

## Spain

We have already looked at the largest Southern European economy, Italy, with Barilla's LGBT+ turnaround story. In the second largest, Spain, with about 47 million inhabitants, there has been a significant increase in recent years in the number of organizations and employers working for LGBT+ inclusion in the workplace.

For instance, there is EMIDIS, a program focused on advancing LGBT+ inclusion and external positioning in local companies. It was launched by FELGTB, short for *Federación Estatal de Lesbianas, Gays, Transexuales y Bisexuales*, the country's main organization working for LGBT+ equality in society in general.

A brief aside: in Spain, the internationally mainstreamed terminology for LGBT – with different endings such as "+," as preferred in this book, or "Q," "Q+," "LGBTI," "LGBTIQ," or many other options – has not been accepted so far. Very often the initials used are "LGTB" – putting the "T" before the "B."

EMIDIS explicitly acknowledges being inspired by the work and indices of the US HRC and British Stonewall, aiming to deliver tools and benchmarks for businesses in Spain to help them push LGBT+ D&I forward. In 2016 the first EMIDIS report was published. Based on 25 companies taking part in a survey on their LGBT+ D&I strategies, it aimed to highlight best practice and thereby contribute to the business case for LGBT+ D&I.[65]

The questions were grouped into five areas: equality policies; training; seminars and workshops; business culture; employee networks;

and external communications.[66] About 40% of the firms participated anonymously, 60% openly. The latter were invited to be part of a ranking. The five employers in the lead, scoring more than four-fifths of the available points, were, in this order: Procter & Gamble, SAP, IBM, Accenture, and IE University.

A second survey was also carried out, but with no ranking. Instead companies that achieved a high enough score were entitled to use a label certifying them as being committed to LGBTI D&I.[67] 15 companies made the grade.

## REDI

In 2015, a year before EMIDIS started, another Spanish organization was set up: REDI, short for *Red Empresarial por la Diversidad e Inclusión LGBTI* ("Business Network for LGBTI Diversity and Inclusion"). In the beginning, REDI was a network of LGBT+ D&I professionals. In 2018, it was formally founded as nonprofit, based on member organizations. REDI has supported EMIDIS' work from its beginning.

REDI as a nonprofit developed fast. It started with 13 founding companies. They included multinationals such as Accenture, AXA, Procter & Gamble, SAP, and corporate law firm Hogan Lovells. And they also included Spanish-based companies such as Uría Menéndez, a business law firm, and Amadeus, a provider for the global tourism and travel industry.

The nonprofit's goals, programs, and tools are similar to those of its cousin organizations in the liberal Western world such as German Prout at Work, Dutch Workplace Pride, Italian Parks, American Out & Equal, or Stonewall in the UK, though it is still less sophisticated. Like those organizations, however, as the country's first cross-company network of LGBT+ leaders, experts, and activists in business, it seeks to advance LGBT+ inclusion in workplaces. And like them, it is designed as a forum for consultation, training, and sharing best practice in workshops, conferences, and other events and formats.

REDI's proximity of mission and means to these other organizations is no coincidence. One of its co-founders, Miguel Castro, is a senior director and leading D&I manager at SAP, with experience in business development and consulting all over the world: in Europe, North America, the Asia Pacific region, Latin America, and Africa. Before he went back to his home country, Castro, who is openly gay, lived and worked in other European countries such as Germany, the UK, and Denmark, and speaks both English and German fluently. He has known many relevant players at REDI's European cousin organizations for many years and served in various roles on advisory boards and special committees at Prout at Work Foundation, Workplace Pride, and OUTstanding, the aforementioned initiator of the first Out Executive role model lists.

Currently, beyond his role at SAP, Castro serves, among other things, as guest professor for D&I in the Inditex-sponsored program for sustainability and social innovation at the University of A Coruña, and as chairman of REDI's board.

## Fast growth

The network is financed mainly by its member companies, with its annual membership fees varying according to the size of business. It has no formal employees but collaborates on a permanent basis with a team of external people composed of two specialist consultants (acting as codirectors), communication and administrative suppliers, and external collaborators on an ad-hoc basis.

Currently, Óscar Muñoz Hernández and Marta Fernández Herraiz serve as REDI's managing directors. Fernández is also an activist on lesbian issues on multiple fronts. For example, currently she is a member of the core team at EL*C, short for Eurocentralasian Lesbian* Community. This community, sometimes also referred to as European Lesbian Conference, is focused not on the working world in particular but on overall inclusion. The current core team covers a range of nationalities beyond Spain: French, Italian, Dutch, Belgian, Austrian, Greek, Swiss, Serbian, Albanian, Moldovan, and Kazakhstani.

Moreover, this time specifically focused on the working world, Fernández is the CEO of LesWorking (LW), a platform she founded in 2014. LW's website says, "We are lawyers, consultants, artists, entrepreneurs, doctors, journalists ... We live in Spain, Latin America, and the rest of the world. We form a global community of restless, hard-working women who connect through LW to weave networks and move our projects forward."[68] Basically, LW aims to create an international professional network, providing participants with tools and best practice examples to cope with the specific challenges facing lesbian and bisexual women at work. So far, the focus is primarily on Spain.

The list of LW's supporting partners – companies and other organizations – is still short, though it includes the US Embassy in Madrid. Nevertheless, LW's resonance in the Spanish media and at universities is significant. For example, Fernández has been invited to speak at the highly regarded IE Business School, part of private Spanish IE University, which offers tuition in Spanish and English[69] (see box).

---

## IE University, the IE Out & Allies Club, and the LGBT@Work conference

As mentioned above, Spain's IE University made the top five in the first EMIDIS ranking of Spanish employers advancing LGBT+ D&I in the workplace. Its Latin motto may have predetermined its commitment: *Unus Mundus Mentes Diversae*: "One World, Diverse Minds."

For many years already, the university has had an LGBT+ student's network on campus, the IE Out & Allies Club, which has grown substantially to about 40,000 members currently, including alumni. The club is led by active students and organizes events open to all members of the IE University community. They include scholarly, educational, networking, and cocktail events. The club also engages socially beyond its activities on campus by supporting *Fundación Eddy-G*, the first LGBT+ shelter for youth in Spain, through biannual fundraising events and volunteer opportunities. Overall the club aims to raise awareness and broaden understanding and support for LGBT+ at the university, in workplaces, and in societies.

Every year, the university also hosts the LGBT@Work conference, fully managed by the IE Out & Allies Club. Established in 2006, it is the longest-running LGBT+ work conference in Europe, and the third largest business school LGBT+ conference in the world.

The two largest, ROMBA in the US and EurOUT in the UK, I will describe in detail in Part IV, Chapters 9. Similarly to them, LGBT@ Work aims to promote the exchange of LGBT+-related ideas and provide a networking platform for LGBT+ students, professionals, and allies. Although there is no job fair with separate company booths, the conference is, in a certain sense, also a career event: IE students and general conference attendees can share their CVs with the organizers to be included in a CV book given to the sponsors for their recruitment and talent acquisition departments.

Usually the conference takes place in early July, with speakers, sponsors, and attendees from around the globe. In 2020, due to the COVID-19 pandemic, it went virtual. For this event, it also added the "+" to its name – making it "LGBT+@Work" – to acknowledge other sexual orientations and gender identities.

It's not just the student-led conference itself that stands out in Spain. Some of its speakers also represent an innovative and global scope. The 2020 edition, which is still accessible on the conference website, provides two interesting examples.

One of these was Phyll Opuku-Gyimah, also known as Lady Phyll. She identifies as black lesbian or queer and has been an LGBT+ rights and anti-racism activist, especially in the UK, for over 20 years. In 2005 she co-founded and is now Executive Director of UK Black Pride, Europe's largest Pride event for LGBT+ people of African, Asian, Caribbean, Latin American, and Middle Eastern descent. In 2019, she became the first black woman to be appointed Executive Director of the British Kaleidoscope Trust, which works for equal rights in countries where it is legally and/or culturally difficult or dangerous to be LGBT+. Long before the Black Lives Matter movement took center stage in spring 2020, Opuku-Gyimah was strongly engaged in drawing attention to the challenge of structural racism in society, including the LGBT+ community.

Another standout speaker at the 2020 LGBT+@Work conference was Jay Lin, founder and CEO of Portico Media, a Taiwan-based media company specializing in content development, production, and distribution for film, TV, and the internet. In 2017, Lin also co-founded the Taiwan International Queer Film Festival. And in 2019, he was included in Newsweek's prestigious "Creative Class" for the year.[70]

Perhaps most importantly, in 2016, Lin launched GagaOOLala,[71] Asia's first LGBT+ streaming service.[72] It aims to share Asian LGBT+-centered stories and characters, breaking clichés and prejudices.

The service is available worldwide and has grown fast, also reaching non-LGBT+ people interested in good films and the reality of LGBT+ people's lives. GagaOOLala was also one of five founding members of the Marriage Equality Coalition Taiwan,[73] the country's main lobbying group working for this aim, which in 2019 led to Taiwan becoming the first Asian country to allow same-sex partners to marry.

The IE Out & Allies Club announced that almost 2,000 people from 92 countries attended the 2020 LGBT+@Work conference, an even higher number than before. And, as it has done every year, the event not only had some outstanding speakers, it also worked with some big-name partners including, for example, software giant Salesforce, Glamazon (Amazon's ERG),[74] US pharmaceutical corporates Gilead and Johnson & Johnson, Spanish banking primus Santander – and REDI.

REDI's second managing director, Óscar Muñoz, is also one of the network's co-founders. And like Fernández and Castro, he has been a speaker at earlier editions of the IE University LGBT+@Work conference described in the box.

Until 2016, Muñoz had been with consumer goods giant Procter & Gamble (P&G) as a consumer expert and marketing manager for almost 18 years, focused for part of that time not just on Spanish but on European markets. Although, at a global level, US-headquartered P&G was quite active in advancing LGBT+ D&I and supported an employee network, in Spain – often characterized by its "macho culture" – things were different. After his late coming out to his boss and in the firm, Muñoz, alongside his core job, quickly became involved with D&I issues. He was appointed a member of P&G Southern Europe's Diversity Committee and leader of its LGBT+ D&I activities. As such he laid the groundwork – ensuring top management support, initiating regular employee surveys and trainings, integrating with HR – on which P&G climbed to the top position in the aforementioned EMIDIS ranking.

When Muñoz left P&G in 2016, he set up his own business, mpátika*, the name derived from the Spanish word *empática*, meaning "empathetic." Among other things, it provides consultancy to companies on D&I issues, including LGBT+ D&I. This includes, for example, designing a D&I roadmap linked to business, awareness workshops, product positioning, and campaigns for diverse target groups such as LGBT+ people.

Muñoz also teaches diversity management at the masters and undergraduate levels, and conducts research, sometimes in conjunction with mpática*. For example, he was, among other things, responsible for the research design of the ADIM project, on Advancing in LGBT Diversity Management in the Public and Private Sector in Spain and Portugal, which was funded by the European Union and led by the Secretary of State for Equality in Spain, the equivalent in Portugal, and Complutense University of Madrid.[75] It involved 16 sixteen global and local companies and eight public universities in Spain and Portugal that wanted to improve LGBT+ inclusion. One result of the research was the ADIM LGBT+ Guide for businesses and organizations.[76]

Mpátika*'s LGBT+ work is defined by the paradox that Spain, with respect to its legal situation, is considered one of the most advanced in Europe for LGBT+ inclusion, but it is actually significantly behind in workplace inclusion. ILGA Europe's 2020 Rainbow Europe ranking, to which I referred in Part I, Chapter 2, ranks Spain seventh after Malta, Luxemburg, Belgium, Norway, and Denmark.[77] Across a wide variety of criteria – including employment – the ranking reflects the human rights situation, as defined by law and policy, for LGBT+ people in 49 European countries.

## Support by studies and universities

On the other hand, a 2019 study on LGBT+ inclusion in Spanish workplaces[78] showed that only 38% of LGBT+ people in Spain are completely out at work. ILGA Europe in its 2020 report refers to this finding,[79] and gives its source: mpátika*. Muñoz directed this recent quantitative study on LGBT+ D&I in the Spanish workplace, teaming up with the aforementioned nonprofit FELGTB, the global market researcher IPSOS, REDI and – on the academic side – Complutense University of Madrid. The prestigious university, founded in the 13th century, is one of the oldest in the world and, with currently about 85,000 students, one of the largest in Europe. In September 2019, it launched a master's program in LGBT+ studies.

Among many other things, Muñoz's study also ranked brands – products or companies – on LGBT+ friendliness (see box).

---

## Top 15 LGBT+-friendly brands (products or companies) in Spain[80]

1) Ikea
2) Google
3) Apple
4) Coca-Cola
5) IBM
6) Absolut
7) Room Mate Hotels
8) Nike
9) Vips (Restaurants)
10) Ben & Jerry's
11) Facebook
12) Netflix
13) Procter & Gamble
14) Levi's
15) Adidas

---

"LGBT+ people clearly reward brands – companies or products – that make their commitment to the LGBT+ community visible," consumer, brand, and LGBT+ D&I expert Muñoz says. "For those brands, as role models on innovation, it makes sense to develop marketing campaigns directly targeted to the LGBT+ community – to reinforce companies' visibility as an open-minded, tolerant employer and corporate citizen. Of course, this can only be credible if they have internal LGBT+ D&I programs and a corresponding working climate."

Within just over two years, REDI has grown extraordinarily fast from 12 members to more than 90 (as of December 2020),[81] and come to represent over 100,000 people.[82] Member companies – which range from small to large – come from a variety of countries, industries, and sectors, including consulting, communications, technology, banking, insurance, and higher education.

REDI has also managed to attract the attention of the influential organization CEOE, short for *Confederación Española de Organizaciones Empresariales*[83] ("Confederation of Employers and Industries in Spain.") On the news section of its website, CEOE covered a major February 2020 REDI event in Madrid at length.[84]

REDI also plans to launch role model lists like the ones we have seen in this book for other countries such as Germany, France,

Australia, and – with global reach – the trailblazers OUTstanding from the UK.

"And in July 2020, we signed an agreement with Spanish Ministry of Transport, Mobility, and Urban Agenda," says REDI's Chairman of the Board Castro." It will facilitate public sector entities like ministries, cities, and state-owned universities to join REDI as well." This is the same approach Dutch cousin organization Workplace Pride has been pursuing successfully for many years. As we have seen, Workplace Pride has several ministries, cities, and universities among its members.

Although a late starter compared to other larger European countries, Spain, with active REDI leading the charge, is on its way to catching up fast on LGBT+ inclusion in the workplace.

# 5. Out around the world: Latin America, South Africa, India, and much more

In countries that are considered emerging markets, an increasing number of organizations working for LGBT+ workplace inclusion and beyond have also emerged. Here are some very brief examples. Let's have a first short look at Latin America.

## Mexico

In Mexico, Latin America's second largest economy in terms of overall GDP, there is Pride Connection Mexico, founded in 2014, a network of companies pursing LGBT+ workplace equality. Its goals and most of its tools are the same as those of the organizations we have met before in this book. Currently, Pride Connection Mexico has almost 140 companies across all industries, mostly multinationals but also local businesses.

Since 2016, the country also has had a workplace equality index, compiled by US Human Rights Campaign (HRC), every two years. For its 2020 edition, almost 130 companies participated. As with the American index, top-scoring companies can locally market their LGBT+ friendliness using a label, in this case reading *HRC Equidad MX:*

*Mejor Lugares para Trabajar LGBT* ("Equality MX: Best place to work for LGBT"). In its design and text, it is adapted from the American label and includes HRC's logo. In 2020, the number of top-scoring companies increased strongly to 120.[85]

## Chile

In terms of GDP per capita, Chile ranks high on the South American continent. Here, as in Mexico, the HRC helps certify businesses for LGBT+ inclusion, cooperating with *Fundación Iguales*, a Chilean foundation for LGBT+ equality.

Fundación Iguales took Mexico as a role model and initiated the Chilean chapter of Pride Connection to address the local working world specifically. Currently, the network has about 50 member companies and its strategic committee consists of representatives from the foundation, Uber, Walmart, Procter & Gamble, McKinsey, German pharmaceutical giant Bayer, and the Chilean Empresas SB, a consumer goods group specializing in health and beauty.

The Chilean-based survey was HRC's first in-country program in South America and the second in Latin America after Mexico. In 2020, in cooperation with the foundation, HRC released the results of its second workplace equality program for Chile. 20 major employers – out of 63 assessed – achieved the top score. These top-scorers included some local operations, but were mostly global players such as Accenture, BASF, Bayer, BCG, Deloitte, H&M, McKinsey, SAP, Uber, and Walmart.

Based on the numbers of participating and top-scoring companies, Chile sounds significantly behind Mexico. But it only has about 20 million inhabitants in contrast to Mexico's more than 127 million, so proportionally, it has moved on significantly too.

This is also reflected in a survey by Pride Connection Chile, published in April 2020. Sixty-five companies participated in this fourth assessment of progress, gaps, and challenges in organizations on LGBT+ D&I. Seventy-eight percent of participating companies said they had an LGBT+ D&I policy that had been formalized, disseminated and applied in Chile. Three years earlier, in 2017, only 39% said this. Also, of those companies, 87% deal with other diversity dimensions – gender, disability, sexual orientation, race, etc. – at the same level, meaning LGBT+ D&I is not secondary.[86]

## Brazil

Brazil, Latin America's largest and only Portuguese-speaking country, has the continent's highest GDP. The US Human Rights Campaign is not active as it is in Mexico and Chile. Anti-LGBT+ violence, hate speech, and discrimination is particularly high in Brazil, so organizations working for LGBT+ workplace inclusion are particularly challenged. *Fórum de Empresas e Direitos LGBTI+* ("LGBT+ Business and Rights Forum") is one such organization. Founded in 2013, its members are mostly global corporates, but some are locally headquartered, for example some banks and law firms. Further partners are nonprofits and NGOs, including US advocacy Out & Equal (Part IV, Chapter 5), and aforementioned UN Free & Equal campaign.

The Forum has launched the *10 Compromissos da Empresa com a Promoção dos Direitos LGBTI+* ("10 Commitments to Advance LGBTI+ Rights"), to be signed by companies with a *Carta de Adesão* ("Letter of Acceptance").[87] So far, more than 90 businesses have signed. The Commitments aim at guiding LGBT+ D&I policies and practices, setting the kind of business agenda we have seen in similar organizations in other countries, including the UN LGBTI Standards of Conduct for Business. Despite some differences, idea and focus are similar to Dutch Workplace Pride's aforementioned ten recommendations in its Declaration of Amsterdam.

There is also Pride Connection Brazil, founded in 2016 with Pride Connection Mexico as a model. It likewise aims to advance LGBT+ workplace equality. That includes attracting LGBT+ talents to its member organizations, representing some crossover with the Forum's approach. The first national chapter was created in São Paulo, where it holds bimonthly meetings and other activities. There is now a second in the south, in Rio Grande do Sul.

## South Africa

Let's have a brief look now at South Africa; after oil-exporting Nigeria, it is Africa's second largest economy, measured in overall GDP.

It's one thing to have perfect laws, but daily life can still be a very different thing. In South Africa, the post-Apartheid constitution refers explicitly to the rights of LGBT+ people. If you travel to Johannesburg's O.R. Tambo Airport via the local Gautrain rail network – as I did researching this book – you are greeted by a large sign with a big blue headline reading "Discrimination" and displaying abstracted human silhouettes in rainbow colors. A prominent text takes up the constitution's message: "The Gautrain celebrates diversity in South Africa and serves people of all races, nationalities, sexes, colors, religions, beliefs, genders, ages, sexual orientations, and disabilities. Valuing and respecting people's differences on board the Gautrain is in the best interests of nation-building."

## Perfect law is not enough

In fact, South Africa, in its post-Apartheid constitution, approved in 1996, was the first country globally to outlaw discrimination based on sexual orientation. This position was also publicly supported before that by Nelson Mandela. In the workplace and economic life in general, the legal situation is equally positive. LGBT+ people are granted constitutional and other forms of protection from discrimination in provision of goods and services and in employment. South Africa was also one of the first nations in the world to legalize same-sex marriage – as early as 1998 – and is still the only one on the continent to have done so. Same-sex couples are allowed to adopt children, use surrogate parents, and arrange in vitro fertilization.

However, the discrimination against LGBT+ people in South Africa in daily life, even with its young population – currently the estimated age median is about 27 years[88] – remains high, at times very high. I learned this directly via interviews in Johannesburg, where I attended the first South African LGBTI Business Summit,[89] also a first anywhere on the continent.

## Premieres in Africa: a summit, a forum and an index

The Summit was set up by the PLUS LGBTI+ Business Network, an initiative that aims "not only to empower LGBTI people to become more active within the business sector in South Africa, but also to address the homophobia and discrimination that still exists, in the workplace," says its website.[90] The summit was sponsored by local and multinational companies such as Absa – a leading South African financial services company – EY, Shell, Uber, and others.

It was also supported by the Other Foundation, which, in 2016, initiated the PLUS LGBTI+ Business Network and works in general for the equality and freedom of LGBT+ people in southern Africa. Finally, another Summit partner was the South African LGBT+ Management Forum, also known as the "LGBT+ Forum." Set up in 2015, the nonprofit works with large companies to advance LGBT+ inclusion and D&I best practice in local workplaces.

One of its co-founders is Luke Andrews, who has worked with consultancy Monitor Deloitte for more than eight years. Since 2015, he has been living in Johannesburg and is now a senior manager. A UK native, he holds a bachelor's degree from Cambridge University and a master's from the University of Toronto. Already, his under-graduate thesis in Cambridge focused on South Africa and was rec-ognized with an award. His thesis in Toronto was related to Africa too, with a special section on South Africa. "I am an Africa optimist," Andrews says, telling me that before his studies in Cambridge, he worked as a teacher in Nairobi, Kenya, for almost a year. Alongside his job at Monitor Deloitte, he is now about to finish his MBA at the University of Cape Town.

In the context of the LGBT+ Forum, Andrews co-authored work-place guides on D&I at work, including one on the business case for LGBT+ inclusion and one on how to develop best-in-class employee networks. He also initiated South Africa's Workplace Equality Index (SAWEI),[91] the first of its kind in Africa and now the flagship project of the Forum. It was launched at the end of the Summit at a different location in Sandton, Johannesburg's business district, with a panel, award ceremonies, and a festive reception.

Like other indices I have referred to in this book, SAWEI aims to measure participating firms' progress in ensuring an inclusive, safe, and affirming workplace for LGBT+ people,[92] but also benchmarks and shows where there are gaps. "Sixteen companies participated, mostly in the major cities of Johannesburg, Cape Town, Pretoria, and Durban, employing more than 30,000 people," says Andrews, who is also coordinator of the index on behalf of the Forum. All partici-pating companies said they provide a variety of channels for LGBT+ employees to report harassment and discrimination. Nearly all had policies in place prohibiting discrimination on the basis of sexual ori-entation along with other elements such as gender, race, or language. The majority had an LGBT+ employee network or affinity group. Consultancy Bain and multinational oil and gas company Shell took the lead and were ranked at the top gold tier. Other companies also scored well, such as Absa, Accenture, Deloitte, Procter & Gamble, PwC, and Thomson Reuters.

## Fears, safe havens and signs of progress

While I was in Johannesburg in September 2018 (and later via Skype), I interviewed a few members of employee networks from the companies participating in the index. Those I am referring to were LGBT+ people of color and all preferred to remain anonymous. They shared a common message: they were proud that their home country has such a progressive constitution with respect to legal equality of LGBT+ people, but they also said culture and daily life are far behind the legal promises. Specifically, all of them had experienced bullying, many even having been beaten up or suffered other forms of violence, some several times, as teens and young adults.

Almost all were enthusiastic about the first LGBT+ Business Summit and the index launch. Almost all also perceived their (multinational) company's LGBT+ employee network and their employer as a whole as safe havens. Some feared, however, that South Africa's difficult economic situation, which has been ongoing for many years, could lead companies to further cut their workforces, reduce investment into diversity programs, and even close their offices in the country completely.

The severe economic and social impact of the COVID-19 pandemic in South Africa might have reinforced that fear significantly. On the other hand, there are also strong positive signs for more engagement to advance LGBT+ inclusion in the local business world. In November 2019, the second Business Summit took place, and the second SAWEI edition was launched, this time with a lot more companies participating: 27, collectively employing more than 140,000 people. "SAWEI also moved to a fully digital platform," Andrews explains. "We want to accelerate the LGBT+ Forum's ambition to grow participation to 100 companies by 2025." In 2019, Accenture, Bain, EY, Microsoft, P&G, and PwC reached the gold tier, and there were also more silver medalists. "One major finding, among many others, was that nearly all companies that had taken part the year before improved their scores, illustrating the growing momentum behind ensuring LGBT+ inclusion in South African workplaces," says Andrews.

And there is more, for example, from the National Business Initiative (NBI). NBI is a more than 25-year-old voluntary coalition of South African and multinational companies working for sustainable growth and development. In 2020, it published a research report on LGBT+ employees' experiences in the local workplaces of both global corporates and South African companies. It showed that discrimination and hiding sexual and gender identity were still high. Still, the fact that such research was done – and presented with global best practice for LGBT+ workplace inclusion – shows business-driven progress's momentum in the country.

## India

India is not only large, with a bit more than 1.3 billion inhabitants, its GDP has also grown to the fifth largest globally. And it is young: in 2020, the median age of the population was an estimated 28.4 years. In the US, for example, the median age is ten years higher, in Japan 20 years.

As for LGBT+ equality, the country was for a long time governed by a colonial-era law known as Section 377, which categorized gay sex as a criminal offence punishable by a ten-year jail term. There was an appeal against this law in 2013, but its validity was upheld. It was only in early September 2018 that India's Supreme Court overturned the law, ruling that discrimination on the basis of sexual orientation is a fundamental violation of human rights.

However, the country's high level of discrimination, bullying, harassment, hate-speech, and even violence against openly or presumed LGBT+ people did not stop overnight. As in South Africa (and other countries) – as in all large organizations – changing rules is not enough; the culture has to change too.

## Emerging role models

But India not only has a young population, it has also shown a capacity to move fast in advancing LGBT+ inclusion in the workplace. In Part IV, Chapter 8, I briefly look at SAP India's LGBT+ D&I journey in Bangalore, India's "Silicon Valley" with its more than 12 million inhabitants, and a senior developer there. The company's currently only openly gay employee locally, he now leads Pride@SAP India and, supported by his employer and a fast-growing number of straight allies, pushes strongly for awareness and LGBT+ inclusion in blogs, training sessions, on panels, and more.

Role models are still lacking in India, in general and in the business world, which is no surprise given the legal history and the conservative society and corporate world. But they have begun to emerge. One of them, for example, is Suresh Ramdas, who has worked at US IT giant HP for over 12 years now. Based in Bangalore, he is currently the Global Training Lead and serves as a global communications chairperson for the company's Global Pride section.

Ramdas and his endeavors have become very visible very quickly. He has not only completed the LGBTQ Executive Leadership Program from Stanford (for more on which, see Part II, Chapter 4). Beyond his job at HP he is also one of several co-founders from the corporate world of Working with Pride (WWP), a community of D&I professionals, LGBT+ employees and straight allies that aim to make India and Indian workplaces more LGBT+-inclusive.[93] They do so by creating resources on the business case for LGBT+ inclusions, supporting with sensitization and training, and sharing best practice and tools for LGBT+ D&I journeys. Within WWP, Ramdas has helped to set up a leadership program for LGBT+ people in the early stages of their careers, called Leading With Pride (LWP). In 2019, he was elected Mr. Gay India and included in OUTstanding's 50 LGBT+ Future Leaders list.[94]

## Pride Circle, RISE, and more

The same speed is much in evidence in the work of Pride Circle, which, in only a short time since the end of Section 377, has become India's premier D&I advisory, pushing strongly for LGBT+ equality. It focuses on companies, but also advising nonprofits and government institutions. On its website, Pride Circle claims to already work with over 150 Indian and global companies. It offers audits, assessments, training and sensitization, managing roundtables, research, meetups, mentoring programs, and job placements. It also advises on supply chain diversity, CSR and more.[95] Among its educational offerings are publications – for instance an ally guide, a parents' guide and a trans inclusion report – and webinars, for example a series on six steps to LGBT+ inclusion.

In 2019, only a few months after the country got rid of Section 377, Pride Circle also organized RISE – short for Reimagining Inclusion for Social Equity – Asia's first LGBT+ conference and job and career fair, in Bangalore. Pride Circle provides a detailed overview on its website. There were 50 speakers, executive breakfasts and lunches, marketplaces for LGBT+-owned businesses and more. Over 40 companies participated, many of them big names, and over 400 conference attendees and 300 job seekers showed up.[96]

## New partnerships

The COVID-19 pandemic also hit India, but Pride Circle soldiered on. In August 2020, it announced a new cooperation involving three further partners. The first was the UK LGBT+ nonprofit Stonewall, which, among many other things has more than 15 years of successfully experienced in conceptualizing and managing workplace equality indices. (For more on Stonewall, see Part IV, Chapter 6.) The second partner was the Federation of Indian Chambers of Commerce and Industry (FICCI).

The third was Keshav Suri Foundation, which works to "embrace, empower and mainstream the LGBTQAI+ Community in India." Launched in 2018 in Delhi, it is named after Keshav Suri, heir and Executive Director of the large Lalit Surit Hospitality Group, which owns and manages hotels.[97] The well-educated Suri, among other things, holds a master's in international management from King's College in London. In 2018 he married Cyril Feuillebois, a French businessman who runs an organic cosmetics company out of Delhi that aims to bring together French expertise with Indian ingredients. Their glamorous Paris wedding was covered in the Indian media.[98] Suri has been an active campaigner for LGBT+ rights in India, not least through his foundation.

This level of activism is matched, although in a different way, by Ramkrishna Sinha, one of the co-founders of Pride Circle, whose early engagements saw him included in the OUTstanding 50 LGBT+ Future Leaders list in 2017, so even before Section 377 was thrown out. (Pride Circle's second co-founder is Srini Ramaswamy, who also engaged early on and was recognized for this with several awards too.)

In 2020, Sinha, Suri, and their two partners announced the creation of IWEI (India Workplace Equality Index),[99] a benchmarking tool to support organizations on their journey of LGBT+ inclusion.

They issued invitations to the digital IWEI launch event in early September of that year.

Around the same time, Parmesh Shahani, one of India's queer icons in the business and culture world, published the book *Queeristan: LGBTQ inclusion in the Indian workplace*. Shahani, among many other things, is founder of the award-winning Godrej India Culture Lab in Mumbai, a D&I expert and a WEF Young Global Leader with a master's from MIT. India's LGBT+ in business arena is moving fast.

## Out around the world

In a lot of countries, LGBT+ inclusion is still a greater struggle. To help them, a new alliance of companies was formed in 2015: Open for Business (OFB), a nonprofit coalition of leading global companies, now with more than 30 members (as of December 2020, see box).

### Open for Business – member firms

| | | |
|---|---|---|
| Accenture | Allen Overy | American Express |
| AT&T | BCG | BD |
| Brunswick | Burberry | Deloitte |
| Deutsche Bank | Diageo | Dow |
| EY | Facebook | Google |
| GSK | IBM | Ikea |
| Inditex | Kearney | KPMG |
| L'Oréal | LinkedIn | Linklaters |
| Mastercard | McKinsey | Microsoft |
| PwC | Relx Group | Standard Chartered |
| Tesco | Thomson Reuters | Unilever |
| Virgin | WeWork | |

OFB's motto is "Business action for LGBT+-inclusive societies." The nonprofit aims to improve LGBT+ people's legal and social situation around the world, it says, via private sector influence, working on the assumption that diverse and inclusive societies are better for business and thus for economic growth.

The grounding is the existing theoretical and empirical findings on D&I's positive economic effects. The OFB aims to improve this research foundation for the LGBT+ D&I business and economic cases, and foster social change by providing this information on a global level and to local policy and business decision-makers.

OFB is led by a small team that brings in resources as needed, including from member companies. Founder and OFB Advisory Board Chair Jon Miller, a partner in the London office of large global PR and communications agency Brunswick, is an important driving force today. Openly gay, his LGBT+ engagements have been recognized by inclusion in the OUTstanding Top 100 LGBT+ Executives role model list.

Early on, in 2016, Miller received support from American Drew Keller, then a young McKinsey management consultant seconded to OFB. Keller finally left the consultants to be OFB's global program director, but recently moved on to start an MBA at Harvard. Kathryn Dovey, previously at OECD in Paris, is the new executive director.

One main OFB focus is on countries that are actively hostile on LGBT+ rights. For example, in 2019 OFB published a report on the business and economic benefits of overcoming discrimination and promoting LGBT+ inclusion in Kenya.[100] It shows this discrimination costs Kenya up 1.7% of GDP, equal to 144% of government spending on healthcare. The costs are mainly underutilized human capital, lost tourist income and poorer health outcomes.

The report made waves in the country and triggered substantial media coverage, and, with it in hand, OFB's Country Director, Yvonne Muthoni, who took office in February 2019, can seek to convince Kenyan business and political leaders that laws and initiatives against anti-LGBT+ discrimination would also be good for them. Beyond the activities in Kenya, recently, some new programs have been set up, for example, in Eastern Europe and the Caribbean.

Another study was on the positive economic effect of same-sex couples marrying in Taiwan.[101] It concluded that "marriage for all" in Taiwan would improve competitiveness and create an environment in which companies could be even more successful. As briefly mentioned before, Taiwan has, in the meantime, adopted equal marriage.

A recent report, launched in September 2020, addressed the connection between LGBT+ inclusion and each of the 17 UN SDGs (for more on these, see Part 1, Chapter 6). A further report focuses on

*Channels of Influence: How Companies Can Promote LGBT+ Inclusive Societies.* It is also available in Simplified Chinese, translated by the Beijing LGBT Center.

Some studies, to increase raise awareness, well-networked OFB founder Miller presented in strategically important locations, for example at Davos or at events in European Parliament (EP) offices in Brussels, supported by the EP's LGBTI Intergroup.[102] This is currently the largest of the EP's 27 cross-party Intergroups, composed of 150 EP Members. It monitors the related work of the EU and the situation of LGBT+ people in EU states, liaising with civil society groups. At a summer 2018 event in the offices of the EP in Brussels I attended, Miller presented an OFB report on the positive correlation between LGBT+ inclusion in cities and their innovative capacity, international competitiveness and economic growth.[103] It was released earlier that year at one of the aforementioned offsite meetings at the WEF in Davos. In summer 2020, OFB provided an update report, new data and ratings for 144 cities, showing Amsterdam in the lead as the world's most LGBT+-inclusive city.

## The Rainbow Cities Network

As OFB research suggests, being LGBT+-friendly pays off for cities everywhere. Not least supported by this finding, Rainbow Cities Network (RCN) seeks to amplify local approaches on LGBT+ inclusion and ensure efficient budget allocation through exchange and joint activity between cities. Mayors or deputy mayors of member cities guarantee political support by signing a Memorandum of Understanding.

Started in 2012 under the umbrella of the Dutch Government, RCN became an independent international organization in 2018. Today it consists of 32 cities, the vast majority European, from 16 countries: Aarhus, Amsterdam, Barcelona, Bergen, Berlin, Bern, Bruges, Brussels, Reykjavik, Cologne, Cork, Esch-sur-Alzette, Frankfurt, Geneva, Ghent, Hamburg, Hannover, Heidelberg, Kotor, Leuven, Linz, Ljubljana, Mannheim, Mexico City, Munich, Nuremberg, Oslo, Paris, Rotterdam, São Paolo, Vienna, and Zurich.

Every member city pays an annual fee pegged to population size, though low-income cities can join via the "solidarity reduction mechanism," effectively a discount. At annual meetings, member cities deliver "one-pagers" – brief progress reports on their local LGBT+ policies and initiatives to facilitate learnings and exchange of best practice.

The network's main governing body is the board, composed of three to five active city members, rotating every two years. The current coordinator, Manuel Rosas Vázquez, who is openly gay, works full time. Originally from Puebla, Mexico, he has lived and studied in Germany since 2014. He facilitates communication between members, establishes relations with other international networks and relevant stakeholders, actively seeks out new cities to join, and represents the network in international forums.

Although OFB is still small in terms of people working for the nonprofit it has grown fast in terms of member companies. However, much of the globe is still not covered. Barely examined is, for example, the whole Islamic world with its LGBT+-hostile legislation and culture, including, for example, Indonesia, the Middle East, North Africa, and Turkey.

China remains barely examined too – by the OFB or any similar body – although in terms of population the largest country in the world with its fast-increasing wealth should now have one of the largest LGBT+ consumer markets. But China is very conservative in LGBT+ matters in general and it is a difficult and at times dangerous environment for members of the LGBT+ community.[104] On the other hand, sometimes there are signs of progress. US nonprofit Out & Equal, for example, for some years has held a China Forum addressing local LGBT+ D&I issues (for more on Out & Equal, see Part IV, Chapter 5). Chinese e-commerce and tech giant Alibaba, as another example, in 2015 launched a contest on its Taobao online marketplace to send 10 gay couples on an all-expenses-paid trip to California, culminating in a group wedding in Hollywood.[105] In an interview with the *Wall Street Journal*, Alibaba announced that it aimed to show respect to gay couples but would not provide benefits for same-sex partners. In China, same-sex marriage is not legalized. In January 2020, Alibaba released an ad that featured a gay couple returning home for Chinese New Year, as part of a series of commercials on the company's online marketplace Tmall to advertise special deals for the upcoming Spring Festival.[106]

Until recently, there was also Shanghai Pride, where, some time ago, global corporates began to showcase their LGBT+ friendliness at least a little. Now news reports say Shanghai Pride has stopped all operations,[107] presumably because of "political pressure." Almost all my interview partners in global companies shied away from discussing their activities in China in more depth. It seems almost all prefer to follow the aforementioned Embassy LGBT+ engagement approach here (see Part II, Chapter 8), limiting their endeavors to the internal sphere.

Even Hong Kong is not dealt with very often, though, for many years already, there is a quite sophisticated nonprofit, Community Business, working for workplace inclusion in the region, with a unit focusing on Hong Kong's corporate LGBT+ D&I, including an index, awards, and more. Also, especially the corporate law and financial services industries have their own platforms, networks, and other informal tools to advance exchange and progress on LGBT+ equality, mainly driven by firms from the Anglo-Saxon sphere.

HKGala, Hong Kong's attorney network, aiming to promote LGBT+ D&I in the legal profession there. According to its website, HKGala represents a network of more than 60 supporting firms and over 800 individual members and supporters, including "lawyers, trainees, paralegals and staff of law firms and in-house legal departments, law students, legal recruiters, and those in the legal field in academia, government and non-profit organizations."[108]

Now, however, due to the new security situation and increasing repression against advocates for more democracy in Hong Kong, uncertainties and anxieties have increased, resulting in corporates being more cautious, as some of my interviewees report. Many of them are frustrated about recent developments in Hong Kong and expecting companies to be less visible in working for greater LGBT+ inclusion.

# Postscript with a GaYme Changer: Bridging business and the social

This section, Part III, has been about a powerful global development: the emergence of a variety of game-changing institutions and the individuals driving it. These individuals are diverse in many ways, but all act – and prefer to do so – at an intersection, aiming to do both good business and good in the world. For some this may sound naïve but, as we have seen so far, it is not.

I am closing this section with an interview with Elliot Vaughn, one of the visible drivers of this change. Vaughn is a Managing Director and Partner at consultancy BCG, based in the UK, but working globally. He is British, grew up near Oxford, is now in his mid-40s and holds a bachelor's degree from Cambridge University and an MBA from London Business School (LBS). Since joining BCG some 15 years ago, in his core job as consultant he has done client work in a variety of industries but has primarily focused on healthcare and social impact. For many years, he has been an active member of his firm's LGBT+ network Pride@BCG, which he currently leads globally.

Outside BCG, he serves on the board of aforementioned NGO OutRight, advocating for LGBT+ human rights nationally and globally and is the founder and Chairman of GiveOut, a charity that raises funds for global LGBT+ advocacy. He has been included in the OUTstanding 100 Executive list ranking several times. For his work with GiveOut, specifically, he was recognized with a Point of Light award from the UK Prime Minister.[109]

## Let's start with some early personal stories – of coming out and beginning activism.

I came out to my family at 15, in 1990. I found it incredibly stressful (my dad grew up in the south of Texas and I had no idea how he would react), but they were amazingly supportive. At 16, I was bringing home boyfriends, and when I graduated from my high school, my then boyfriend came with my parents to see me give the valedictorian speech.

At Cambridge University I got deeper into student activism and led the LGB group for the student union for two of my three years.

There was no visible "T" or "I" at that time. I ran a campaign called Assume Nothing and I'm still proud of that work – it was about encouraging people to be themselves. After a stint as a full-time elected student union officer, and some other engagement, I went to do an MBA, and then joined BCG.

## What happened there?

There I experienced exactly what we now find in our student surveys: I went back into the closet thinking this big corporate world couldn't handle who I really was.

Fairly quickly, I got comfortable being out with colleagues, but I found it really hard to be open with clients. I even had one client who invited me to a rugby match. But I couldn't bring myself to accept because I couldn't imagine having to pretend to be straight and interested in rugby! That's, of course, also a cliché, as I know now. But at that time, I finally thought, enough, I'm not going to live my life like this and came out to this client. And the funny thing is he has gone on to be one of my main clients, and I'm pretty sure that if I hadn't come out to him I might not now be at the firm.

After I was elected partner at BCG, I was starting to have this feeling that I was enjoying my work, but I wasn't actually getting the things done in life that I always meant to. And it made me think, what's the point of all this privilege if I'm not using it for any real purpose?

Honestly, I even started by assuming that I had to leave BCG. And over the past five years I've come to realize that was really old-school thinking. I guess my philosophy kind of shifted from one of "playing the game" to get ahead, to one of "changing the game," where I am hopefully having an impact both within and beyond BCG. And that does involve at times an attitude internally of "take me as I am or not at all."

I've found BCG to be incredibly supportive, which now makes sense but was an unknown to me until I took the leap. I've worked at 80% for the past four years; I have two external board roles.

This is personally important. I founded a charity called GiveOut and am on the board of OutRight. The LGBT+ movement is underfunded, and I saw an opportunity to help. I realized the impact that I could have and have a rising sense of the importance of using my privilege for a purpose other than my own advancement.

BCG has started funding research in LGBT+ and other diversity topics. And surprisingly to me, the firm started celebrating me as a role model BCGer for the very thing that had at first made me feel like an outsider.

For me that's been a lot to process, but it has been in many ways a wonderful journey. Now I am seeking to use my energy to help move our Pride network forward and to elevate the profile and advance the careers of LGBT+ colleagues.

## What does it mean for you to be a LGBT+ role model?

This comes back to the title of your book. Are you in your career to play the game to get ahead or to change the game? Changing the game also benefits me as it allows me to balance interesting work with purposeful impact.

It also means being prepared to share. We all have the potential to use our power and privilege to support our LGBT+ communities, no matter where we work. Increasingly the challenges facing the world are ones that require action today rather than in 20 or 30 years' time, when traditionally leaders would at the end of their careers start to get involved. No one can decide for you how out you should be, but be aware that there is a tendency to be too risk averse.

## What do you think about Lord Browne's story?

I personally asked him, if he could live his life again would he have made the same decisions to remain covered up until such an advanced stage. He said no, in hindsight the loss of personal life fulfillment was not worth the gain. (For more on John Browne's story, see Part II, Chapter 2.)

But the mistake would be to imagine that it is somehow a story from the past. We know from our research that many people all around the world are still calibrating toward risk aversion – in countries like the US, UK, France, and Germany, as well as countries like India, Japan, Brazil, etc. While no one can tell someone else to come out, we need to highlight this risk aversion and help people – and companies – be aware of the consequences. (For more on some of this research, see Part IV, Chapter 1.)

### How many members does your Pride network currently have and what would be your highlights in recent BCG LGBT+ D&I activity?

We are now at 600+ members globally, not including straight allies, and growing every year by 15% or more. As for the highlights, here are four:

One: Doubling down on driving our network growth beyond the US, Western Europe and Australia. We have activated our network in many offices with difficult cultural contexts.

Two: Our support for OFB in general and on their first ever study of LGBT+ support among emerging market multinationals.[110] (For more on OFB, see previous chapter.)

Three: Being founding members of the Partnership for Global LGBTI Equality, connected to the WEF and the UN LGBTI Standards of Conduct for Business, as I mentioned before. (For more details on the Partnership, see Part II, Chapter 8.)

Four: Our study, *A New LGBTQ Workforce Has Arrived – Inclusive Cultures Must Follow*,[111] for which we partnered with New York City's Lesbian, Gay, Bisexual & Transgender Community Center, a nonprofit service and advocacy organization. We surveyed 2,000 LGBT+ employees and 2,000 non-LGBT+ (straight) employees across the US to try to understand the experiences of today's LGBT+ workforce and how companies could specifically respond to them by creating more inclusive workplaces. We also conducted another research report, *The Diversity Dividend in South East Asia*, which covers all diversity dimensions. Among other things, it shows that there is high correlation between a more diverse workforce and greater innovation – with a higher share of revenue coming from new products."[112]

### Can you say more about the progress of your Pride&BCG network in those difficult cultural contexts?

In India, over the past six months, we moved from four members and 15 allies to eight members and 80+ allies.

In Japan, our network was largely dormant, largely for cultural reasons. We undertook a visibility and awareness campaign during Pride month in 2020 and now have two members and 15 allies. That's encouraging.

In China, our network is thriving with 25 members, including at senior levels. We actively engage externally as well, e.g. with a social impact project pro bono. We were also a financial sponsor for Shanghai Pride 2020.

In South Africa, we launched Pride@BCG in 2018. The year after, among other initiatives, it was one of the corporate sponsors of Johannesburg Pride, the largest Pride parade on the continent. (For more on South Africa, see Part III, Chapter 5.)

We also have our own chapter of Pride@BCG in Africa now. It spans three countries and has a low double-digit membership.

Beyond that, we continue to focus on similar geographies in emerging markets and have appointed task forces to continue this agenda. Currently, they focus on six countries. Thailand is one example.

## Finally, what do you see as the challenges and emerging trends related to LGBT+ D&I?

Purpose-driven business is already a powerful megatrend – not only but *also* very relevant for LGBT+ inclusion: we increasingly find the workforce is keen on having a sense of "purpose," which is not limited to business value alone but includes contributions to society. (For more, see Part I, Chapters 5 and 6.)

A big theme will be gender identity and expression, so whether people feel supported to express their gender identity and do they feel accepted at work on that basis. My sense is that the "clock" is probably 25 years behind compared to today's acceptance of alternative sexual orientations.

With regard to Millennials and Generation Z, we have learned a lot from the latest research, summarized in our aforementioned report with New York City's Lesbian, Gay, Bisexual & Transgender Community Center. It shows that the LGBT+ workforce of Millennials and Generation Z is now significantly more racially diverse, has a higher proportion of women, and is increasingly averse to identifying with any single "label" from the LGBT+ alphabet. This calls for a reappraisal of how to best recruit and include a workforce identifying as LGBT+. The new approach highlights the need to create daily moments of inclusion, "micro-inclusion," which necessitates a combination of systemic culture change and a "segment of one" approach (which means seeing each person as a unique individual) to help diverse employees feel a sense of belonging. While the study refers to research conducted in the US, we think it has relevance more broadly.

Further, recent events in the US and beyond including the Black Lives Matter protests have elevated the importance of businesses standing up in support of racial justice in particular. This absolutely extends to LGBT+ diversity and inclusion at work in a corporate setting where, historically, racial identity has not been sufficiently prioritized as a consideration. Going forward, there will be a much greater focus on intersectional inclusion – bridging different diversity dimensions such as gender, race, sexual orientation, and gender identity.

Finally, I expect this to give rise to an increasing focus on the aforementioned "segment-of-one" inclusion approaches and a focus on the "thousand daily moments" that go into making people feel included or excluded at work. This will raise the bar on what we expect of businesses to show they are not just speaking on LGBT+ D&I, but also acting credibly.

# Part IV

**Changing cultures,
a revolution among
the young, and its impact
on the business world**

# 1. Maintained obstacles, ideal environments, and overcoming bias

In recent years, in many countries and companies, a lot of progress in LGBT+ equality has been made with respect to credible LGBT+ D&I management, external support for LGBT+ communities, including support for same sex marriage, implementation of nondiscrimination laws, and much more.

## The continuing problems of coming out at work – even among the young

Even today, however, it's not always that easy for many, even among the young, to come out at work. Studies stress this finding, and a study published by BCG in 2019 confirms it in an exemplary way. (An 2020–21 BCG update survey confirms it too.)

For their 2019 Out@Work Barometer, BCG surveyed around 4,000 LGBT+ talents under 35 with over 60 different nationalities in more than ten countries. Only 52% overall had come out to all work colleagues.[1] The box below breaks this down into the proportion of LGBT+ employees out to all colleagues in ten major countries.

---

### BCG study: percentage of young LGBT+ employees out to all peers

| | |
|---|---|
| Great Britain 63% | Brazil 60% |
| USA 55% | Canada 55% |
| France 48% | Mexico 47% |
| Italy 46% | Netherlands 43% |
| Spain 42% | Germany 37% |

---

This gives rise to a key conclusion: many young LGBT+ people still do not fully reach their productivity potential at work. Within the top ten countries shown, this is least true of the British, most true of the Germans, but applies to all. To give an indicative, more detailed breakdown of one country's figures: though 85% of young German LGBT+ employees would prefer to come out at work, only 37% have actually done so to all colleagues, 36% have done so with some colleagues, and 27% keep quiet about it completely.[2]

So, there is still a lot many employers would need to do to improve conditions for coming out and thus harvest the ensuing economic fruit. As one of the study authors, Annika Zawadzki, Partner at BCG, puts it, companies must "do better at creating a safe and supportive environment for LGBT+ employees if they want to attract and retain this talent in the future."[3] Indeed, companies that are not successful in this could lose large parts of this age cohort as candidates for their employee pools – and, depending on the industry they are in, also as customers, business partners, and other stakeholders.

## A supportive environment, diversity, merit-orientation, and better results

As Zawadzki has put it, "creating a safe and supportive environment is key," which basically means creating and sustaining a respectful working climate and culture.

I have referred to this argument in this book before. Let's look at it in a little more detail. For some years now, practice-oriented science has been emphasizing that a working climate that embraces diversity of all kinds to become open and inclusive is beneficial for companies. In concrete terms, it sees this working climate – at least to a large extent – as an expression of a specific culture. This culture does not rely on negative egalitarianism but on positive respect and recognition for other people as they are, as individuals, with all the facets they identify with, their self-perceptions, talents, and skills.

In a culture with such an open working climate, no one is excluded, stigmatized, discriminated against, or preferred, whether on the basis of their gender, age, ethnicity, religion, culture, sexual orientation, or gender identity. Everyone experiences inclusivity and can therefore exist and work undisguised, expressing their true selves – concepts that John Browne and Richard Quest refer to and that have, as we have seen, found their way into Barilla's new language of diversity and inclusion as well. The same applies, as we have also seen, to the globally growing number of organizations helping bring about LGBT+ inclusion in the workplace (and societies).

In an open, inclusive working climate understood this way, with not just formal but lived equal rights for all, there is no "minority stress" and "emotional tax" – causing reduced well-being and increased health problems – due to some form of exclusion. Instead there are equal opportunities for everyone to make something of themselves and contribute to the company and its success. An open, inclusive working climate and culture thus supports individual performance, leading to better company performance and to justice and fairness at the same time.

In view of this argument, the business case and the human rights or moral case for D&I are thought of together. As we have seen, this is reflected, for example, in Barilla CEO Claudio Colzani's very visibly featured leading D&I statement, which I'll repeat here: "Our diversity and inclusion journey starts with the recognition that supporting diversity and inclusion is the right thing to do and it is also good for business."

Also, given the talent, skills, and potential of all employees, including that of LGBT+ people, companies not working toward equal LGBT+ rights and opportunities simply cannot claim to be truly merit-based. And what would a company be in today's modern dynamic economy without credible merit-focused rules, working climate, and culture?

Companies have to rely on merit as a guiding principle for hiring, retaining, framing career development, and paying salaries and bonuses. And they have to promise this merit-focus to ensure competitiveness, setting expectations that their promise will be fulfilled.

That's highly important especially today since, as described earlier in this book, the younger generations in particular are paying more and more attention to how credible and fair companies are – to everybody, whatever their true self is.

But what would a promise to be merit-based be worth if talented, ambitious, hard-working LGBT+ employees wanted to seize their promised (equal) opportunities – whether in terms of function, company division, hierarchical level, or career goal – and were not given the chance to do so? They would discover that the promise was a lie – for example, by finding that the prevailing working culture does not encourage them to come out or that after coming out "suddenly," the next career step was delayed. They would walk away or be less productive and perform more poorly.

From this perspective, on the organizational level there is an inseparable link between diversity, an open, inclusive working climate and culture, equal rights and opportunities, credible merit-orientation and productivity.

## Changing the culture

That's not all in matters of culture. Sustaining a diverse and inclusive working culture means allowing and enabling permanent change into the unknown to embrace the potential of creativity and innovation. Once this culture has become reality, the people working in it, through their shared lived values, talents, and skills, are able to continuously reproduce it.

But without diverse personnel, talented, skilled, and motivated, the promised diversity dividend harvest of benefits remains void. So how to attract the desired personnel? For example, the young LGBT+ talents, the cited BCG study had described?

Not every company has the same prerequisites for this. What is most important is the shape of the existing corporate culture because it also shapes the recruitment processes.

Homogeneous, less-open cultures tempt those responsible in the company to unconsciously recruit on the external personnel markets according to the principle of self-similarity. Examples:

- A man from a certain university hires a man from the same university.
- A man with a clothing style or habitus perceived as "feminine" – because he is classified as "gay" – does not advance any further in the application process.
- A white computer scientist resists hiring a female nonwhite computer scientist, although she has the best qualifications.
- A white US HR manager does not even invite in for interview a candidate with an Arabic or "black"-sounding name, despite him having the same qualifications as candidates they do invite.

Comparable patterns can also be found in homogeneous, diverse, nonappreciative corporate cultures when it comes to the design of personnel, career, and management development. It goes without saying that personnel recruited and developed in this way can hardly contribute to the economic advantages of diversity summarized above. Simply getting started with successful D&I management is difficult in such set-ups because the entire culture is so biased against it.

Sometimes, even a revolution is needed, often initiated by an exogenous crisis/shock that puts a company under great pressure to change. Again, the Barilla example applies.

Companies that have already embarked on the path to a diverse, inclusive work culture tend to behave differently. Employees and managers in such a culture are less at risk of having their recruiting and career development processes unconsciously shaped by the principle of self-similarity. Rather, their own diversity and openness also stimulate recruitment and promotion of a diverse workforce.

The members of this diverse workforce will also be all the more motivated to activate the economic potential of diversity the more they feel in their everyday work that they belong and are needed as they are – with their true authentic selves. It is obvious that this then also strengthens their loyalty to the company and their willingness to work and perform.

## Beyond awareness: the special challenge of unconscious bias

Taylor Cox with his work on the "multicultural organization" and diversity basically starting in the early '90s is one of the pioneers of modern diversity management. He stressed early on that neither diversity management's beginning nor its sustainable practice in a company were straightforward. Rather, diversity management had to be strategic. It required systems and practices for managing an organization's members so diversity's potential benefits – e.g. varied views, better decisions, higher productivity – would outweigh potential disadvantages, such as increased conflict. Today, this finding is undisputed.

Cox also identified some key potential pitfalls in D&I management – and a very crucial one is unconscious prejudice or bias. Supported by D&I research and practice, it is today undisputed that an open organizational culture that values diversity – that is, respects, recognizes, and appreciates every employee with all their facets – cannot develop without dealing with each participant's unconscious biases. Such an open organizational culture is a preeminent precondition for harvesting the diversity dividend of higher productivity.

Briefly summarized, unconscious biases – or just bias – refers to beliefs that affect our perception, assessment, decisions, and actions unconsciously. Research shows how biases widely held about diversity dimensions such as gender, ethnicity/race, age, sexual orientation, and gender identity are the products of lifelong conditioning. It starts with direct and indirect messages from parents, teachers, etc. and continues via the media, peer groups, organizations, and more.

These biases are pervasive. We all hold them, even those committed to impartiality, such as judges or referees. They are often so ingrained in society, organizations, and groups that they go unnoticed by many members.

Sometimes, unconscious biases are also called "implicit biases" – to differentiate them from explicit (conscious) biases. For example, if asked whether we think heterosexual people are "better" than gays and answer "yes," this is explicit, conscious bias: homophobia.

Contrarily, though we are unaware of implicit biases, they still influence us. For example, we might, without realizing it, consider lesbian mothers inferior to heterosexual mothers – even if we would not rationally defend this. This is very different from deliberately hiding an explicit bias for reasons of social cohesion/political correctness.

Of course, conscious and unconscious biases affect each other. If we have always heard that women are too weak and emotional to be good managers, scientists, or soldiers, our decisions regarding recruitment, career development, and promotion may well be adversely affected.

## Advantages and disadvantages of bias – and how to overcome them

As I said, everyone holds unconscious biases – and not all are negative. They can be useful mental shortcuts to faster decisions or support for group harmony.

But clearly, they can also lead to pigeonhole thinking, blind spots, and denial of others' viewpoints, blocking access to the new, shutting down exploratory thinking, and diversity's potential advantages. Given modern society's pressure to compete creatively and innovatively, this is a major disadvantage.

The list of (conscious and) unconscious prejudices against LGBT+ people is long and well-known. Here are two examples from Vienna's Anti-discrimination Office for Same-sex and Transgender Lifestyles:

- "Gay men are particularly sensitive." At work, the mental short-cut can be: he's gay, ergo sensitive, ergo not assertive, ergo not a leader. The truth is, of course, there are insensitive gays and sensitive heterosexuals and all points in between.
- "Lesbian women are misandrists (hate men)." At work, this can mean lesbian women are considered poor team players, supposedly likely to exclude men. The truth is, although lesbians have romantic relationships with women, most of them have successful and fulfilling professional and personal relationships with everyone, as most heterosexuals do.

Moreover, it is well known today that working with people clearly different from yourself – in whatever respect – can challenge the brain to overcome ingrained thinking, often associated with conscious and unconscious prejudice, and thus improve performance.

The good news is, implicit biases are malleable. The unconscious associations we have formed can be gradually unlearned, e.g. through a variety of debiasing techniques. Today, workshops with unconscious-bias training are standard for almost all global companies that have professional D&I management. Ideally, all managers and employees receive such training regularly.

As mentioned in Part I of this book, Barilla has had each of its managers and employees take part in such training since the beginning of its LGBT+ turnaround, and the group emphasizes this point in its own performance record. Today, the same applies at many global corporates that want to be perceived as advanced on LGBT+ inclusion.

All global institutions that promote and evaluate LGBT+ friendliness in the workplace are as one in emphasizing the great importance of targeted sensitization to unconscious biases. This includes institutions such as the HRC and Out & Equal in the US, Stonewall and INvolve in the UK, Parks in Italy, L'Autre Cercle in France, Workplace Pride in the Netherlands, Prout at Work and Uhlala in Germany, REDI in Spain, Pride at Work Canada/Fierté au Travail in Canada, Pride Circle in India, Community Business in Hong Kong, ACON in Australia, and more.

A brief note: in recent years, there have been some discussions about whether artificial intelligence (AI) can support the overcoming of human unconscious bias, for example, with algorithms checking resumés in recruitment processes. There may by pitfalls. In October 2018, *Reuters*, for example, summarized one of the challenges in a headline: Amazon scraps secret AI recruiting tool that showed bias against women.[4] Though it is certain that digital technology can help to overcome biases in many ways – through webinars, digital awareness trainings, and much more – it must not be forgotten that AI-based tools are made by human beings who have biases too, and/or are based on experience and data from the past that (may) reflect or embody bias.

At any rate, in the course of research for this book, one (white, heterosexual) top executive who wanted to remain anonymous told me that, for him, overcoming conscious and, even more, unconscious bias against LGBT+ people is the key to an open, appreciative working culture in general. He acknowledged the problem of other prejudices. But, he added, "It's like that *New York* song by Frank Sinatra … 'If you can make it there, you can make it anywhere.'" If the organization, he explained, succeeds in overcoming the conscious and unconscious prejudices and clichés about LGBT+ people, which are the most deeply rooted and the most stigmatizing, then we have done it: "… we really have an open culture that values everyone, encouraging more creativity and productivity."

Perhaps that's not the whole story. In view of the Black Live Matters movement, some parts of the LGBT+ community in liberal Western societies – for example in the US, the UK, France, and the Netherlands – started to reflect critically about their own biases and unconscious practice of excluding LGBT+ people of color. Those engaging in these reflections included members of the business world, detecting, confessing, and discussing unpleasant realities, for example, the fact that the dominant figures in most of the firm's ERGs or other organizations working for LGBT+ equality were white gay men, reproducing in some way the overall prevailing societal gender and ethnic/race power structures.

In view of this insight, the cited top executive might want to adapt his statement and, taking an intersectional perspective, now say, "If the organization succeeds in overcoming the conscious and unconscious prejudices and clichés about LGBT+ people of color, we really have an open culture that values everyone, encouraging more creativity and productivity."

## (Power) Position in the social fabric and its importance for the benefits of diversity

This leads to another important line of thought: the increasingly numerous research examples on the benefits of diversity can also be associated with some findings from what is known as "standpoint theory."

According to this, one's perspective depends on which social group one belongs to and whether this group is dominant in the social structure and thus represents the norm, or whether it is subject to domination by others and thus does not represent the norm.

Of course, any social group's perspective likely entails conscious and unconscious bias or prejudice against other groups. However, certain group perspectives could enable a more "objective" perception and analysis of the world than others.

The reason will be clear shortly. The inequalities between social groups not only create a power imbalance, they also favor different standpoints, points of view. In order to secure its position of power, the dominant group's point of view implies the desire to maintain the status quo. It is therefore likely to be less interested in new things. In contrast, the dominated groups are more likely to be open. On the one hand, they have an interest in understanding the dominant group in order to be able to deal better with its greater power. This creates incentives for enhanced empathy and greater awareness of diverse viewpoints. On the other hand, in contrast to the dominant group, the dominated groups are often less interested in maintaining the status quo. Instead, they tend to seek the new, because this could also improve their position in the social fabric.

Viewed in this way, the affiliation of a person to a dominated social group is better for an "objective" perception and analysis of the world than that of a dominant group:

* For example, membership of the group of women compared to the dominant group of men, or
* Membership – in the West – of a group of people with dark skin compared to the dominant group of whites, or
* Membership of the LGBT+ community compared to the dominant group of heterosexuals.

Of course, exceptions exist in which sometimes extreme narrowness is found among members of the otherwise dominated groups, but these are far less likely to apply where members of those groups actively seek to achieve mainstream success alongside members of the dominant group. This is where the impetus to greater openness comes into play for the dominated groups.

In a global economy dynamically driven by creativity and innovation with ever-increasing competitive pressure, sensitivity to diverse perspectives and openness to the new thus represent real potential advantages. But that alone is not enough. It is important that these potential advantages are also made use of.

So how do you start and then continue? In other words: how does one succeed with diversity management? Looked at through the lens of standpoint theory, diversity management in companies will ideally be aimed at creating a forum for productive conflicts in order to enable and exploit the coexistence of competing viewpoints. The first focus of such diversity management is obviously not on strengthening the dominant group, which already has an audible voice and, as I've said, tends not to be as open to the new. The most important focus is therefore naturally on strengthening the dominated groups. They contribute the additional perspectives and openness – which are particularly necessary for creativity and innovation-driven business.

The obvious challenge at the start is that the narrowly focused group at the top will be resistant, first and foremost, to the change represented by the introduction of greater diversity itself: the hiring, especially at senior level, of more women, members of ethnic minorities, LGBT+ people, etc.

From this point of view, it is no coincidence that a change toward professional diversity management often only begins when exogenously triggered crises make this unavoidable. The dominant group often only moves when there is no other way and they themselves see a previously nonexistent advantage in it, e.g. avoiding a worsening of the crisis, from which they themselves would suffer greatly. Again, the story of the Barilla's LGBT+ turnaround told in Part I can serve as an example of this dynamic.

On the other hand, a shock is not always required. It is also true that a dominated group's standpoint can gradually change the dominant group's standpoint alongside slowly changing social values. The dominant groups come to understand that a gradual change of direction is worthwhile for its business and for it.

The quick response of United Airlines, Baker McKenzie, and others to the extraordinarily fast rise of more diverse gender identities among the younger age cohorts Millennials and Generation Z can serve as an example. This rise and these responses I describe in the next chapters.

# 2. Millennials and Generation Z: The rise of more diverse and nonbinary identities

Millennials already have a strong presence in companies and now Generation Z is quickly entering the workforce. This represents not only a fast and significant change in everyday life and business, it also implies a change of prevailing values and attitudes with respect to sexual orientation and gender identity – with consequences for companies.

## Rejecting old classifications

Survey data show how drastic this change is, especially in the liberal Western world – notably, for example, in the LGBT+ trendsetter country, the US. In the spring of 2017, GLAAD, the influential media-focused LGBT+ organization, published its new Accelerating Acceptance study on Millennials and their self-assessments of gender identity and sexual orientation.[5] By "Millennials," the survey meant 18- to 35-year-olds at the time of the survey in November 2016 (approximately those born between 1982–1998). It compared this age cohort with the older Generation X (35 to 51) and Baby Boomers (52 to 71), but also to the generation 72+ (less relevant for the workplace, because its members have retired.)

The survey looked at how strongly younger people question the convention according to which there are only two genders – "male" or "female" – and two for sexual orientation: "homosexual" or "heterosexual." It showed a clear and fast change in attitudes around these, especially the former. It is not an exaggeration to say that we are about to experience a gender revolution – already a reality in major parts of the business world.

Some simple brief notes on terminology related to gender first.[6]

1. The term "gender identity" refers to an individual's sense of their own gender, which is not necessarily governed by their physical attributes.

2. The term "cisgender" is used to distinguish from "transgender." The prefix "cis" comes from Latin and means "on this side of," while "trans" means "on the other side of." Transgender people do not identify with the biological sex assigned to them at birth. Both terms – cis and transgender – refer only to gender identity, not sexual identity/orientation, which refers to whom we feel emotionally, sexually, and/or romantically attracted to. Cis and transgender people can be homo- or heterosexual or otherwise sexually oriented, for example bisexual or asexual.

3. "Gender expression" is how people express themselves by their behavior, mannerisms, interests, and appearance (including clothing, make-up etc.) associated with gender in a particular cultural context.

4. "Nonbinary" is an umbrella term referring to those whose gender identity doesn't sit comfortably with "male" or "female." Alternative or similar terms are "gender-noncompliant," "gender-nonconforming," or "gender-neutral." Nonbinary people can identify with some aspects of male and female identities, while others reject them entirely. With respect to their gender expression, nonbinary people can present as masculine, feminine ("femme"), or both or in another way and this can change over time ("gender-fluid"). (In the acronym LGBTQ, all these are also part of the "Q," covering a variety of forms of queerness.)

5. Pansexuals – or omnisexuals – are people who feel emotionally, romantically, or sexually attracted to other people, regardless of their biological sex or gender identity. In the initials LGBTQ, pansexual people are also part of the "Q," for "queer."

In the GLAAD survey, managed by Harris Poll, a stunning 20% of Millennials self-identified as *other* than strictly heterosexual or cisgender. In a generational comparison, this is a drastic change:

- Millennials:       20%
- Generation X:      12%
- Baby Boomers:      7%
- Over 71s:          5%

Let's break this down to look at the survey's findings for each of the two categories individually: sexual orientation and gender identity.

## A strong increase in "atypical" sexual orientations

The survey figures for people self-identifying as neither heterosexual nor homosexual rose markedly from older to younger generations:

- Millennials:       6% identified as bisexual and 2% as pansexual
- Generation X:     4% bisexual, 1% as pansexual
- Baby Boomers:   2% bisexual, 1% pansexual

Another finding: 3% of Millennials and Generation X identified as exclusively gay or lesbian, compared to 2% of Baby Boomers, so very little had changed here.

What had changed greatly, however, was the proportion of asexual people, i.e. those not sexually attracted to anyone. Among Millennials, 4% identified as asexual, compared to 1% of both Generation X and Baby Boomers. In the acronym LGBTQ, asexual people are also part of the "Q" – that is, one version of "queer."

Finally, if we add up gays, lesbians, bisexuals, pansexuals, and asexuals, the size of the generational leaps with respect to sexual orientation becomes even clearer:

- Millennials:       15%
- Generation X:     9%
- Baby Boomers:   6%

## New categories beyond the old gender classifications

There were also significant changes when it came to gender identity. Two percent of Millennials identified as transgender, compared to 1% for Generation X and 0.5% for the Baby Boomers.

Millennials were also much more frequently located outside the traditional binary understanding of gender. In the survey, in total, a high 10% of Millennials identified as nonbinary.

This means, that overall, a total of 12% of Millennials either identified as transgender or as "nonbinary/gender-noncompliant." Compared to Generation X (6%), this represented a doubling.[7]

## Changed self-descriptions

So, attitudes have changed greatly within one generation and extraordinarily strongly within two. The changes are likely related to the increased media visibility and cultural acceptance that have arisen during Millennials' lifespans, as GLAAD emphasized in its assessment of the survey results in spring 2017.[8]

But increased cultural acceptance was not the automatic correlative of all this, as became clear one year later when a new GLAAD survey showed that acceptance of sexual and gender minorities in the US had actually declined after a year of the Trump presidency.[9]

## Public discussions – and a message to businesses

Change continues nonetheless. *Time* magazine even used the 2017 GLAAD survey as the basis for a cover story – *Beyond He or She – How a new generation is redefining the meaning of gender*.[10] And it was not the first influential publication to respond to these new developments. Two months earlier, in January, the US magazine *National Geographic* had published a special issue entitled *Gender Revolution*,[11] attracting a lot of attention. It organized a major discussion on its content at Davos, three years after the historic off-piste breakfast described in this book's Part II. In the US, interest was so high that the magazine put out a *Discussion Guide for Parents and Teachers* about its contents as a free PDF.[12]

The generational shift on gender identity and sexual orientation is highly relevant for companies that take their equality and inclusion efforts seriously. It sends a message to them. As US politics and culture site *The Daily Beast* wrote in fall 2018, *Workplaces need to prepare for the nonbinary future*.[13]

Indeed, Millennials have already become the largest age cohort in the US workforce (36%), as the Pew Research Center reported in spring 2018, based on the official 2017 US census 2017.[14] With an about 5% presence in the workforce, Generation Z adds to this. At the end of 2017, this accounted for 41% of the total workforce.[15] The trend has risen rapidly since. And there are similar developments in almost all liberal Western societies and companies.

Shortly after the Pew figures were published, Deloitte's Millennial survey 2018 reinforced the picture of how companies must adapt.[16] Its results were based on the views of more than 10,000 Millennials in 36 countries and more than 1,800 Generation Z respondents in six countries. This took into account where in the world Generation Z had already entered the labor force. The results showed, among other things, Millennials' expectations of companies to act, on the one hand, ethically/responsibly toward society and, on the other, to offer them, as employees, a diverse and inclusive corporate culture.

I have already reported on the first of these changed expectations in Part I. There is more: according to the survey, only a minority of Millennials think that companies behave ethically (48% compared to 65% in 2017) and that corporate leaders are committed to improving society (47% compared to 62% in 2017). These are major slumps in just one year.

The Deloitte survey also showed how companies should deal with this alarming finding against the background of rapidly advancing demographic change. Both Millennials and Generation Z attach great importance to factors such as tolerance, respect, and inclusion within companies, as well as different ways of thinking at work, i.e. diversity. Specifically, 74% of those surveyed believed that an organization is more innovative if it has a culture of inclusion. And those who work for companies that have diverse workforces and management teams are more likely to want to stay with their employer for five or more years.

## Generation Z overtakes Millennials

The change of values and attitudes regarding sexual and gender identities from generation to generation does not stop at Millennials. It is continuing rapidly, as other studies have suggested.[17]

In the fall of 2018, Pew Research Center surveyed over 900 teenagers and over 10,000 adults on various social issues. The Generation Z results combined teenagers' and 18–21-year-old respondents' survey data.[18] They suggest that Generation Z outperforms Millennials in their familiarity with nonbinary gender identity and their transgender acceptance – while both outperform all older generations.[19]

Thirty-five percent of Generation Z said they knew someone who used gender-neutral pronouns such as "they," "their," and "them," compared to 25% of Millennials and only 16% and 12% of Generation X and Baby Boomers respectively. Majorities of Generation Z and Millennials also express higher levels of comfort using gender-neutral pronouns than previous generations.

Fifty-nine percent of Generation Z said that forms or online profiles should contain options other than "man" or "woman." Among Millennials, only around 50% agreed. Social media companies had already understood this years before. Facebook, for example, introduced more than 50 new possible gender identity options as early as 2014.

Generation X and Baby Boomers, at 40% and 37% respectively, showed significantly less agreement with the idea.

In addition, Pew noted that about half of Generation Z and Millennials – 50% and 47%, respectively – agreed with the thesis that society is insufficiently accepting of people who do not clearly identify as men or women. About the same percentages of both generations also said that they would like to use gender-neutral pronouns to refer to someone, where appropriate.[20]

## 3. "Welcome Aboard, Mx.," with support from little Trevor, a superstar's journey, and some interface challenges

Some US states have already reacted to the change in values and attitudes. By the end of 2019, roughly a dozen either already offered an "X" in gender fields for driver's licenses instead of just "M," or "F," or had announced the step.[21] Oregon was the first to add a third option in mid-2017,[22] just some months after the aforementioned GLAAD/Harris Poll study was published. Since then, the number has grown quickly, especially in 2019.

IT and other challenges around this are immense for public authorities. What are called the "input masks" in computer programs have to be changed coherently, and communications with other authorities and institutions have to be adapted, including use of language, reporting, and much more. As the headline of a *Fortune* article puts it: *Adding a nonbinary gender option to driver's licenses has become a huge expense for states.*[23] But it seems the costs have not been an obstacle.

The US's leadership on social developments like this sends a strong signal, reflecting a change that global companies cannot ignore.

## United Airlines: "Fly how you identify"

Some have already started to adapt rapidly in terms of personnel, marketing, training, clients, internal and external diversity, inclusion activities, and more. It is a change that especially challenges older generations, for whom the binary concept of gender is often deeply embedded. The concept has shaped the understanding of gender in liberal Western societies (and almost everywhere else) for so long, it seems to many simply unquestionable.

United Airlines provides an example of how global corporations are already willing to vigorously promote the counterview. United is one of the five major US airlines along with American, Delta, Southwest, and Alaska, and had some 95,000 employees in mid-2019.[24]

Due to COVID-19 and related travel restrictions, all airlines are under huge pressure, some laying off hundreds of thousands of employees. It remains to be seen which will fold or be forced to merge. In such a context, United's story remains highly relevant because the struggle to attract customers – more and more dominated by Gen Y and Z – will certainly remain fierce and may even increase post-pandemic.

Prior to the pandemic, on March 22, 2019, the aviation giant posted a short message on its Twitter account: "Fly how you identify. Our new nonbinary gender options are now available."[25] Below this text there were three simple white tick boxes: "Mr.," "Mrs.," and "Mx." – with a check against "Mx." Below that it said: "Welcome Aboard, Mx. – United Continues to Lead in Inclusivity."[26]

If you clicked this, you learned that nonbinary gender options were now offered on all booking channels. Customers could now identify themselves as "M" (male), "F" (female), "U" (undisclosed),or "X" (unspecified).[27] They could also use "Mx." instead of "Mr.," "Mrs.," or "Ms."[28] Toby Enqvist, United's customer executive, said the airline was determined to lead aviation in LGBT+ inclusion and proud to be the first US airline to offer these options.[29]

## Sam Smith's coming out in series

British superstar Sam Smith, among other things winner of the Golden Globe and Oscar for the song *Writing's on the Wall* in the James Bond movie *Spectre*, should be pleased with the offer.

Millennial Smith, born in 1992, revealed himself to be gay in 2014, but soon moved on. In fall 2017, he told the British *Sunday Times* he did not know what the term for this was, but he felt he was "just as much woman as I am a man."[30] While in his youth his wardrobe had mostly been women's clothes, half of it was now men's attire.[31]

The media reported that Smith was one of the first people in public life to come out as gender queer[32] – a kind of second coming out. But his journey was not over. In spring 2019, he came out as nonbinary, saying "I've always had a little bit of a war going within my body and my mind." The headline was, *I am not male or female.*[33]

Shortly afterwards he said that, despite identifying as nonbinary, he wanted to stick to male pronouns, but a few months later he stated a preference for the English nonbinary pronouns "they/them," not "he/him."[34]

(Please note: I have stuck to "he/him" as pronouns in the paragraphs above when describing earlier stages of Sam Smith's identity journey because they reflect Smith's preferences at that time.)

Recently, an International Nonbinary People's Day has been declared, July 14.[35] Analogous to the LGBT+ rainbow flag and the much more recently introduced transgender flag, there is now also a nonbinary flag, with four horizontal stripes – yellow, white, purple, and black.

## The Trevor Project's support

In its press release, United Airlines also announced that it had worked with the Human Rights Campaign, and another nonprofit, The Trevor Project, on its new initiative.

The Trevor Project was an interesting choice. The nonprofit owes its name to a short film entitled *Trevor* that won numerous awards, including an Oscar. In summary, *Trevor* is about a gay 13-year-old with a weakness for Diana Ross, theatrical self-staging, and his school friend, Pinky. When Pinky and other friends and classmates reject Trevor because of his longing for Pinky, he tries to commit suicide with a lot of aspirin tablets and fortunately fails. After his return from hospital, Trevor tentatively finds his way back to life through an inner dialogue that is funny, touching, thoughtful, and positive, and still plausibly and movingly suffused with uncertainty.[36]

When HBO wanted to broadcast the film in 1998, its three film-makers were worried that young viewers might be inspired to make real suicide attempts. Unsuccessful in their search for a professional telephone hotline, they did something even better, creating the first round-the-clock telephone hotline for at-risk LGBTQ youth. It launched with the TV premiere, but this was only the beginning. Over time it became the Trevor Project.

As the leading organization of its kind in the US, it today offers crisis intervention and suicide prevention for LGBTQ people aged 13 to 24, including the 24-hour telephone hotline, known as The Trevor Lifeline. It also comprises an instant messenger service, TrevorChat, and TrevorSpace, the world's largest secure social network for young LGBTQ people, including their friends and allies, plus an educational program for parents, teachers, and other adults professionally involved with young people.[37]

Those seeking to join TrevorSpace are greeted with the words: "Customize your profile to let your friends know how you identify."[38] Options include: "I am gay," "I am transgender," "I am a Demigirl," "I am questioning," "I am pansexual," and others.

## Beyond Barilla: United moves fast for competitive advantage

The United press release announced that it had sought advice from the HRC and the Trevor Project on operational training initiatives for its employees. For example, colleagues were to be trained in workplace LGBT+ competency, gender norms, and preferred pronouns "to make United an inclusive place for both customers and employees."[39]

This kind of work with LGBT+ organizations and the way the new gender booking option was communicated is reminiscent of Barilla's approach described in Part I. However, there are also significant differences.

First, United's engagement with gender identity represents a recent development in companies' efforts to achieve greater LGBT+ equality and inclusion. When Barilla initiated its LGBT+ turnaround some years earlier, this new awareness was not yet so apparent, though in a way, the pasta-makers acknowledged it with their *Dinner's Ready* video (See Part I, "Postscript with a diva").

Second, unlike Barilla, United was not responding to a global outcry that threatened it economically but positioning itself proactively as an LGBT+ pioneer, aiming to gain a competitive advantage.

On the day United made its new booking options public to widespread media attention, *USA Today* asked the airline's major US competitors for reactions. A few weeks earlier, American, Southwest, Alaska, JetBlue, and United had announced new gender booking options in the near future. Now Delta, Alaska, and Southwest made similar statements.[40] By end of 2019, American announced it would be the second large US airline to offer nonbinary gender booking options.[41]

## Challenges with global interfaces?

Right after United's press release, airlines outside the US like British Airways and Air New Zealand also said that they would consider the move. In the fall of that year, a memo sent to Air Canada employees said that soon they would stop using "ladies and gentlemen" in onboard or airport greetings, switching instead to terms like "everyone."[42]

Like United and many other airlines, Air New Zealand and Air Canada are members of the global Star Alliance. With respect to the new booking options, precisely the global nature of this alliance may lead to some technical and other challenges in the near future. For example, most likely the Star Alliance booking systems will have to be aligned to capture the new options. What if some members resist including the new terms in their systems? A nonbinary United passenger, who has booked a ticket at United, might ultimately fly with Star Alliance partner Egypt Air, which would then, presumably, only be able to issue a boarding card listing the passenger as either male or female.

Twenty-six airlines are currently members of the Star Alliance (as of July 2020).[43] It remains to be seen whether airlines from China, India, Turkey, Egypt, and Poland, where legal situation and/or life are difficult for LGBT+ people, will follow United down the path of inclusion.

# 4. More responses to an ongoing development

Other industries have also reacted to the identity explosion. Among them are the global commercial law firms that struggle particularly hard to attract talent, not just against one another but with large companies in other fields.

Take 2020's top five business law firms in the US: Baker McKenzie, DLA Piper, Norton Rose Fulbright, Latham & Watkins, and Hogan Lovells, each with turnovers in the billions.[44] All are known to be making increased efforts toward LGBT+ inclusion in the US. All have, for many years, achieved the perfect score of 100 on the Human Rights Campaign's Corporate Equality Index.

## Preparing for a nonbinary world: Baker McKenzie

In the summer of 2019, Baker McKenzie – with over 75 offices in more than 45 countries – announced diversity targets set at 40:40:20: 40% women, 40% men and 20% flexible (women, men, or nonbinary persons).[45]

The press release stressed, "Once again Baker McKenzie is leading the way in the legal sector."[46] Just like United, it was seeking a D&I advantage over its industry rivals, although in a different way, combining gender and LGBT+ diversity.

The extent to which everyone in this elite industry has been striving to become global LGBT+ leaders for a few years already was again made clear in summer 2020, when Stonewall, the large London-based nonprofit working for LGBT+ equality, published its annual list of the world's best multinational LGBT+-friendly employers. Inclusion on this list is hard won. Companies submit an extensively documented application, which can take many days to compile. The documents are reviewed by Stonewall according to strict criteria. Companies that make the list usually market their success extensively.

That year, of the 17 companies Stonewall put on the list, the bulk were nine global law firms: Freshfields Bruckhaus Deringer, Simmons & Simmons, Pinsent Masons, Hogan Lovells, Allen & Overy, Bryan Cave Leighton Paisner, Dentons, Herbert Smith Freehills, and Baker McKenzie.

## Netflix and its gender-nonconforming stars as new role models

Baker McKenzie's step is important "because it's inviting nonbinary people into the conversation," Beck Bailey, current Director of HRC's Workplace Equality Program, told the *Washington Post*.[47]

### Clifford Chance: introducing LGBT+ targets

In summer 2020, another global law firm made waves. Clifford Chance announced it had set global and regional targets to advance gender, ethnic, and LGBT+ inclusion.

This was big news; what Clifford Chance does has impact. The company usually makes it into the global top ten of multinational law firms measured both by number of lawyers and revenue. It is headquartered in London and a member of the prestigious "Magic Circle," encompassing global law firms headquartered in London that show the largest revenues and highest profits.

The press release said, "Change the rules, change the culture, and change the lived experience."[48] The company now aims to have at least 40% female and 40% male global partners by 2030, and promises that this will be extended throughout the firm's structures at a global and regional level. It also set minority ethnicity targets for the US and UK, specifying 15% of partners and 30% of senior associates and business professionals by 2025. Finally, the law firm introduces an LGBT+ global partner target of 3% by 2025.

Tiernan Brady, the firm's Global Director of Inclusion, said in the press release, "There is no hidden arc of progress that will make it happen automatically."

### Tiernan Brady's campaigning for change

Appointing Brady as Head of Inclusion was a smart move, although surprising for some. Before taking up the role in 2019, Brady led a colorful professional life. He was Director of Organization to the Irish Deputy Prime Minister (*Tánaiste*); mayor of his Irish hometown, Bundoran; policy officer for GLEN, the Gay and Lesbian Equality Network, Ireland's leading LGBT+ organization; and a successful international LGBT+ campaigner. As Political Director of the Yes Equality campaign in Ireland in 2015 and as Director of the Equality Campaign in Australia in 2017, he substantially contributed twice to equal marriage legislation.[49] In both referendums, about 62% of voters said yes to this legislation. Australia and Ireland were the only two countries in the world to enact marriage equality by public vote.

After the success in Australia, Brady also worked for a couple of months in a leading role at Equal Future 2018,[50] an international humanitarian campaign aiming to raise "awareness of the damage done to children when they feel that being LGBT would be a misfortune or a disappointment."[51] The campaign was launched at the World Meeting of Families of the Catholic Church in Dublin in August 2018. It has since attracted support around the globe, especially from countries with a significant Catholic population. They include Global Network of Rainbow Catholics, musicchildren. org, *Grupo Lesbico Feminista Artemisa* (Nicaragua), Gay Christians Slovakia, *Diversidade Católica* (Brazil), Australian Catholics for Equality, HRC, GLAAD, and many more.[52] Among other things, the campaign urged people to use its website to tell their stories, especially if they were LGBT+ religious people. It gave this feedback directly to the Catholic Church's bishops prior to the event.[53]

There is no doubt, then, that Brady is an expert at campaigning on challenging topics. And, it seems, Brady is still using his elaborate skills in his new job. Referring to the Clifford Chance's new targets, he says, "If we want to build an inclusive firm and society, we have to work hard and campaign for it, set goals, and when we achieve them, defend and champion them."[54]

But at the same time, Bailey was looking further ahead. In fact, a few larger companies have also begun to make initial efforts to include nonbinary people, he added, for example, by introducing gender-neutral language in communications or updating clothing regulations and toilet facilities. It is therefore no coincidence that the *Post* ran an article headlined, *How employers are preparing for a gender nonbinary world* in early July 2019.[55]

Mastercard provides a further example. During a summer 2019 discussion event with the New York City Commission on Human Rights, the credit card giant announced the True Name Program, giving cardholders the option of changing their birth name if it conflicts with their gender identity, for the name they actually use.[56]

Netflix is also on the case. Its recruiters are now being asked to name their preferred personal pronoun and ask candidates about theirs in their first telephone contact.[57] The streaming service and media producer has many young people among its viewers, customers, business partners and, not least, its stars. Some of these have come out as nonbinary, gender-nonconforming or genderqueer and now are increasingly viewed as role models.

Jonathan Van Ness and Lachlan Watson are examples. Van Ness, from the reality show *Queer Eye*, currently has long hair and a beard, often wears women's clothes, and almost always sports painted fingernails. He is gay and prefers the pronouns "he/his/him," but in an interview with *Out* magazine that described his gender identity as nonbinary, gender-nonconforming and genderqueer, he added, "Some days I feel like a man, but then other days I feel like a woman."[58]

As for Lachlan Watson, in 2016, they – that's Watson's preferred pronoun, along with "them" and "theirs" – was given a permanent role in the Netflix series *Chilling Adventures of Sabrina*. Watson played a genderqueer character from the series' second season, their character revealing themselves as a transman and changing their name from Susi to Theo Putnam. At the time of their debut, Watson, born 2001 in North Carolina, was one of the youngest Hollywood actors to come out as nonbinary. In sexual preference terms, they identified as pansexual.

In November 2018, Watson was featured in a five-minute Netflix production entitled *What I Wish You Knew: About being nonbinary*[59] with other nonbinary celebrities such as Australian actor Liv Hewson, Indian artist Shiva Raichandani,[60] and Jacob Tobia, a US writer, producer, and LGBT+ activist.[61]

Netflix stars like Van Ness and Watson are regularly included on role model lists of nonbinary/gender-nonconforming/genderqueer stars – as are Sam Smith or Jacob Tobia.[62]

## "Boston's largest all-female, femme and nonbinary hackathon!"[63]

US universities have also been responding. In spring 2019 in Boston, a 36-hour hackathon called TechTogether Boston was organized by several universities. A hackathon is a technology-oriented event in which people work together intensively on programming.

The event, called SheHacks when launched in 2018, had revised the conditions of participation. Participants now had to consider themselves as female or nonbinary. The rebranded event was a success.

Advertising for the subsequent event in 2020 used the slogan, "Boston's largest all-female, femme and nonbinary hackathon!"[64] The term "femme" refers to a queer person whose gender expression is seen as feminine. There is also an International Femme Appreciation Day celebrated on the first Saturday of July.

The website says the organizers want "to shape the way women and nonbinary people get involved with tech," adding they aim "to create an inclusive environment to encourage more underrepresented people" to get into technology.[65]

## McKinsey's awards – modern language, including "queer" and "questioning"

Consultancy McKinsey reacted to this development too. In April 2020, amid the COVID-19 pandemic, it announced the launch of new McKinsey Achievement Awards designed "to recognize and support talented people who may be currently underrepresented in leadership roles."[66] The awards are clearly not focused on generations over 40. They offer mentoring and some money, either for academic or professional development, and for support toward a later application to work at McKinsey.

One such award, the Women Achievement Award, is for "individuals who self-identify as women," not just "women."[67] Another, the McKinsey LGBTQ+ Achievement Award, is "for individuals who self-identify as lesbian, gay, bisexual, transgender, queer, or questioning,"[68]

## Young, highly talented, black, nonbinary, femme, Accenture, and more

Titi Naomi Tukes was recognized with this award – young, highly talented, engaged and an employee at Accenture. Tukes' LinkedIn business profile shows "they/them" as preferred pronouns, they are black, identify as nonbinary femme, and give "Mx." as their preferred honorific.

In 2018, just a couple months after starting their work with Accenture as a consulting analyst, Tukes suggested adding a field for identifying pronouns to the company's online directory. The idea was quickly implemented.[69] Being a nonbinary employee, Tukes said in a *Washington Post* interview, can be full of ups and downs. Sometimes, they have to help other colleagues use "they/their/them," sometimes there are "moments when I'm being championed and endorsed."[70]

It seems that at Accenture they experience more of the latter. Speaking to the *Post* for the same article, Ellyn Shook, Accenture's Chief Leadership and Human Resources Officer, said Tukes had inspired her to add the pronouns "she/her" to her own emails.[71] "If you are in a 'battle for talent,'" Accenture's HR boss said, "you have to help people both professionally and personally." It would be her job and the job of her colleagues "to make sure that each and every one of us feels like we belong."[72]

Tukes grew up in the greater area of Atlanta, Georgia, and studied at Morehouse College, a historically black men's college in Atlanta founded in 1867, a prestigious college, especially among people of color. Martin Luther King, Jr. got his bachelor's degree there.[73]

Tukes received not only their bachelor of arts in cinema, television, and emerging media studies at Morehouse, they also received several grants, including the merit-based Oprah Winfrey Charitable Foundation Scholarship. They became a member of the elite Phi Beta Kappa too, the more than 240-year-old academic honor society, known for its selectivity.[74] In addition, they were part of a presidential task force for LGBT+ D&I and the campus climate survey on sexual violence. And they served as the college ambassador to the Obama Administration's White House Initiative on Historically Black Colleges & Universities (HBCUs).

A quick explanation: most HBCUs were established after the American Civil War, which ended in 1865, to serve African Americans.

Despite the formal end of slavery, African Americans were fully banned from or severely discriminated against in many ways in schools, universities, politics, workplaces, and public life. It was only the US Civil Rights Act in 1964 that outlawed discrimination based on race, color, religion, sex, or national origin, prohibiting racial segregation in schools, universities, workplaces, and public accommodation, and the unequal application of voter registration requirements. As the Black Lives Matter movement has – again – made very clear, even new laws are not enough as long as cultural attitudes do not also change profoundly.

Tukes made their way up nevertheless. Now living in New York City, they got promoted to management consultant at Accenture at the end of December 2019. Around that time, they were also the first nonbinary person to join the board at Rainbow Railroad, a nonprofit founded some fifteen years ago that focuses on LGBT+ people globally who need help quickly against serious threats to their lives and safety.[75]

Beyond that they "invest in emerging LGBT, black-led startups addressing society's sociopolitical failings,"[76] Tukes stated until recently in their LinkedIn business profile. There, they also said of themselves, "Titi Naomi leads in the movement for racial, sexuality, and transgender equity and justice in society" though this has now changed too. Meanwhile Tukes has changed these remarks. Their purpose-led message remains.

# 5. Out, equal, and the business of belonging

Out & Equal Workplace Advocates – Out & Equal for short – reports similar developments and responses in companies to the gender revolution. It works with companies, government agencies, and organizations for LGBT+ equality by providing D&I training, consultation, networking opportunities, and executive leadership development. Although it engages in some programs in Brazil, China, and India, by far its primary focus is the US.

## A major conference – and data by self-identification?

Every fall in different American cities, Out & Equal holds the world's largest multi-day event on LGBT+ equality at work. This annual conference, legendary for many, shapes trends. Every year, companies send more and more participants, who use the event as a networking, communication, and learning platform, and as a marketing instrument to show off their LGBT+ friendliness. Their sincerity is not always clear, but simply attending the event exposes them to greater scrutiny.

In October 2018, the conference took place in Seattle, Washington, and I attended. According to the organizers, there were more than 5,000 participants, a strong increase from the previous year, and a new attendance record. About a third came from abroad, also a record, the organizers said on stage. About one-third were not LGBT+ but allies – as was probably known thanks to the registration process' self-identification feature.

I hesitated with respect to this feature as I filled out the form when picking up my conference passport and documents. Some data protectionists would probably find the collection, storage, and use of data on sexual and gender identity alarming.

I was not the only one with a slightly strange feeling about it. After the following year's annual Out & Equal conference, which took place in Washington, DC, I spoke with a lesbian tech expert, who prefers to remain anonymous. She said she had tried to talk about her data protection concerns in a conference workshop that was actually about improving LGBT+ D&I measures based on voluntary self-identification data.

She asked critical questions, pointing out that data, though handled in accordance with strong compliance rules, could be misused and/or hacked. This would be especially dangerous for LGBT+ people working in countries where they are strongly stigmatized or even criminalized, but even in liberal Western countries, people could get into trouble with their personal data on sexual and gender identity online. "To me, and many Europeans in general, these security and data protections are major topics, also to Millennials," she said, "But at this very US-focused event, absolutely nobody was interested in discussing this topic." To her it seemed "that in Europe, we view these things a lot more critically."

## A quick additional note

The same tech expert was also irritated by the fact that Out & Equal had accepted Northrop Grumman as a leading sponsor the year she attended. As already mentioned in Part II, Northrop Grumman is one of the world's largest military technology and weapons manufacturers.

"Regarding the purpose of companies, i.e. in the case of Northrop Grumman producing killing devices, there are, I think, limits to engaging with businesses on advancing LGBT+ equality," she said. "But at the US conference, there was no discussion at all. In continental Europe there would have been a critical discussion and a reputation risk for the conference organizers and also for the other participating companies." She is right – and once again draws attention to the sometimes severe cultural differences in the handling of LGBT+ inclusion globally.

For example, an expert from South Africa, who also prefers to remain anonymous, told me, in an interview for this book, a story about Shell. In 2018, in Johannesburg, South Africa's first Workplace Equality Index (SAWEI) was launched at an event I attended (see Part III, Chapter 4). This was without doubt a major step in raising awareness of LGBT+ workplace and societal inclusion in this economically and socially unsteady country. That year, Shell South Africa was ranked at the top gold tier, scoring 80% or more.[77] However, the following year, prior to the index's second edition, the organizers posed some critical questions on the company's dealing with oil pollution in Nigeria, an issue with a long and extremely troubled history, considered by many to represent one of the worst corporate atrocities in the world.[78] Shell finally decided not to participate again in the index evaluation – not giving an official reason but most probably wanting to avoid reputational risks beyond its status as an LGBT+-friendly company.

## A wealth of events, sponsors, and knowhow

In the end, at the Out & Equal conference in Seattle, when I filled in my registration form, I decided on openness and made a cross next to "gay." But although my sexual orientation is broadly known in many ways, including through social media, the strange feeling stayed with me.

The conference offered such a wealth of lectures, panel discussions, workshops, networking events, and artistic performances that it was hard to keep track. A conference booklet of over 120 pages – with countless company advertisements – provided some orientation.

There was also a well-designed conference app with detailed information about programs and people, functionality for commenting on conference events and networking, and news updates. For example, it would let you know who had won the awards known as "Outies" presented by the organizers. There was one for a single LGBT+ champion, one for an exemplary company, and one for an LGBT+ employee resource group.

The 2018 conference was supported by more than 100 companies and organizations, divided into ten categories. Standing in front of the huge sponsorship board peppered with logos was bewildering. Among the most important sponsors in the top five categories were American Airlines, Apple, HP, Disney, Deloitte, Starbucks, Boeing, Pepsi, and major banks such as JPMorgan Chase, HSBC, and Bank of America.

Further conference partners might be surprising for some: the US Department of Agriculture and even the CIA. Germany, Europe's strongest economy, was only present in lower sponsorship categories, via companies such as SAP, T-Mobile, Bayer, and Volkswagen.

The conference program included well over a hundred events, some of which ran in parallel. Simple terms made clear each event's level, e.g. beginner, advanced, D&I expert, and its content focus, e.g. LGBT+ marketing, bi+/queer leadership, general/global, LGBT+ allies, corporate networks/employee resource groups, and transgender/gender expansion (also including all things nonbinary).

There were also "tracks," i.e. paths on which one could travel to pursue a particular content focus on successive conference days. The Transgender/Gender Expansive track covered an amazing 11 events taking place over three days. Nine of them were purely transgender related, with only one having a clearly recognizable reference to non-binary inclusion.

## Not just D&I, but also B - the next big thing?

I asked Erin Uritus, Out & Equal's then quite new CEO, which LGBT+ workplace trends she saw as important. She immediately said, "belonging": making LGBT+ employees feel part of their workplaces, teams, and organizations. Uritus had emphasized this topic repeatedly already in her main conference speech, so it was no surprise.

Out & Equal's homepage now shows "The Business of Belonging" as the leading claim, marketing it as the differentiating factor in its work to "help LGBTQ people thrive and support organizations creating a culture of belonging for all."[79]

Will the addition of "belonging" to the D&I discourse have an impact on how D&I – and LGBT+ D&I in particular – are discussed in the near future? Will belonging be the "next evolution of diversity and inclusion,"[80] as the headline of a recent article on this topic suggested?

Perhaps. It is worth having a quick look back. Diversity, understood as offering potential economic benefits, started to gain more and more visibility in both theory and practice from the mid '90s. Initially, the focus was on just that: difference.

But over time, it became clear that in order to unleash the hidden economic potential of diversity, one would need to be able to manage the potentially growing conflicts it could cause in teams and workforces, and promote cultural learning within the organization. A new concept needed to be added to cover these concerns: inclusion.

A few years ago, the *Harvard Business Review* (*HBR*) published an article entitled: *Diverse teams feel less comfortable – and that's why they perform better*.[81] In contrast, homogeneous teams may feel lighter – but "light," according to the article, is bad for performance. It is precisely the "perceived uneasiness" of heterogeneity that companies and their teams, departments, and workforces can benefit from.

But the *HBR* article also rightly added that more diversity can also mean more conflicts. This is good if these conflicts are used constructively for better solutions. It is precisely then that the potential benefits of diversity – i.e. better handling of facts, better decisions, better ideas, more innovation, growth, and profit – can be exploited. However, increased conflicts resulting from greater diversity can also be destructive.[82] The "perceived uneasiness" of various teams, referred to in the *HBR*, must not be allowed to boil over. The line between success factor and destroyer of value may be thin and must be found.

To head off potentially damaging conflicts, many companies also nurture their workforces in being more diverse in terms of knowledge, emotional intelligence, empathy and understanding of otherness, as well as awareness of conscious and unconscious prejudices or biases. All of this equates to the workforces becoming more actively inclusive.

For example, white employees are helped to better understand nonwhite colleagues, heterosexual employees to understand LGBT+ colleagues, and so on. This is why it is now commonly understood that companies not only practice diversity management but rather engage in diversity *and inclusion* management – D&I or sometimes I&D for short.

In sum, "diversity" refers to the mix of different employees in a company, "inclusion" to how well companies succeed in integrating all members a diverse workforce. The one does not work without the other. *Diversity doesn't stick without inclusion*[83] says the title of another *HBR* article.

Some ten years ago, the terms diversity manager, diversity advisory board, or diversity management tended to dominate in companies. Those times are over in many places. Today, it's all D&I or I&D – for example: D&I manager, D&I management, D&I advisory board, or I&D council. This reflects a growing sensitivity around integration and inclusion in an economic world with increasing pressure to innovate and compete but also increasing centrifugal forces and conflict potential. Even if the "I" is not mentioned, it now overwhelmingly tends to be part of strategy and concrete operational measures.

Now, with the idea of widening the focus to "belonging," the discourse around D&I may shift again. The way Erin Uritus repeatedly said, "You belong here" on stage at the conference in Seattle stressed the emotional side in contrast to the more emotionally distant notions of "diversity" and "inclusion."

## Fast development

At the time of the conference, some companies had already begun to switch from talking only about D&I or I&D to DIB, meaning: diversity, inclusion, and belonging. Just a few months later, a leading business school, the Wharton School of the University of Pennsylvania, hosted an event with panelists from companies titled Fostering Belonging at Work as part of Wharton's Leading Diversity lecture series. Wharton Assistant Professor Stephanie Creary, who teaches a seven-week elective course to undergraduate and MBA students called Leading Diversity In Organizations, summarized the message of the event in the title of a LinkedIn article, *Keeping the diversity conversation emotional: why we need to keep talking about belonging at work.*[84]

One of the panelists was Sam Lalanne, Senior Vice President of Global Diversity and Talent Management at Citi, stressing that this diversity message related to emotions. While diversity is often linked to numbers and percentages, Lalanne said, belonging was "about how you feel." Do you feel that you should be where you are and that your insights, commentary, and perspectives matter? Do you feel valued?

As a means of advancing the experience of belonging among the entire workforce, he stressed the power of storytelling to senior figures "about the struggle to fit in or to be their authentic selves at work."[85] The proximity to the language and concepts used for a couple years to advance LGBT+ D&I is evident.

In November 2019, Yale University followed the fast-developing discourse by setting up the Belonging at Yale initiative to advance the university's effort "to foster a more diverse, inclusive, and welcoming campus."[86]

Both Wharton and Yale, were, it seems, following a competitor, Harvard University, where, in the spring of 2018, the college's Presidential Task Force on Inclusion and Belonging had already issued a report.[87] It set out recommendations and a framework "to serve as a blueprint for advancing Harvard's practices and culture of inclusion and belonging."[88] Today Harvard has a website (https://dib.harvard.edu/) featuring the Harvard Diversity Inclusion & Belonging mission, goals, and everything related to DIB at the university.

Others have also picked up the baton of "belonging," for example, the NYU School of Law's Center for Diversity, Inclusion, and Belonging.[89]

Universities, especially those in the top tier, are not only at the front line of up-to-date research but also of the young and their changing values, expectations, and feelings, including those with more diverse sexual and gender identities. In this light, it may be no coincidence that there is a very evident parallel between the significant increase in diverse gender identities among the young and the steady rise of "belonging" in (LGBT+) D&I discourse.

At the end of December 2019, Jena McGregor in the *Washington Post* started an article with the words: "Move over, 'diversity.' Make room, 'inclusion.' Today, the hot corporate buzzword in the diversity field is 'belonging.'"[90]

Out & Equal CEO Erin Uritus might have a good intuition about the direction trends relevant for her business are going in, and leading

US universities may be at the forefront of the development. Still, it remains to be seen whether "belonging" is just another new "buzzword," as the *Post* put it, or whether it can prove more substantial than is visible today.

At any rate, a more emotional dimension for LGBT+ D&I seems a good fit for a time when emotional intelligence, empathy, and the ability for self-refection have become indispensable skills for successful leadership in modern business.

# 6. An inflection point in the US, language issues, and Stonewall's work

In our interview, Uritus also cited the "inclusion and belonging of nonbinary persons" in efforts to achieve LGBT+ equality in companies and other organizations as a second important trend. For a moment I was a little surprised, given that that year's conference program did not really reflect this.

But the event was also about identifying future developments through the less formal mechanism of discussions during coffee breaks, lunches, dinners, and other occasions. Out & Equal, in any case, quickly picked up the ball. In mid-November 2018, just six weeks after the conference, the organization compiled a guide, made available as a PDF, entitled, *Best practices for nonbinary inclusion in the workplace*,[91] giving handy advice on definitions, policies, dress codes, facilities, talent acquisition, tips for ERG engagement, how to show support as a straight ally, gender-neutral language, and pronoun usage.[92]

In line with this, a recent study by Margit Tavits from the University of St. Louis and Efrén O. Pérez from UCLA showed that gender-neutral pronouns improved feelings toward LGBT+ people. Sabine Sczesny, Professor of Social Psychology at the University of Bern, Switzerland, in an interview with the *Guardian*, classified the research as further evidence that gender-related language can reduce gender-specific prejudices and "contribute to the promotion of gender and LGBT equality and tolerance."[93]

It was only shortly after Out & Equal made available the nonbinary guide in March 2019 that United announced its new third booking option, and Baker McKenzie, Netflix, and Mastercard followed a little later with the other initiatives described above. In the summer of 2019, Noam Shelef, communications director at Out & Equal, in an interview with the *Washington Post*, said they had recently conducted well over two dozen training sessions that included the use of gender pronouns.[94] There "clearly is an inflection point where nonbinary inclusion is becoming of interest," he said.

## Germany's "third gender" option

He's right. There's movement on many fronts. For example, there is also a fast-growing awareness of gender-neutral language in Europe's largest economy, Germany, not just in state agencies but also in larger companies. And there is a fast-growing sensitivity to personal preferences indicated by the inclusion of preferred pronouns on social media profiles, including globally leading business site LinkedIn, and on email signatures.

In addition, as of January 1, 2019, Germany became the first country in the European Union to offer a "third gender" option (in German: *drittes Geschlecht*) on birth certificates. Parents of intersex babies and grown-up intersex people themselves, can now choose to register as diverse (in German: *divers*), on birth certificates, instead of having to choose between male or female.

Six years before, Germany had already become the first European country allowing parents of intersex babies to leave the gender box blank on a birth certificate. And only a few years later, a young intersex person had gone to court to demand a third option. Germany's Constitutional Court finally ruled that the existing system had been unconstitutional, violating basic rights in failing to provide the third option. It had set a deadline for lawmakers to change the system by December 31, 2018.

According to the United Nations, between 0.05 and 1.7% of the global population are born with intersex traits.[95] The umbrella term "intersex" is usually used to describe a variety of conditions in which a person is born with sexual and/or reproductive anatomy that does not fit into (historically and culturally developed) binary definitions of female or male.

Babies or small children born with visible variations in their sexual characteristics are often subjected to painful and irreversible surgery to make them appear to have a "normal" male or female gender, says an Amnesty International report.[96] In general, intersex people are at high risk of human rights violations in the form not only of surgery but also discrimination and torture, according to the UN.[97]

Although the new German law was celebrated as a revolution for intersex people, it does not include the whole range of nonbinary gender identities 1 have described in this book. However, the law contributes to advancing the gender revolution driven by the young.

### Axel Springer: a German "gender star" and a growing sensitivity to language issues in the media

An example of how young Germans are taking up language reflecting changing perceptions of gender is provided by the Axel Springer Group. The German-based European media house, headquartered in Berlin, generates about €3 billion in annual revenue and employs over 16,000 people (as of December 2019).[98] It is active in about 40 countries.[99] In Germany, by far the group's most important market, it runs, among other things, newspapers, a news channel, and various websites. One of its brands is Europe's bestselling tabloid newspaper, *Bild*.

For decades now, the group has also run a journalism school, the Axel Springer Academy, which, at the end of December 2018, launched an interesting project: Divers*land. The school's website explains, "A change in the law now allows a third gender option in the birth register: 'diverse,' designating people who don't identify as male or female ... We, 18 young journalists from Berlin, are entering a media industry in which ... personal stories of trans* and inter* people often remain untold. In a just society, however, everyone must be visible ..."[100] Divers*land, the website says, has been created as a platform for these stories.

Note: the asterisk * in Divers*land, known as the "gender star" – in German, *Gendersternchen* – has become increasingly common in recent years. German has male and female forms for certain nouns, e.g. *Spieler* (male player) and *Spielerin* (female player). The "gender star" is usually placed in the female form before the female suffix to render the word gender-neutral, e.g. *Spieler\*in* (player). Using it is considered to be progressive.

The Divers\*land project is even more remarkable because for decades Axel Springer was – in continental European terms – conservative or liberal-conservative. However, it is also especially subject to pressure from the young generation, having strongly increased its revenue share from digital business to more than 70%. It is mainly the young for whom digital media is the norm.

Axel Springer's response to this changing world is also reflected in the fact that, after many years of resistance to even dealing with LGBT+ D&I, in 2014 it finally allowed employees to launch an LGBT+ employee network, queerseite. It is now quite active and visibly supported by CEO Mathias Döpfner, already the driving force behind the company's major move into the digital media. The network has a website, in both German and English,[101] and also uses special instruments to check the company's news, articles, and other media for language and presentation that reinforce LGBT+ stereotypes and prejudices.

Such prejudices can still turn up almost anywhere, of course, but especially for tabloid *Bild*, this is sometimes appropriate because the very nature of tabloids is to simplify drastically. However, it is worth noting that *Bild* has for some time had a queer section on its website, with a constant stream of stories. This is a notable development, perhaps indicating that even in the world of tabloid newspapers, the LGBT+ business case is winning out.

So, while Germany's companies have not yet been engulfed by the non-binary wave triggered primarily by the young in the US, sensitivities are clearly growing, especially in terms of language, form of address, and pronouns. It is probably only a matter of time before the trend makes itself fully felt in Germany and continental Europe in general – no doubt, again, as the Axel Springer example shows (see box), driven by the young. In the United Kingdom, it is already becoming apparent. Just after the law came into force, the German Prout at Work Foundation published a how-to-guide for companies and other organizations. It introduced gender in the new way reflected in this book and gave tips on how to implement the law in the workplace. It also looked in more detail at the challenges of the third gender option in relation to labor law. And it showed which norms can be interpreted a bit more broadly but still in alignment with the third option's spirit, and which norms still require a legislative response. The guide is currently being revised, with new best practices and more.[102]

However, the German language – in common with many others – does not yet offer a third "pronoun family" for nonbinary people, like "they/them/theirs" in English. This is a major disadvantage because sensitive language usage contributes, as we have seen, strongly to LGBT+ inclusion – in daily life and in the workplace.

It remains to be seen if non-English languages will see new pronouns soon, perhaps invented by the creative young in their day-to-day communication, to advance the gender revolution they want to live.

## Merriam-Webster's change

The English-speaking world, in contrast, has already seen a major linguistic move reflecting the nonbinary revolution. In the fall of 2018, the influential Merriam-Webster dictionary updated the description of the word "they" with an entry describing its use as a pronoun for nonbinary people.[103]

Merriam-Webster is a subsidiary of the world-famous Encyclopaedia Britannica, an American company, despite the name. On its free-to-access website, Merriam-Webster explains that there are examples of the word being used as a singular pronoun in various contexts in speech and writings going back hundreds of years, even in literary and formal contexts.[104]

In the entry on its newest usage, it says that, in recent years, the pronoun has been adopted by individuals whose gender identity is nonbinary, and includes an example of how it can be used today: "I knew certain things about ... the person I was interviewing ... They had adopted their gender-neutral name a few years ago, when they began to consciously identify as nonbinary – that is, neither male nor female. They were in their late 20s, working as an event planner, applying to graduate school."[105]

## "10 ways to step up as an ally for nonbinary people"

UK-based Stonewall, Europe's largest LGBT+ organization, impacting the whole English-speaking world, also reported on this Merriam-Webster news.[106] And it now provides some resources to support nonbinary inclusion, too, although not yet a comprehensive guide like that of the aforementioned US nonprofit Out & Equal. On the occasion of International Nonbinary Peoples' Day on July 14, for example, Stonewall published *10 ways to step up as an ally to nonbinary people* on their website.[107]

Most of the tips refer to gender-neutral language and pronouns, including inviting (potential) allies to put in their own pronouns on their social medial profiles and email signatures. Stonewall recommends that, when highlighting LGBT+ people in events or as role models, one should make sure to include some nonbinary role models, too.[108]

Stonewall's ten recommendations are presented in such a way as to be usable in the workplace or in schools, both areas where Stonewall has been active for decades. The charity was founded in 1989, 20 years after the Stonewall riots in New York City described in Part I. In its approach and work, it is both much broader and deeper than the continental European nonprofits working on LGBT+ inclusion I have referred to in this book, such as the Netherlands' Workplace Pride, Italy's Parks, Germany's Prout at Work, or Spain's REDI. These are only focused on workplace inclusion.

## A big player in LGBT+ workplace issues – with more on nonbinary

Well-funded Stonewall is also one of the leading organizations working for LGBT+ workplace inclusion in the UK, setting standards in many ways in Europe and globally.

Here is a selection of its wealth of initiatives, programs, and resources.

There is the annual Workplace Equality Index for the UK and a global equivalent. Both are high-standard, detailed benchmarking tools reflecting organizations' efforts, progress, and level with regard to LGBT+ inclusion. As key benefits for organizations taking part in analysis for the index, Stonewall lists assessing status, showing commitment, receiving recognition, and building an action plan for next steps.[109]

Every year in September, based on employers' submissions for their Global Workplace Equality Index, Stonewall also compiles the Top Global Employer list, recognizing the best multinational employers for LGBT+ staff.

Stonewall also offers a Diversity Champions program, guiding paying member employers in the UK in ensuring LGBT+ inclusion for all staff. Currently this program works with hundreds of companies and public organizations, representing almost a quarter of the UK workforce. One member of this program is Metro Bank, a very early mover in nonbinary inclusion in the UK, even preceding America's United Airlines. The high-street bank was founded only in 2010 and is small compared to British banking giants like HSBC or Barclays. Yet as early as 2016, it became the first bank in Britain to welcome customers who do not identify as male or female, by adding the nonbinary gender option "Mx." on its account application form.[110]

Stonewall also offers a Global Diversity Champions program, with about 200 employers in 18 categories, most of them from business industries, but also from other sectors such as education (including the renowned London School of Economics and Political Science and many other universities), government agencies, and sport (including the world's best-known soccer league, the Premier League). The program provides the tools for paying member employers to take a strategic and structured approach to LGBT+ equality initiatives globally, even in countries where people may not be protected by workplace law, LGBT+ people face discrimination, same-sex relationships are criminalized, etc.

There are also Stonewall's Global Workplace Briefings for many countries, which provide practical guidance on how to support LGBT+ staff through a mixture of legal, cultural, and workplace best-practice information. The briefings are usually supported by local nonprofits working for LGBT+ equality in their country.

Furthermore, Stonewall offers programs for LGBT+ leadership, trans allies, workplace allies, and role models, the last two also having versions for Scotland. There are conferences, workshops, and webinars. There are guides to LGBT+ advocacy for businesses, for getting data on sexual orientation and gender identity in the European Union, for trans inclusion in the workplace, for setting up an ERG and maximizing its impact, for LGBT+ inclusion in procurement, and for advancing LGBT+ inclusion in higher education. And there is a toolkit called The Employee Lifecycle that shows how an organization can be LGBT+-inclusive at every step of an employee's journey – from recruitment and induction to development and exit.

In addition, based on the result of its aforementioned annual Workplace Equality Index in the UK, Stonewall publishes rankings. The most prestigious lists the 100 most LGBT+-inclusive workplaces in Britain. Those that are included in the list are entitled to use the seal Stonewall Top 100 Employer for internal and external communications. Another list showcases the best 20 trans-inclusive employers (in 2020).

Based on the index, Stonewall also showcases the past year's best practices for different categories. In the category Monitoring, for example, it listed UK-based global business law firm Pinsent Masons as Employer of the Year in 2019, praising it for monitoring the sexual orientation and gender identity of their applicants and staff, and for analyzing that data to identify areas for improvement.[111] Specifically, Pinsent Masons "ask separate questions on their monitoring forms about sexual orientation, gender, and trans identity, always including the option to self-describe for those who don't identify with the options offered in the survey."[112]

Based on their annual UK Workplace Equality Index as well, Stonewall distinguishes individuals for outstanding work in their organizations and beyond. There are awards for lesbian, gay, bi, trans, ally, and senior champion role models of the year.

At this point, Stonewall does not offer awards for nonbinary role models – although in their own ten recommendations, discussed above, they suggest making such role models visible. Also, so far, although Stonewall annually applauds several trans-friendly companies of the year, it has not showcased companies that set an example for strong nonbinary inclusion.

Both gaps may have to do with the fact that the topic of nonbinary inclusion in the workplace is still in an early phase of being addressed by companies and other organizations. Also, US-based companies may be more advanced in responding to these trends than those in Britain – which are more advanced again than continental European companies or companies in other areas such as Asia.

# 7. A Berlin tribute to a Scottish grandmother, contests for leaders around the world, and new female power

Another strong indicator of changed business responses to new realities is the growing landscapes of options for meeting, recruiting, and educating young LGBT+ talents.

## LGBT+ Entrepreneur

Stuart Cameron, whom we have met before, offers workshops, audits, consulting, and more to support businesses in being LGBT+-inclusive and credibly promoting this as a brand value. He has consolidated his many ventures into the Uhlala Group. "We are a social business," he says. "Working professionally for a good, meaningful purpose for us also means we want to earn good money. We are not doing this to get rich, but we are growing and our salaries have to be paid."

Among his initiatives is Unicorns in Tech, a technology-oriented LGBT+ community founded in 2014 that has grown to about 4,000 members. It usually meets once a month, hosted by LGBT+-friendly companies primarily in Berlin, but also others.

Another initiative is Alice, an LGBT+ career network for lawyers, law students, and trainees, with a conference, the Alice Summit, held every two years. It is named after the Cameroonian lawyer and LGBT+ activist Alice Nkom.

In December 2019, Cameron launched the DAX 30 LGBT+ Diversity Index, ranking the 30 companies on Germany's leading stock market index, the DAX. Companies answered ten categories of question on LGBT+ diversity, including internal and external communication, participation in LGBT+ events, ERGs, awareness and other forms of training, language use, and anti-discrimination protection. Over two thirds of DAX companies participated.[113]

Some specific findings: 23 of the firms have an LGBT+ ERG, of these are financially supported, more than two-thirds consider the diversity dimension of sexual orientation and gender identity part of systemic D&I management.

After criticism from the LGBT+ community, some weeks after the index launch, Uhlala Group asked companies for proof of the information provided and some results had to be corrected. But the original top three companies – in this order, SAP, Allianz (including Allianz Global Investors), and Siemens, together employing more than 630,000 people – remained the leaders. (For more on SAP, Siemens, and Allianz Global Investors, see Chapter 8.)

Another Uhlala initiative is Proudr, which claims to be the world's first LGBT+ business and networking app, though it also welcomes straight allies. Cameron activated it on the tenth anniversary of his business in summer 2019, with free access in German and English.

Cameron and his team also offer paid audits. For the Pride 500 seal, they evaluate companies and other organizations and, if they meet the criteria, certify them "LGBT+ Diversity Champion" for one year. The organizations can use the seal for internal and external communication. In 2020, certified companies included SAP, Enterprise Rent-A-Car, and Arvato, part of German billion-dollar multinational Bertelsmann Group. The Pride 500 seal is obviously modeled on the tough, long-established LGBT+ workplace equality ratings in the Anglo-Saxon world: those of HRC in the US and Stonewall in Great Britain. Cameron has simply learned from these global best-practice examples – as is only right, since Germany workplaces lag behind both countries in LGBT+ inclusion.

Recently, Cameron announced a new Uhlala's program: We Stay Pride, designed to support a company as a whole and each LGBT+ individual within it on their goals and development for a year. Cameron claims the focus is unique. It is rare, certainly, but its basic idea has some elements of Stonewall's toolkit, The Employee Lifecycle, which shows organizations how to be LGBT+-inclusive at every step of an employee's journey. At any rate, the new program seems to be attractive. Four companies signed within just a month of the launch: software giant Adobe, consultancy Alix Partners, SAP, and Metro, the German multinational wholesale specialist.

## Harvey Milk and the inspiration for a fair

The most important and most visible Uhlala endeavor, however, is what is now by far Europe's largest LGBT+ career fair, Sticks & Stones. "Work where you're celebrated, not where you're tolerated," was the fair's motto on its tenth anniversary and it's still one of Cameron's favorite slogans today.

Founded in Munich, it was initially called Milk – after the legendary LGBT+ activist and politician Harvey Milk, whose life story was told in an Oscar-winning film starring Sean Penn (see box). For legal reasons, Cameron was unable to use the name Milk for long and renamed the fair Sticks & Stones – "A reference to my Scottish grandmother," he says. "From her I learned the nursery rhyme: 'Sticks and stones may break my bones. But words will never hurt me.' There's hardly a better message for me, on a very personal level and on the level of my business." The rhyme calls on people not to let mockery get them down. Cameron knows what he's talking about, having been bullied at companies he worked for "just because I was gay."

As an entrepreneur, Cameron had some turbulent early years. After launching his fair, he found himself in dispute with his business partner, separated from him, and upped sticks from Munich for Berlin. Things were hard there at first financially, but he stuck with it and turned the fair – and Uhlala Group – into a success story.

## Harvey Milk – LGBT+ civil rights activist with early business sense

Harvey Milk is one of the world's best-known LGBT+ rights icons. Born in 1930 in a New York City suburb, the youngest son of pious Lithuanian Jews, he studied mathematics and served in the US Navy during the Korean War, making lieutenant. Afterwards he led a rather unsettled life, working, for example in the insurance industry, on Wall Street, and in the cultural scene. He had a number of same-sex partners but was not open about his homosexuality. He was even critical for a long time of LGBT+ rights militancy, which he experienced through one of his lovers.

In the early 1970s, he moved to San Francisco – the turning point in his life. Together with his partner at the time, he initially lived on his savings and then opened a photographic shop.

The US's military activities in South East Asia had increasingly politicized him. Finally, in San Francisco he found his own central political concern. The city was already a magnet for gays and

LGBT+ people, especially its Castro district, where Milk's shop was located. He quickly became an innovative and widely visible activist and politician, fighting for LGBT+ protections and rights and seeking – three times unsuccessfully – to become a city supervisor.

At the same time, he remained flexible, changing not only programmatically, but also with regard to those he wanted to address. Left-wing and liberal LGBT+ groups did not follow him for long, as he was considered too unpredictable. Ideologically undefined, he turned to the economy, the mechanisms of which he knew well from his work in business.

He also understood retail through his own small-business activity and that of his grandfather. In his political campaign in 1974, he repeatedly emphasized that gays (today's LGBT+) should buy from gay businesses (today's LGBT+ companies). He also initiated a lobby for LGBT+ retailers, after some were denied licenses to open their own stores. In other words, he had the LGBT+ economic factor in his sights very early on.

Above all, however, he led the group that initiated the Castro Street Festival. Already in its first year, 1974, it had 5,000 visitors. Three years later there were 70,000. It quickly became clear that not only LGBT+ businesses profited hugely, but almost everyone in the neighborhood, whether in hospitality, tourism or other fields. Milk thus gradually drew non-LGBT+ retailers on-side. The festival with its extensive program is still going strong, attracting around 300,000 visitors, and can be considered a model for today's countless city festivals in neighborhoods characterized by LGBT+ culture worldwide.

Milk was finally elected a member of the San Francisco Board of Supervisors in 1977, thereby becoming California's first openly gay elected official. Soon after that he aspired to be elected to California's Parliament, but this was not to be. In 1978, he and Mayor George Moscone were assassinated.

US President Barack Obama honored Milk posthumously in 2009 with the country's highest civilian award, the Presidential Medal of Freedom. And in 2019, San Francisco Airport named its Terminal 1 after him, the first airport terminal in the world ever named in honor of a member of the LGBT+ community.[114]

The same year, Europe also paid tribute. In June, on occasion of the 50th Stonewall anniversary events, Paris dedicated four squares to four global LGBT+ icons. One, in gay quarter Le Marais, was named Place Harvey-Milk.

Sticks & Stones takes place every summer in Berlin, with workshops, speeches, panel discussions, résumé checks, and more. The fair's spirit is open, colorful, and innovative. "We are the wild ones, we like to try new things," says Cameron.

When Cameron moved to Berlin, there were very few activities in Germany's capital by companies and their LGBT+ networks. This has changed. For some time now, there has been a Queer Staff Network Berlin, bringing together LGBT+ employee networks mostly from larger organizations headquartered in Berlin or with an office there. It aims to advance LGBT+ equality in local workplaces and communities through exchange of best practice, events hosted by member networks' companies, and more. Representatives are from more than 40 networks, including those of Coca-Cola, Siemens, Volkswagen, Axel Springer Group, and Deutsche Bahn (German Railways). Cameron sometimes partners with the Staff Network and he gives it a booth at Sticks & Stones.

Among exhibiting companies are many big names, and the rush to be present at the fair has increased greatly over the years. The tenth edition in 2019 was attended by well over 100 paying exhibitors and over 3,000 job seekers (who have free admission), with around 50 lectures and panel debates. These were record numbers. In June 2020, due to COVID-19, the fair took place virtually. The box gives an overview on the 2019 edition.

---

## Sticks & Stones – selected participating employers

- Consultancy brands such as Accenture, Boston Consulting Group, EY, KPMG, McKinsey, PwC, and Oliver Wyman
- German industrial icons such as BASF, Bayer, BMW, Bosch, Daimler, Porsche, Siemens, and Thyssenkrupp
- Leading corporate law firms such as Baker McKenzie, Freshfields Bruckhaus Deringer, Hogan Lovells, Latham & Watkins, and White & Case
- Key players from the world of communications, media and technology such as Amazon, Axel Springer, Bertelsmann, Bloomberg, ebay, Google, IBM, Netflix, SAP, and Vodafone
- Finance giants such as Allianz (including Allianz Global Investors), AXA, and BNP Paribas
- Other strong brands such as Coca-Cola, Deutsche Post DHL, Enterprise Rent-A-Car, Inditex, Johnson & Johnson, L'Oréal, Metro, and Richemont
- Public employers such as the Federal Financial Supervisory Authority, the German Armed Forces, and the European Central Bank

---

Some of the employers at Stick & Stones have been active in LGBT+ D&I for many years and attended the fair since its inception. Some are taking first steps. German and English are spoken almost everywhere there now. "This started about five or six years ago. Today it is taken for granted," observes Cameron. At some company booths, English is the only language used. Media attention is high, including from leading quality weeklies such as *Spiegel* and *Zeit*, a variety of TV stations, and quality business news publications such as *Handelsblatt* or *Wirtschaftswoche*.

## A global leadership contest: the cream on the milk

Since Harvey Milk sought contact with the local economy, Cameron thinks, he "would have been pleased to see how strongly the business world is now moving toward LGBT+ equality."

The German regularly names one of the Sticks & Stones stages after Milk. And for a few years now, he has done the same with one of the seminar rooms in his international English-language leadership contest for LGBT+ talents, RAHM, already mentioned briefly in this book (Part II, chapter 4.)

RAHM launched in 2017. The contest's name also pays tribute to Harvey Milk. The German word "*Rahm*" means "cream on the milk." In theory, RAHM welcomes participants of all ages, but in practice Millennials dominate, followed by Generation Z. At its premiere, the contest took place in Berlin, but then expanded quickly.

In 2018, there were two events, in London and Berlin. In 2019, there were three, in Dublin, Toronto, and Berlin. For 2020, further premieres were planned, for example in Vancouver, but these had to be canceled due to the Corona pandemic.

Each RAHM event is hosted by a different company. Sometimes now, there is competition among companies to host. This happened in 2019 in Berlin, for example, which is where Holger Reuschling comes in. We have met the then Commerzbank middle manager before in Part II, Chapter 6, in which he became a spokesperson the bank's LGBT+ ERG. In that capacity, he approached the bank to host RAHM. This was agreed and Reuschling began establishing financial and organizational requirements, then negotiated with Cameron. His negotiations were successful. Commerzbank got the Berlin event. Reuschling also joined the jury and succeeded in getting a Commerzbank executive colleague to join it too.

Lindsay Krakauer, a manager at Siemens Healthineers, traveled from the US to be part of the RAHM jury too. Siemens Healthineers combines the medical technology subsidiaries of German technology icon Siemens. Listed on the TecDax and MDax, it is headquartered in Erlangen, Germany, and employs around 50,000 people worldwide, many in the US. The openly lesbian Krakauer had attended RAHM before. At the 2017 premiere in Berlin, she had won. Since then she has been loyal to the contest and to Cameron. The following year I met her at the first RAHM competition abroad, in London, where she was on the jury – as she was again in Berlin the following year. "An experience of a lifetime," she summarized, "both as a participant and a jury member." The latter, she said, was also a "great opportunity to give something back." (For more on Siemens, see this section, Part IV, Chapter 8.)

Matthias Weber joined the RAHM jury in Berlin too. The bank manager also serves as Chairman of Völklinger Kreis, aforementioned Germany's LGBT+ association of gay managers, entrepreneurs, and self-employed people. Recently he was appointed President of European Pride Business Network (EPBN), launched in April 2020 as the new umbrella organization for European LGBT+ professional associations. Founder members were Völklinger Kreis, Network, and AGPRO (the equivalent networks covering Switzerland and Austria), Wirtschaftsweiber (the aforementioned German Lesbian business women's network), Wybernet (its equivalent for Switzerland), and EDGE and L'Autre Cercle (the LGBT+ professional networks for Italy and France). EPBN replaces a predecessor organization founded several years ago that was neither visible nor active.

## Young, gifted, LGBT+, and a more female future

The application process to participate at RAHM is elaborate: completion of a questionnaire, submission of a résumé and letter of recommendation, and a video interview. Most participants work for prestigious companies, but some are still in late phases of their studies.

Those selected face further trials at the event: group work, challenging discussions, presentations – for example, a fictitious pitch to secure funds for an LGBT+ project. They must also defend ideas that run counter to their views, mutually evaluate each other via an app, and more. All this happens at top speed, with the tightest deadlines. There's nowhere to hide: personality, leadership skills, and learning capacity are pretty much inevitably revealed in this thoroughgoing format.

With the mutual evaluations as a starting point, the jury decides on the winner. I followed one of the final jury sessions and other debates in London. There were tough discussions on the candidates and some about matters of principle. For example, though heterosexual candidates can participate, should they be allowed to win? After all, the competition's aim is to bring LGBT+ leadership to the forefront.

In Dublin in 2019, Jeannine Ferreira, openly lesbian Marketing Manager at the South African company Vodacom, won the contest. Vodacom is majority-owned by Vodafone and, in addition to South Africa, also focuses on other African countries. I spoke to Ferreira in detail during a research stay in Johannesburg. The white South African grew up in a small town in the Northwest province. After studying at the University of the Witwatersrand in Johannesburg, she spent over ten years in international businesses in a variety of marketing functions across several industries: finance, IT, automotive, and then telecommunications at Vodacom. There she became one of the youngest female executives and the most senior out leader. She praised her employer, with good reason, for substantially supporting her as an out lesbian.

Talking about her success in Ireland, she said that at RAHM, because of its setup and dynamics, participants are forced "to take a stand, be innovative and creative, and really dissect current LGBT+ issues to find workable solutions." In the end, "Walking away with a great network, mentors, coaches, and opportunities is really the cherry on top!"[115]

But Ferreira was also very reflective on societal issues, for example, the role of LBT women in the LGBT+ community as a whole. Historically, she says "We played a supportive role," referring to the dominance of gay (mostly white) men in many LGBT+ ERGs, and related endeavors. But now "young women want to see someone like them succeed while being different and comfortable in their own skin ... The future is female."[116]

By fall 2019 she was back in Europe, moving with her wife and two children to Utrecht, Netherlands, to become Head of Marketing for VodafoneZiggo – a joint venture of Vodafone and telecom giant Liberty Global.

There was more female power at RAHM that year, with Meike Imberg the winner at RAHM Berlin. Describing the benefits of her participation, she cited, "New methods for reflection and self-reflection, strong people, friends for life" – and a growing awareness of what it means to be a lesbian role model. Originally from Aachen, Germany, Imberg studied sociology and psychology at Greenwich University in the UK. There, she took up "various jobs with the university as well as various elected positions, such as being the President of the LGBTQ+ Society," she says. At a lecturer's recommendation, she also joined the LBTQWomen.org network outside the university – avoiding the gay male dominance in certain LGBT+ contexts that Ferreira had pointed to. Imberg also succesfully ran for the Greenwich Students' Union presidency in her final year becoming, "the first female, lesbian, German president," Imberg says. She was re-elected in the spring of 2018, her presidency finishing around the time she went to RAHM.

Perhaps these multiple distinctions are related to her birthday: May 17, IDAHOBIT, the International Day Against Homophobia,

Biphobia, and Transphobia. And perhaps it also carried her on to her first job. She got the call "a day before London Pride to say I got my dream job as Client Account Manager for Insurance and Financial Tech at Stonewall."

## A minority within a minority, Westernized views ...

The same year in Toronto, the RAHM winner was Salar Shoaiby. Born to Iranian parents in the United Arab Emirates, he immigrated to Canada at an early age. He got his MBA at McMaster University's DeGroote School of Business after he had won the contest. He is now a business analyst at LoyaltyOne, a subsidiary of the billion-dollar Alliance Data group.

As a gay man with origins in the Middle East, Shoaiby is part of "a minority within a minority,"[117] as an interviewer at RAHM put it. "Something I've had difficulty with is conflating identities that have, at times, felt conflicting," Shoaiby said, stressing that it could be "challenging to find a space within either of these communities that I identify with because there is rarely space given to those who are considered an 'other.'"[118]

Since Canada is a country of migrants, his double identity is fairly common. "A lot of us are born into families where acceptance and love are conditional," he went on, convinced that what was needed was the creation of environments enabling lines to be crossed and intersectional diversity to be welcomed.[119]

He also pointed to what he sees as a major deficit: many LGBT+ programs in companies and society "that focus on inclusivity look at equity through a Westernized lens." He therefore pledged to rethink the way LGBT+ D&I programs are framed today.[120]

## ... and the impact of the Black Lives Matter movement

He may be right. The topic he raised is worth reflecting upon. Related questions may be: are LGBT+ D&I discourse and practices culturally inclusive enough? Do they have, so to speak, an unconscious bias?

About a year after Shoaiby made his remarks, the Black Lives Matter movement started to force global businesses to admit huge shortcomings on inclusivity with respect to people of color, especially but not solely black people.

This matters for LGBT+ inclusion in theory and practice. In the US and in other Western liberal countries like the UK, the Netherlands, and France, it is becoming undeniable that societies and organizations have failed to include people of color sufficiently, reflecting most probably an unconscious bias (even unconscious racism), though the continuing influence and power of *conscious* racism surely can't be discounted. This also applies to the white majority, typical in Western countries, within the societal minority of LGBT+ people.

Globally in summer 2020, more and more companies and non-profits working for LGBT+ inclusion in the workplace started to use an "extended" version of the "traditional" rainbow flag to celebrate Pride (for more on the background of both, see Part 1, Chapter 7). The new version, above the "traditional" six stripes, adds a brown and a black stripe standing for people of color within the LGBT+ community. The idea goes back to 2017 and a growing awareness of racism in the gay neighborhood in Philadelphia at that time. Working with the city's Office of LGBT+ affairs, Tierney, a subsidiary of billion-dollar advertising giant Interpublic Group (IPG), designed the new flag for the city's Pride 2017, supported by the motto "More colors, more pride."[121]

## A growing community

Analysis of 2019 RAHM contestants, which the RAHM team provided as a service to a selected audience, shows that:

- 60% are Millennials, about 22% belong to Generation Z and almost 15% to Generation X
- More than 50% have a master's degree, 31% a bachelor's, and 5% a PhD
- A bit less than 50% work in business and finance or computers and technology. Around 25% work in either sales and marketing, management, engineering, or politics and public administration.

Cameron was smart enough to set up RAHM as an exclusive global LGBT+ leadership community built on participants, hosting companies, and jury members, but designed to grow beyond these three pillars. To become a member one has to apply, but once accepted, membership is free. The community is growing, supported globally by meet-ups and so-called RAHMbassadors, who spread the word face-to-face and in social media to bring in new members. The community covers the whole career spectrum: students, young professionals, team leaders and middle managers, freelancers, founders, and executives. "Allies are also welcome," says Cameron.

How far will Cameron's reach extend to senior levels? At RAHM 2019, there were senior managers among participants and jury members. And when, in October 2019, the second edition of Germany's LGBT+ role model lists was published, they numbered many "RAHMers," as former participants and jury members are sometimes called. The two rankings, Top 100 Out Executives and Top 20 Future Leaders, showed 32 in total, with former jury members on the former and former participants on the latter. (For more on these lists, see Part II, Chapter 4.)

## An "LGBT+ Evangelist" who knows what it is to be in a minority

Number one on the 2020 Top Voices list (replacing the Future Leaders ranking) was Nikita Baranov, who had been a finalist at the first contest in Berlin 2017. His LinkedIn business profile currently states not only his job, but also, very visibly, "LGBT+ Evangelist."

Baranov's background is quite diverse. Born in Russia, his family belonged to the small Jewish minority there and, as members of this group, thanks to a treaty between Russian and Germany, were able to emigrate. I first met him at the annual conference of German Prout at Work Foundation. We later had a Skype conversation. "I really know what it means to belong to a minority from early childhood," Baranov says. "And I know it even more because I am gay and Jewish." In his youth in a small German city, his "foreign"-sounding name and the fact that he was allowed to forego the Christian-focused religious education classes increased his awareness of being an outsider. Baranov often stresses his triple minority experience when speaking in public.

After studying logistics management, he began work in the retail industry before moving to Metronom, Metro's IT subsidiary, in 2015. Until recently, he was responsible for external IT partners and the innovation lab. His current job is at the top level of the HR department, potentially allowing him to have more impact in strategically framing his employer's corporate culture and operations simultaneously.

For some years already, he has also been one of the spokespeople for Metro Pride, the firm's LGBT+ employee network and – as a gay ally – a core member of the firm's women's network.

## But is he "too gay to donate blood"?

One of Baranov's more recent efforts, for which he was very active both internally and externally, was advocating to change the German guidelines prohibiting gays from donating blood. He did this, for example, in a December 2019 English-language article for RAHM's website: *Too gay to donate blood?*[122]

"Ninety percent of people eligible to donate do not currently do so in Europe," says Baranov, "Among those technically deemed eligible are homosexual men, bisexual men, and trans people, who are excluded from donating blood for 12 months after they have sex with men, which is a *de facto* ban."

In 2018, he received an email from his employer about its annual blood drive, set up in partnership with the German Red Cross. He immediately understood that he would not be allowed to donate, though he wanted to. One of his gay colleagues, also a member of Metro Pride, tried and was rejected.

As a spokesperson for Metro Pride, Baranov felt it legitimate to investigate. He looked at whether the rules were discriminatory and how other countries handled the question. Working with his employer's D&I, public policy, communications, and work council departments, "We quickly learned that if we continue to offer blood donations within the company framework, we will not be able to live up to our claim of offering a nondiscriminatory workplace. At the same time, we also want to clearly communicate that blood donations are very important and encourage employees to continue to do so in their private lives."[123] A dilemma, but also a challenge to be addressed.

In his article on the RAHM website, Baranov wrote, "As a company with social responsibility, we want to work toward the amendment of the current guidelines for the preparation of blood and blood components and for the use of blood components (hemotherapy)."[124] And he also drew attention to the fact that other countries in and beyond the European Union enable (at least) a less discriminatory blood donation regimen with regard to LGBT+ people without compromising on safety and security.

This led to a draft positioning paper, laying down the background and calling for a reconsideration of the current medical guidelines in Germany. On behalf of his employer, he gave this to the Prout at Work Foundation for legal and other checks. In April 2020, Prout at Work – now the leading actor on this – launched an official positioning paper directed at *Bundesärztekammer*, the German doctors' association, and other relevant actors. It was officially supported by global corporates and multinationals headquartered in Germany.[125] These included Microsoft, Ikea, consultancy Oliver Wyman, and global law firm White & Case. Supportive German companies, beyond Metro, were Continental, SAP, railway giant DB, Otto, Uhlala, and two Bertelsmann firms, Arvato and Ufa.

The paper's message was clear: no compromise should be made in blood products and blood transfusions with regard to safety for donors and patients, but Germany can learn from other countries. For example:

- Great Britain and Canada have recently reduced the provision to three months, and the first evaluations in the UK show no significant increase in HIV-positive blood donations.
- Japan is practicing a six-month delay.
- In France and Denmark, health ministers have announced their intention to reduce the provision from 12 to four months with, in Denmark, donors living in a monogamous partnership subject to no delay at all.

The paper also lists modern yet safe approaches in Italy, Portugal, Spain, South Africa, and Israel.[126]

Media coverage appeared in local papers, *bild.de*, and *Thomson Reuters* in the UK. The *bild.de* article included the logos of all supporting organizations. *Thomson Reuters'* headline, read, *Ikea and Microsoft join call for Germany to relax ban on gay men giving blood*.[127]

"Let's see, what happens," says Baranov. "Whatever the outcome ... it's relevant because more blood donations save lives and because it advances nondiscrimination."

# 8. Europe's largest software company engages globally, a German technology icon changes fast, and an investment house catches up

As we saw in the previous chapter, three German-based global companies led Uhlala's first DAX 30 LGBT+ Diversity Index: SAP, Allianz (including Allianz Global Investors, AllianzGI for short), and Siemens. It is worth looking at their LGBT+ efforts in turn – in Allianz's case, focusing on their subsidiary AllianzGI. The three represent different industries – software (SAP), industrial technology (Siemens), and financial services (AllianzGI). SAP has been leading on LGBT+ inclusion for years, not just in Germany but globally, while the other two are still at earlier stages. All three, however, are examples of fast learning on LGBT+ issues in companies from Europe's largest economy.

## SAP

Very connected to some of Uhlala's ventures, SAP is Europe's largest software corporate, employing about 100,000 people from more than 150 countries globally.[128] "SAP has been at Sticks & Stones with their own booth right from the start and also have speakers and panelists on stage there," says Uhlala CEO Cameron. "They sent participants to the RAHM contests, they asked to be screened to get the Pride 500 seal, and registered on Proudr as an employer offering jobs. Their HR boss spoke at our recent LGBT+ diversity conference. There are colleagues in the Unicorn in Tech community and hosted community events."

SAP even sent three representatives to the Berlin RAHM jury in 2019 and has agreed to send them again in the future. I will get back to one of the representatives from this jury in a moment. But let's look at another protagonist at SAP first.

As mentioned, SAP made first place on the new German LGBT+ Diversity Index. Openly gay Ernesto Marinelli, a high-level human resources manager and the most senior out executive at the firm, was one spokesperson for this success in interviews.[129] Born Italian, Marinelli moved to Germany as a young man to study linguistics, finally leaving Bavaria's University of Würzburg with a PhD. It was also in Würzburg that he met his husband, to whom he has been married for almost 20 years. This partner is one of the main reasons he stayed in Germany.

But not the only. In 2005, Marinelli joined SAP as a recruiter and has remained there since. "At the beginning of my career, I decided to look for a job where I did not have to hide,"[130] the manager said in an interview with a German business daily.

## Making a career: an Italian going shopping with his husband as a start

Marinelli relates how he was first interviewed for a job at SAP in Walldorf, the small German city near the French border, where the software giant is headquartered. In this interview, to check whether the firm would have a problem with his homosexuality, he mentioned that afterwards he was planning to go shopping in Walldorf – with his husband. He got the job and understood: "This is the right place for me."[131]

I first met Marinelli at an LGBT+ event, hosted by IBM in Munich. We then continued our conversation in a number of phone calls, and in the context of a reading of early (draft) sections of this book's English edition at a major SAP software developer conference.

After about 15 years with the company, Marinelli, now in his mid-50s, is currently serving as a Senior Vice President and Global Head of Human Resources for SAP's sales organization. Previously, he held a variety of other HR roles as a senior executive, covering many parts of the globe including Eastern Europe, the Middle East, Africa, and Greater China. In fact, Marinelli has become a leading human resources expert not only in his firm, but far beyond it.

The international focus obviously meant Marinelli traveled a lot, which helped him quickly understand the difficulties of being open in certain regions. For instance, an Arab sheik once asked him whether he had married a German woman. His "No, a German man," was followed by a surprised silence, then an abrupt change of topic. The previously jovial mood had turned to freezing cold.[132] This was only one of several challenging experiences. Nevertheless, he climbed the career ladder fast.

During his years at SAP, Marinelli has impacted the firm's D&I strategies and practices and supported its LGBT+ ERG Pride@ SAP, which has grown to about 8,000 members globally. He is also involved with various nonprofit ventures, for example at Aidshilfe, the German nonprofit working for people with HIV/AIDS. One of the projects he supports is #positivarbeiten, the name of a German declaration opposing workplace discrimination against people with HIV, launched in 2019.[133] SAP along with Accenture, Daimler, Deutsche Bank, IBM, and PwC were among the first to sign. Since then, over 70 companies, associations, cities, ministries, small-to-medium enterprises, and some large businesses have followed suit.[134]

In 2018 and 2019, he made it into the top ten of the German Out Executive ranking. In a portrait photo of him published with the ranking, some other small photos are visible. One shows him giving a presentation, conveying the message that he's an active senior business professional. Another shows him, his husband Thomas, and their dog – hardly just a personal message.[135]

## Beyond Europe ...

Beyond Germany and Europe, too, SAP is today considered very active in advancing LGBT+ equality. On a global level, it signed the UN LGBTI Standards of Conduct for Business early on and was also named a Stonewall Top Global Employer 2019. In Latin America, for example, the firm partners with the organizations working for LGBT+ inclusion in the workplace in Brazil, Chile, and Mexico that I referred to in Part III, Chapter 5.

The European software giant is also engaged with these issues in North America, especially the US, as a major market. For, example, SAP supports Lesbians Who Tech,[136] which claims to be the largest LGBT+ technology community in the world, encompassing around 50,000 LGBT+ women, nonbinary, and trans people in and around tech, including supporting allies.[137] Its major event today is a large three-day summit in the US with speeches, panels, speed mentoring, recruitment elements, and more. SAP was also a summit partner for Out & Equal's large annual conference in the US (for more see Part IV, Chapter 5). And for many years already, SAP has achieved the top score on the Human Rights Campaign's Corporate Equality Index, to which I've frequently referred in this book.

In Canada and well beyond it, Rachel Ho, who works as a senior marketing manager, is a central figure. She co-led the Pride@SAP activities in North America, currently leads the firm's Pride@SAP activities in New York, where she is based, and has launched the first LGBT+ ERG for SAP Canada, with members across the country now. She is also visible externally. For example, she has sat on panels at the Out & Equal summit, appeared for three years at the Lesbians Who Tech conference, and attended the UN General Assembly LGBT+ global policy panel. Ho also made it onto the EMpower Top 100 Ethnic Minority Future Leaders ranking for 2020, sending a signal for D&I intersectionality. EMpower is a sister initiative of OUTstanding, both managed by UK social business INvolve, I have referred to earlier.[138]

## ... with a journey in India

With respect to Asia, for some time already, SAP has also been quite active in India. Erik Lüngen, with the firm for more than 15 years now, has traveled to the country often. The software company has many locations there, including their development hubs, known as SAP Labs, in Bangalore, Mumbai, and Gurgaon.

As already mentioned, it was not until September 2018 that Section 377 of the Indian criminal code, which criminalized, among other things, same-sex intercourse between adults, was dropped. Still, living and working as a member of the LGBT+ community remains tough, the level of discrimination and violence high.

"There is a quote from the legendary management thinker Peter Drucker: 'Culture eats strategy for breakfast,'" Lüngen notes. "Every experienced leader in an organization understands what this means. You can strategize as much as you want – if you don't include a focus on organizational culture and cultural change in your daily work, then you might as well not strategize. It also means that the organizational culture has to be adapted to the local cultures, companies are operating in. What is needed is a common global ground but also some local flexibility."

In fact, in India, despite legal change, the cultural pressure remains very high, he says. "People mostly don't have the chance to come out and be their true selves, not at home and not in the workplace.

"For me this is, of course, different. As a white manager in India belonging to a Western company, I've never had problems so far. My colleagues know that I am married to a man. They know that my husband and I have children who live with their mothers, a lesbian couple." But Lüngen has been very aware from early on, that "I have a very special status and am privileged. I decided to make use of this and help the LGBT+ community in India fight for their rights and against stigmatization and discrimination."

He has fallen in love with the country and its people, he says. "I am more than happy that with my new role at SAP, which I took up in March 2020. I am still responsible for some hundreds of colleagues in Bangalore, which means that I can continue to support Pride@SAP India and local LGBT+ D&I activities in many ways."

Lüngen has worked in the IT industry for more than 20 years. He briefly left SAP but has now been back for more than seven years and is a Vice President. He currently manages the product delivery unit of one of SAP's major resource planning software offerings for large enterprises. Lüngen holds an MBA from the Mannheim Business School, Germany, and ESSEC Business School, France. (Short for: *École Supérieure des Sciences Economiques et Commerciales*, ESSEC is one of the so-called *Grandes Écoles*, which are among the most prestigious and selective French higher educational institutions.)

He is still in close contact with his German alma mater and recently gave the keynote speech at Mannheim Business School for the launch of its LGBT+ students club. One of his charts showed his husband and him in the small village they are living. For many years already, he has also been not just one of few out executives in his firm, he has also been actively engaged with Pride@SAP. In recent years, he made both Germany's Top 100 Out Executives list and OUTstanding's global Top 100 LGBT+ Executives ranking.

Also for many years already, Lüngen has supported the Pride@SAPLabsIndia initiative. "It started," he says, "in 2017 with the first Pride Event at SAP Labs India, even before Section 377 had been dropped. The event included a video to sensitize attendees to the challenges the LGBT+ community in India faces. Local HR Head Shraddhanjali Rao and the Chief Operating Officer of SAP Labs India Mahesh Nayak were present, and more than 200 SAP colleagues participated, both of which were great signs – a good start."

## "Liberation at SAP" India on Valentine's Day

In June 2018, the first Pride march on the grounds of SAP Labs India took place, the start of what was to become a tradition in the following years. Also, the Ally@SAP India group was launched, aiming to support colleagues belonging to the LGBTQIA+ community.[139] LGBTQIA+ or LGBTAI+ have become some frequently used terms in India (by way of a reminder, the "A" usually stands for people who identify as asexual/agender/aromantic).

In 2019, SAP started to work with social business Pride Circle, which I have already referred to in Part II, Chapter 5. In a very short time it has become the country's leading consultancy focused on advancing LGBT+ inclusion in Indian workplaces. Supported by it, SAP Labs India for the first time invited external speakers. Among them was not only Ramkrishna Sinha, Pride Circle's co-founder but also a human rights activist from Amnesty International and the technology department HR leader for ANZ India (ANZ is short for Australia and New Zealand Banking Group). Another event, for the firm's ally group, at the Solidarity Foundation in Bangalore covered the challenges the trans community faces in India, and how to support it in a variety of ways in the workplace and beyond.

Since India got rid of Section 377, SAP's local activities have grown. "It's fantastic," says Lüngen. "For example, there is the work of Sameer Ranjan Kumar, who is the only openly gay colleague at SAP India in Bangalore." In fact, Kumar, a senior software engineer who has worked at SAP for over eight years, is very visible both internally and externally. In January 2020, for example, he shared his story in a blog article: *Liberation at SAP: Coming out as gay*.[140] There, he talked not only about depression, anxiety, and mental health problems before this coming out, and the lies he told at home, but also about the positive experiences: coming out to his parents in 2016; coming out to his manager and his colleagues the year after; coming out across the firm in a blog post on Valentine's Day 2018.[141] That piece, titled *Love knows no gender*, was shared many times. SAP's local HR Head Rao even called him after it, suggesting he become engaged in D&I issues.

Today Kumar leads Pride@SAP India – and continues to be very active. For example, recently, during the COVID-19 pandemic, he took part in in a virtual session co-hosted by Pride Circle. Or, as another example, in March 2020, he posted a blog, titled *Women as strong LGBTQ allies #PrideatSAP*. There he focused on intersectionality and, among other things, stated, "Irrespective of the biases, stigma, and stereotypes, women and the LGBTQ community have experienced similar discrimination at the hands of society.

This is the precise reason women can understand the plight of LGBTQ community."[142]

"I strongly believe change is achieved via small steps," Lüngen explains. "That's why I participated in the RAHM contest as a jury member. If we want to make our companies and leadership teams more diverse, more inclusive, and more empathic, we need to build a diverse pipeline of leaders for tomorrow. It will be great to see these LGBT+ ambassadors in senior management roles tomorrow." To foster such future leaders, Lüngen also arranged for SAP to host the first-ever Asian RAHM event – in Bangalore. This was supposed to have happened in 2020, but because of COVID-19, was postponed.

## Allianz Global Investors: a short story of catching up fast

Change to advance LGBT+ inclusion can happen fast, as we saw in the case of Barilla in Part I. Here is a short account of a slightly different quick-change story, that of Allianz Global Investors (AllianzGI).

The global investment management company is owned by German icon Allianz Group, the global insurance and financial services giant. It operates in 25 locations in the US, Europe, and the Asia-Pacific region, and with its roughly people currently manages assets of around €540 billion for private and institutional investors (as per of June 30, 2020). Among the institutional investors using AllianzGI services is, most importantly, parent company Allianz Group, active in more than 70 countries with over 145,000 employees.

In May 2017, around the time of the International Day Against Homophobia, Biphobia, and Transphobia (IDAHOBIT), I traveled to Germany's financial capital Frankfurt, where AGI held its annual Inclusion & Diversity Day. Sven Schäfer, Managing Director, employed by the firm for almost 20 years, welcomed me at the reception.

When we spoke a few weeks before, he had said, "It's time to become more visible, both within the company and externally." He was right. Compared to other firms in the global financial industry, AllianzGI was late – though it had a quick route to progress via its parent company. For a book on LGBT+ D&I in Germany's society and economy, published in 2014, I had researched the first steps at Allianz Group toward becoming a more LGBT+-inclusive workplace. They had started to support development of an LGBT+ employee resource group and to gradually integrate LGBT+ D&I into overall D&I strategy and action.

Schäfer, who is openly gay and one of the co-founders of Allianz-GI's LGBT+ ERG, knew that he and his colleagues could learn a little from the parent company's LGBT+ journey when they started their own. When he contacted me, he invited me to participate in their first panel discussion on coming out in business, which was the reason for my trip to Frankfurt.

## A kickoff with the CEO

The hall in which the panel discussion was to take place offered a beautiful view of Frankfurt's skyline. And it was full. On the one hand, this was due to the topic for which there had previously been no stage here. On the other, it was due to the presence of Andreas Utermann, then CEO of AllianzGI. He had announced his intention to appear at short notice, but not so late that it stopped the message from getting out. Everyone wanted to know what he had to say.

Utermann's first important message on the panel was quickly apparent: a relaxed approach to the topic based on a very personal experience from an early age. "My uncle is Erwin Haeberle, one of the important German sexologists, and he's gay," he said. Haeberle and his partner often visited his family. "Although he was a professor in the US until the early 1990s, we saw each other often." Utermann grew up in a liberal home. "That has shaped me."

A bit later, I asked him in an interview why exactly he had joined the panel discussion. "My family lived in London, for many years now a very LGBT+-friendly place. I had actually thought that this was also the case in our firm. I had thought people could be as they are." But then some members of the firm's LGBT+ employee network made clear to him that there was a need for some action. "People are very much aware of what their CEO says and does. I wanted to send the message that diversity enriches and benefits us, and that no one has to hide in our firm with its about 3,000 people. I wanted to show that the CEO stands for this attitude."

Recently, Utermann retired as a CEO for family reasons. He continues to live in London and is, among other things, active as a private investor. But the impact of his contribution has remained. Looking back, Schäfer, who moderated the panel discussion, says,

"That was exactly the kickoff we needed – with a strong message and a lot of attention."

## Being global

Another gay colleague active in the firm's LGBT+ employee network, Michael Sandstedt, was also on stage. Like Schäfer, he is a Managing Director, and after Schäfer had initiated the firm's first LGBT+ activities, he took over their leadership.

Sandstedt has been working at AllianzGI for more than 15 years. For even longer he has been with his husband, whom he met in 2000 and married three years later. Like Sandstedt, his husband advocates for LGBT+ equality, but he does so in a truly different area, as part of the German platform Gay Farmer, an organization for gays and lesbians working in rural professions such as agriculture, viticulture, market gardening, forestry, landscape planning, veterinary medicine, or fisheries.[143]

Today, Sandstedt himself is not only an active member of the firm's LGBT+ ERG in Germany but also part of the company's global LGBT+ workstream, set up in 2018. It is dedicated to ensuring an open, LGBT+-inclusive working climate through a variety of measures and to building a global network for LGBT+ staff and allies. Beyond that, Sandstedt is a member of the Global Allianz Group Pride Board. It aims to share knowledge and best practice, use synergies, and join forces to bring bundled insights to the attention of the Group's Global Leadership in order to impact strategies related to LGBT+ D&I.

In sum, within a short time, an institutional set up across AllianzGI, embedded in some way in parent company processes, has developed, reflecting fast progress toward more LGBT+ inclusion. For example, in Hong Kong, this was supported by a straight ally. Daniel Lehmann is a managing director, heading the firm's operational business for the Asia-Pacific region, and is also senior sponsor and active member of its global LGBT+ workstream. "When I came to Asia five years ago, I noticed how much of a taboo LGBT+ is compared to Europe and what a difficult environment it can be for people who identify as LGBT+," he recently posted on his LinkedIn business profile.

We missed each other during my research visit to Hong Kong, so I talked to him on the phone later. The global goal, he says, is clear: "We want to show AllianzGI is an LGBT+-friendly company." This applies to all major financial centers, including those in the Asia-Pacific region. The competition in Hong Kong for the best financial minds is particularly tough.

"That is why it is also an important signal that AllianzGI signed the UN LGBTI Standard of Conduct for Business in spring 2019," Sandstedt says. The firm did so as an independent legal entity – with parent company Allianz having already signed. (For more on the Standards, see Part II, Chapter 8.)

## Role models in the industry

Recently, Lehmann and Sandstedt were honored by LGBT Great, a London-based global membership organization founded in 2017. It works to advance LGBT+ D&I within the investment and savings industry through a variety of measures, including research,[144] education such as webinars, tools such as benchmark trackers, and campaigns. Members include, for example, Fidelity, Northern Trust, Schroders, and many more. In summer 2020, LGBT Great honored Lehmann and Sandstedt by including them on their Global Top 100 Executive Allies ranking, recognizing their work in that year's Pride media campaign. (In contrast to the usual usage of the term "ally" to mean "straight ally," LGBT Great uses it in a broader sense that can encompass openly gay people like Sandstedt.)

"In the long term, we also aim to be included in one of the indices of Stonewall or the Human Rights Campaign in the US," Lehmann says. "We know how impactful these indices are globally. And we want to increase our global impact."

In other words, he wants to increase the firm's global reputation as an LGBT+-friendly employer and brand. He has good reasons to stay with this goal. The competition in the financial industry to get the best talents and keep them is and will stay tough, especially in the world's major financial centers such as New York, Chicago, London, Hong Kong, Tokyo, Singapore, Frankfurt, and Paris, but also beyond.

Recently, in March 2020, AllianzGI published a 20-page guide entitled *Fostering LGBT+ workplace inclusion*, to "improve understanding of sexual orientation and gender identity."[145] It gives some figures on why LGBT+ inclusion matters economically, some background information on misconceptions, a glossary, and more. Its foreword is signed by the AllianzGI Executive Committee, which is responsible for strategic decision-making and includes a small team of four senior executives. Among them is new CEO Tobias C. Pross. Messages from the top remain an important factor in Allianz-GI's LGBT D&l journey.

## Siemens: another quick change and some digitized answers

"Over the years, we have had many strong candidates," Matthias Weber says. "But the Siemens application beat everything in terms of presentation, scope, richness of detail, and documentation. Even the data volume was enormous: about 500 megabytes."

In his day job, Weber is a member of the Board of Postbank's North Western Area, Postbank being a brand of Deutsche Bank. But, as mentioned, he also serves as Chairman of aforementioned Völklinger Kreis. In that capacity, he was a member of the jury for an award his association gives out every two years to recognize outstanding diversity management, especially with regard to LGBT+ D&l. In 2018, Siemens, applied and won in the category "Companies" – resulting in the above praise from Weber.

The win reflected a dramatic cultural transformation. Until 2014, there were major blocks against any form of LGBT+ D&l management. I experienced this very directly during my research for the aforementioned earlier book, published in 2014. "We don't have gays and lesbians at Siemens," the employees I spoke to said. Or they expressed no interest in the subject or gave no answer at all.

Today, the group has a structured and systematic LGBT+ D&l management, an active LGBT+ network, called Siemens Pride, and is very visible on the subject internally and externally, not only in Germany but around the world. The company is present at Pride events and LGBT+ job and career fairs such as Sticks & Stones. It has global steering committees and processes and holds company-wide seminars to sensitize people to unconscious bias. It supports LGBT+ employees (and straight allies), sending them to congresses and seminars, sometimes abroad. This seismic revolution has taken only a couple years.

Siemens CEO Joe Kaeser has been clear in his support for the change. In particular, when it was suggested to him that he sign the UN LGBTI Standards of Conduct for Business in 2018, he did so, accompanied by a clear statement: "As a global company with more than 386,000 employees worldwide, we consider it our responsibility to stand up for human rights and to advocate openness and understanding in a connected world."[146] It is said that there were advisors in the firm who would have preferred Kaeser not to use the phrase "human rights" for fear of alienating leaders in the many authoritarian countries where Siemens does business. However, so the story goes, Kaeser insisted on exactly this formulation in his statement.

## Global grassroots work

Among Siemens' grassroots corporate LGBT+ activists is Arthur Schmid, who joined the firm in mid-2017. Schmid, who holds a PhD in computer science, worked at the University of Munich, specializing in databases, until he thought it was time to move into the business world. When, in the course of his job interviews at Siemens, he wanted to know "how the company deals with someone like me – a gay man – I was invited to immediately talk to a representative of Siemens Pride, the firm's network," he says.

Today, he is not only a data scientist at the firm and an internal digital consultant, he is also one of the hands-on movers and shakers at Siemens Pride. Coordinating internal and external initiatives, he is, among other things, not least an important interface with other local and national network chapters.

However, things are also moving forward quickly at international locations. "In Europe, above all in Austria, Great Britain, Norway, Portugal, and Spain," but further afield too, "For example, in the US, Brazil, Mexico, and India."

Recently, in fact, he traveled to the group's location in the South Indian high-tech center Bangalore. As already mentioned, it was not until September 2018 that Section 377 of the Indian criminal code was dropped. Among other things, it had criminalized same-sex intercourse between adults. The law has gone, but everyday discrimination has not. "It was an important signal that someone from Munich was there, who also brought along small gifts with the Siemens and Pride logos in rainbow colors for the network activities," says Schmid. Since then, the Indian Pride offshoot has grown strongly, both in terms of numbers and activities.

## Changing course – and sticking with it

"When we as Siemens Pride talked with Janina Kugel in her capacity as Chief Diversity Officer about the firm's LGBT+ strategy, she recommended to us to get as many stones rolling as possible as quickly as possible," Schmid says. "That is exactly, what we did – to keep up the momentum."

Changing direction on a controversial topic is not easy for a large company such as Siemens, which operates in more than 200 countries. It is not at all a hidden secret in the firm and the business world that the technology giant's quick journey to becoming an LGBT+-friendly company is closely connected to Janina Kugel, who for five years was the firm's Chief HR Officer and Chief Diversity Officer and as such a member of the Management Board. "When she started her job, we were in hell; when she left in 2020, we were in paradise," a Siemens colleague who wanted to remain anonymous said of her.

Supported by CEO Joe Kaeser, Kugel strategized and pushed the firm's D&I agenda from the top. There was a strong focus on LGBT+ D&I and also on gender diversity – in which Siemens needed to catch up to – very visibly, both internally and externally.

When, in January 2020, Kugel left Siemens, her achievements were highly praised. Since May 2020, there has been a new Chief Diversity Officer, Natalia Oropeza.[147] Oropeza, originally from Mexico, knows large German technologically driven global corporates well. She has a background in electrical engineering and worked for Volkswagen for more than 25 years before she joined Siemens in 2018 to become the firm's cyber security officer. She now has two roles.

## Webcast surprise – and continuity

Oropeza made herself visible very quickly. For May 17, the International Day Against Homophobia, Biphobia and Transphobia (IDAHOBIT), there had been plans for some live events, but due to the COVID-19 pandemic, the new idea of creating a truly global webcast event emerged, proposed by Siemens Pride. The human resources department, where the firm's D&I strategies and actions are coordinated and managed, supported the idea from early on. It got the necessary top-level approvals and arranged for the setup, including hiring a media service provider and ensuring that internal and external communications would run smoothly.

Along with Arthur Schmid, moderating the two-hour webcast was Katja Ploner, HR and D&I leader at the firm's headquarters in Munich, Germany, a straight ally and supporter of the firm's LGBT+ journey for many years already. Several hundred participants and viewers from throughout the Siemens universe attended. Beyond Germany and the EU, there were colleagues from the US, Brazil, Mexico, India, and many more. On colorful sets with rainbows and Schmid wearing high heels (to break expectations related to "normal" gender expression), the moderators talked about LGBT+ history, Siemens Pride, and the firm's and the network's past, present and future LGBT+-related activities. Before the event, members of Siemens Pride from around the globe had helped develop ideas and spread the word to maximize attendance. There were also live interactions with the virtual audience, which could make comments, pose questions, and take part in discussions, and live broadcasts to other Siemens locations. A panel discussion with managers took place, and there was a longer interview with Oropeza, just a couple days after she had taken office as the firm's CDO.

"The feedback was very strong," reports Schmid, "already during the event but also thereafter. Many were enthusiastic, and no one was negative, which is unusual." Some colleagues were also asking for advice or other forms of support. "Those we could connect to our internal mentoring program immediately."

Shortly after the event, Siemens shared the video on LinkedIn. "Very soon, we also got a variety of positive response from other companies, especially from members of their LGBT+ employee network." Schmid says. Some weeks later he would present the Siemens experience with its network and corporate LGBT D&I at German headquarters of the Italian Banking Group UniCredit, which is also in Munich.

After Siemens Chief HR Officer and diversity leader Kugel announced that she would leave the company, there had been internal worries about what would follow. These were reinforced a couple months later when CEO Kaeser also announced that he would step down in 2021 – after seven years as Chief Financial Officer and almost eight as CEO.

Business is people, as the saying goes. But it seems the company now not only has a coherent LGBT+ D&I strategy, it has also created self-sustaining practices and processes – not least reflected in the awards it has received and the firm's third-place ranking on Germany's aforementioned LGBT+ Diversity Index.

## 9. Reaching out to MBA students in the US, a business conference managed by a university club in London, and an entrepreneurial Mexican Canadian

Learning is at the heart of activity at universities – and increasingly, that includes initiatives that aid business and societal learning on LGBT+ inclusion.

Above all, in the US, there is ROMBA, short for Reaching out MBA, the superstar among high-end LGBT+ business student activities for both content and recruitment.

At the heart of ROMBA is the world's largest conference of LGBT+ MBA students and companies and other organizations seeking to recruit them. Held annually in October, the conference's subtitle is "LGBTQ MBA and graduate conference." There are panels with corporate board members, workshops, competitions in which students can win monetary awards, a career fair with many corporate partners across many industries, and more.

Over 20 years ago, students from Harvard and Yale Business Schools had the idea of a national space for LGBT+ business students to meet. Only ten business schools then had on-campus LGBT+ clubs. The innovative students succeeded and in 1999 about students from six schools gathered at ROMBA's premiere.

It grew fast, becoming a nonprofit five years later and, after 2013, went from being volunteer-led to a fully staffed, full-service organization. Today, there is a paid leadership team that mainly leaves conference activity to be managed by regularly changing groups of LGBT+ students from top US business schools. They set themes and develop content, but they are supported by the leadership team, an advisory council, and board. Board members are from well-known firms, except for one from the HRC.

In 2019, the conference took place in Atlanta, welcoming more than 1,800 business students and alumni, and 100 corporate partners. Planning is long-term: in 2021 the event will be held in Austin, in 2022 in Washington, DC, in 2023 in Chicago, and in 2024 in Los Angeles. In October 2020, due to the COVID-19 pandemic, the conference was virtual, its motto was: "Technicolor future: Life through a new lens." A good claim in the time of COVID, Black Lives Matter, and riots? Perhaps not really.

At any rate, ROMBA again had Human Rights Campaign as an organizational ally – alongside, for example, NGLCC (the National LGBT Chamber of Commerce, see Part III, Chapter 3), and StartOut (a US nonprofit founded in 2009, working to increase the number, diversity and impact of LGBTQ+ entrepreneurs).[148]

Every year, numerous companies line up to be sponsors. For 2020's virtual version, less corporate budget was available, but ROMBA nevertheless acquired a large sponsor cohort. At the highest level, the so-called "underwriters" were consultancy primus BCG, and Discover, the billion-dollar US financial services company that operates through its Discover Bank. The second sponsor league, the so-called "Diamond level," was filled by McKinsey and Deloitte, followed by another five levels with a further 40 companies. Although most of the sponsors operate globally, less than 10% were non-US businesses.

Like every year, there were tough contests, each sponsored by a company. For example, there was a consulting case competition. Participating business students could win up to $5,000. There were also competitions in mergers and acquisitions and in start-ups, both also offering monetary prizes.

## Not just a conference

ROMBA has gradually developed a universe of further initiatives. In 2014, in partnership with top business schools, the ROMBA Fellowship was launched, a national scholarship program that, only four years later, already had 50 business schools participating.[149] Currently, each ROMBA fellow receives a minimum $20,000 scholarship and a place on a leadership program and fellowship retreat.[150]

There is also the LGBT+ Student Leadership Summit, the first of which took place in 2008. Since then, every year in Chicago, it has brought together leaders of affiliated LGBT+ clubs at Business Schools around the world.

With this network continually growing, the number of participants coming from these schools has also grown continuously. Currently, ROMBA boasts a global network totaling 66 LGBT+ business school club affiliates. It must be said, however: though global is the goal, only seven affiliates are non-US (as of August 2020):

- Two in France (HEC in Paris with its LGBT+ Business Club, and INSEAD in Fontainebleau with OUTSEAD)
- Two in Spain (ESADE Business School in Barcelona with its LGBT+ Allies Business Club, and IE Business School at IE University in Madrid with its IE Out & Allies Club (for more on IE Business School and their own LGBT+ conference managed by the Club, see Part III, Chapter 4)
- One in the UK (London Business School with its Out in Business Club, OiB)
- One in Canada (Ivey Business School at University of Western Ontario with its Ivey Pride Club)
- One in Australia (the Australian Graduate School of Management at University of New South Wales with its Pride@AGSM Club).[151]

Another example of a fast-succeeding initiative within the ROMBA universe is the Out Women in Business (OWIB) conference, bringing the LBT+ community together and encouraging the building of strong networks for connecting, learning and inspiration. Since its launch in 2015, it has taken place annually in New York City. In 2020, because of COVID-19, it took place virtually, dealing with topics like the pay gap, inclusive leadership, and strategizing, and overcoming mental health issues such as anxiety by creating suitable environments.

Further annual ROMBA events include Summer Treks, another way of connecting LGBT+ MBA students to companies seeking talent. They are held in June and July in different cities, each with an industry focus. In summer 2020, they were virtual: San Francisco Tech Trek with companies like Google, BCG, and Walmart e-commerce: and Seattle Tech and Retail Trek, with companies such as Starbucks, Amazon, Nike, Deloitte, and Microsoft.

In its over 20 years, ROMBA has become a role model, the best platform globally for recruiting young LGBT+ MBA talents and a legendary dynamic force for change. In particular, it was an inspiration in Europe, in the UK especially, where, in 2010, the London Business School's LGBT+ affinity group – the Out in Business Club (OiB) – launched a new project called EurOUT.

## London Business School's EurOUT

EurOUT was set up as a conference and, like ROMBA, achieved quick success. Within ten years, it grew from one day, 12 participants and a single sponsor to over 400 delegates, attendees from over 20 business schools, 21 corporate sponsors, and over 50 participating companies at a two-day-event in 2019.

EurOUT takes place in London every November, hosted by the London Business School (LBS). Today it is Europe's largest LGBT+ postgraduate business student conference.

"In contrast to ROMBA, our conference is fully organized by students," says Alberto Padilla Rivera, an LBS MBA graduate and former Co-President of the OiB with Nicholas Deakin. Together they led the conference management team in 2016. Deakin, both an MBA and an MD (medical doctor), today works at Citibank, London as Vice President in the healthcare investment banking team. He has been included twice in the OUTstanding LGBT+ Future Leaders list. Since 2018, he has co-chaired EurOUT's board.

As one of the few non-US LGBT+ student clubs in ROMBA's universe, the OiB was well connected before EurOUT's start. "Of course, we have learned from our US colleagues, and still today we exchange views," Padilla says. "But while ROMBA is mainly focused on the US and North America, we cover Europe, which has a lot fewer business schools and is also culturally more diverse."

EurOUT's target group is larger – top business school graduate students, MBAs, PhDs, and alumni – but it is itself smaller, focusing on the conference almost exclusively.

EurOUT 2019 was a success, achieving new records for attendees and partners. Lead sponsor was consultancy BCG, which hosted a session of its own and a dinner. McKinsey hosted a women's lunch, and Salesforce threw a closing party. Discussion topics included the media's role in pushing LGBT+ visibility in business, next levels for companies' Pride activities, and LGBT+ identities globally.

## A personal mission with multiple ventures

Born Mexican, Padilla now also has Canadian citizenship. At age 18, he moved to Edmonton for his bilingual (English-French) bachelor's degree in commerce at the University of Alberta, followed by six years in consulting at Monitor Deloitte and Bain.

Today in his early 30s, Padilla is a Senior Director at Insight Partners, the American venture capital and private equity firm investing in high-growth technology and software. In his free time, he also works voluntarily for some innovative LGBT+ nonprofits – "My personal mission," he says. For example, he is a founding board member at Out Investors (OI), a new global network for LGBT+ investment professionals with a mission is "to make the direct investing industry more welcoming for LGBT+ individuals."[152]

"We plan to run events and programs involving LGBT+ investment professionals and investment-adjacent roles," Padilla summarizes. "Plan" is the correct word. OI was launched in June 2020, in the middle of the COVID-19 pandemic. But from the beginning, leading firms became members. Just a few weeks after launch, the list already comprised 30 names, including Apollo, Bain Capital, Barings, Blackstone, Carlyle, and Permira. Soon, the Mexican Canadian says, "They will champion our events and programs."

Padilla is also a founding board member of Series Q, a network for LGBT+ people at startups primarily in the UK. A registered nonprofit based in London, Padilla Rivera says it plays a similar role to a large company's LGBT+ employee network, but for entrepreneurs and start-up employees across smaller operations. Among Series Q's partners is EurOUT.

## Club work, board work

The OiB represents LBS's LGBT+ students and allies and raises LGBT+ awareness and facilitates interaction between club members and other LGBT+ business networks. With almost 1,000 members, including alumni and straight allies, it is considered "one of the most active clubs on the LBS campus," Padilla Rivera says, adding, "EurOUT, fully run by OiB, is not only the club's highlight event but also one of the school's flagship conferences."

The EurOUT board currently consists of 20 people, many of them working for well-known brands such as Amazon, BCG, Burberry, Citi, Google, HSBC, Levi Strauss, and Salesforce. There are also five LBS representatives. "One of our core jobs as a board member," says Padilla, "is to ensure that EurOUT does not lose its knowhow and networks during the annual transition of responsibilities from one student team to the next." Board members also act as mentors and help with ideas and networks – as their colleagues at ROMBA.[153]

## "Crowning our new queens" – and leadership beyond EurOUT

Recently the OiB has announced its two new presidents for the 2020–2021 school year, Charul Pant and Maury Ueta. They were also to manage EurOUT 2020 in November – virtual due to COVID-19. The news was sent out in April by a mailer nicely titled, *Crowning our new queens.*

Pant and Ueta hail from India and Brazil respectively, so their co-presidency is the first time neither chair has come from Europe or the US. Though this does not yet mean EurOUT affiliating with other universities and LGBT+ business students clubs globally, or having regionally more diverse sponsors, it is still a strong signal. Pant is also the first straight ally to co-lead the club and EurOUT.

In October 2019, LBS launched an LGBTQ+ Executive Leadership Programme.[154] After the programs in Stanford and Berlin – managed by the German branch of the world's oldest business school, ESCP, Paris – LBS is offering a third high-end option in the field of professional LGBT+ leadership education. "LBS school asked us for advice when they were designing the curriculum and also for support from the club and its board to promote the program within our networks," Padilla Rivera says. "And I like the photo on the brochure. It shows Allie Fleder, OiB's club president, in 2018."

# 10. Lawyers' worlds, an invitation to Moscow, and a young Russian working for change

It was winter and terribly cold when I landed at one of the huge Moscow airports, just a few weeks before lockdowns would begin to freeze the world in a different, previously unknown way. A driver was waiting to bring me to the city center and a nice hotel close to the office, where, the next day, I would be speaking at an event hosted by business law firm Hogan Lovells.

My presence in Russia's capital was in some ways a surprise to me. Coinciding with the launch of the German edition of this book at the world's largest book fair in Frankfurt in October 2019, I received a variety of invitations to read and speak. Among the first, which I accepted even before the book was published, was from Hogan Lovells, one of the world's largest corporate law firms. They wanted me to give a reading and participate in a discussion at their Munich office with some of their lawyers, other colleagues, and representatives of clients and other companies. The large room turned out to be packed, and the event was a success and inspiring for me, too.

A bit later, Alexey Kozlov contacted me. I had met Kozlov, who was a born Muscovite, at the Munich event, after which we had a few drinks with some colleagues. It was a nice and long evening, and I enjoyed it. Kozlov, who studied in Moscow and Tübingen, Germany, has worked for Hogan Lovells for more than 15 years and at different locations. First, he was in the Moscow office, then in Germany, then in the UK. Now, in Hogan Lovells' New York office, Kozlov not only works as a manager, taking care of the firm's knowledge management and document automation. In his capacity of a co-chair of the firm's ERG for LGBT+ employees and straight allies in continental Europe he is also involved in the firm's global LGBT+ D&I activities. As part of this, for example, he hosted and moderated an event on LGBT+ refugee crisis in the firm's Frankfurt office and did pro bono work for Human Rights Campaign and Transparency International.

"In Moscow, we will host a meeting on LGBT+ D&I in the Russian business world," he told me in an email and then on the phone. "That's a major step. I will be there, too. We would like to invite you to give a presentation on the results of your book." This sounded interesting. But should I go?

I had already started research for this English edition and was also involved in some other projects. In addition, my husband and friends had concerns because of the difficult situation for LGBT+ people in Russia, both legally and in daily life. I would have to take the book with me in my luggage. We all also knew a bit about the Russian so called "propaganda law" related to LGBT+ people that had come into force just the year before the world's eyes were turned to Sochi for the Winter Olympics in 2014. During the research for my book in New York I had also met Russians who had left the country because their lives as politically engaged LGBT+ people had become dangerous.

But still this knowledge was only vague, and I finally decided to accept the invitation wholeheartedly. I was curious because of the business context of the event, I appreciated Hogan Lovells' initiation of it, and I wanted to contribute. Kozlov and his colleagues in Munich and Moscow took care of everything. So there I was.

## Discretion in the law business and how it is changing

Let's start with some background on the law industry. There is no question that lawyers must be discreet, wherever they operate around the globe. This is also true for corporate lawyers. After all, for both corporate lawyers and clients there is a lot of money at stake and the outcome of the legal proceedings they engage in is all.

So what about information from one's private life? In the past, for a long time there was a kind of imperative that only rational legal argument should count in this world. The private sphere should not be of interest to anybody else, especially when it comes to issues seen as outside the norm. Lesbian, gay or bi, trans, or nonbinary? Private issue – "not normal," no issue.

At best, such matters have tended to be passed over in silence. After all, you don't want to spook the client – or the colleague or boss. Normality builds trust, as it has done for a long time, with the reassuring mutual mentioning of a wife and kids. As we saw in looking at unconscious biases (Part IV, Chapter 1), such norms neglecting the value of diversity and diverse perspectives let people feel comfortable (though without producing better results.)

These or similar cultural patterns have long governed the corporate law world, dominated as it was by straight middle-aged or older white men as both clients and lawyers just about everywhere around the globe. But as the world changes, the world of the law firms is changing with it, and changing fast, though partly for its own reasons.

Important among these is simply the sheer rising demand for top-quality new personnel. In the past decade, large corporations have had to considerably upgrade their legal departments in the face of growing demands from legislators. In addition, globalization, with its growing opportunities related to large international mergers and acquisitions, IPOs, spin-offs, and much more, has increased the market for corporate law advice, and thus for business lawyers substantially.

In parallel, the expectations regarding quality and speed of legal services for the corporate world have also grown. "The pressure from clients on lawyers to work even better, faster, and more creatively is increasing," says Sian Owles, a Partner at Hogan Lovells, working in the London office.

As a result, the salaries for young talented lawyers entering the industry have increased quickly. They are reaching six-figure sums now, with no upper ceiling in sight.

As we have seen in this book already (Part IV, Chapters 4 and 6), major corporate law firms such as Baker McKenzie, Clifford Chance, and others have become very active and innovative in reaching out to and retaining LGBT+ talents, especially those based in Anglo-Saxon countries. For an increasing number of them, it is no longer enough to be as good as their competitors on LGBT+-friendly policies and cultures – they want to be better, faster, and more creative too. And they know they don't just have to perform that way with respect to recruiting and retaining personnel. Rather – as this book has shown in many ways – their corporate clients are also pushing for greater LGBT+ inclusion with increasing intensity. This includes asking their suppliers to trackably commit to advancing LGBT+ equality themselves.

Though in a slightly less dynamic way than in the Anglo-Saxon countries, the same has been happening in continental Europe for a couple of years. For example, since 2013, business law firms have been the biggest industry cohort at Europe's largest LGBT+ job fair, Sticks & Stones, in Berlin (Part IV, Chapter 7). In its 2019 edition there were international players such as Allen & Overy, Baker McKenzie, Freshfields Bruckhaus Deringer, Hogan Lovells, Latham & Watkins, Simmons & Simmons, and White & Case. Even German-headquartered small- or medium-sized business law firms such as GSK Stockmann or Gleiss Lutz have been present with their own booths or shared their experience on the fair's panels, having understood that they must present themselves as LGBT+-friendly. There are similar developments in the job markets for young lawyers in other European countries, as is visible, for example in rates of membership or other forms engagements with local organizations working for LGBT+ inclusion such as Parks (in Italy), L'Autre Cercle (France), and REDI (Spain).

## Promises to be kept and a new spirit

Today, all major corporate law firms have LGBT+ employee net-works. "When I joined Hogan Lovells in 2012, I was attending the firm's first LGBT+ event in London already on my third day of work," says Owles, who today is one of the spokespersons for the firm's Pride+ network in the UK. Even young non-LGBT+ talents increasingly look for LGBT+ employee networks and their activities because they too want to work in open, diverse, tolerant, and, in that sense, modern corporate climates.

Of course, just letting it be known that a globally operating business law firm is practicing LGBT D&I and/or has an LGBT+ ERG, is not enough, especially if one can only point to such activities in other countries such as the US or the UK. As with so much else, equality – conveyed via policies, practices, networks, and various forms of internal and external communications – begins at home. One must be able to point to it locally.

During the research for this book I saw this firsthand, meeting several young business lawyers of different nationalities who worked for law firms that had promoted their LGBT+ friendliness with primary reference to US or UK activities. Now, specifically referring to a lack of local network activities, events, and other publicly visible initiatives, they were disappointed. They felt that they had implicitly been promised an active culture of LGBT+ inclusion in which they would feel a real sense of belonging, and the promise had not been kept. As a consequence, they were considering leaving their companies soon.

Such a situation is bad for the company in question, too. Its broken promise is expensive because the investment in recruiting and then educating a young law talent is high. And there is future economic damage too in loss of reputation. People talk, especially in small worlds – and compared to many of their multinational clients, corporate law firms are small, not in terms of revenue but numbers of employees – and the business law world as a whole is also small.

## All in one: professional, private, political

Many law firms have understood this dynamic and are engaging actively and visibly to advancing LGBT+ equality. For instance, they let their young lawyers participate in RAHM, the aforementioned international LGBT+ leadership contest in cities like Berlin, Toronto,

London, and Dublin (Part IV, Chapter 7). As did, for example, Malte Stübinger, a young employee of leading global law firm Latham & Watkins, who made the top ten at RAHM's 2017 premiere in Berlin. Hired by the firm just two years earlier and based in its Hamburg office, Stübinger says he strongly believes in the law's power to make change. In this he expresses the attitude of many younger-generation law talents looking beyond the ends of their own noses toward societal concerns.

On his LinkedIn business profile, Stübinger, next to Litigation Associate, also describes himself as a "Proud Out Father" and "Feminist." These designations can be understood not just as personal descriptions but the statements of an activist with a political conscience. They can also be understood as an invitation – again in line with other well-educated members of his generation – to perceive him as a human being with many facets, not reducible merely to his impersonally rational professional competence.

Linked to the publication of the German edition of my book, I was invited to an event with a panel discussion on LGBT+ inclusion in Frankfurt. It was hosted by the local Latham & Watkins office in partnership with Deutsche Bank and Prout at Work Foundation. Before the event started, I happened to be part of a conversation between one of the firm's Partners and Stübinger, who at that time was on sabbatical because he and his husband had recently become fathers of a daughter. It was "normal" private talk about Stübinger's new family situation, the lack of sleep and short nights – a "new normality."

The large room in which the panel event took place was full. Two other lawyers speaking were Jonas Menne, who made the introducing and closing remarks, and Maria Eisgruber, who joined me on the panel for discussion. Together with Stübinger, both were managing the German chapter of the firm's LGBT+ employee network. Some months later, both were part of a Latham & Watkins pro bono team that advised the Prout at Work Foundation on a major project on blood donation, the background of which I explained before: they helped formulate a positioning paper directed at German lawmakers and medical institutions. Its aim, learning from other countries, is to amend German blood donation directives to end their discrimination against gays, bisexual men and trans people in blood donations. Being active in the human rights domain, which includes fighting against any form of discrimination against LGBT+ people, has also become a "new normal" at many business law firms.

## Back to Moscow: open and careful at the same time

Prior to my Moscow trip, I met Tomas Schurmann, a marketing expert from Hogan Lovells' Munich office. He managed the afore-mentioned reading event there and is also a member of Pride+, the firm's LGBT+ employee network. "As a company, we have become much more active in recent years, globally and also in Germany," he says. That fits my research.

In Italy, for example, in collaboration with the Parks team, it organizes an event every year with external speakers. In the past, they came, for instance, from Gucci, Ikea, P&G, Pfizer, and Barilla. In Germany, Hogan Lovells partners with Prout at Work. In Spain, in 2016, the company was one of the founding members of REDI, alongside other global players such as Accenture, AXA, Procter & Gamble, and SAP.

Hogan Lovells is also quite active in the US. Beyond scoring top in the HRC's Corporate Equality Index for many years now, the company has also been engaged with Out Leadership (OL), having joined the globally oriented social business as one of its first inter-national law firm members in 2014. Among other things, Hogan Lovells has supported a variety of OL initiatives since, including the OutWOMEN program (for more on OL, see Part III, Chapter 1).

Hogan Lovells was also one of the main partners behind OL's European Summit on the business case for LGBT+ inclusion in fall 2019, which included a VIP Dinner series in London and Paris. Together with French-based AXA and UK-based bank giant HSBC, the law firm co-sponsored OL's first VIP dinner in Paris. It was hosted by HSBC and its then UK CEO António Simões, whom we have met in this book before (Part II, Chapter 4) and was attended by top and senior executives only.

Beyond engagements in liberal Western countries, in recent years, Hogan Lovells has also become active in countries that are difficult for LGBT+ people, at times even dangerous – such as Russia. As early as 2017, the firm hosted an internal event at their Moscow office with Ty Cobb, HRC Senior Director. His speech on the benefits and value of greater LGBT+ equality in the workplace was broadcast live via video conference to all Hogan Lovells offices worldwide. The following year, there was a seminar on LGBT+ discrimination protection and workers' rights, again set up as an internal event, but with guests from Microsoft and the firm's new pro bono client, the Russian LGBT+ organization Coming Out.

It was finally Coming Out that partnered with Hogan Lovells, setting up their third event for which I traveled to Moscow. A few years ago, the nonprofit had launched their Business as an Ally initiative, which had led to variety of contacts with the corporate world. Also, this time representatives from more companies were invited including, alongside a Hogan Lovells group, attendees from a variety of global businesses such as Accenture, SAP, Microsoft, and law firm DLA Piper.

All of them are headquartered in Western countries and have LGBT+ employee networks with chapters around the globe. This is important here, since, for some years already, the overwhelming majority of those networks has welcomed straight allies. This has not only led to growth but also fostered intersectionality and inclusion. However, in countries characterized by a difficult or even hostile legal and/or cultural environment – like Russia – this also contributes to an interesting situation: very often, the membership of the local chapters consists exclusively or almost exclusively of employees identifying as straight allies. This might reflect genuine willingness to learn and engage on the one hand and a self-protection strategy on the other. At the Hogan Lovells event in Moscow, a significant proportion of participants said, at least in informal talks, that they were straight allies.

The room in Moscow was packed. And attendees not only included representatives of the corporate world, but also a small team from Coming Out, including an interpreter who, since the event took place in Russian, sat next to me to whisper the translation so that I could follow.

Proceedings began with opening remarks from Hogan Lovells addressing the history of the firm's engagement on LGBT+ workplace equality in general and in Russia in particular, stressing the economic benefits of it there. Speeches followed, including mine, and breakout-sessions on how to advance LGBT+ inclusion in Russian workplaces specifically, including but not only focused on global companies with a subsidiary in the country.

Ruslan Savolainen from Coming Out took the stage to present a new study conducted by the organization: an online survey investigating "The Conditions for LGBT+ People in the Workplace." The survey's target group was LGBT+ people aged 18 and above with work experience in cities of more than a million inhabitants, such as Moscow or St. Petersburg. Beyond the basic data – such as sexual orientation, gender identity, age, education, employment, etc. – the questions addressed topics such as whether the employer in question could ensure a safe and open working environment for LGBT+ people, whether coworkers contributed to such an environment, and whether there had been discrimination and violence in the workplace based on sexual orientation and gender identity.

This is not the place to look in detail at the findings of this nonrepresentative study, though they were very interesting. But overall, it was no surprise that they showed:

- A much lower ratio of LGBT+ employees out at work than in liberal Western societies
- Far less feeling of safety in the workplace
- A much higher level of discrimination and violence experienced.

The most important thing I learned, however, was simply that it is possible to do studies of this kind at all in Russia – managed by an organization like Coming Out – and to make them public at an event held by Hogan Lovells in partnership with Coming Out.

I asked Savolainen for a longer interview, at which I began by asking him to help me understand what the so-called "propaganda law" means for Coming Out's activities and for advancing LGBT+ inclusion in Russian workplaces (see box on next page). I also wanted to learn more about him, his motivation, and the work of Coming out, including its work with companies in Russia.

## The so-called "propaganda law" in Russia and its relevance for businesses

On June 30, 2013, the Russian law on "propaganda for nontra-ditional sexual relations among minors" came into force. Once adopted, it not only increased fear in the LGBT+ community, but also confusion as to what it really meant, not least for the corporate world and workplaces. In an interview, Max Olenichev, legal advi-sor to the LGBT+-nonprofit Coming Out, based in St. Petersburg, answered my questions on this.

**Q: What is the essence of this law for firms operating in Russia – either headquartered in the country or operating as a subsid-iary of a foreign company?**

A: If there are no minors in the company, then there can be no "propaganda" and the law cannot be applied.

In practice, this also means:

- If a company employs only people above 18 years, then any questions about sexual orientation, gender identity, and LGBT+ (D&I) can be freely discussed throughout the firm.
- If in a department there are only people above 18 years (but minors in other parts of the company), then in this department the discussion of issues related to sexual orientation, gender identity, and LGBT+ (D&I) is not prohibited by law.

**Q: What does this mean for the whole world of companies oper-ating in Russia?**

A: Most companies employ only people above 18 years. For them, the "propaganda law" does not apply. This also means that limiting the possibilities for discussing issues related to sexual orientation and gender identity in the firm is not what the law asks for. To the contrary, it is not helpful and inappropriate if one wishes to advance LGBT+ equality in the workplace.

**Q: What does "propaganda" in the context of the law mean?**

A: It basically refers to education and dissemination of information related to "non-traditional sexual relations" – i.e. related to the sexual orientation and gender identity of LGBT+ people. And it must be targeted at minors. At the same time, "propaganda" is not just information, but purposeful activity aimed at forming in minors an idea of the advantages of non-heterosexual orientation over heterosexual. To me, this is farfetched, and it is impossible to compare forms of sexual orientations this way.

**Q: What, then, in the context of workplaces, is not "propaganda"?**

A: For example:

1. The mere fact that a person who identifies as LGBT+ works in a company
2. A photo of one's same-sex partner on the desktop
3. Discussion of any questions about sexual orientation and the gender identity of LGBT+ people in the absence of minors
4. Organizing special events supporting equality, creating support groups, disseminating information via corporate email about the need to support the transgender transition of an employee etc.
5. Providing same-sex partners (although not married) with the same benefits as straight married couples.

**Q: Beyond the "propaganda law" – what does Russian legislation say about discrimination against people based on their sexual orientation or gender identity?**

A: Article 3 of the Labor Code of the Russian Federation specifies that any distinction not based on the employee's work function is discrimination and prohibited.

**Q: Has there been any prosecution based on violation of this law in workplaces so far?**

A: No. More than six years of lack of judicial practice demonstrates the impossibility of applying this law related to "propaganda" in the workplace.

**Q: What does the European Court of Human Rights say?**

A: In 2017, the European Court of Human Rights in the case of Bayev and Others v. Russia[155] classified the law as violating human rights, the right to freedom of expression and the prohibition of discrimination and recommended that Russia repeal it.

## Setting up an LGBT+ organization in Russia

Savolainen is one of the founders of Coming Out, set up in 2008.[156] "At that time, I was only 18 years old, studying psychology at the Faculty of Family and Childhood Culture at the University of Culture and Arts in St. Petersburg, my hometown," he says.

"We – some activists and myself – gathered for a Day of Silence to raise awareness of the harmful effects of bullying, harassment and discrimination of LGBT+ people in schools," he continues (for more on the Day of Silence idea, see box). "After that experience, we had a discussion and decided that we should not stop. That was the moment when Coming Out was born."

The organization, dedicated to working for LGBT+ inclusion and equality, has grown fast since. "Now it is one of the largest and oldest in Russia. We have more than 100 volunteers supporting our work, and employ about 15 people, some full time, some part time." The focus of Coming Out's work is St. Petersburg and its greater area. "But our Business as an Ally initiative extends to all regions," Savolainen adds.

---

### The Day of Silence

The Day of Silence was initiated in the US and first took place at the University of Virginia, went national the year after, and has been held each year all around the country since, usually on the second Friday of April. Basically, it is a demonstration in which LGBT+ students and allies take a vow of silence to protest the harmful effects of bullying, harassment, and discrimination against LGBT+ people in schools. Often, the day ends with Breaking the Silence events to share experiences from the protest and draw attention to ways in which schools and communities can become more inclusive.[157]

For about 20 years now, the Day of Silence has been sponsored by GLSEN (an acronym for Gay, Lesbian, and Straight Education Network), a US awareness campaign and education lobbying organization founded in 1990.[158] Currently, GLSEN coordinates 43 chapters in 30 US states. It encompasses more than 1.5 million people, including students, families, educators, and education advocates working to ensure LGBT+ students in the US are able to learn and thrive in a school environment free

---

from bullying, harassment and discrimination.[159] Since GLSEN has started to support and promote the Day of Silence, this has led to the fast growth of these initiatives nationwide.

Meanwhile, the idea of practicing a Day of Silence has been taken up in a few other countries, such as in New Zealand, where it has taken place since 2007 and done so nationwide. Or in Russia, although there, due to widespread anti-LGBT+ hostility, it is held only very selectively. Nonprofit Coming Out has not held a Day of Silence for some years now but provides legal support to institutions that plan to do so.

## The group's work

"Coming Out is a public initiative and all the services that we provide are free," says Savolainen. "This is possible thanks to the support of international funds, the work of dozens of volunteers, as well as to other people who donate to help us do this – sometimes difficult – work."

The group has several programs. For example, it provides free psychological and legal support to LGBT+ people and those close to them. It also engages in educational activities such as setting up meetings, seminars, and roundtables, and releasing information materials on LGBT+ issues and related topics.

Coming Out also initiates cultural events in St. Petersburg to provide platforms for dialogue and discussion. "For example, due to our work, since 2009 the city of St. Petersburg, has been hosting the Queer Fest." An international festival of queer culture, Queer Fest has taken place more than ten times already and Savolainen coordinates it on behalf of Coming Out. "Its concept is similar to those of large Pride events in Europe, with ten days full of exhibitions, concerts, lectures, discussions, parties," Savolainen says. Each year, it has about 3,000 visitors.

"As Coming Out, we are not a political party or interest group. We are a human rights initiative that aims to ensure that any legitimate authority respects human rights and ensures human dignity to everyone," Savolainen says, explaining the group's mission. "To us, human rights are the highest value to refer to. To us, everyone, regardless of sexual orientation, gender identity, gender, race, nationality, and other characteristics, has the same rights and should be treated with equal respect." This also means, that "our work is based on the principles of non-violence, feminism, respect for personal life, respect for human rights, and the rule of law."

## A personal experience of violence

In 1993, homosexuality was decriminalized in Russia. The age of protection is 16 and sex reassignment has been legal since 1997. Nevertheless, discrimination is not against the law and bullying and hate speech is widespread, not to forget violence. This in no coincidence. "There is a strong homophobic tradition that goes back to Soviet times," says Savolainen. "But now there is a real propaganda of state, state-controlled media, and the Russian Orthodox Church that aggressively claims LGBT+ is something foreign to Russian values and Russian people."

Savolainen has experienced severe violence himself. In February 2018, he was invited to attend the the HagueTalks. On the 70th anniversary the Universal Declaration of Human Rights, he, alongside seven other LGBT+ and gender rights activists from Colombia, Bangladesh, China, Egypt, Nigeria, Ukraine, and Kenya, shared his story and how it changed him.

The HagueTalks got their name from The Hague, seat of the government of the Netherlands and the International Court of Justice. Some years ago, the HagueTalks were set up by the Hague Project for Peace and Justice, a joint initiative of the Dutch Ministry of Foreign Affairs, the Municipality of The Hague, and the Hague-based international organizations. It is basically a platform or meeting place "for creative minds, peace inventors, and game changers in the field of peace and justice," as its website says, setting up international events and more.[160]

In his three-minute videotaped statement at the HagueTalks, which is still accessible,[161] Savolainen reports with a hoarse voice how he was harassed on the sidewalk, people calling him "faggot" and "freak" before pushing him onto the street just as a car approached. The driver braked but could not avoid hitting Savolainen. He ended up with broken bones and had to spend several months in bed. "I had a lot of resentment, including anger, hatred, and feeling like a victim," Savolainen says, confirming his statement from the video. "But I did not want to be a victim. I decided that this should make me stronger," not stronger by training the body, but "stronger in my will and mind. Helping others in the LGBT+ community would make me stronger."

Thus, in addition to his work for Coming Out, he started to work in a program to evacuate LGBT+ people from Chechnya, whose lives are in danger. The program is coordinated by Russian LGBT Network (Российская ЛГБТ-сеть), a leading nonprofit headquartered in St. Petersburg that works for LGBT+ equality nationwide and is also a member of ILGA Europe (for more, see Part 1, Chapter 2).

## A mixed picture: some positive developments and some major remaining difficulties

Over roughly the past five years, the situation in Russia has changed in some ways. "On the one hand, the community of activists has become stronger and more professional," Savolainen observes. "There are now organizations and initiatives set up even in the most remote parts of the country. Celebrities are supporting LGBT+ people. And some politicians and political parties have begun to include LGBT+ issues in their agenda." But at the same time, the situation remains very different throughout the country. "We still have a high level of internal migration of LGBT+ people to the large cities, for example, St. Petersburg and Moscow. Or they leave the country."

Savolainen fully understands why LGBT+ people migrate to the main large cities, as there is still a hostile or even dangerous climate in the Russian countryside and in smaller cities. "For LGBT+ people, overall, St. Petersburg is the country's most tolerant and safest city. Here we have the oldest and largest LGBT+ organizations, and we have successful festivals," he says. "In addition, the local human rights authorities even support the LGBT+ agenda. For our events, Queer Fest in particular, for many years now, we have had experience working with the police to ensure safety and security. Also, courts decide in favor of LGBT+ people more often now."

Coming Out's primary target is to work for the LGBT+ community of St. Petersburg, but since the business program that the organization launched a few years ago has a national focus, Savolainen is looking even more intensely at other areas than he did before. He is part of the team coordinating this program and the Hogan Lovells event in Moscow was part of it.

"There are powerful human rights organizations in Moscow, too," Savolainen says. "And the nightlife for LGBT+ people is also more diverse there." Overall, compared to 2006, when Savolainen was about 16, he says, the situation for young LGBT+ people in Russia is, in some ways better now, with more accessible information through the internet and organizations like Coming Out. But for many LGBT+ people, even living and working in the more open environments of St. Petersburg or Moscow is still not satisfactory. "As an organization, we very often receive requests for consultations on how to obtain political asylum in other countries, especially for the young. They want to live openly and safely without looking around every day, build a career and relationships," Savolainen adds.

Several times, he has been called to the police for interrogations at which attempts were made to recruit him for "special services." "There is always a risk – especially when you are an activist," he says. "There were times when I was scared every day. But today, it's more dangerous for minors. I am openly gay in public and do not hide anything about myself. This makes my work safer."

## Courage

To be out in Russia and an LGBT+ activist requires courage, something Savolainen had to learn from early age. Even without his LGBT+ identity, he already had a Finnish-sounding last name and a colorful family background that made him a poor fit for the conventional Russian mainstream.

"Yes, I am half Finnish; historically a part of my family comes from Finland." But his father was also a Palestinian refugee whose family had to flee to Jordan when he was a child. Later he moved to Leningrad – today St. Petersburg – where he studied at the local medical university and met Savolainen's mother.

When he was a child, Savolainen also spent a lot of time in Jordan. "But during one of those visits, everything changed," he reports. "The unwritten cultural laws were saying that the oldest person in the family is its head." In the case of his family, this turned out to be his great grandmother from Saudi Arabia. "Due to her position, it was up to her to decide where I should live and other things." Savolainen had never met her. But then "she came to meet me in Jordan, when I was already ten years old, and decided to take me away from my parents and raise me in Saudi Arabia by herself. My mother and I had to leave the country secretly, went back to Russia, and never returned to Jordan again."

Today, his mother is one of his strongest supporters. "I had my coming out to my friends in my first year of university at age 18. At the same time, I was also part of *Ours*, where I became the first openly gay person." (Ours is a political youth organization that includes thousands of people from all over the country.) It took another five years until his brother's wedding party before he had the courage to come out to his mother. "I was crying, and while I was talking, she laughed and asked, 'Have you really thought that I didn't know?' and led me to dance. Today my mother is an activist, too. She helps other parents and LGBT + people to cope with their coming outs, and sometimes she attends Pride events in other countries."

## Business focus

Since 2020, Savolainen has been a member of the "core team" of Coming Out's leadership body. Beyond being in charge of the afore-mentioned Queer Fest and taking care of a variety of studies, he is also engaged in the organization's Business as an Ally initiative, in which "we help companies advancing an inclusive and safe working environment for LGBT+ employees, including offering trainings."

For Savolainen, this initiative is of the highest importance. "The workplace is where many of us spend most of our time. We can be more productive when we feel accepted and respected. To be LGBT+-inclusive is a win-win constellation for all parties. In addition, businesses have a huge impact on society and in many areas and can be a strong ally for change."

Part of this initiative is also the study Savolainen presented at the Hogan Lovells event. "We provide the study's data to employers, to show the challenges LGBT+ people face at work and what is needed to overcome them," he explains. "It was a great revelation for many companies that every tenth LGBT+ employee had faced threats and physical abuse and that one in four LGBT+ people had faced harass-ment and ridicule at work. And if all LGBT+ employees were out at work, this number would be much higher." Moreover, according to the study, LGBT+ employees are ready to support their company in case of a crisis, if it works for LGBT+ inclusion visibly.

For Coming Out, the Hogan Lovells event was the third of its kind. "At the end of each event, we choose a company that will become a co-organizer of the next one. A representative of Hogan Lovells proposed being the next partner." They knew what they were doing, since "Hogan Lovells had already participated in a roundtable meeting we had co-hosted before."

The cooperation continues. Hogan Lovells is taking part in a new study. "Now we don't ask LGBT+ people. We study the experience of introducing inclusive practices in companies and also their willingness to adopt them."

The LGBT+ inclusion journey in Russia's corporate world and society remains difficult. But supported by local civil society organizations, it goes on.

## Postscript from Paris: "What it really means to be a human being"

Coming from Moscow, where I attended the event described in the previous chapter, I landed in Paris, France's adorable capital, just a few weeks before the COVID-19 lockdown.

I have to confess, I have been a Francophile since my early youth, having spent some weeks with a family in a small castle called *La Poterie* while I was at school and worked in Paris for a couple weeks during my student years. Also, I did my master's at the University of Fribourg, a bilingual French-German university in the French-speaking part of Switzerland. I love French movies, French food, the sound of the French language, and a great deal more about the country besides. In other words, I have a bias.

When I started researching the German edition of this book in summer 2018, however, I had some difficulties gaining access to stories and background in France that I would be allowed to share. This was somewhat frustrating; I felt a bit like a rejected lover.

But it was not that surprising as France was, as I said earlier, lagging behind in awareness of the benefits of LGBT+ workplace inclusion and equality, compared to the UK and even to Germany. However, as I also said earlier, for some time now French employers have been bucking this trend. (For more on France, see Part II, Chapter 5.)

When I arrived in Paris, I was invited by Réseau des Réseaux, the aforementioned informal network of local LGBT+ ERG representatives, to attend an informal afterwork get-together in a bar close to the Stock Exchange. Jean-Luc Vey, well-networked French co-founder of German Prout at Work Foundation whom we have met in this book before, had helped me to be put on the guest list.

There were at least 40, if not 50 people from a variety of firms, industries, ethnicities, and ages. In some way, I was surprised, but this upsurge of engagement also tallied with my research showing changes recently in the French corporate world.

At the event, I met many people and had some inspiring discussions. One of these was with Tarique Shakir-Khalil, a Brit with Egyptian roots who recently took French nationality. He has worked for PwC's Corporate Finance practice for nearly 30 years, first in London, and now, for over 20 years, in Paris. He is a Partner there and led the French Corporate Finance business for many years before taking on a new role leading PwC's fundraising business for private equity clients globally, a business he initiated.

In the bar, we began a long conversation that continued two weeks later in Berlin. It turned out that he is a straight ally of LGBT+ people and engages in many ways, for example for Shine, PwC's LGBT+ inclusion network, set up in the country only in 2017 and covering not just France but also the Maghreb states.

"I thought I had three daughters – and recently discovered that I have two daughters and a son," Shakir-Khalil says, summarizing in a few words the motivation that led to his LGBT+-related activities, which include panel discussions, staging talks, writing articles, and more. Part of this is about how companies should deal with and support trans people at PwC and in all French workplaces, but his engagement covers a lot more. And he does not hide his activities. To the contrary, he showcases his role as an ambassador for Shine on his LinkedIn business profile very visibly.

"When, Jason – that's our son's name now – finally decided to tell us, as parents, what he feels and who he actually is, that came as a surprise to us," Shakir-Khalil reveals. "But at the same time, there was this strong love. There was no question that we wanted to support him."

His very personal experience changed a lot, says Shakir-Khalil, "... if not everything. It was a wakeup call to me to start to truly appreciate the potential challenges that Jason and others are prone to face in society whether due to narrow-mindedness, lack of understanding or unconscious biases on the part of others, whether at school, in the workplace, or elsewhere."

"Perhaps the most moving, the most important moment, happened," Shakir-Khalil reports, "when we shared the news with Jason's two younger sisters, who love him. As a family, we sat down, of all places, on the corner of a bed in a hotel room in Japan. And when Jason actually said that he is boy, not a girl, despite his initial physical endowment, the reaction from his then-six-year-old sister was totally spontaneous: 'I always wanted to have an older brother!' she exclaimed as she threw her arms around Jason's neck and hugged him. And the whole family joined the two in the hug – no more words, only tears of relief and joy."

Since then, Shakir-Khalil says, "I sensed that I also have to do something." While PwC has come to understand that companies need to work for LGBT+ inclusion in the workplace and contribute to society beyond just business, he realized that in France the LGBT+ inclusion journey was at a very early stage and felt increasingly compelled to act.

But there was more. "The journey of Jason's introspection to discover and fully embrace who he really is, whatever the challenges, has been quite humbling to me. Above all, I think, I have become more aware of what it really means to be a human being – in his, her, their uniqueness."

# Acknowledgements

The idea of writing this book consolidated in the Frankfurt offices of Allianz Global Investors in May 2017, when I read from an earlier work and participated in a panel discussion. I have Sven Schäfer, Michael Sandstedt, and former CEO Andreas Utermann to thank for this inspiration and their special support. Thanks are also owed to Eliza Young in New York for enabling me to share and discuss early research findings in a presentation at the firm's offices there, streamed to other offices in the US.

Many people have contributed to this book: as storytellers and content suppliers, idea and advice providers, sparring and interview partners, background clarifiers and contact mediators, companions and much more. My helpers probably number over a hundred, so I sadly cannot list them all. Though I valued every aspect of their information and suggestions, for reasons of space or because plans changed, not everything made it in. They should all know how much they have enriched this book and my experience of writing it nevertheless. I owe them the greatest thanks.

Very special thanks are owed to the following:

Kristen Anderson, Chief Diversity Officer at Barilla, Parma, was wonderfully prompt and forthcoming with her insights on the Barilla story I tell in Part I and gave feedback on this section.

Antonio Zappulla, CEO of the Thomson Reuters Foundation, London, engaged in many fascinating and fruitful conversations with me.

Igor Suran, Executive Director at Parks – Liberi e Uguali, Milan, helped me understand the Italian context, Parks' history and work, and Barilla's engagement.

Jürgen Petrasch of BNP Paribas Group arranged for me to attend his firm's second global LGBT+ business conference in Rome as the only external participant, and also reviewed Part I of this book's German version. Giovanna Spinazzola of BNP Paribas's Italian arm, BNL, which hosted the conference, shared precious insights and reviewed some pages in the English version of Part I.

Jean-Luc Vey, Deputy Chairman of Prout at Work Foundation and a manager at Deutsche Bank, gave helpful support in reviewing major sections of the book and was vital in helping me access and understand some French backgrounds. Also at Prout at Work, its Chairman Albert Kehrer gave insights and reviewed some pages in the German version.

Dan Bross, former Senior Director at Microsoft (retired) and now Co-Chair at the new Partnership for Global LGBTI Equality (PGLE), connected to the World Economic Forum (WEF), spoke with me about the WEF and much more. He invited me to a wonderful break-fast in Manhattan at an early stage of work on this book, we contin-ued our conversation in Seattle and Dan gave precious feedback on some chapters related to WEF, UN and PGLE.

Beth Brooke, former Global Vice Chair – Public Policy at EY (retired) and now sitting on several boards and acting as Co-Chair at PGLE, allowed me to interview her twice and gave precious insights.

Sander van 't Noordende, for many years and until recently a Group CEO at Accenture and also today a top executive, opened doors in an early phase of work and shared helpful views.

Beyond that, many people at Accenture were supportive. Javier Leonor-Vicente, part of his firm's global D&I team and leading the LGBT+ programs on all continents, shared his network and insights, and gave feedback on a subchapter of this book. The same applies to his colleague Christine Rauh, managing director and co-sponsor of Accenture's global Pride employee network, and Wenche Fredrik-sen, who leads the company's D&I programs in the Nordic states. Thomas Cusson, senior analyst in Paris, shared his view on French developments, especially among students, and helped open doors. Ulf Henning, Chief Marketing Officer Europe, and Christian Win-slow were very supportive at an early stage of this book.

Angela Matthes, CEO of Baloise Life Liechtenstein, shared her tran-sition story with me and gave feedback on the German version of it.

Stuart Bruce Cameron, founder and CEO of Uhlala Group, Ber-lin, shared his insights several times and reviewed the pages about him and his endeavors.

Armand Jouhet, senior consultant at Strategy&, Paris, arranged for me to attend a meeting of LGBT+ employee network represent-atives (Réseau des Réseaux), shared his detailed views in two inter-views and reviewed the parts on France.

Marc Sollin, HR Project Director at Société Générale, Paris, opened doors and arranged insightful interviews with his colleague Vincent François in London, and Ezequiel Corral in Manhattan.

Holger Reuschling shared his story of a father's late coming out, supported by his former employer Commerzbank in Frankfurt.

Ralph Breuer and Brian Rolfes, both Partners at McKinsey, helped me understand their firm's engagements at an early stage of my research.

Todd Sears, founder and CEO of New York City-based Out Leadership (OL), reviewed the pages about OL in Part III and shared valuable new information in a longer interview.

Fabrice Houdart, until recently a Human Rights Officer at the United Nations in New York, one of the co-authors of the UN LGBTI Standards of Conduct for Business, and now a Global Managing Director at OL, provided me with valuable access points and shared his equally precious background knowledge. He also reviewed some pages in Parts I, II and III.

Ty Cobb, Senior Director at Human Rights Campaign, Washington, DC, shared his insights at an early stage of my research. The same applies to Erin Uritus, CEO of Out & Equal Workplace Advocates, and to Jon Miller, founder and Chair of OFB, London, their former Global Program Director Drew Keller and their current Kenya Country Director Yvonne Muthoni.

Pavel Šubrt and Ludo Swinnen, co-founders and Co-Chairs of East meets West and the EGLCC (European LGBTI Chamber of Commerce), Vienna and Brussels, helped me understand Central and Eastern European situations, shared their story, and reviewed the respective parts in the book.

Fabienne Stordiau, co-founder and Co-Chair of GGLBC (German LGBTIQ* Business Chamber), shared her story and reviewed some pages on new chambers of commerce.

Czeslaw Walek and Adéla Horáková from Prague Pride/Pride Business Forum and Jsme fér, the Czech equal marriage campaign, have shared their stories and insights on the Czech context and Adéla gave important feedback on the respective part.

Alexander Dmitrenko and Naosuke Fujita, co-founders and Co-Chairs of Lawyers for LGBT & Allies Network (LLAN), Tokyo, provided rich stories and insights on the Japanese context and gave precious feedback on the respective chapter.

Dawn Hough, Director at ACON, Sidney, shared helpful insights at an early stage of research.

David Pollard, Executive Director at Workplace Pride Foundation in Amsterdam, reviewed the chapter on the Netherlands and provided invaluable insights and support in earlier phases of my research, as well as a very gratefully accepted invitation to a Workplace Pride conference in Hong Kong.

Leon Pieters, Partner at Deloitte Netherlands, also shared his story and reviewed material on his home country.

Marijn Pijnenburg, Executive of IBM's LGBT+ business development team, shared his insights and reviewed the respective parts.

Miguel Castro and Óscar Muñoz, co-founders of REDI (Red Empresarial por la Diversidad y la Inclusión LGBTI), Madrid, shared their knowledge on REDI's work and on the Spanish context in general and reviewed the respective chapter.

Luke Andrews, Senior Consultant at Monitor Deloitte and co-founder of the South African LGBT+ Management Forum, was generous to a fault to me in Johannesburg, with hospitality, insights, and conversation time. He also reviewed the South Africa chapter.

Manuel Rosas Vázquez, of Rainbow City Network (RCN), helped me understand RCN's goals and work.

Ernesto Marinelli, Senior Vice President at SAP, helped me understand his story as an out Italian making a career in a German software company.

Erik Lüngen, Vice President at SAP, who fell in love with India and its people, shared his story, opened up his rich box of insights and reviewed some pages in the respective chapter. Also, his colleagues Sameer Ranjan Kumar and Vishalakshi Khizhakhe helped me understand the specific Indian context.

The same applies to Suresh Ramdas of HP who is also co-founder of Working With Pride (WWP), to Ramkrishna Singha, co-founder of Pride Circle, and to Khandhar Kushal of BCG. Kushal generously invited me to join an internal BCG webinar with Parmesh Shahani, who presented his book *Queeristan: LGBTQ inclusion in the Indian workplace.*

Elliot Vaughn, Partner at BCG and Chair of his firm's global LGBT+ network, shared his precious insights, gave me a rich interview with which Part III of this book ends and reviewed it.

Fern Ngai, former CEO of Community Business, Hong Kong, shared her helpful insights and network in an early phase of research.

Cecilia Leung helped me understand local daily life in Hong Kong and invited me to stay a couple of days at her home.

Meike Imberg gave helpful insights and reviewed some pages in Part IV, including those on Stonewall, London, where she works.

Jeannine Ferreira, shared her views and knowledge in an interview in Johannesburg, before she moved to the Netherlands, where she now works as Head of Marketing for VodafoneZiggo.

Nikita Baronov, of Metronom, shared his story and gave useful feedback on the respective part.

Katja Ploner, D&I manager at Siemens, opened doors and shared precious stories. The same applies to Arthur Schmid, a research scientist, who co-leads the firm's LGBT+ employee network. Lindsay Krakauer of Siemens Healthineers was helpful at an early stage of work too.

Alberto Padilla Rivera, Senior Director at Insight Partners, shared his views and stories, and inspired me to look more into the student-managed conferences ROMBA and EurOUT.

Many people at Hogan Lovells in Germany, the US, and Russia were very supportive, especially Oxana Balayan, Alexey Kozlov and Tomas Schurmann. Among other things, they invited me to present the findings of my German book in Moscow and helped me understand more about the special challenges in Russia, including those related to the workplace. They also reviewed the respective chapter in this English book version.

Ruslan Savolainen, from LGBT+ NGO Coming Out in St. Petersburg, helped me understand more on Russia, discussed his engagement with Russian workplaces, shared his moving story, and reviewed the respective chapter. Max Olenichev, legal advisor to the same NGO, gave me an insightful interview on the so-called "propaganda law" and its impact on Russian workplaces, and reviewed my write-up of the material.

Martina Eisenberg, Jonas Menne, and Malte Stübinger, laywers at Latham & Watkins, shared helpful information on their employer's activities, and personal stories.

Tarique Shakir-Khalil, Partner at PwC France, had many inspiring and very personal conversations with me in Paris, Berlin, and on the phone. He reviewed the passages on France and, in particular, with great trust and openness, shared the very moving story of his own family with which this book ends.

Matthias Weber, Chairman of Völklinger Kreis and an executive at Postbank/Deutsche Bank, shared his views on the German context.

Petra Thorbrietz enriched the German version of this book from concept development to the printing phase with constructive comments and also read Part 1 of this English version.

The colleagues at my English publisher LID were very supportive and patient at every stage of the project, in particular Aiyana Curtis, Caroline Li, and Martin Liu.

Finally:

A big thank you goes to the many who took time to write endorsements praising this book in advance, as shown on the first pages. I am flushed by their generosity and strong support. They make me humble.

John Moseley was my private editor in London. His work was just extraordinary. I owe him a lot.

My biggest thank you goes to my husband, Karsten Østergaard Nielsen. For everything. He knows what for. What would I be without him?

# The author

**JENS SCHADENDORF** is an author and keynote-speaker on top-ics related to diversity and inclusion (D&I), primarily LGBT+ D&I, corporate social responsibility (CSR), and leadership. He also advises companies, scientists, and managers on book projects globally and consults on communications, change, and CSR matters. Alongside this, he is also an independent researcher at the Peter Löscher Chair of Business Ethics/TUM School of Governance at Technical University of Munich, Germany.

Previously, he was for many years an editorial and publishing director. As a publisher of general nonfiction books, he worked at leading media houses such as Bertelsmann, Axel Springer, Bonnier, and Herder, with international bestselling authors such as Jack Welch, Bill Clinton, the Dalai Lama, Hans-Werner Sinn, Elie Wiesel, Don Tapscott, Michael Porter, Peter Drucker, Louis Begley, Gary Hamel, Anita Roddick, and many more. Further accomplishments include publication of the first critical biographies in German of French far-right presidential candidate Marine Le Pen, Volkswagen tycoon

Ferdinand Piëch and Turkish president Recep Tayyip Erdoğan. His work as a book publisher has received several awards.

After studying economic and social sciences in Hamburg, Germany, where he was born, Schadendorf earned a Master's in Political Economy and Business Administration at the bilingual French-German Fribourg University, Switzerland. His thesis, for which he received a *summa cum laude*, was at the intersection of arts, culture, business strategies of banks, and communications. Subsequently, he worked as a research associate at the bilingual Seminar of Political Economy at Fribourg University, followed by postgraduate studies on East Asian development economics and culture in Bangkok, and Singapore, funded by the Swiss National Fund.

For some years, he has taught at universities on topics related to intercultural management, D&I, and media economics, and has also supervised bachelor and master's theses. Today, he still lectures intermittently.

He has written for the *Financial Times Deutschland*, *Zeit online*, *Spiegel online*, *Tagesspiegel*, and others. Among his books, *Der Regenbogen-Faktor* (The Rainbow Factor), a book on gays and lesbians in German business and society, was widely covered by German media. There is also *Gut!* (Good!), co-authored with philosophy professor Christoph Lütge, a book of thought-provoking short stories about how to act well in ordinary life.

In October 2019, the German edition of this book, *GaYme Changer*, was published, again with extensive media coverage. This resulted in Schadendorf being invited to read and speak at universities, nonprofits, and many companies. The book was also the trigger for his authorial activism being recognized in Vienna with an East meets West Award in the category "Individual."

Schadendorf lives in Munich and has a long-distance relationship with his Danish husband Karsten, who lives in Hannover, Germany, with their dachshund Nelly.

# Glossary of terms and abbreviations

**Affinity group** – See "ERG."

**Ally** – Typically, a straight, cisgender person who works to support the LGBT+ community.

**Asexual** – Refers to individuals with a lack of desire for sex and/or sexual partners.

**Bias** – See "Unconscious bias."

**Bisexual** – Refers to individuals with a capacity for sexual attraction to more than one gender.

**CEI** – The "Corporate Equality Index" put out by the HRC measuring companies on their policies and practices for LGBT+ employees and external stakeholders.

**Cisgender or Cis** – Adjectives describing people who continue to identify with the gender identity assigned to them at birth. The terms come from the Latin "cis," meaning "on this side of" to distinguish from "trans" meaning "on the other side of." Both terms – "cis" and "transgender" – refer only to gender identity, not sexual identity/ orientation, which are about whom we feel emotionally, sexually, and/or romantically attracted to. Cis and transgender people can be homo- or heterosexual or otherwise sexually oriented, for example bisexual or asexual.

**Closeted** – See "In the closet."

**Coming out** – The process of revealing a previously hidden sexual or gender identity to others.

**"Conversion therapy"** – A pseudoscientific therapy promising to "return" LGBT+ people to a "natural," i.e. straight sexual orientation. It can cause severe long-term psychological damage, even increasing suicide risk. The UN Independent Expert on protection against violence and discrimination has called for a global ban.

**CSR** – Corporate social responsibility.

**D&I** – Diversity and inclusion. Sometimes also written as "I&D." "D&I management" refers to the running of a company's strategies, policies and programs on D&I, but "D&I" alone can often be read as standing for this, e.g. "He is Head of LGBT+ D&I." Recently, "belonging" has also come to be seen as important, meaning "DIB" has replaced "D&I" in some instances.

**Employee network** – See "ERG."

**Equal marriage/marriage equality/same-sex marriage** – The right for people to marry the partner of their choice, regardless of gender. It has recently become legal in many countries in the West, Latin America, or even Taiwan, but the fight for it continues in many other countries around the world.

**ERG** – Employee resource group. Refers to groups of employees sharing similar concerns or identity markers working together for one another's interests in a company. Other terms include "affinity group," "business resource group (BRG)" and "employee network."

**Gay** – Emotionally/romantically/sexually attracted to people of the same sex. Most commonly used to refer to men with same-sex attraction, though many lesbians also use the term to describe themselves.

**Gender identity** – Refers to the gender with which an individual identifies, regardless of whether it conforms to the gender assigned to them at birth. Gender identities can be male, female, or nonbinary (see "Nonbinary").

**Gender-nonconforming** – See "Nonbinary."

**Gender-noncompliant** – See "Nonbinary."

**GLAAD** – The influential US nonprofit organization working for better representations of LGBT+ people in the media, and for LGBT+ rights and inclusion in the media industry. Originally the name stood for Gay & Lesbian Alliance Against Defamation. Since 2013, it has stood only for itself – without referring to gays and lesbians, making it clear that the organization also works for bisexual, transgender, and queer people.

**Heterosexual** – Refers to individuals solely experiencing sexual/romantic attraction to individuals of the "opposite" gender. See "Straight."

**Homosexual** – Refers to individuals solely experiencing sexual/romantic attraction to individuals of the same gender (see "Gay"). Now widely seen mainly as a scientific term, not commonly used by gay people to refer to themselves.

**Homophobia** – Prejudice against, anxiety about and ill-treatment of lesbian and gay people, though it often refers more generally to mistreatment of any LGBT+ person. Related terms are "biphobia" and "transphobia."

**I&D** – See "D&I."

**In the closet** – Refers to an individual who has not yet come out (see "Coming out"), that is, revealed their true sexual/gender identity publicly.

**HR** – Human Resources, often standing for "Human Resources Department." D&I management is often part of HR or closely aligned to it, especially as HR oversees recruiting, career development programs etc.

**HRC** – Human Rights Campaign, the influential US LGBT+ nonprofit that, among many other initiatives, puts out the Corporate Equality Index (see "CEI").

**IDAHOBIT** – International Day Against Homo-, Bi- and Trans-phobia. The day is May 17, because it was on that date in 1990 that homosexuality was removed from the WHO's list of diseases.

**ILGA** – International Lesbian, Gay, Bisexual, Trans and Intersex Association.

**Intersectionality** – A theoretical and practical framework for under-standing and managing discrimination and under-representation not simply as a matter of individual minority groups – women, peo-ple of colour, the disabled, LGBT+ people – but via the way these fac-tors combine. For instance, a company might have a strong LGBT+ ERG, but it might still be dominated by men, with ethnic minorities, women, and others remaining marginalized.

**Intersex** – Refers to individuals born with either a mix of male and female or non-gender-specific genitalia and/or other biological attributes. Intersex people may identify as male or female or non-binary, but many people who identify as nonbinary are not intersex.

**Lesbian** – Primarily refers to women emotionally/romantically/sex-ually attracted toward women, though some nonbinary people also use the term to describe themselves.

**LGBT+** – Initials standing for lesbian, gay, bi, and trans. The "+" stands for other less clearly definable sexual and/or gender identities such as "asexual," "questioning," and "pansexual." Variants include LGBTQ, with the "Q" standing for "queer" or "questioning," LGBTI, with the "I" standing for "intersex," and LGBTIA, with the "A" stand-ing for "asexual/aromantic."

**"LGBT-free zones"** – This term refers to areas of Poland, totaling about a third of the country's territory, that have declared them-selves unwelcoming to LGBT+ people and/or so-called "LGBT ide-ology", thereby legitimizing bullying, harassment, hate speech, and even violence.

**Nonbinary** – A catch-all term referring to those whose gender iden-tity cannot simply be defined as "male" or "female." Alternative or similar terms are "gender-noncompliant," "gender-nonconforming," or "gender-neutral." Some nonbinary people identify with aspects of male and female identities, while others reject them entirely. With respect to their gender expression, nonbinary people can present as masculine, feminine ("femme") or both or neither and this can change over time ("gender-fluid"). (In the acronym LGBTQ, all these are also part of the "Q," covering a variety of forms of queerness.)

**Out, or Out of the closet** – Refers to individuals who have come out (see Coming out). Not to be confused with the terms "outed" or "outing," which generally refer to the revelation being made by someone else, generally without the individual's consent.

**OutRight Action International** – OutRight for short, based in New York City and founded in 2008, aims at helping to improve LGBT+ rights and protection in the US and worldwide, including within the UN framework.

**Pansexual** – Refers to individuals with the capacity to be attracted to anyone, regardless of sexual and gender identity.

**PGLE** – Partnership for Global LGBTI Equality (a project within the WEF.)

**Pinkwashing** – This describes strategies aimed at promoting products, brands, or companies through the appealing appearance of being LGBT+-friendly without really being so.

**Pronoun** – The basic meaning is words like "she," "he," or "they" used to refer to individuals without naming them. The singular, gender-specific terms become problematic when referring to individuals who do not identify with a specific gender. Many such individuals now opt to be referred to by what are called "gender-neutral pronouns," which, in practice, usually means using "they" and "them" as singular pronouns – as is already commonly done in instances where gender is not known, e.g. "If anyone wants to know more, they can get in touch with..." The new pronouns "ze" and "zir" are also sometimes used.

**Queer** – Originally a derogatory term for LGBT+ people, it was long ago repurposed as a badge of pride and identity by the community. Today it is often used similarly to "nonbinary" or the "+" in "LGBT+" to refer to the wider spectrum of gender and sexual orientations.

**Questioning** – Describes a process of exploration of one's sexual/ gender identity, or of being in a permanent or long-term state of uncertainty about it.

**ROMBA** – Stands for Reaching Out MBA. Based in the US, this is the leading LGBT+ business student initiative both for content and recruitment. At its heart is the world's largest conference of LGBT+ MBA students.

**Section 377** – Part of the Indian criminal code, criminalizing, among other things, same-sex intercourse between adults. This was only dropped in September 2018.

**The Standards** – See "The UN Standards."

**Straight** – Standard colloquial terminology for "heterosexual."

**Trans** – An umbrella term for individuals who do not identify with or only partially identify with the gender assigned to them at birth. Terms falling within this broad category include transgender, transsexual, gender-queer (GQ), gender-fluid, nonbinary, gender-variant, crossdresser, genderless, agender, nongender, third gender, bi-gender, trans man, trans woman, trans masculine, trans feminine and neutrois. "Transgender man" or "trans man" refers to someone assigned a female gender identity at birth who now identifies as male. "Transgender woman" or "trans woman" refers to someone assigned a male identity at birth who now identifies as female. Both fall within the category "Transgender."

**Transitioning** – A trans individual's process of adopting the gender identity with which they identify. Most commonly understood to be the medical process, involving surgery and/or hormone therapies, but not all trans people go through this. It can also describe the process they go through of altering their gender identity publically, both in official documents such as passports, coming out to friends and family, and wearing different clothes.

**Unconscious bias** – In the context of D&I, e.g. LGBT+ D&I (see definitions of these terms here), "bias" refers to predispositions that can lead to discrimination against minority groups, e.g. top managers who are predominantly white and male may be more likely to hire – or even just select for interview – people like themselves. Such tendencies are often so habitual as to go unnoticed by those perpetrating them, which leads to the concept of "unconscious bias." "Unconscious bias training," helping people see beyond their unquestioned assumptions, has therefore become a key element in corporate D&I.

**The UN Standards** – The UN's "Standards of Conduct for Business. Tackling Discrimination against Lesbian, Gay, Trans, & Intersex People," also known as the UN LGBTI Standards of Conduct for Business. Sometimes referred to as just the Standards.

**WEF** – World Economic Forum.

# Endnotes

## Introduction

1. https://open-for-business.org/kenya-economic-case; accessed October 21, 2020
2. https://outleadership.com/; accessed October 21, 2020
3. https://www2.deloitte.com/global/en/pages/about-deloitte/articles/millennialsurvey.html; accessed 20 October 2020

## Part I

1. https://www.queer.de/detail.php?article_id=20132; https://ricerca.repubblica.it/repubblica/archivio/repubblica/2013/09/27/mai-spot-con-gay-bufera-su-barilla.html; accessed December 21, 2020
2. https://www.change.org/p/tell-barilla-where-there-is-love-there-is-family; accessed June 10, 2020
3. https://eu.usatoday.com/story/money/business/2013/09/26/barilla-boycott/2877487/; accessed December 21, 2020
4. https://www.washingtonpost.com/politics/human-rights-campaign-says-barilla-has-turned-around-its-policies-on-lgbt/2014/11/18/9866efde-6e92-11e4-8808-afaa1e3a33ef_story.html; accessed December 20, 2020
5. https://twitter.com/miafarrow/status/383592871196381184; accessed December 21, 2020
6. https://www.huffpost.com/entry/barilla-boycott-gay-friendly-pasta-brands_n_4003543; accessed December 21, 2020
7. https://www.bloomberg.com/news/features/2019-05-07/barilla-pasta-s-turnaround-from-homophobia-to-national-pride; accessed March 15, 2020
8. https://www.washingtonpost.com/politics/human-rights-campaign-says-barilla-has-turned-around-its-policies-on-lgbt/2014/11/18/9866efde-6e92-11e4-8808-afaa1e3a33ef_story.html; accessed June 10, 2020l
9. https://www.bloomberg.com/news/features/2019-05-07/barilla-pasta-s-turnaround-from-homophobia-to-national-pride; accessed March 15, 2020; https://www.forbes.com/sites/susanadams/2014/04/08/the-worlds-most-reputable-companies/?sh=417e71ac4024; accessed December 21, 2020
10. https://www.forbes.com/sites/susanadams/2014/04/08/the-worlds-most-reputable-companies/?sh=417e71ac4024; accessed December 21, 2020
11. Ibid.
12. https://tylerclementi.org/; accessed March 16, 2020
13. The results of a representative US-wide study published in the Journal of the American Medical Association (JAMA) at the end of 2017 are alarming. Nearly 25% of the LGBQ youth* surveyed said that they had attempted suicide at least once in the past year (2015). Among heterosexual young people, this figure was just 6%, i.e. about four times lower. The risk of suicide was equally alarming: 40% of LGBQ youths said they had already thought about suicide, compared to just under 15% of heterosexual respondents. The suicide risk is even higher among the non-outed, as another study adds. (*Note: The study did not include trans people, but – as per the acronym LGBQ – "Q people," the "Q" in this case meaning "questioning." https://www.ncbi.nlm.nih.gov/pmc/articles/PMC5820699/; https://www.reuters.com/article/us-health-teens-lgbq-suicide/one-in-four-gay-lesbian-bisexual-teens-attempt-suicide-idUSKBN1ED2LS
14. https://www.ncbi.nlm.nih.gov/pmc/articles/PMC6583682/; accessed December 20, 2020
15. https://www.bloomberg.com/news/features/2019-05-07/barilla-pasta-s-turnaround-from-homophobia-to-national-pride; accessed March 16, 2020
16. https://www.ilga-europe.org/who-we-are/what-ilga-europe; https://ilga.org/; accessed March 16, 2020
17. More information on the list of criteria and their weight on the total score can be found at http://www.rainbow-europe.org/about; accessed June 10, 2020

18. https://www.rainbow-europe.org/country-ranking; accessed December 20, 2020. Beyond the ranking, the annual review provides a more differentiated and detailed overview of the progress made by each country over the last twelve months and of developments at international level.

19. https://www.bloomberg.com/news/features/2019-05-07/barilla-pasta-s-turnaround-from-homophobia-to-national-pride; accessed December 20, 2020

20. Ibid.

21. https://www.panorama.it/news/dolce-gabbana-lunica-famiglia-quella-tradizionale; accessed March 17, 2020

22. https://www.vogue.com/article/dolce-and-gabbana-synthetic-babies-apology; accessed March 17, 2020

23. Ibid.

24. In the very fluid Italian political arena, Renzi has meanwhile founded a new party, Italia Viva, which is part of the current national government. Scalfarotto is now a member of Italia Viva and serves as Under Secretary of State for Foreign Affairs (as per August 2020).

25. https://eu.usatoday.com/story/money/business/2013/09/26/barilla-boycott/2877487/; accessed June 12, 2020

26. https://eu.usatoday.com/story/money/business/2013/09/26/barilla-boycott/2877487/; https://www.change.org/p/lindsay-hawley-stop-carrying-anti-gay-pasta; accessed June 10, 2020

27. https://www.glaad.org/about; accessed June 10, 2020

28. https://www.glaad.org/mediaawards/31/categories; accessed August 10, 2020

29. https://www.bloomberg.com/news/features/2019-05-07/barilla-pasta-s-turnaround-from-homophobia-to-national-pride; accessed June 10, 2020

30. Ibid.

31. Ibid.

32. Ibid.

33. https://www.aliforneycenter.org/homeless-for-the-holidays/; accessed June 10, 2020

34. https://www.washingtonpost.com/politics/human-rights-campaign-says-barilla-has-turned-around-its-policies-on-lgbt/2014/11/18/9866efde-6e92-11e4-8808-afaa1e3a33ef_story.html; accessed June 10, 2020

35. https://assets2.hrc.org/files/assets/resources/HRC-HRCF-Combined-2019-FS.pdf?_; accessed December 21, 2020

36. https://www.washingtonpost.com/politics/human-rights-campaign-says-barilla-has-turned-around-its-policies-on-lgbt/2014/11/18/9866efde-6e92-11e4-8808-afaa1e3a33ef_story.html; accessed June 10, 2020

37. https://www.hrc.org/campaigns/corporate-equality-index; accessed June 10, 2020

38. https://www.washingtonpost.com/politics/human-rights-campaign-says-barilla-has-turned-around-its-policies-on-lgbt/2014/11/18/9866efde-6e92-11e4-8808-afaa1e3a33ef_story.html; https://www.youtube.com/watch?v=vdgTlkQ1yRo; accessed June 10, 2020

39. Ibid.

40. Ibid.

41. Ibid.

42. https://eu.usatoday.com/story/money/business/2013/09/30/barilla-executive-gays-apology/2895831/; accessed June 11, 2020

43. https://money.cnn.com/2013/11/04/news/companies/barilla-diversity/index.html; accessed June 11, 2020

44. https://www.williamcfrederick.com/articles/GrowingConcern.pdf; accessed October 11, 2020

45. https://www.weforum.org/agenda/2019/12/davos-manifesto-1973-a-code-of-ethics-for-business-leaders; accessed June 12, 2020

46. Ibid.

47. https://www.weforum.org/about/world-economic-forum; accessed June 11, 2020

48. Ibid.

49. https://www.nytimes.com/2018/01/15/business/dealbook/blackrock-laurence-fink-letter.html; accessed June 11, 2020

50. https://bridgingthegapventures.com/the-change-generation-report/; accessed June 11, 2020

51. https://www.pewresearch.org/fact-tank/2019/01/17/where-millennials-end-and-generation-z-begins; accessed June 11, 2020

52. https://www.nytimes.com/2018/01/15/business/dealbook/blackrock-laurence-fink-letter.html; accessed March 10, 2020

53. https://www.blackrock.com/corporate/about-us/contacts-locations; accessed December 20, 2020

54. https://www.blackrock.com/corporate/investor-relations/2018-larry-fink-ceo-letter; accessed June 10, 2020

55. Ibid.

56. Ibid.

57. https://www.blackrock.com/sg/en/about-us; accessed December 16, 2020

58. https://de.statista.com/statistik/daten/studie/200520/umfrage/staatseinnahmen-und-staatsausgaben-in-den-usa/; accessed December 16, 2020

59. https://www.nytimes.com/2019/01/17/business/dealbook/blackrock-larry-fink-letter.html; accessed June 16, 2020

60. https://www.nytimes.com/2018/01/15/business/dealbook/blackrock-laurence-fink-letter.html; accessed March 10, 2020

61. Ibid.

62. https://www.nytimes.com/2019/01/17/business/dealbook/blackrock-larry-fink-letter.html; accessed June 16, 2020

63. https://money.cnn.com/2018/02/22/news/companies/blackrock-gun-questions/index.html; accessed June 16, 2020

64. https://money.cnn.com/2018/03/02/investing/blackrock-gunmakers/index.html?iid=EL; https://money.cnn.com/2018/04/05/news/companies/blackrock-gun-sellers/index.html; accessed June 16, 2020

65. https://www.blackrock.com/corporate/investor-relations/2019-larry-fink-ceo-letter; accessed June 16, 2020

66. Ibid.

67. Ibid.

68. https://hbr.org/2019/01/the-backlash-to-larry-finks-letter-shows-how-far-business-has-to-go-on-social-responsibility; accessed June 16, 2020

69. https://www.foxbusiness.com/business-leaders/blackrocks-larry-fink-rattles-employees-amid-political-posturing; accessed June 16, 2020

70. https://hbr.org/2019/01/the-backlash-to-larry-finks-letter-shows-how-far-business-has-to-go-on-social-responsibility; accessed June 16, 2020

71. https://www.foxbusiness.com/business-leaders/blackrocks-larry-fink-rattles-employees-amid-political-posturing; accessed June 16, 2020

72. Ibid.

73. https://www2.deloitte.com/global/en/pages/about-deloitte/articles/millennialsurvey.html; accessed June 27, 2020

74. https://www2.deloitte.com/global/en/pages/about-deloitte/press-releases/deloitte-millennial-survey-reveals-resilient-generation.html; accessed June 27, 2020

75. https://www2.deloitte.com/global/en/pages/about-deloitte/articles/millennialsurvey.html; accessed June 27, 2029

76. https://www.unglobalcompact.org/what-is-gc/mission/principles; accessed December 20, 2020

77. https://www.unglobalcompact.org/what-is-gc/mission/principles/principle-1; accessed June 24, 2020

78. https://shiftproject.org/wp-content/uploads/2020/01/GuidingPrinciplesBusinessHR_EN.pdf; accessed June 20, 2020. In a year-long process, they were developed by John Ruggie from Harvard University's John F. Kennedy School of Government. As UN Secretary-General's Special Representative, Ruggie had already been one of the architects of the Global Compact.

79. https://www.ohchr.org/Documents/Publications/HR.PUB.12.2_En.pdf; accessed June 20, 2020

80. Ibid.

81. https://www.unglobalcompact.org/take-action/action/human-rights-open-letter-to-academics; accessed June 20, 2020

82. https://www.unglobalcompact.org/take-action/action/human-rights-policy; accessed June 24, 2020

83. https://d306pr3pise04h.cloudfront.net/docs/issues_doc%2Fhuman_rights%2FResources%2FHR_Policy_Guide_2nd_Edition.pdf; accessed June 24, 2020

84. https://www.unglobalcompact.org/what-is-gc/our-work/sustainable-development; https://ungc-communications-assets.s3.amazonaws.com/docs/publications/UN-Global-Compact-Progress-Report-2020.pdf; accessed June 9, 2020

85. Ibid.

86. https://s3-us-west-2.amazonaws.com/ungc-production/commitment_letters/139578/original/UN_Global_Compact_-_Letter_of_Commitment_-_BlackRock_-_Final.pdf?1587137024; https://www.unglobalcompact.org/what-is-gc/participants/139578-BlackRock-Inc-; accessed June 20, 2020

87. https://www.unglobalcompact.org/what-is-gc/our-work/sustainable-development; https://ungccommunications-assets.s3.amazonaws.com/docs/publications/UN-Global-Compact-Progress-Report-2020.pdf; accessed June 9, 2020

88. https://unsdg.un.org/2030-agenda/universal-values; accessed June 11, 2020

89. https://sustainabledevelopment.un.org/post2015/transformingourworld; accessed June 11, 2020

90. https://www.barillagroup.com/en/barilla-standards-onu-against-lgbti-discrimination; accessed June 30, 2020

91. https://www.trust.org/documents/trf-2020.pdf, accessed June 25, 2020

92. https://www.trust.org/contentAsset/raw-data/98b348c9-b99d-4d84-8aa6- 30da4d61aae3/document; accessed June 20, 2020

93. https://news.trust.org/profile/?id=003D000002WZGYRIA5; accessed June 20, 2020

94. https://www.barillacfn.com/en/dissemination/food_sustainability_media_award/; accessed June 20, 2020

95. https://www.theguardian.com/world/2019/apr/01/brunei-cruel-and-inhuman-law-on-stoning-for-gay-sex-condemned-by-un; accessed June 10, 2020

96. https://www.trust.org/documents/trf-2020.pdf; https://news.trust.org/item/20190403181959-iyic6; accessed June 25, 2020

97. https://news.trust.org/item/20191010103819-wbt6x/; accessed June 26, 2020

98. https://www.trust.org/documents/trf-2020.pdf; accessed June 26, 2020

99. https://www.proutatwork.de/en/the-foundation/our-purpose/; accessed December 16, 2020

100. https://www.parksdiversity.eu/; accessed June 28, 2020

101. https://www.parksdiversity.eu/rassegna-stampa/vanity-fair-david-mixner-storico-attivista-gay-2/; accessed June 12, 2020

102. https://www.barillagroup.com/en/diversity-inclusion; accessed June 20, 2020

103. https://www.barillagroup.com/en/claudio-colzani-en; https://www.barillagroup.com/en/diversity-inclusion; accessed June 20, 2020

104. https://www.bloomberg.com/news/features/2019-05-07/barilla-pasta-s-turnaround-from-homophobia-to-national-pride; accessed June 29, 2020

# Part II

1. https://www.weforum.org/about/world-economic-forum; accessed June 30, 2020

2. https://www.huffingtonpost.com/2014/01/23/fareed-zakaria-davos_n_4638124.html?1390468133; accessed June 30, 2020

3. https://fortune.com/2012/03/26/mitt-romneys-hedge-fund-kingmaker/; accessed July 1, 2020

4. https://www.nytimes.com/2012/06/10/opinion/sunday/the-gops-gay-trajectory.html; accessed July 1, 2020

5. Ibid.

6. https://www.americanunityfund.com/; accessed July 1, 2020

7. https://www.freedomforallamericans.org/about/; accessed July 1, 2020

8. http://fortune.com/2015/01/23/davos-gay-rights/; accessed July 1, 2020

9. https://www.linkedin.com/pulse/davos-why-lgbt-radar-now-c-suite-sander-van-t-noordende/; accessed July 1, 2020

10. https://www.theguardian.com/media/2006/nov/13/mondaymediasection16; https://www.queer.de/detail.php?article_id=9056; accessed December 20, 2020

11. https://www.bp.com/content/dam/bp/business-sites/en/global/corporate/pdfs/investors/bp-annual-report-and-form-20f-2019.pdf; accessed December 16, 2020

12. Versions of the story differ on the exact sequence of events, on whether there really was blackmail, and on various other details.

13. https://www.dailymail.co.uk/news/article-452983/The-TRUE-story-Lord-Browne--ex-rent-boy-lover.html; accessed June 20, 2020

14. Browne, John, *The Glass Closet: Why coming out is good business*, (London: WH Allen, 2014), 60

15. Ibid. 16

16. Ibid. 60

17. https://www.theguardian.com/society/2014/may/24/lord-browne-thought-being-gay-wrong-interview-bp-boss-homophobia; accessed July 1, 2020

18. https://www.nytimes.com/2014/06/28/business/john-browne-former-chief-of-bp-on-being-a-closeted-executive.html?_r=0; accessed July 1, 2020

19. Browne, *The Glass Closet*, 159

20. https://www.pinknews.co.uk/2014/06/28/cnn-host-richard-quest-my-worst-fears-never-materialised-after-coming-out/; accessed July 1, 2020

21. Ibid.

22. Ibid.

23. https://www.advocate.com/politics/media/2014/08/24/gay-cnn-anchor-my-work-better-coming-out; https://www.pinknews.co.uk/2014/06/28/cnn-host-richard-quest-my-worst-fears-never-materialised-after-coming-out/; accessed July 1, 2020

24. https://www.nytimes.com/2014/05/18/upshot/there-are-still-no-openly-gay-major-ceos.html; accessed July 31, 2020

25. https://www.forbes.at/artikel/das-richtige-richtig-tun.html; accessed July 14, 2020

26. https://www.suedostschweiz.ch/sendungen/2017-10-15/im-falschen-koerper-geboren; accessed July 14, 2020

27. https://www.forbes.at/artikel/das-richtige-richtig-tun.html; accessed July 14, 2020

28. Ibid.

29. https://www.suedostschweiz.ch/sendungen/2017-10-15/im-falschen-koerper-geboren; accessed July 14, 2020

30. Browne, *The Glass Closet*, 127

31. https://www.adcouncil.org/; accessed July 14, 2020

32. https://www.nbcnews.com/know-your-value/feature/lisa-sherman-how-my-coming-out-corporate-closet-sparked-cultural-ncna1063681; accessed July 14, 2020

33. https://store.hbr.org/product/lisa-sherman-b/408116?sku=408116-PDF-ENG; accessed July 31, 2020

34. https://www.suedostschweiz.ch/sendungen/2017-10-15/im-falschen-koerper-geboren; accessed July 14, 2020

35. Ibid.

36. https://www.bloomberg.com/news/articles/2014-10-30/tim-cook-speaks-up; accessed July 14, 2020

37. Ibid.

38. Ibid.

39. https://www.zeit.de/gesellschaft/2014-11/homosexualitaet-tim-cook-management; accessed July 14, 2020

40. https://www.managementtoday.co.uk/hsbc-boss-antonio-simoes-slams-closeted-gay-bosses/article/1321293; accessed July 14, 2020

41. Ibid.

42. https://www.theguardian.com/business/2015/jan/18/hsbcs-antonio-simoes-says-being-gay-was-key-to-career-success; https://www.telegraph.co.uk/finance/newsbysector/retailandconsumer/11353678/HSBC-boss-Being-gay-helped-me-rise-to-the-top.html; https://expresso.pt/sociedade/antonio-simoes-se-nao-fosse-gay-provavelmente-nao-seria-ceo-do-banco=f906769; accessed July 15, 2020

43. https://www.gsb.stanford.edu/exec-ed/programs/lgbtq-executive-leadership-program; accessed October 12, 2020

44. https://www.escpeurope.eu/programmes/open-programmes/lgbt-leadership; accessed July 15, 2020

45. https://www.theguardian.com/business/2015/jan/18/hsbcs-antonio-simoes-says-being-gay-was-key-to-career-success; accessed July 15, 2020

46. https://www.santander.com/en/press-room/press-releases/2020/05/banco-santander-appoints-antonio-simoes-as-regional-head-of-europe; accessed July 15, 2020

47. https://www.theguardian.com/business/2015/jan/18/hsbcs-antonio-simoes-says-being-gay-was-key-to-career-success; accessed July 15, 2020

48. https://outstanding.involvepeople.org/old-previous-role-models/2014-top-100-lgbt-executives/; accessed July 14, 2020

49. https://www.ted.com/talks/martine_rothblatt_my_daughter_my_wife_our_robot_and_the_quest_for_immortality/transcript; accessed August 20, 2020

50. Ibid.

51. https://outstanding.involvepeople.org/2019-hall-of-fame/; accessed August 20, 2020

52. https://www.ibm.com/thought-leadership/lgbt-plus-pride/; October 17, 2020

53. https://www.fidar.de/; accessed August 16, 2020

54. https://www.autrecercle.org/sites/default/files/Federation/CHARTES/charte_lautre_cercle-_english_version_24th_april_2018.pdf; September 10, 2020

55. https://www.autrecercle.org/sites/default/files/Barometre/communique_de_presse_barometre_autre_cercle_ifop_2020_-_english.pdf; accessed September 5, 2020

56. Ibid.

57. Ibid.

58. https://start.lesechos.fr/apprendre/universites-ecoles/ecoles-dingenieurs-les-etudiants-lgbt-sous-pression-1175513; accessed September 14, 2020

59. Ibid.

60. Ibid.

61. https://www.autrecercle.org/sites/default/files/RolesModeles/17_mai_2019_dp_top_60_lgbt_v2.pdf; accessed 16 July 2020

62. Ibid.

63. https://www.radiofrance.fr/; accessed 16 July 2020

64. https://www.thejustinfashanufoundation.com/; accessed 21 August 2020

65. https://www.vk-online.de/was-wir-machen/max-spohr-preis/die-person.html; accessed 23 September 2020

66. https://www.mckinsey.com/careers/meet-our-people/glam-colleagues-at-mckinsey/the-alliance; accessed July 17, 2020

67. https://www.mckinsey.com/our-people/brian-rolfes; https://www.mckinsey.com/careers/meet-our-people/glam-colleagues-at-mckinsey; accessed July 19, 2020

68. https://www.mckinsey.com/careers/meet-our-people/glam-colleagues-at-mckinsey; accessed July 19, 2020

69. Ibid.

70. https://www.mckinsey.com/about-us/new-at-mckinsey-blog/one-hundred-leaders-commit-to-advancing-lgbtq-diversity; accessed July 15, 2020

71. Ibid.

72. https://www.startproud.org/joinus/; accessed July 17, 2020

73. https://outstanding.involvepeople.org/100-lgbt-executives-2019/; https://www.ft.com/content/f42dbba8-48ba-11e8-8c77-ff51caedcde6; accessed July 17, 2020

74. https://www.mckinsey.com/our-people/diana-ellsworth; accessed July 17, 2020

75. https://www.mckinsey.com/about-us/new-at-mckinsey-blog/one-hundred-leaders-commit-to-advancing-lgbtq-diversity; accessed July 17, 2020

76. Ibid.

77. Ibid.

78. Badgett, M.V. Lee, The Economic Cost of Stigma and the Exclusion of LGBT People: A case study of India. (Washington DC: World Bank Group, 2014)

79. https://www.mckinsey.com/about-us/new-at-mckinsey-blog/a-mckinsey-lgbtq-leader-building-a-global-alliance; accessed July 18, 2020

80. Ibid.

81. Ibid.

82. https://www.mckinsey.com/careers/meet-our-people/glam-colleagues-at-mckinsey/the-alliance; accessed July 17, 2020

83. Ibid.

84. Ibid.

85. Ibid.

86. https://www.ohchr.org/Documents/Publications/BornFreeAndEqualLowRes.pdf;https://www.ohchr.org/EN/NewsEvents/Pages/BornFreeAndEqual.aspx; accessed July 20, 2020

87. Ibid.

88. https://www.youtube.com/watch?v=sYFNfW1-sM8&feature=youtu.be; accessed July 21, 2020

89. https://newsarchive.ohchr.org/EN/NewsEvents/Pages/DisplayNews.aspx?NewsID=13335&LangID=E; accessed July 21, 2020

90. Ibid.

91. https://www.bbc.com/news/world-africa-23464694; https://news.un.org/en/story/2013/07/445552-un-unveils-free-equal-campaign-promote-lesbian-gay-bisexual-transgender-rights; accessed 21 August 2020

92. https://www.businessinsider.com/jason-collins-number-98-matthew-shepard-2013-4?r=DE&IR=T; accessed December 20, 2020

93. https://www.unfe.org/wp-content/uploads/2019/03/2018_Progress_Report.pdf; accessed December 20, 2020

94. https://www.unfe.org/about/; https://www.unfe.org/wp-content/uploads/2018/03/2017-Progress-Report.pdf; accessed December 20, 2020

95. https://www.unfe.org/wp-content/uploads/2019/03/2019_Progress_Report.pdf; accessed July 20, 2020

96. Ibid.

97. https://www.unfe.org/standards/; accessed July 21, 2020

98. https://www.db.com/newsroom_news/2017/deutsche-bank-signs-up-to-un-standards-of-conduct-for-business-to-tackle-discrimination-against-lgbti-people-en-11670.htm; accessed July 21, 2020

99. https://news.un.org/en/story/2017/09/567252-un-rights-office-issues-business-standards-treatment-lgbti-employees-major; accessed July 21, 2020

100. https://www.unfe.org/wp-content/uploads/2017/09/UN-Standards-of-Conduct.pdf; p.4; accessed July 21, 2020

101. Ibid.

102. Ibid.

103. Ibid.

104. Ibid.

105. Ibid.

106. http://www3.weforum.org/docs/WEF_AM16_Programme.pdf; accessed July 21, 2020

107. https://www.youtube.com/watch?v=o0wHlRkmY3E; https://www.reuters.com/article/us-davos-meeting-biden-lgbt-idUSKCN0UY1N5; accessed July 21, 2020

108. Ibid.

109. https://www.weforum.org/agenda/2016/02/joe-biden-business-lgbt-rights/ https://www.euronews.com/2016/01/20/joe-biden-urges-executives-at-davos-to-end-lgbt-repression; accessed July 21, 2020

110. https://www.talentinnovation.org/Research-and-Insights/pop_page.cfm?publication=1510; accessed December 20, 2020

111. https://hbr.org/2016/02/lgbt-inclusive-companies-are-better-at-3-big-things; accessed July 21, 2020

112. https://www.talentinnovation.org/Research-and-Insights/pop_page.cfm?publication=1510; accessed December 20, 2020

113. https://hbr.org/2016/02/lgbt-inclusive-companies-are-better-at-3-big-things; accessed July 21, 2020

114. https://hbr.org/2019/08/how-multinationals-can-help-advance-lgbt-inclusion-around-the-world; accessed 24 August 2020

115. https://www.weforum.org/agenda/2016/01/explainer-the-state-of-lgbt-rights-today/; accessed July 21, 2020

116. https://www.weforum.org/agenda/2016/01/the-real-cost-of-lgbt-discrimination/; accessed July 21, 2020

117. https://www.weforum.org/agenda/2016/01/the-real-story-of-the-gay-middle-east/; accessed July 21, 2020

118. https://www.weforum.org/agenda/2016/02/lgbt-equality-in-workplace/; accessed December 20, 2020

119. https://www.weforum.org/agenda/2016/05/lgbt-rights-africa-business/; accessed July 21, 2020

120. https://www.weforum.org/agenda/2016/01/why-commonwealth-countries-need-to-wake-up-to-lgbt-rights/; accessed July 21, 2020

121. https://www.weforum.org/agenda/2016/01/my-30-years-of-being-out-and-proud-in-leadership/; accessed July 21, 2020

122. https://www.accenture.com/_acnmedia/PDF-127/Accenture-Getting-to-Equal-2020-Pride-Visible-Growth-Invisible-Fears.pdf#zoom=40; accessed 20 September 2020

123. https://www.global-lgbti.org/news-updates/press-release-partnership-for-global-lgbti-equality-launched-in-davos; accessed July 21, 2020

124. https://www.global-lgbti.org/steering-committee; accessed August 22, 2020

125. Ibid.

126. Ibid.

127. Ibid.

128. https://outstanding.involvepeople.org/2019-hall-of-fame/; accessed August 22, 2020

129. http://fortune.com/2015/01/14/why-im-proud-to-be-gay-at-home-and-at-work/; accessed August 22, 2020

130. https://www.youtube.com/watch?v=XHa6rFWNX9M; accessed December 20, 2020

131. https://www.aspeninstitute.org/our-people/beth-a-brooke/; accessed August 22, 2020

132. https://www.global-lgbti.org/what-we-do; accessed July 21, 2020

133. Ibid.

# Part III

1. https://outleadership.com/about/; accessed August 5, 2020

2. Ibid.

3. https://williamsinstitute.law.ucla.edu/M; accessed August 5, 2020

4. https://williamsinstitute.law.ucla.edu/publications/econ-impact-obergefell-5-years/; accessed August 4, 2020

5. Ibid.

6. https://williamsinstitute.law.ucla.edu/publications/cost-discrim-so-africa/; accessed August 5, 2020

7. https://williamsinstitute.law.ucla.edu/publications/gdp-and-lgbt-inclusion/; accessed August 5, 2020

8. https://www.lambdalegal.org/about-us/board-nlc; accessed August 6, 2020

9. https://www.prnewswire.com/news-releases/out-leadership-unveils-15-state-ceo-briefs-empowering-business-leaders-to-invest-in-equality-protect-lgbt-employees-300998691.html; accessed December 20, 2020

10. https://outleadership.com/content/uploads/2019/04/State-_LGBT_Business_Climate_Index_Report.pdf; accessed August 5, 2020

11. https://outleadership.com/content/uploads/2020/06/StateClimateIndex_June_2020_WebVersion.pdf; p.2, accessed August 6, 2020

12. https://hbr.org/2016/02/lgbt-inclusive-companies-are-better-at-3-big-things; accessed July 21, 2020

13. https://outleadership.com/content/uploads/2020/06/StateClimateIndex_June_2020_WebVersion.pdf; accessed August 5, 2020

14. Ibid.

15. Ibid.

16. http://www.interbanklgbtforum.co.uk/about-us/; accessed September 16,2020

17. https://www.scmp.com/news/hong-kong/article/1990941/hong-kong-banks-lead-way-forging-path-sexual-minorities-workplace; accessed December 20, 2020

18. http://openfinancenyc.org/participating-firms/; accessed September 16,2020

19. https://www.gaystarnews.com/article/fabrice-houdart-%E2%80%98coming-out-relieved-me-shame-i-had-felt-so-many-years%E2%80%99260215/; accessed December 20, 2020

20. https://www.pinknews.co.uk/2020/07/25/mexico-city-ban-conversion-therapy-mental-health-suicide-regional-congress/; accessed 23 September 2020

21. https://www.ohchr.org/Documents/Issues/SexualOrientation/ConversionTherapyReport.pdf; accessed 23 September 2020

22. https://www.gaystarnews.com/article/fabrice-houdart-%E2%80%98coming-out-relieved-me-shame-i-had-felt-so-many-years%E2%80%99260215/; accessed August 5, 2020

23. Ibid.

24. https://www.worldbank.org/content/dam/Worldbank/document/SAR/economic-costs-homophobia-lgbt-exlusion-india.pdf; accessed December 20, 2020

25. https://www.worldbank.org/en/topic/socialdevelopment/publication/investing-in-a-research-revolution-for-lgbti-inclusion; https://documents.worldbank.org/en/publication/documents-reports/documentdetail/196241478752872781/investing-in-a-research-revolution-for-lgbti-inclusion; accessed August 23, 2020

26. http://documents1.worldbank.org/curated/en/196241478752872781/pdf/110035-WP-InvestinginaResearchRevolutionforLGBTIInclusion-PUBLIC-ABSTRACT-SENT.pdf; August 22, 2020

27. https://medium.com/@fabricehoudart/confessions-of-a-single-gay-dad-on-parenting-during-the-2020-confinement-d556ba08868a; accessed August 8, 2020

28. https://eastmeetswest.eu/; accessed August 8, 2020

29. https://www.rainbow-europe.org; accessed September 5, 2020

30. https://www.sbarvouven.cz/; accessed September 5, 2020

31. https://www.rainbow-europe.org/#8653/0/0; accessed September 6, 2020

32. https://eur-lex.europa.eu/legal-content/EN/TXT/?uri=CELEX:12012P/TXT; accessed September 6, 2020

33. https://edition.cnn.com/2020/07/31/europe/poland-lgbt-eu-funding-intl/index.html; accessed September 6, 2020

34. Ibid.

35. https://www.theguardian.com/world/2020/sep/16/ursula-von-der-leyen-says-polands-lgbt-free-zones-have-no-place-in-eu; accessed December 20, 2020

36. http://polishlgbtawards.pl/; accessed September 6, 2020

37. http://www.nglcc.org/; accessed August 10, 2020

38. http://www.nglcc.org/get-certified; accessed August 10, 2020

39. http://www.nglcc.org/cei; accessed August 10, 2020

40. http://www.nglcc.org/get-certified; accessed August 10, 2020

41. http://www.nglcc.org/corporate-partners; accessed August 11, 2020

42. https://eglcc.eu/de/about-us/; accessed December 16, 2020

43. https://asia.nikkei.com/Spotlight/Japan-immigration/Worker-shortage-in-Japan-to-hit-6.4m-by-2030-survey-finds2; accessed October 18, 2020

44. http://llanjapan.org/en; accessed October 18, 2020

45. http://www.workwithpride.jp/pride.html#prideEnglish; accessed October 2020

46. https://www.softbank.jp/en/corp/news/press/sbkk/2019/20191011_01/; accessed October 18, 2020

47. https://static1.squarespace.com/static/5eb491d611335c743fef24ce/t/5eca5ef6063db750f2664 cd6/1590320893440/1806_marriage_equality__hrc__.pdf; accessed October 21, 2020

48. Ibid.

49. https://accj-old.accj.or.jp/uploads/4/9/3/4/49349571/180912_joint_chamber_-_press_release_3.pdf; accessed October 21, 2020

50. Ibid.

51. https://www.nippon.com/en/japan-data/h00771/; accessed October 18, 2020

52. https://www.australianmarriageequality.org/open-letter-of-support/; accessed August 19, 2020

53. https://www.accenture.com/_acnmedia/PDF-127/Accenture-Getting-to-Equal-2020-Pride-Visible-Growth-Invisible-Fears.pdf; accessed September 9, 2020

54. https://www.sglba.org.au/; accessed August 19, 2020

55. https://www.sglba.org.au/the-fund/; accessed September 9, 2020

56. https://www.universiteitleiden.nl/en/news/2015/06/leiden-university-considers-establishing-chair-for-workplace-pride; https://workplacepride.org/organisation/; accessed September 2, 2020

57. https://workplacepride.org/download/membership-benefits-2020/?wpdmdl=6409&refresh=5f4fb dc9399191599061449; accessed September 2, 2020

58. https://workplacepride.org/download/declaration-of-amsterdam-2/?wpdmdl=6114&refresh=5f4f83d d9c5da1599046621; accessed September 2, 2020

59. https://workplacepride.org/declaration-of-amsterdam/; accessed September 2, 2020

60. https://workplacepride.org/download/declaration-of-amsterdam-2/?wpdmdl=6114&refresh=5f4f83d d9c5da1599046621; accessed September 2, 2020

61. https://abs.uva.nl/news-events/uva-in-carre/uva-in-carre-2019-autumn/uva-in-carre-2019-autumn. html#Leadership-and-inclusion-in-global-companies; accessed 17 September 2020

62. https://werkenbijdeloitte.nl/en/blogs/781-781; accessed September 2, 2020

63. Ibid.

64. https://workplacepride.org/download/2018-moscow/?wpdmdl=6818&refresh=5f4f8b7 ea76891599048574; accessed September 2, 2020

65. https://ilga-europe.org/sites/default/files/Attachments/es_-_executive_report.enlg_.pdf; accessed September 3, 2020

66. Ibid.

67. https://felgtb.org/participa/empresas/emidis/; accessed September 3, 2020

68. https://www.lesworking.com/; accessed September 3, 2020

69. https://www.ie.edu/insights/videos/diversity-the-importance-of-references/; accessed September 3, 2020

70. https://www.newsweek.com/sponsored/creative-class-2019/jay-lin; accessed 4 September 2020

71. https://www.gagaoolala.com/en/home; accessed September 3, 2020

72. https://www.screendaily.com/features/portico-media-ceo-jay-lin-on-launching-asias-first-gay-themed-ott-service/5131741.article; accessed September 3, 2020

73. https://parasolprojects.com/projects/marriage-equality-coalition-taiwan/; accessed September 3, 2020

74. https://www.aboutamazon.com/working-at-amazon/diversity-and-inclusion/affinity-groups; accessed 4 September 2020

75. https://en.adimlgbt.eu/; accessed 4 September 2020

76. https://eprints.ucm.es/59902/1/200408%20-%20Gu%C3%ADa%20ADIM%20-%20EN.pdf; accessed 4 September 2020

77. https://www.ilga-europe.org/rainboweurope/2020; accessed September 3, 2020

78. Munoz, Oscar. *La Diversidad en el contexto laboral en Espana*. (Spain: Center IE Center for Diversity, 2019), 65

79. https://www.ilga-europe.org/annualreview/2020; accessed September 3, 2020

80. Muñoz, *La Diversidad en el contexto laboral en España*, 65

81. https://www.redi-lgbti.org/asociadas; accessed December 20, 2020

82. https://www.redi-lgbti.org/; accessed August 19, 2020

83. https://www.ceoe.es/en/; accessed September 2, 2020

84. https://www.ceoe.es/es/contenido/actualidad/noticias/la-alta-direccion-empresarial-une-fuerzas-para-hacer-visible-su-compromiso-con-la-inclusion-de-la-diversidad-lgbti-en-los-entornos-laborales; accessed September 2, 2020

85. https://www.hrc.org/news/hrc-reconoce-a-mas-de-100-empresas-comprometidas-con-la-inclusion-lgbt-en-m; https://assets2.hrc.org/files/assets/resources/HRC-Mexico-2020-Working.pdf?_ga=2.55058924.656610861.1597670411-2085832741.1591717609; accessed August 17, 2020

86. https://www.prideconnection.cl/wp-content/uploads/2020/04/Radiografi%CC%81a-Pu%CC%81blica-Pride-Connection-2020.pptx.pdf; https://www.iguales.cl/; accessed December 16, 2020

87. https://www.forumempresaslgbt.com/10-compromissos; accessed August 18, 2020

88. https://de.statista.com/statistik/daten/studie/255289/umfrage/durchschnittsalter-der-bevoelkerung-in-suedafrika/; accessed August 17, 2020

89. https://lgbtiplus.com/first-south-african-lgbti-business-summit-a-groundbreaking-success/; https://www.youtube.com/watch?v=KDb9tLZxosQ&list=PLBa5O_6R0VGgwNAASNFELI57Tv3_zJ16J; accessed August 17, 2020

90. http://theotherfoundation.org/plus-the-lgbti-business-network/; accessed September 10, 2020

91. https://www.timeslive.co.za/news/south-africa/2018-09-13-leading-companies-for-lgbti-staff-in-sa/; accessed August 17, 2020

92. https://lgbtiplus.com/first-south-african-lgbti-business-summit-a-groundbreaking-success/; accessed August 17, 2020

93. https://workingwithpride.org/; accessed September 9, 2020

94. https://www.ungender.in/change-mindsets-for-an-inclusive-workplace-says-suresh-ramdas-wwp-group/; accessed September 9, 2020

95. https://thepridecircle.com/#czqpcxkpteqqbbfxuhqjuplpwqntvyctjlou; accessed September 9, 2020

96. Ibid.

97. https://keshavsuri.foundation/profile/; https://www.thelalit.com/media-coverage/keshav-suri-delhi/; accessed September 9, 2020

98. https://mumbaimirror.indiatimes.com/mumbai/other/hotelier-keshav-suri-weds-partner-in-paris/articleshow/64755463.cms?utm_source=contentofinterest&utm_medium=text&utm_campaign=cppst; accessed December 20, 2020

99. https://workplaceequalityindex.in/; accessed September 9, 2020

100. https://drive.google.com/file/d/1qBeumxNW55O99ib4lTJ0ToryCHYScGw5/view; accessed December 20, 2020

101. https://open-for-business.org/taiwan; accessed December 20, 2020

102. https://lgbti-ep.eu/; accessed December 20, 2020

103. https://open-for-business.org/special-focus; accessed December 20, 2020

104. https://daxueconsulting.com/the-lgbt-market-in-china/; https://www.cn.undp.org/content/china/en/home/library/democratic_governance/being-lgbt-in-china/; accessed October 22, 2020

105. https://qz.com/379195/alibaba-is-sending-10-same-sex-couples-on-all-expense-paid-trips-to-us-to-get-married/; October 22, 2020

106. https://www.reuters.com/article/us-china-homosexuality-alibaba-idUSKBN1Z80RN, https://supchina.com/2020/01/09/alibaba-features-gay-couple-in-chinese-new-year-ad-campaign-for-tmall/; October 20, 2020

107. https://edition.cnn.com/2020/08/14/asia/shanghai-pride-shutdown-intl-hnk/index.html; accessed October 22, 2020

108. https://www.hkgala.com/; accessed November 15, 2020

109. https://www.bcg.com/en-gb/press/15may2019-elliot-recognised-for-outstanding-international-lgbt-activism; accessed September 6, 2020

110. https://open-for-business.org/new-global-champions; accessed September 10, 2020

111. https://www.bcg.com/publications/2020/inclusive-cultures-must-follow-new-lgbtq-workforce; accessed September 10, 2020

112. https://www.bcg.com/en-gb/publications/2020/diversity-dividend-in-southeast-asia; accessed September 10, 2020

# Part IV

1.  https://media-publications.bcg.com/pdf/out-at-work-barometer.pdf; https://www.bcg.com/de-de/d/press/BCG_2019_Jan28_PM_LGBT-212748; accessed July 1, 2020

2.  https://www.bcg.com/de-de/d/press/BCG_2019_Jan28_PM_LGBT-212748; accessed July 1, 2020

3.  Ibid.

4.  https://www.reuters.com/article/us-amazon-com-jobs-automation-insight/amazon-scraps-secret-ai-recruiting-tool-that-showed-bias-against-women-idUSKCN1MK08G; accessed 15 August 2020

5.  http://www.glaad.org/files/aa/2017_GLAAD_Accelerating_Acceptance.pdf; accessed July 1, 2020

6.  Part of these brief definitions have their roots here: https://www.stonewall.org.uk/about-us/news/10-ways-step-ally-non-binary-people; accessed July 22, 2020

7.  https://www.glaad.org/blog/new-glaad-study-reveals-twenty-percent-millennials-identify-lgbtq; accessed July 1, 2020

8.  http://www.glaad.org/files/aa/2017_GLAAD_Accelerating_Acceptance.pdf; accessed July 1, 2020

9.  https://www.glaad.org/publications/accelerating-acceptance-2018; accessed July 1, 2020

10. https://time.com/4703058/time-cover-story-beyond-he-or-she/ accessed July 1, 2020

11. https://www.researchgate.net/publication/317689276_Review_National_Geographic_-_Gender_Revolution_Special_Issue_The_Shifting_Landscape_of_Gender_January_2017; https://www.nationalgeographic.com/pdf/gender-revolution-guide.pdf; https://www.nationalgeographic.com/magazine/2017/01/; accessed July 1, 2020

12. https://www.nationalgeographic.com/magazine/2017/01/; https://www.nationalgeographic.com/pdf/gender-revolution-guide.pdf; https://www.weforum.org/agenda/authors/eric-vilain/; https://www.youtube.com/watch?v=nY5KcPU4iCg; accessed July 1, 2020

13. https://www.thedailybeast.com/workplaces-need-to-prepare-for-the-non-binary-future; accessed July 1, 2020

14. https://www.pewresearch.org/fact-tank/2018/04/11/millennials-largest-generation-us-labor-force/; accessed July 1, 2020

15. Ibid.

16. https://www2.deloitte.com/content/dam/Deloitte/global/Documents/About-Deloitte/gx-2018-millennial-survey-report.pdf; accessed July 1, 2020

17. https://www.vice.com/en_us/article/kb4dvz/teens-these-days-are-queer-af-new-study-says; accessed July 1, 2020

18. https://www.pewsocialtrends.org/2019/01/17/generation-z-looks-a-lot-like-millennials-on-key-social-and-political-issues/; accessed July 1, 2020

19. Ibid.

20. https://www.pewsocialtrends.org/essay/on-the-cusp-of-adulthood-and-facing-an-uncertain-future-what-we-know-about-gen-z-so-far/; https://www.pewsocialtrends.org/2019/01/17/generation-z-looks-a-lot-like-millennials-on-key-social-and-political-issues/; accessed July 11, 2020

21. https://www.seattletimes.com/explore/careers/employers-prepare-for-a-gender-nonbinary-world/; https://edition.cnn.com/2019/08/01/health/washington-pennsylvania-gender-x-id/index.html; accessed July 11, 2020

22. https://edition.cnn.com/2017/06/16/us/oregon-third-gender-id-approved-trnd/index.html; https://edition.cnn.com/2019/08/01/health/washington-pennsylvania-gender-x-id/index.html; accessed July 11, 2020

23. https://fortune.com/2019/12/11/nonbinary-gender-x-drivers-license/ accessed July 11, 2020

24. https://hub.united.com/united-airlines-achieves-highest--2639211870.html; accessed July 11, 2020

25. https://www.theblaze.com/news/united-airlines-non-gender-booking; https://hub.united.com/united-non-binary-gender-booking-2632449328.html; https://twitter.com/united/status/1109050841200250880; accessed July 11, 2020

26. Ibid.

27. https://www.theblaze.com/news/united-airlines-non-gender-booking; https://hub.united.com/united-non-binary-gender-booking-2632449328.html; accessed July 11, 2020

28. https://hub.united.com/united-non-binary-gender-booking-2632449328.html; accessed July 11, 2020

29.  Ibid.

30.  https://www.thetimes.co.uk/article/interview-sam-smith-on-coming-out-and-the-thrill-of-it-all-3235l3n78; http://whatstrending.com/pop/24989-sam-smith-comes-out-as-gender-queer/; accessed July 11, 2020

31.  Ibid.

32.  Ibid.

33.  https://www.bbc.com/news/newsbeat-47612616; accessed July 11, 2020

34.  https://www.bbc.com/news/entertainment-arts-49688123; accessed July 11, 2020

35.  https://www.hrc.org/blog/breaking-binaries-this-international-non-binary-day; accessed July 11, 2020

36.  https://www.thetrevorproject.org/about/history-film/; accessed July 11, 2020

37.  https://www.thetrevorproject.org/about/programs-services/; accessed July 12, 2020

38.  https://www.trevorspace.org/; accessed July 12, 2020

39.  https://hub.united.com/united-non-binary-gender-booking-2632449328.html; accessed July 12, 2020

40.  https://eu.usatoday.com/story/travel/flights/2019/03/22/united-first-airline-offer-new-non-binary-gender-booking-options/3243718002/; accessed July 12, 2020

41.  https://www.foxbusiness.com/lifestyle/american-airlines-non-binary-gender-option; accessed July 12, 2020

42.  https://www.autoevolution.com/news/airlines-are-going-overboard-to-accommodate-non-binary-gender-options-138417.html; accessed July 12, 2020

43.  https://www.staralliance.com/de/home; accessed July 12, 2020

44.  https://abovethelaw.com/2020/06/the-500-largest-law-firms-in-america-2020/; accessed July 12, 2020

45.  https://www.bakermckenzie.com/en/newsroom/2019/06/gender-targets; accessed July 12, 2020

46.  Ibid.

47.  https://www.washingtonpost.com/business/2019/07/02/how-employers-are-preparing-gender-non-binary-world/?noredirect=on; accessed July 12, 2012

48.  https://www.cliffordchance.com/news/news/2020/07/clifford-chance-commits-to-new-global-and-regional-gender-ethnicity-and-lgbt-plus-targets.html; accessed July 19, 2020

49.  https://www.cliffordchance.com/people_and_places/people/directors/tiernan-brady.html; accessed August 11, 2020

50.  https://www.forbes.com/sites/caiwilshaw/2020/05/23/meet-tiernan-bradythe-man-who-won-equal-marriage-on-two-continents/#28a594c4677e; accessed August 12, 2020

51.  https://equalfuture2018.com/; accessed August 13, 2020

52.  Ibid.

53.  Ibid.

54.  https://www.cliffordchance.com/news/news/2020/07/clifford-chance-commits-to-new-global-and-regional-gender-ethnicity-and-lgbt-plus-targets.html; accessed July 19, 2020

55.  https://www.washingtonpost.com/business/2019/07/02/how-employers-are-preparing-gender-non-binary-world/?noredirect=on; accessed July 12, 2020

56.  https://www.washingtonpost.com/business/2019/06/18/mastercard-launching-true-name-its-transgender-nonbinary-cardholders/; accessed July 12, 2020

57.  https://www.washingtonpost.com/business/2019/07/02/how-employers-are-preparing-gender-non-binary-world/?noredirect=on; accessed July 12, 2020

58.  https://www.youtube.com/watch?v=eoNO6yeKGis; https://www.out.com/lifestyle/2019/6/10/queer-eyes-jonathan-van-ness-im-nonbinary; https://www.seventeen.com/celebrity/g27702340/non-binary-celebrities; accessed July 13, 2020

59.  https://www.youtube.com/watch?v=qA8z0_tXIpg; accessed July 12, 2020

60.  https://www.shivaraichandani.com/; accessed July 12, 2020

61.  https://jacobtobia.com/; accessed July 12, 2020

62.  https://www.youtube.com/watch?v=qA8z0_tXIpg ; https://www.youtube.com/watch?v=eoNO6yeKGis; https://www.out.com/lifestyle/2019/6/10/queer-eyes-jonathan-van-ness-im-nonbinary; https://www.seventeen.com/celebrity/g27702340/non-binary-celebrities; assessed July 13, 2020

63. https://boston.techtogether.io/; accessed July 13, 2020

64. Ibid.

65. Ibid.

66. https://www.mckinsey.com/careers/mckinsey-achievement-awards/overview; accessed July 13, 2020

67. Ibid.

68. Ibid.

69. https://www.washingtonpost.com/business/2019/07/02/how-employers-are-preparing-gender-non-binary-world/?noredirect=on; accessed July 11, 2020

70. Ibid.

71. Ibid.

72. Ibid.

73. https://www.morehouse.edu/; accessed December 20, 2020

74. https://www.pbk.org/; accessed August 13, 2020

75. https://www.rainbowrailroad.org/; https://www.rainbowrailroad.org/bios/titi-naomi-tukes; accessed July 13, 2020

76. https://www.linkedin.com/in/titinaomitukes/; accessed August 13, 2020

77. https://www.timeslive.co.za/news/south-africa/2018-09-13-leading-companies-for-lgbti-staff-in-sa/; accessed August 13, 2020

78. https://www.amnesty.ch/de/themen/wirtschaft-und-menschenrechte/fallbeispiele/nigeria/dok/2020/shell-muss-endlich-verantwortung-tragen/report-on-trial-shell-in-nigeria-legal-actions-against-the-oil-multinational.pdf; accessed 14 August 2020

79. https://outandequal.org/; accessed July 13, 2020

80. https://www.gqrgm.com/belonging-the-next-evolution-of-diversity-and-inclusion/; accessed July 13, 2020

81. https://hbr.org/2016/09/diverse-teams-feel-less-comfortable-and-thats-why-they-perform-better; accessed July 13, 2020

82. https://journals.sagepub.com/doi/full/10.1177/1745691615598513; accessed July 13, 2020

83. https://hbr.org/2017/02/diversity-doesnt-stick-without-inclusion?referral=03759&cm_vc=rr_item_page.bottom; accessed July 31, 2020

84. https://www.linkedin.com/pulse/keeping-diversity-conversation-emotional-why-we-need-keep-creary/; accessed July 27, 2020

85. https://knowledge.wharton.upenn.edu/article/belonging-at-work/; accessed 15 August 2020

86. https://news.yale.edu/2019/11/11/kimberly-goff-crews-oversee-campus-wide-belonging-yale-initiative; accessed 22 July 2020

87. https://news.harvard.edu/gazette/story/2018/03/harvard-issues-task-force-report-on-inclusion-belonging/; accessed 22 July 2020

88. Ibid.

89. https://www.law.nyu.edu/centers/belonging; accessed 26 July 2020

90. https://www.washingtonpost.com/business/2019/12/30/first-there-was-diversity-then-inclusion-now-hr-wants-everyone-feel-like-they-belong/; accessed 24 July 2020

91. https://outandequal.org/app/uploads/2018/11/OE-Non-Binary-Best-Practices.pdf ; accessed July 13, 2020

92. Ibid.

93. https://www.theguardian.com/science/2019/aug/05/he-she-or-gender-neutral-pronouns-reduce-biases-study; https://www.pnas.org/content/116/34/16781; accessed July 13, 2020

94. https://www.washingtonpost.com/business/2019/07/02/how-employers-are-preparing-gender-non-binary-world/?noredirect=on; accessed July 13, 2020

95. https://www.unfe.org/wp-content/uploads/2017/05/UNFE-Intersex.pdf; accessed 23 July 2020

96. https://www.amnesty.org/en/documents/eur01/6086/2017/en/; accessed 23 July 2020

97. https://www.unfe.org/wp-content/uploads/2017/05/UNFE-Intersex.pdf; accessed 23 July 2020

98. https://www.axelspringer.com/data/uploads/2020/03/geschaeftsbericht_2019-1.pdf; accessed 29 August 2020

99. https://www.ringieraxelspringer.com/about/who-we-are/; accessed 29 August 2020

100. https://divers.land/about/; accessed 29 August 2020

101. https://www.queerseite.de/en/home-2; accessed 29 August 2020

102. https://www.proutatwork.de/aufklaerung/how-to/; accessed December 20, 2020

103. https://www.outinperth.com/merriam-webster-dictionary-adds-they-as-a-pronoun/; https://www.merriam-webster.com/dictionary/they?src=search-dict-box; accessed 23 July 2020

104. Ibid.

105. https://www.merriam-webster.com/dictionary/they?src=search-dict-box; accessed 23 July 2020

106. https://www.stonewall.org.uk/about-us/news/merriam-webster-adds-they-singular-non-binary-pronoun; accessed 22 July 2020

107. https://www.stonewall.org.uk/about-us/news/10-ways-step-ally-non-binary-people; accessed 22 July 2020

108. Ibid.

109. https://www.stonewallscotland.org.uk/global-workplace-equality-index; accessed 22 July 2020

110. https://www.buzzfeed.com/patrickstrudwick/british-bank-becomes-the-first-to-welcome-gender-nonbinary-c; https://www.stonewall.org.uk/node/36957; accessed July 21, 2020

111. https://www.stonewallscotland.org.uk/what-best-employers-do; accessed July 21, 2020

112. Ibid.

113. https://uhlala.com/dax-30-2019/; accessed December 20, 2020

114. https://www.nbcnews.com/feature/nbc-out/harvey-milk-terminal-opens-san-francisco-international-airport-n1033021; accessed 25 July 2020

115. https://app.rahm.ceo/news/210692; accessed 25 July 2020

116. Ibid.

117. https://app.rahm.ceo/news/210414; accessed 26 July 2020

118. Ibid.

119. Ibid.

120. Ibid.

121. https://hellotierney.com/work/more-color-more-pride-2/; accessed December 20, 2020

122. https://app.rahm.ceo/news/236592; accessed 15 August 2020

123. Ibid.

124. Ibid.

125. https://www.proutatwork.de/wp-content/uploads/2020/09/PAW_Positionspapier_Blutspende_V1_92020.pdf; accessed December 20, 2020

126. Ibid.

127. https://news.trust.org/item/20200420152107-yqrn4/; accessed August 17, 2020

128. https://www.sap.com/corporate/en/company/diversity.html; accessed August 19, 2020

129. https://uhlala.com/wp-content/uploads/2019/12/DAX30_LGBT_Diversity_Index2019_Report.pdf; accessed August 16, 2020

130. https://www.handelsblatt.com/unternehmen/beruf-und-buero/buero-special/karriere-grenzen-der-toleranz-wenn-details-zum-privatleben-auf-der-dienstreise-zum-lebensrisiko-werden/25255268.html; accessed August 16, 2020

131. Ibid.

132. Ibid.

133. https://www.aidshilfe.de/sites/default/files/documents/positivarbeiten_-_deklaration_zur_unterschrift_einseitig_0.pdf; accessed August 16, 2020

134. https://www.aidshilfe.de/positivarbeiten#tab-2; accessed August 16, 2020

135. https://www.outexecutives.de/germanys-top-100-out-executives-2019/; accessed August 17, 2020

136. https://lesbianswhotech.org/about/; accessed August 17, 2020

137. Ibid.

138. https://empower.involvepeople.org/100-ethnic-minority-future-leaders-2020/; accessed August 19, 2020

139. https://blogs.sap.com/2020/05/29/pride-events-sap-labs-india/; accessed September 7, 2020

140. https://news.sap.com/india/2020/01/liberation-sap-coming-out-gay/; accessed September 7, 2020

141. https://blogs.sap.com/2019/02/13/love-knows-no-gender/?preview_id=780971; accessed September 9, 2020

142. https://blogs.sap.com/2020/03/16/women-as-strong-lgbtq-allies-prideatsap/; accessed September 9, 2020

143. https://www.lgbtgreat.com/role-model/michael-sandstedt; https://www.gayfarmer.de/; accessed August 26, 2020

144. https://www.lgbtgreat.com/research; accessed August 26, 2020

145. https://www.allianzgi.com/-/media/allianzgi/globalagi/our-firm/inclusion-diversity/20-1823-fostering-lgbt-workplace-inclusion.pdf; accessed August 26, 2020

146. https://new.siemens.com/global/en/company/sustainability/diversity/siemens-takes-a-stand-for-more-openness.html; accessed September 6, 2020

147. https://press.siemens.com/global/en/pressrelease/siemens-sets-course-establishing-next-generation-management; accessed September 6, 2020

148. https://startout.org/about-us/; accessed September 30, 2020

149. https://reachingoutmba.org/who-we-are/; accessed July 27, 2020

150. https://reachingoutmba.org/fellowship/; accessed July 27, 2020

151. https://reachingoutmba.org/club-affiliates/; accessed July 27, 2020

152. https://www.outinvestors.com/about; accessed July 31, 2020

153. https://www.EurOUTconference.org/board-members; accessed July 31, 2020

154. https://www.london.edu/executive-education/leadership/lgbtqleadership#Your-learning-journey; accessed August 4, 2020

155. https://globalfreedomofexpression.columbia.edu/cases/case-bayev-others-v-russia/; accessed August 30, 2020

156. https://comingoutspb.com/eng/; accessed August 31, 2020

157. https://www.glsen.org/day-of-silence; accessed August 31, 2020

158. https://www.glsen.org/about-us#snt--1; accessed August 31, 2020

159. Ibid.

160. http://www.hagueproject.com/project/project-1/; accessed September 1, 2020

161. https://www.haguetalks.com/event/lgbti-gender-rights/; accessed September 1, 2020

# Index